American Drama of
the Twentieth Century

Gerald M. Berkowitz

Longman

London and New York

Addison Wesley Longman Limited
Edinburgh Gate,
Harlow, Essex CM20 2JE, England
and Associated Companies throughout the world.

Published in the United States of America
by Addison Wesley Longman Inc., New York

© Longman Group UK Limited 1992

First published 1992
Third impression 1997

ISBN 0 582 01602 9 CSD
ISBN 0 582 01601 0 PPR

British Library Cataloguing-in-Publication Data
A catalogue record for this book is
available from the British Library

Library of Congress Cataloging-in-Publication Data
Berkowtiz, Gerald M.
  American drama of the twentieth century / Gerald M. Berkowitz.
    p.   cm. – (Longman literature in English Series)
  Includes bibliographical references (p.) and index.
    ISBN 0–582–01602–9 (csd) – ISBN 0–582–01601–0 (ppr)
    1. American drama – 20th century – History and criticism.
I. Title.   II. Series.
PS350.B47   1992
812'.509–dc20   92-9396 CIP

Set 7L in 9/10pt Bembo
Produced by Longman Singapore Publishers (Pte) Ltd
Printed in Singapore

Contents

Editors' Preface

The multi-volume Longman Literature in English Series provides students of literature with a critical introduction to the major genres in their historical and cultural context. Each volume gives a coherent account of a clearly defined area, and the series, when complete, will offer a practical and comprehensive guide to literature written in English from Anglo-Saxon times to the present. The aim of the series as a whole is to show that the most valuable and stimulating approach to the study of literature is that based upon an awareness of the relations between literary forms and their historical contexts. Thus the areas covered by most of the separate volumes are defined by period and genre. Each volume offers new and informed ways of reading literary works, and provides guidance for further reading in an extensive reference section.

In recent years, the nature of English studies has been questioned in a number of increasingly radical ways. The very terms employed to define a series of this kind – period, genre, history, context, canon – have become the focus of extensive critical debate, which has necessarily influenced in varying degrees the successive volumes published since 1985. But however fierce the debate, it rages around the traditional terms and concepts.

As well as studies on all periods of English and American literature, the series includes books on criticism and literary theory, and on the intellectual and cultural context. A comprehensive series of this kind must of course include other literatures written in English, and therefore a group of volumes deals with Irish and Scottish literature, and the literatures of India, Africa, the Caribbean, Australia and Canada. The forty-seven volumes of the series cover the following areas: Pre-Renaissance English Literature, English Poetry, English Drama, English Fiction, English Prose, Criticism and Literary Theory, Intellectual and Cultural Context, American Literature, Other Literatures in English.

David Carroll
Michael Wheeler

Longman Literature in English Series

General Editors: David Carroll and Michael Wheeler
Lancaster University

Pre-Renaissance English Literature

* English Literature before Chaucer *Michael Swanton*
  English Literature in the Age of Chaucer
* Engish Medieval Romance *W. R. J. Barron*

English Poetry

* English Poetry of the Sixteenth Century *Gary Waller (Second Edition)*
* English Poetry of the Seventeenth Century *George Parfitt (Second Edition)*
  English Poetry of the Eighteenth Century, 1700–1789
* English Poetry of the Romantic Period, 1789–1830 *J. R. Watson*
  (Second Edition)
* English Poetry of the Victorian Period, 1830–1890 *Bernard Richards*
  English Poetry of the Early Modern Period, 1890–1940
* English Poetry since 1940 *Neil Corcoran*

English Drama

  English Drama before Shakespeare
* English Drama: Shakespeare to the Restoration, 1590–1660
  Alexander Leggatt
* English Drama: Restoration and Eighteenth Century, 1660–1789
  Richard W. Bevis
  English Drama: Romantic and Victorian, 1789–1890
  English Drama of the Early Modern Period, 1890–1940
  English Drama since 1940

English Fiction

* English Fiction of the Eighteenth Century, 1700–1789 *Clive T. Probyn*
* English Fiction of the Romantic Period, 1789–1830 *Gary Kelly*
* English Fiction of the Victorian Period, 1830–1890 *Michael Wheeler*
  (Second Edition)

* English Fiction of the Early Modern Period, 1890–1940 *Douglas Hewitt*
  English Fiction since 1940

English Prose

* English Prose of the Seventeenth Century, 1590–1700 *Roger Pooley*
  English Prose of the Eighteenth Century
  English Prose of the Nineteenth Century

Criticsim and Literary Theory

Criticism and Literary Theory from Sidney to Johnson
Criticism and Literary Theory from Wordsworth to Arnold
Criticism and Literary Theory from 1890 to the Present

The Intellectual and Cultural Context

The Sixteenth Century
* The Seventeenth Century, 1603–1700 *Graham Parry*
* The Eighteenth Century, 1700–1789 *James Sambrook (Second Edition)*
  The Romantic Period, 1789–1830
* The Victorian Period, 1830–1890 *Robin Gilmour*
  The Twentieth Century: 1890 to the Present

American Literature

American Literature before 1880
* American Poetry of the Twentieth Century *Richard Gray*
* American Drama of the Twentieth Century *Gerald M. Berkowitz*
* American Fiction 1865–1940 *Brian Lee*
* American Fiction since 1940 *Tony Hilfer*
* Twentieth-Century America *Douglas Tallack*

Other Literatures

Irish Literature since 1800
Scottish Literature since 1700
Australian Literature
* Indian Literature in English *William Walsh*
  African Literature in English: East and West
  Southern African Literatures
  Caribbean Literature in English
* Canadian Literature in English *W. J. Keith*

* *Already published*

Acknowledgements

We are indebted to the author's agent on behalf of the Estate of Thornton Wilder for permission to reproduce extracts from the play *Our Town* by Thornton Wilder (Coward-McCann, Inc., 1938), copyright 1938, © 1957 by Thornton Wilder, an extract from the play 'Pullman Car Hiawatha' from *The Long Christmas Dinner and Other Plays in One Act* by Thornton Wilder (Coward-McCann, Inc., 1931), copyright 1931 by Yale University Press & Coward-McCann, Inc. Copyright © 1959 by Thornton Wilder, and extracts from the play *The Skin of Our Teeth* by Thornton Wilder (Harper & Bros, 1942), copyright 1942, © 1970 by Thornton Wilder.

Author's Preface

I want to thank the General Editors of this series, David Carroll and Michael Wheeler, first for offering me the opportunity to write this book, and, second, for wisely knowing when to give me my head and when to crack the whip.

The Department of English of Northern Illinois University granted me a partial relief from teaching at a point in my research when extra time was particularly valuable and appreciated.

Alfred Weiss, who taught me most of this in the first place, generously read the manuscript to help make sure I got it right; my debts to him continue to mount. Having grown up in what I refer to later in this book as the Broadway era, when virtually the only venue on the continent for the best in American theatre was New York City, I was doubly fortunate in living near New York and in having parents who introduced me to the theatre and encouraged my interest in it. For that, among the innumerable gifts they have given me, this book is offered as an inadequate tribute.

Gerald M. Berkowitz
October 1991

To My Parents

Chapter 1
Introduction

The American drama is, for all practical purposes, the twentieth-century American drama. There were plays written and performed on the American continent well before there was a United States, and during the nineteenth century the American theatre was widespread and active. But, as was also true in much of Europe, it was, with rare exceptions, not the home of a particularly rich or ambitious literature. The theatre was a broadly popular light entertainment form, much like television today; it is possible to do artistically ambitious work on American commercial television, but television is not likely to be the first medium to come to the mind of a serious writer. This is not to say that the playwrights of the nineteenth century were without talent, but that, like television writers, they were more likely to be artisans skilled at producing the entertaining effects that audiences wanted, than artists looking to illuminate the human condition or challenge received values.

Yet in America, as in Europe, a change in the kind of literature being written for the theatre began to become apparent in the last years of the nineteenth century. As with many historical and artistic developments in American culture, this was much less a matter of an organized 'movement' than of trial and error and accidents of personality; an individual writer might not be consciously innovating, but something in his work might attract audiences or inspire other writers, so that the art form lurched forward a step. There is, for example, little evidence that James A. Herne considered *Margaret Fleming* (1890) revolutionary in any way, but with hindsight we can see that his version of the mildly sensational melodrama typical of the period raises moral questions that its contemporaries do not, and that those questions give the play a distinctly twentieth-century feel. The process was slow and unsteady, with false starts and relapses, but by the second decade of the twentieth century artistically ambitious writers were venturing into drama and finding it able to carry a weight of psychological insight and philosophical import it had not been asked to carry before.

This was very much a rebirth of an art form; with little in the recent history of the genre to build on, the first generations of twentieth-century American dramatists had to discover for themselves what shape the twentieth-century American drama would take. It is not surprising, then, that the years from, say, 1900 to 1930 saw a great variety of dramatic styles and vocabularies, as playwrights experimented with epic, symbolism, expressionism, verse tragedy and the like, finding out as they went along what a play could and could not do. Foremost among the experimenters was Eugene O'Neill, of whom it is only a slight exaggeration to say that during the 1920s he never wrote two plays in the same style. O'Neill, whose father had been a star of the nineteenth-century theatre, and who thus had a sharp awareness of its literary limitations, was consciously experimenting, trying to shape and stretch the medium so it could do what he wanted it to – express his profoundly thought-out insights and philosophies. But even the less determinedly innovative writers of the period found themselves making up the rules as they went along.

Inevitably, some experiments failed. One reason O'Neill kept changing styles was that many of them disappointed him, while some of the '–isms' that were briefly successful in Europe proved unamenable to American topics and tastes, or simply uncommercial. Through trial and error, however, one particular dramatic mode came to the fore. Theatrically effective, easy for audiences to relate and respond to, remarkably flexible in its adaptability to the demands of different authors, the natural voice of American drama was revealed by the 1930s to be in realistic contemporary middle-class domestic melodrama and comedy.

Realistic contemporary middle-class domestic melodrama – each of those words is worth examining and defining. 'Realism' does not mean the uncensored photographic and phonographic record of external reality. Dramatic realism is an artifice as much as any other mode, violating reality in order to give the illusion of reality; to take one simple example, characters in 'realistic' plays generally speak one at a time, and in grammatical sentences. The important point is that the illusion of reality is maintained; realism avoids gross violations of the laws of nature (People don't fly) or the introduction of purely symbolic characters or events (the Little Formless Fears of O'Neill's *The Emperor Jones*), while presenting characterizations and behaviour that are at least possible. And thus a realistic play asserts the claim that it speaks the truth, that what happens on stage is a reflection of the world its audience inhabits.

Historical plays were a mainstay of the nineteenth-century American drama, and continued to be written in the twentieth; most Broadway seasons in the 1920s saw at least one play about eighteenth-century France or nineteenth-century Mexico, and the 1930s had a thin but constant stream of plays about Washington, Lincoln or other American heroes. But the overwhelming majority of twentieth-century American plays are set in the present, again implying a close parallel to the real world. Moreover, a play set in the here and now is likely to reflect the external reality of the here and now, be it the Depression of the 1930s, the middle-class anxieties of the 1950s or the profound social changes of the 1960s and after; and one of the first important discoveries about domestic realism was that it could address large social and historical issues in theatrical terms.

Shakespeare wrote about kings, O'Neill wrote about Lazarus and Marco Polo, and Maxwell Anderson wrote about Elizabeth I and Mary of Scotland. But the overwhelming majority of modern American plays are about people from the same social and economic world as the play-goers – the urban middle class. That is not a narrow range, and can stretch from the barely-getting-by and underemployed to the comfort-ably well-off. But the extremes of the economic ladder, along with other fringes of society – blacks, rustics, etc. – are rarely represented before the 1960s, except as stereotypes, and infrequently thereafter except in plays specifically addressing minority subjects. Audiences for American plays are likely to see themselves or people like them, or people they might believably, with good or bad luck, be like.

Of all these adjectives being defined, 'domestic' may be the most significant. Not only are American plays about recognizable people in a recognizable world, but they are about the personal lives of these people. Whether a play is actually set in a living room, with a cast made up solely of family members, as an extraordinary number are, or whether the 'domestic' setting extends to an office and a circle of friends, the issues and events are presented in small and localized terms. Whatever the deeper meanings of an American play, on one solid level it is about love and marriage, or earning a living, or dealing with a family crisis.

Of course Americans did not invent domestic drama. Ibsen and Chekhov (to name just two) had written of realistic characters in domes-tic situations, and even hinted at larger social and moral issues through this mode. The gradual discovery of American dramatists, starting in the 1930s, was that domestic realism was their most effective vehicle for talking about larger issues – that the small events in the lives of small people could be presented so that they reflected the world outside the living room. Put another way, the insight becomes more than merely technical. Dramatists discovered that the real story of, say, the Depression was not in statistics and large social changes, but in the ways it affected a family in its living room. From there it was a small step to the dis-coveries of the 1940s and 1950s that purely personal experiences, even those without larger social implications, were valuable and dramatic in themselves. A national literature of plays set in living rooms is a deeply democratic national literature, one that assumes that the important sub-jects are those that manifest themselves in the daily lives of ordinary people.

And finally 'melodrama,' a word with unfortunate and undeserved negative connotations. Although 'melodramatic' is popularly used as a criticism of literature that invokes shallow or excessive emotional effects, the noun merely refers to a serious play with no pretension to tragedy. It is worth noting that few American dramatists aspire to high tragedy; indeed, the other characteristics already enumerated, particularly realism and the domestic setting, militate against any such ambition. Once again an essentially democratic impulse is at work, in the assumption that the important events of life, the things worth writing plays about, are the things that happen to the essentially ordinary, not the heroic.

As with the rebirth of serious drama at the beginning of the century, the discovery of domestic realism's power and potential was not the result of conscious artistic manifestos or collusion among writers. The form worked, and so individual writers were drawn to it; indeed, in a number of cases dramatists who began as non-realistic writers or who went through a period of experiment found themselves drawn back to domestic realism in later works: Eugene O'Neill most strikingly, but also Maxwell Anderson, Edward Albee, Sam Shepard and others. The remarkable accomplishment of domestic realism lies in its richness and adaptability, as writers as different in their styles, subjects and ambitions as Eugene O'Neill, Tennessee Williams, Arthur Miller and August Wilson have been able to say what they want to say in this mode.

Just as there have been few stylistic schools or movements in the American drama, so there have been few conscious agreements among writers about subject matter. Individual dramatists wrote about what interested or moved them, and cases of direct influence (e.g. of Tennessee Williams on William Inge) are far less common than situations in which playwrights responding to a similar reality independently found their way to similar subjects and approaches. Still, similar realities, or the discoveries of particularly strong or insightful writers, are likely to produce some similarities among contemporaries. It is both coincidental and (with hindsight) inevitable that the Great Depression of the 1930s would lead some dramatists to explore and even criticize the social and economic forces that were affecting the lives of millions; and the drama of social and political criticism remains a small but significant part of the American repertoire. (It may be the American theatre's commercial constraints, the need to sell tickets and make a profit, that kept political drama from becoming as dominant or as angry as it did in some European countries.)

Similarly, Tennessee Williams wasn't trying to move the American drama into new subject areas when his own personal empathy for the lost and weak led him to explore their experience in the 1940s and 1950s; it was the fact that these plays spoke to a perhaps unexpected hunger for counsel and reassurance in the hearts of his audiences that made them succeed, and allowed other writers with their own forms of counsel and reassurance to voice them in drama. Clear evidence that this was no conscious 'movement' is the fact that O'Neill's late and posthumous plays, some written as early as 1940 but not released until the 1950s, address some of the same emotional questions as the Williams plays that preceded them in the theatre but were written later; the two authors (and others) independently found their ways to subjects that only became a recognizable genre when audiences responded to them, making reassurance that the pains and insecurities of life can be endured a recurring theme in plays from the 1950s to the 1990s.

This, then, is a literary history with a plot. For various historical and artistic reasons the stylistic outline of the twentieth-century American drama has a clearly discernible arc. An art form that was essentially born afresh at the beginning of the century went through a period of exploration and experiment culminating in the discovery that one style was more amenable to American tastes and more adaptable to the demands that different writers made on it. That style – realistic contemporary middle-class domestic melodrama – was to become the dominant and artistically most fertile and flexible mode, the one in which the greatest American dramatists were able to create the greatest American plays, and in which writers with widely varying agendas could offer psychological insights, political criticism or spiritual counsel. So absolute was the superiority for American dramatic purposes of domestic realism that when, soon after the middle of the century, some significant changes in the theatrical structure led to another period of experiment and exploration, the centre held. Artistic discoveries were made – some of them greatly enriching the dramatic vocabulary – but domestic realism retained its place as the native and natural American dramatic style as new generations of dramatists continued to discover its flexibility and power.

Theatre history

By its very nature the drama – the literature of the theatre – is more closely bound to the marketplace than any other literary form. Poetry exists even if it is not published, and a novel may sell very few copies but remain on the library shelves to be discovered later. But a play simply is not a play until it is put on a stage, and it is likely not to exist for posterity unless it proves itself on a stage; it is the general rule that plays are not published unless they have had successful productions. So, since forces and events that are really more part of theatrical than literary history have a direct effect on the types of plays that are written and the types of plays that survive, a brief history of the twentieth-century American theatre is in order.

As mentioned earlier, there was professional theatre in colonial America and in the Spanish southwest before there was a United States. In the nineteenth century live theatre was a flourishing entertainment form, with more than two thousand resident professional companies across the continent, in almost every city of more than village size, each with a repertoire of classics and new plays. Though first Philadelphia, and later New York, was acknowledged as the cultural capital of the nation, audiences in Chicago, St Louis, Denver and dozens of other cities were just as likely to see new plays and leading performers in first-class productions.

This situation began to change in the last two decades of the nine-teenth century, in part because New York-based producers began send-ing out touring companies of their biggest hits, drawing audiences away from the less glamorous local theatres. In the 1890s a cartel of producers bought up or sabotaged the competition in many cities, to give them-selves a monopoly. In the new century most of the remaining resident companies succumbed to competition from vaudeville, movies and later radio. By 1920 at the latest, New York City had achieved an absolute dominance and virtually absolute monopoly of the American theatre, with the rest of the country reduced to local amateur fare and touring companies of last year's New York hits.

'Broadway' is the name of a street in New York City, and the label has come to be attached to the commercial theatres of that city (even though most Broadway theatres are in fact on the side streets intersecting Broadway), just as the term Wall Street has come to refer generically to the financial community. And for roughly the first half of the twentieth century 'Broadway' was for all intents and purposes the entire American theatre.

This was obviously an imperfect state of affairs. When virtually all the new plays, all the major playwrights, all the best actors, directors and designers were to be found in one square mile of one city, then the overwhelming majority of the population was being deprived of the opportunity to experience American theatre at its best. Meanwhile the intense competition for a limited audience meant that many talented artists were inevitably squeezed out or not given a chance. On the other hand, the concentration of the best and most ambitious in one place had some salutary effects. Writers and performers could be inspired and chal-lenged by each other, and build on each other's accomplishments. It is surely not coincidental, for example, that the psychologically realistic performance style called 'Method Acting,' the emotionally evocative powers of such directors as Elia Kazan and Jose Quintero, and the major plays of Tennessee Williams and Arthur Miller all appeared at the same time, in the late 1940s and early 1950s. Each of these, along with the responsiveness of an experienced and sophisticated audience, fed on and nourished the others, helping to create an identity, a unified style and a very high standard of accomplishment that a more dispersed theatrical community would probably not have achieved.

Virtually all of the dramatists discussed in the second, third and fourth chapters of this book wrote for the Broadway theatre; and the overall arc of theatre history in the first half of the century – the period of experiment leading to the discovery of a dramatic mode that seemed most amenable to the task of addressing American concerns, and the subsequent development of this mode to its fullest potential – is itself clearly a product of a small community of artists observing and learning from each other's errors and accomplishments. It is quite likely that the shape of the American drama by mid-century would have been quite different, in unpredictable ways, if the performance arena of American theatre had not been so concentrated and localized.

This state of affairs began to alter around 1950, as a result of four distinct changes in the structure of the American theatre. The first was the appearance of an alternative theatrical environment within New York City, as young actors, directors and designers who could not find employment on Broadway formed their own shoestring 'Off- Broadway' companies. Motivated by the desire to be seen and to exercise their craft, they performed in lofts, unused theatres and various converted spaces, free to do uncommercial and experimental work simply because there was so little money or prestige to lose. And because there were so many good young actors, directors and designers in New York, some very good work was done Off-Broadway, leading critics and audiences to discover and appreciate the potential of this new venue.

With its lower budgets, Off-Broadway concentrated in its first few years on classics and revivals. By 1960, though, it found a new function, as a showcase for commercially risky new writers. Its generally younger and more adventurous audiences were open to new styles and subject matters, encouraging a period of experiment and stylistic diversity recalling that of forty years earlier. A generation of American dramatists had their first plays produced Off-Broadway, and the alternative theatre was soon recognized as a significant complement to Broadway, its new respectability inspiring a further expansion of the fringe and avant-garde to the ironically labelled 'Off Off-Broadway'.

About the same time that an alternative theatre was developing in New York, alternatives to New York theatre were being born elsewhere in America. In the late 1940s and early 1950s new professional resident theatre companies were founded in Dallas, Houston and Washington; and by 1960 there were a dozen such companies around the country. By 1966 there were thirty, with, for the first time in the century, more professional actors employed outside New York City than on Broadway. By 1980 there were more than seventy large, permanently established resident theatres in America and, since many of them awakened a hunger for theatre in their areas, at least ten times as many smaller professional companies functioning in local equivalents of Off-Broadway.

The opening of new theatres all over the country did not just mean that high-quality live drama was now available to more people than ever before in the century, though that was accomplishment enough. It meant more opportunities for new writers, particularly those from outside New York City and those doing challenging new work. Unlike the New York theatre, which was structured as a marketplace, with each production an independent commercial enterprise in competition with others, most regional theatres produced full seasons of from four to ten plays a year. This innovation, seemingly just a matter of logistics and organization, actually changed the way in which audiences, at least outside New York, experienced plays.

By buying tickets for the full repertoire in advance instead of waiting for each play to appear and be reviewed, audiences opened themselves to a variety of new theatrical experiences, taking the occasional Shakespeare or new American play along with more familiar fare. Many regional theatre audiences soon surpassed Broadway audiences in their willingness to experiment, and new American playwrights found their plays welcomed by producers in Minneapolis or San Francisco more readily than by their counterparts in New York. Many regional companies declared the encouragement of new writers, particularly from their region, as a central part of their mission; others, particularly the low-budget alternative theatres, were simply more able than commercial producers to take a chance on an unknown. By the 1980s there were routinely up to ten times as many new American plays produced Off- and Off Off-Broadway and outside New York as there were on Broadway.

The third development in theatre history that helped change the shape of American drama around mid-century was a revolutionary alteration in the financial basis of the American theatre. The marketplace structure of the Broadway theatre was in keeping with the American tradition of entrepreneurial capitalism; each production was a business intended to make a profit for its backers. From the start the alternative theatres offered a partial release from market pressures. Most of these companies, at least at the beginning, had such tiny budgets that profit or loss was not a significant consideration. Even more radically, virtually all regional theatres were established as non-profit corporations with (allowing for the constraints of their budgets) the quality of the work more important than its profit-making potential.

Until this point in its history, the United States was one of the very few countries in the world with no tradition of public support for the arts; those artistic institutions (museums, symphony orchestras, etc.) that could not support themselves had to rely on the generosity of individual philanthropists. But this also began to change in the 1950s. Earlier in the century the anomalies of American income tax laws had led the very richest families in America to establish charitable foundations; by giving away a lot of their money they actually got to keep more of it from the taxman. In the 1950s some of the largest charitable foundations in America – the Ford Foundation, the Rockefeller Foundation, etc. – turned their attention to the arts and began making large gifts to non-profit theatres, to fill the gap between ticket sales and production costs. In 1966 Congress created the National Endowment for the Arts to distribute government funds to arts institutions, and many individual states and cities followed with their own arts-funding arms. For the first time in American history the majority of theatres in the country were at least partially liberated from the pressures and constraints of having to make a profit or even to break even.

That, of course, opened new opportunities for new American dramatists. Even a masterpiece by an unknown writer is a risky proposition in the commercial theatre, but a theatre company that is not driven by the profit motive can take the risk. Moreover, such companies can afford to nurture and support promising writers through commissions, grants, or works-in-progress stagings. Even failure is not absolute in the non-commercial theatre; having a first play flop on Broadway can seriously damage a new writer's future; losing money in a theatre whose successes also lose money is no great shame.

This imbalance became even more marked as a result of the fourth development, the decline of Broadway in the last third of the century. Not only was its monopolistic hold on the American theatre audience broken, but many of the most talented theatrical artists and virtually all of the most talented new dramatists in the country were happily finding opportunities and building careers elsewhere. Broadway continued to be the home of musicals, light entertainments and star vehicles, but a loss of artistic energy and creativity was inevitable. Financial constraints also worked against Broadway: as production costs escalated by the natural forces of inflation, it became more and more risky for the commercial theatre to attempt anything but the safest, most conservative fare. By the 1980s Broadway had virtually abdicated the job of producing new American plays, instead becoming a central showplace for the best new plays produced elsewhere in the country.

Thus, while for the first half of the twentieth century the terms 'Broadway theatre' and 'American theatre' are virtually synonymous, the years after, say, 1960 can rightly be called the post-Broadway period. Important new plays and playwrights were as likely to appear in Chicago as San Francisco, Buffalo as Seattle, Louisville as Milwaukee; and many more new plays and playwrights were given the opportunity to appear. If some of the benefits of the Broadway monopoly – the intense concentration of talent, the artistic inbreeding – were lost, the openness of the now truly national American theatre to a variety of new voices and new styles made up for them. The fifth and sixth chapters of this volume show that Broadway's decline did not mean the decline of the American drama.

Outline of this volume

This is a study of American drama rather than of American theatre. Although, as the preceding discussion has implied, it is sometimes difficult to separate the two, the focus will always be on the literature rather than the production history. It is a study of the *staged* drama; and while some of the playwrights included in this book also wrote for television or film, only their theatrical plays will be discussed. It is also a study of the *spoken* drama; the Broadway musical is one of the American theatre's special accomplishments, but its serious consideration requires entirely different approaches that would confuse and diffuse the focus of this book. At the centre of any analysis in this volume is the text, the words of the play, written by an author with the intention of communicating something to an audience or affecting an audience in some way.

Literary study has, willy-nilly, certain prejudices, and one of these is a ranking of serious intention and accomplishment over popularity. It is not impossible for a great work to be popular or a popular work to be great, but in those cases where one must choose, the literary critic will opt for the artistic accomplishment over the commercial success. This volume unashamedly owns up to that prejudice, finding Eugene O'Neill's *Strange Interlude*, for example, more interesting than Anne Nichols's *Abie's Irish Rose*, even though the first ran for only 208 performances and the second for over 2300.

After this Introduction, the chapters of the book are divided chronologically, with all but Chapter 2 covering fifteen years each. (Chapter 2 covers the period from about 1890 to 1930, with its main emphasis, however, falling after 1915, so it fits the general pattern.) The dividing points are not arbitrary; each coincides closely with a historical or theatrical turning point that marks a discernible change in the nature of the drama: the beginning of the Depression in 1930; the start of Broadway's greatest period in 1945; the rise of Off-Broadway around 1960; and the establishment of a truly cross-country theatrical arena around 1975.

The division into periods means that some dramatists' work will be discussed in the course of two or more chapters, rather than all in one place. On the other hand, I have not hesitated to stretch the chapter boundaries when that simplifies things or helps the analysis: although Edward Albee's first plays were staged in 1959, he is clearly a dramatist of the 1960s and is discussed in that chapter; although Tennessee Williams's *The Night of the Iguana* was produced in 1961, it can most profitably be studied alongside his plays of the 1950s.

Finally, two technical points that may be violations of usual practice. Recognizing that plays exist first in the theatre, I date plays by their first production (not counting workshops or previews) rather than by their first publication. Generally the two are the same, but there may be a year's difference in some cases and a considerably longer gap in a very few. Unless otherwise indicated, the place of first production is New York City. And I do not identify quotations from the plays by edition or page number. Virtually none of these authors is published in a recognized Standard Edition, and students and casual readers are most likely to encounter the plays in paperback reprints, acting editions or anthologies of various sorts. Page references to unavailable editions would be useless at best and confusing at worst. In most cases the context of the quotation or the manner of its introduction should help locate it in the play.

Chapter 2
1890–1930: The Beginnings

Antecedents and roots

The nineteenth-century American theatre was an immensely popular and vital form of entertainment, with theatres and resident theatre companies in virtually every city of more than village size. But it was not the home of an artistically significant literature. Serious American drama at its most ambitious reached the level of blank verse pseudo-Shakespearean tragedy along the lines of George Henry Boker's *Francesca da Rimini* (1855) or large-scale costume melodrama filled with spectacle, like Steele MacKaye's *Paul Kauver* (1887); at its less ambitious it produced broader melodrama of the cheer-the-hero-hiss-the-villain kind, like George Aiken's enormously popular dramatization of *Uncle Tom's Cabin* (1852). Much of American comic drama was built on variants of the situation established in Royall Tyler's *The Contrast* (1787), the triumph of a supposedly uncivilized American (or Westerner, or Yankee farmer) over sophisticated Englishmen (or Easterners, or city slickers); among the many of this type were Samuel Woodworth's *The Forest Rose* (1825) and J.K. Paulding's *The Lion of the West* (1830).

The reasons for the general absence of literary depth or quality are many and not restricted to America; in Britain and on the European continent the eighteenth and nineteenth centuries were generally fallow periods for dramatic literature. It wasn't until late in the nineteenth century that serious literary writers, led by Ibsen in Norway, Chekhov in Russia and later Shaw in Britain, rediscovered the theatre as a vehicle amenable to ambitious literature, serious or comic. In America the inspiration was probably less the European dramatic models than the new realistic American novel as practised and championed by William Dean Howells and Henry James among others. Emphasizing depth of characterization and accurate depiction of social milieu, these novelists pushed fiction towards the close analysis of the ways in which individuals were affected by the world they inhabited, thus illuminating both psychology and social forces.

Howells and James both tried their hand at drama, generally unsuccessfully, and at dramatic criticism, with considerable influence on at least some of their contemporary playwrights. Their calls for a drama marked by believable and consistent characters, serious consideration of social and moral issues, and direct reflections of reality, along with the model of their fiction and the audience taste for realism which they developed, led to a variety of experiments in dramatic realism in the last decade of the nineteenth century. Much of this new realism was more a matter of surface than content. Some American theatrical producers, like some of their British colleagues, had already become fascinated with realistic stage settings as ends in themselves, putting real trees, real water, even real locomotive engines on stage. The realistic novel's emphasis on setting, with the story and characters clearly growing out of a specific time and place, was reflected in 'local colour' plays such as Augustus Thomas's *In Mizzoura* (1893) and *Arizona* (1899).

The most interesting and challenging sort of dramatic realism, however, was that which reflected the method of the realistic novel by placing characters in moral or practical dilemmas that required a direct acknowledgement and discussion of larger issues. 'Problem plays' such as Edward Sheldon's *Nigger* (1909), however melodramatic in structure or style, were clearly *about* something beyond their specifics; their action frequently stopped dead while characters debated the larger issues or at least made explicit connections between the specific and the general. It is noteworthy that in the history of the novel the Realism of Howells and James led to the Naturalism of Frank Norris and Theodore Dreiser, with its emphasis on the manner in which the environment – social, economic, biological – comes in conflict with human aspirations, because a similar development took place in the drama. A step beyond the play that raised issues was the one that saw that they were not easily resolved or escaped; and the plays of the twenty years surrounding 1900 that have the clear feel of a twentieth- rather than nineteenth-century sensibility about them are those that raise more questions than they answer and that leave their characters facing a future of continued dilemmas and partial solutions.

Generally cited as the first of these is James A. Herne's *Margaret Fleming* (1890). The title character, wife of a factory owner, discovers her husband's working-class mistress has died giving birth to his child. She adopts the baby and, while not completely breaking with her husband, leaves open the question of whether she will ever fully forgive him. Like other problem plays of the period, *Margaret Fleming* thus raises a number of moral and ethical issues; unlike the others, it quite consciously leaves many of them unresolved. Foremost among these is a significant questioning of received definitions of marital morality. In the early part of the play Fleming shows no particular remorse about his infidelity, only an annoyance at the inconvenience of his mistress's pregnancy, and later he apologizes to his wife with the evident expectation of being quickly forgiven. She shocks him by raising the spectre of the double standard:

> MARGARET   Suppose – I – had been unfaithful to you?
> PHILIP   (*With a cry of repugnance.*) Oh, Margaret!
> MARGARET   (*Brokenly.*) There! You see! You are a man, and you have your ideals of – the – sanctity – of – the thing you love. Well, I am a woman – and perhaps – I, too, have the same ideals. I don't know. But, I, too, cry 'pollution.'

It is that – the realization that a wife might expect of her husband the kind of love and loyalty that he assumes from her – that moves Fleming to a deeper remorse and justifies Margaret's insistence that any reconciliation can only be partial and long in coming. *Margaret Fleming* also raises questions about sexual and economic exploitation, the relationship between class and moral obligation, and the nature of the maternal instinct; and it poses new answers, or at least partial dissatisfaction with old answers, to some of these while leaving others unanswered. It is easy to overstate the play's revolutionary nature; it is recognizably a product of its time, and has its share of coincidence and sensationalism – in the midst of all this conflict Margaret goes blind, and early versions of the text include a kidnapping. Still, as one of the first plays in the American repertoire to challenge received assumptions rather than affirming them, it recognizes and brings into the theatre a more complex image of reality than the American drama had previously sustained.

The double standard and socially defined sexual roles are the recurring subjects of the earlier plays of Rachel Crothers, which also reveal the limits that audience taste or authorial courage put on serious questioning of received values at that time. The heroine of the western melodrama *The Three of Us* (1906) is found in a compromising situation by the man she loves and is unable to defend herself because she is sworn to secrecy on another matter. In justifying her silence she makes a strong argument for a woman's right to a 'masculine' sense of honour, but then submits completely, apologizing for every sign of strength and independence she has shown, and admitting that all she really wants is the love and protection of a strong man. In *A Man's World* (1910) a bohemian feminist victimized by gossip discovers that the man she loves is unapologetically guilty of the sins he falsely accuses her of, and rejects him. But she cannot reject or answer his assertion that her values are irrelevant and impertinent in a world whose morality and assumptions are completely defined by men. *A Man's World* thus complains about an injustice while admitting that the injustice seems uncorrectable; in background action two other women are forced to forsake their attempts to define themselves outside masculine terms, one giving up a career for marriage and the other falling into the socially accepted role of spinster social worker.

He and She (1911) is Crothers' first really successful attempt to address these issues without sensationalism or surrender. A woman sculptor wins a valuable commission, but discovers that her teenage daughter has problems that will require her complete attention, and gives up the project. The difference from *The Three of Us* is that this is not a capitulation to social forces or traditional roles; the woman does not rush happily to find fulfilment as a traditional wife and mother, but regretfully interrupts her career because her personal values recognize a higher responsibility at this moment:

> I'll hate myself because I gave it up – and I'll almost – hate – her.
> You needn't tell me. . . . I've heard people say – 'A woman did
> that' and my heart has almost burst with pride – not so much that
> *I* had done it – but for *all* women. And then the door opened –
> and Millicent came in. There isn't any choice, Tom – she's part
> of my body – part of my soul.

In the subplot two other women pick futures – marriage in one case and a career in the other – that are right for them, and thus *He and She* does not settle for simple victory by either side, but rather presents life as requiring personal and difficult choices.

Admittedly these plays and the few others like them represent a small percentage of the drama of the late nineteenth and early twentieth centuries, and their hints of a new sensibility may be more apparent in hindsight than they were at the time. Contemporary audiences did not find the plays of Herne and Crothers significantly more advanced than, say, Eugene Walter's *The Easiest Way* (1905), in which a fallen woman is redeemed by love, only to fall again and be rejected by her lover, or Edward Sheldon's *The Boss* (1911), about an unscrupulous businessman's rise, fall and redemption. In both cases, and in dozens of others, the trappings of realism and contemporary relevance effectively disguised the conventional morality, contrived plots and cardboard characters. And even the most naturalistic plays of social commentary had a touch of the allegorical about them, with characters functioning more as representatives of The Modern Woman, The Downtrodden Poor and similar types than as individuals.

Meanwhile, some of the most popular playwrights of the period made little or no pretence of writing anything different from the kinds of plays that were the mainstays of late nineteenth-century drama. The light comedies and romantic melodramas of Clyde Fitch have only the surface details of contemporary life and manners to distinguish them from similar plays written twenty years earlier. Even less innovative were the melodramatic plots and striking stage tableaux around which actor-playwright William Gillette constructed starring roles for himself in such successful vehicles as the Civil War spy thriller *Secret Service* (1895) and *Sherlock Holmes* (1899). It was about this time that George M. Cohan began his career as playwright with such successes as *Little Johnny Jones* (1904) and *Forty-Five Minutes from Broadway* (1906), which are far more significant for their contribution to the development of the Broadway musical as an art form than for any special virtues in their romantic comedy plots and characterizations.

The more immediate roots of later twentieth-century American drama appeared in the second decade of the century, when the Little Theatre movement brought a new generation of writers to the theatre. Experimental theatre companies – what would later come to be called Off- and Off Off-Broadway in America and fringe theatre in Britain – had appeared in Europe towards the end of the nineteenth century and in Britain early in the twentieth, but it wasn't until after 1910 that the movement reached America as part of the broader social and intellectual ferment of the time. In a number of cities across the country young writers and political activists gathered with the self-conscious intention of creating new and experimental literature, and many of these young artists turned to the theatre. One such company, a loose collection of poets, artists and socialist activists based in New York City's Bohemian neighbourhood of Greenwich Village, declared themselves the Province-town Players (after Provincetown, Massachusetts, where they spent sum-mers and produced their first plays in 1915). A peripheral member of the group, Eugene O'Neill, had his first play produced by the Provincetown Players in 1916.

Eugene O'Neill: the early naturalistic plays

Before beginning a discussion of O'Neill's plays it is necessary to note that his career spanned more than fifty years, extending beyond his death with the release of several posthumous plays, and dividing into at least three distinct periods. So his work will be dealt with in segments spread over several chapters, with chronology occasionally violated for the pur-pose of discussing plays of similar style together. O'Neill's earliest plays, predominantly one act long or barely sketches, are all naturalistic and anecdotal, small or large episodes in the lives of unremarkable people. Many of the early plays deal with sailors on or recently off the sea; four of them – *Bound East for Cardiff* (1916), *In the Zone* (1917), *The Long Voyage Home* (1917), *Moon of the Caribees* (1918) – have essentially the same cast, the crew of the freighter *S.S. Glencairn*.

In the *Glencairn* plays, as in others of this period, O'Neill breaks with his immediate predecessors in the American drama by making no attempt to preach or to shape his characters or story to reflect some social issue or demonstrate some social thesis. The power of the plays lies in their unadornedly anecdotal quality: in *Bound East* an injured sailor dies and his mates are saddened; in *Voyage* a sailor looking forward to leaving the sea is robbed and shanghaied back onto a ship. By refusing to impose meanings on the anecdotes, O'Neill demands that attention be paid to these people's small adventures for their own sake, and thus announces a basic change, for America, in the definition of what drama does. These short plays are not totally free of thesis, but thesis is not what generates them. They are observational, putting on stage the dramatist's perceptions of reality rather than his moral or social opinions. His characters are conceived of as characters – that is, as presentations of human beings – rather than as issues or problems dressed in human clothing.

Paradoxically, this concentration on the characters as individuals and the plots as anecdotes gives the plays an unstated universality. By emphasizing the realistic and familiar in characterization, O'Neill makes his characters representative – not of social or moral types, but of humanity in general. The barely articulated camaraderie of the *Glencairn* crew, the boundaries of their imaginations and lives, the small but significant private secrets that separate them are all recognizably human, and become the true subjects of the plays. *Bound East* is about death, not as a moral issue but as an experience through which the dying man must find his way and to which the living must react. *Moon* makes us recognize that loneliness and the attempt to find pleasure in distractions are facts of life, things that people feel and do.

If the characters of O'Neill's early plays have anything in common it is obsessiveness, overt or hidden. A few of the plays – for instance, *Ile* (1917), about an Ahab-like whaling captain – are open studies in obsession, whose characters are destroyed by their inability to break free of some fixation. But almost all of O'Neill's characters are limited in their freedom by internal forces, if only the lack of the imagination necessary to make a change. It is not only because he had spent some time as a merchant sailor that he was drawn to what he would call in *Anna Christie* 'dat ole davil, sea' as a subject. Seamen share with farmers, another recurring group of characters in O'Neill's early plays, an emotional and spiritual attachment to their element that is beyond their conscious control. The hint of tragedy in *The Long Voyage Home* is not that the sailor Olson is forced back to the sea after trying to quit, but that he actually thought he could break away in the first place; the horror of *Where the Cross is Made* (1918) is not in the ghostly figures that appear in one of O'Neill's first experiments with non-realistic effects, but in the psychological study of a father and son both driven mad by a fantasy attached to the sea; the O'Henry-like twist in the plot of *The Rope* (1918) is built on the conflicting obsessions of land, family and revenge that drive a farmer and his prodigal son.

The undeniable strength of these early one-act plays made O'Neill's move to longer forms and to the mainstream Broadway theatre inevitable, and by the early 1920s he was firmly established as the most important new playwright in America. His first Broadway plays included a few more in the naturalistic mode of his beginnings, but signs of strain soon appeared. The slice-of-life mode of the shorter works did not lend itself easily to longer plays, and O'Neill began to reach beyond naturalism. As one of the most intellectual and consciously philosophical authors in American literature, he found himself moving more towards thesis drama, not with the political or social agendas of earlier playwrights, but with the desire to dramatize his philosophical and spiritual visions. As these ambitions became more clear to him, so did the apparent inability of realism to encompass them, and he soon rejected that mode for an extended period of stylistic and technical experimentation.

The full weight of philosophical content that O'Neill wanted the drama to bear will be analysed later in this chapter, in the section devoted to his non-realistic plays. The first signs of intentions more complex than the simple depiction of reality come in the extension of the early plays' sense of obsession-generated fate to a more fully developed tragic vision. In many ways his first Broadway production, *Beyond the Horizon* (1920), is a summation of his themes and concerns up to then, with his signature symbols of the sea and the farm, and his characters' uncontrollable ties to one or the other. What is added in *Beyond the Horizon*, and was soon to be seen as even more central to his vision, is an overriding sense of tragic doom that is not merely a function of obsession, as in the earlier plays, but an elemental fact of life.

Beyond the Horizon opens by introducing two brothers: the poetic dreamer Robert, drawn by the 'beauty of the far off and unknown, . . . beyond the horizon', plans to leave the family farm for the life of a sailor, while the more stolid, practical Andrew will stay on. But Ruth, the woman they both love, chooses Robert, and he decides impulsively to stay at home and marry her, while Andrew chivalrously goes to sea in his place. What follows is predictable because O'Neill makes it seem inevitable: totally ill-equipped to be a farmer, Robert fails as manager and husband, but fails himself more deeply by frustrating and repressing his *wanderlust*. Meanwhile Ruth finds that her somewhat whimsical choice of Robert over Andrew was a mistake that traps her in a stultifying, joyless life from which there is no release. And the wonders of the world beyond the horizon are wasted on the unimaginative Andrew, who has moderate success but none of the satisfaction he would have found within the bounds of the farm. The play ends with Robert, broken in body and spirit, dying with a vision of the afterlife that will be the only escape granted any of them: 'I can hear the old voices calling me to come – And this time I'm going! It isn't the end. It's a free beginning – the start of my voyage! I've won my right to my trip – the right of release – beyond the horizon!'

Beyond the Horizon is a play of unrelenting doom, in part the result of the characters' failure to be true to their own natures, but to a greater extent the workings of an ironic and cruel providence. It would be simplistic to say merely that they get what they deserve for not being true to themselves; each makes his or her fatal error for what seem at the time reasonable and honourable motives, and even at his most self-critical Robert insists that he and Ruth 'can both justly lay some of the blame for our stumbling on God'. The sunset that opens the play is as ironic as the sunrise that closes it; the first calls the characters' attention to the horizon at the moment that it is being closed, while the second offers an elusive hope for freedom in death that merely emphasizes the hopelessness of the characters who remain alive.

Anna Christie (1921) is a little lighter in tone, if only because its characters are allowed briefly to experience the fulfilment denied to those in *Beyond the Horizon*, before the gloom closes in on them again like the sea fog that dominates the final act of the play. The title character is a prostitute who is reunited in the first act with her sea-going and sea-hating father, who reluctantly takes her on board his coal barge where, to his horror, she comes under the spell of what he continually curses as 'dat ole davil, sea'. When the barge picks up the shipwrecked Mat Burke, who quickly falls in love with Anna, the play seems to be moving towards the hope of a new life. But Mat's proposal of marriage forces a confession of her past from Anna, leading to his curses and rejection. In the last act they are reconciled, slowly and painfully pushing past each practical and emotional obstacle to their getting together, but their earnest determination only has the effect of emphasizing the size of those obstacles in the audience's mind. The final images of the play are of futility and foreboding, despite the characters' attempts to believe in a happy future: 'Fog, fog, fog, all bloody time. You can't see vhere you vas going, no. Only dat ole davil, sea – she knows!'

A number of non-naturalistic plays (to be discussed later) came next, but the first period in O'Neill's career concluded with *Desire Under the Elms* (1924), a full-length tragedy of obsession and inevitability. Set in a barren New England farm in 1850, the play shows a conflict between father and son complicated when the patriarch marries a younger woman whose first line – 'It's purty – purty! I can't b'lieve it's r'ally mine' – establishes her as a dangerous rival to both. To ensure her do-minance Abbie makes Cabot promise to leave the farm to her child if she bears him one, and then seduces Eben to produce the child. But in the process Abbie falls in love with Eben, killing the baby to prove her loyalty. Eben insists on being arrested with her, leaving the barren Cabot on his barren farm. *Desire Under the Elms* is, then, a drama of obsessions in conflict: Cabot's determination to live fully and to conquer his land; Eben's hatred of his father and need to lay to rest his mother's spirit, which he senses haunting the farm; and Abbie's compulsion to possess and control something after her years of poverty, compounded with the obsessiveness of her love for Eben.

But *Desire*, unlike the earlier realistic plays, reaches consciously for tragedy, invoking the myths of Oedipus (Eben's hatred of his father, and his confusion of his love for Abbie and for his mother), Phaedra (the stepmother's passion for the stepson) and Medea (the mother's sacrifice of the child); and successfully borrowing tragic stature through the resonances. It also uses Freudian psychology effectively in defining and explaining all three characters, most notably Eben, who early in the play attempts to declare his manhood by sleeping with his father's whore, and whose seduction by Abbie takes place in the room haunted by his mother's spirit:

> ABBIE   Don't cry, Eben! I'll take yer Maw's place! I'll be every-
> thin' she was t'ye! . . .   Don't be afeered! I'll kiss ye pure,
> Eben – same's if I was a Maw t'ye – an' ye kin kiss me back's
> if yew was my son . . . .
> EBEN   Maw! Maw! What d'ye want? What air ye tellin' me?
> ABBIE   She's tellin' ye t'love me. She knows I love ye an' I'll be
> good t'ye. Can't ye feel it? Don't ye know? She's tellin' ye
> t'love me, Eben!

O'Neill's interest in dramatic imagery, apparent in the symbolic use of the horizon in *Beyond the Horizon* and 'dat ole davil, sea' in *Anna Christie*, continues in *Desire Under the Elms* in a much more sustained and developed way. Foremost among the play's symbols are the rocks that cover the barren farm, and the stone walls and fences built from them. Repeatedly invoked and cursed by each of the characters, they take on layers of meanings, suggesting first the difficult and Sisyphean life of the farmers, then the cold hardness of Cabot's religion and Eben's hatred (equating them), then the unending harshness of the characters' emotional lives and the fated boundaries within which they must live their tragedy.

It must be admitted that, for all their power, these early plays have flaws which themselves bear O'Neill's signature. Throughout his career he was to be convinced that the best way to show a character's concerns was to have him repeat them again and again, often in the same words. There is a sometimes numbing verbosity to *Anna Christie*, particularly in the scenes in which the essentially non-verbal characters struggle to express themselves; and each play's catch-phrase declares its significance by constant repetition: 'dat ole davil, sea', and *Desire*'s 'dead spit 'n' image', used variously to equate Eben and Cabot, Eben and his mother, the baby and each of them, even Eben and Abbie, thus stressing the tragic bonds that hold them all together. The dialogue in these plays also exposes O'Neill's tin ear for dialect and natural speech, with Anna and her father sounding at times like burlesque comic Swedes and Mat like a stage Irishman, while the Cabots waver between Yankee and hillbilly accents. This was a limitation O'Neill would never overcome; though at his best he could create a kind of stage poetry out of the eloquence or stammering of his characters, to the end of his career he would burden some with broad dialects or speech patterns never spoken by real human beings.

More significant than these technical flaws, and evidently more frustrating for O'Neill, is an obvious and seemingly unresolvable tension between the tragic ambitions of these plays and their realistic trappings. However effective the symbolism or classical allusions, there is something bathetic about the insistently realistic farmers of *Beyond the Horizon* and *Desire Under the Elms* speaking of fate and predetermination; and the gloomy fatalism of *Anna Christie* seems more an authorial vision imposed on the characters than a discovery growing out of the reality of the play. The plays are far from failures, but they were clearly too far from O'Neill's vision of what they should be to satisfy him. O'Neill would wrestle throughout his career with the double challenge of making his philosophical observations and tragic vision seem to grow naturally out of the events and characters of his plays rather than being imposed on them, and of making their darkness dramatically palatable to an audience without falsifying his vision. At this point he developed serious doubts about his ability to do this within the bounds of realism, or about realism's ability to carry the thematic burdens he wanted to put on it; and he began more than a decade of experiments in alternative forms before he finally returned to domestic realism in his last and greatest plays.

Other developments in realism 1915–1930

The mix of new American plays in the early 1920s included romantic comedies, costume dramas, mystery thrillers, local colour pieces and domestic melodramas with only superficial differences from similar plays written twenty or thirty years earlier. Nevertheless, among the young dramatists of the new century there were several others who, like O'Neill, were exploring the possibilities of realism and naturalism in the theatre. As will be seen later in this chapter, they represented only one strand of the various courses the American drama was taking, but it was the one that followed most directly the lead the previous generation had provided.

Susan Glaspell, one of the founders of the Provincetown Players, wrote a number of short satiric comedies and a few realistic dramas of some merit. *Trifles* (1916), her most successful work, is an efficient and effective one-act essay on sexual differences. A farmer has been murdered, possibly by his wife, and the men who come to the farmhouse to investigate leave their wives in the kitchen, on the unspoken assumption that there will be nothing of importance in that woman's room. As the wives idly tidy up, they discover and immediately understand the significance of things the men would never recognize as clues even if they found them: a piece of sloppy sewing, a broken birdcage, a dead songbird. Barely having to verbalize their insights, they reconstruct the story of a brutal husband and a wife driven to the end of her tether; barely having to verbalize their decision, they easily conceal these 'trifles' from the men.

The subject of *Trifles* is thus not just the differing perceptions and preconceptions of the men and women about what is significant, but also the women's growing sense of unity and sisterhood. Starting with sympathy for the murderess, they move through guilt at not having visited and helped her, to a sense of solidarity with her and each other, made concrete in the hiding of the evidence. One of the play's strengths is the elliptical nature of its language, the women acknowledging and expressing most of their discoveries and decisions through a silence and indirection that dramatize their empathy more than open discussion could. The special experience of women is the subject of Glaspell's other serious plays: *The Outside* (1917), about two alienated women forced to recognize their almost forgotten ties to the human world; *Bernice* (1919), about the effect of a woman's apparent suicide on the survivors; *Inheritors* (1921), which echoes *Antigone* in the conflict between an idealistic college student and a temporizing administrator; *The Verge* (1921), in which a woman striving for total, uncompromising liberation can find it only in insanity; and *Alison's House* (1930), in which the heirs of an Emily Dickinson-like poet struggle with their obligation to publish her embarrassingly intimate works.

The drama of unexpected moral complexities, in the tradition of Herne and Crothers, continued in early plays by Maxwell Anderson and Sidney Howard, though both moved to other styles later in their careers. Anderson's *What Price Glory?* (1924), written with Laurence Stallings, is a war story that resists all the received clichés and theatrical conventions about war: its soldiers are neither passionately dedicated patriots nor sentimentalized common men transfigured by the experience of battle, but ordinary Joes somewhat brutalized by their experience and merely trying to do their job and survive. Howard's *They Knew What They Wanted* (1924) gives unprecedented depth to what could have been a conventional romance, as the parties in a sexual triangle talk their way through the crisis to a compromise that each can live with. The conclusion is sentimental, but it is the sentiment inspired by practical little people making the best they can out of life, rather than triumphing over it in a fantasy happy ending.

To contemporary audiences these two plays, along with O'Neill's *Desire Under the Elms* the same year, were notable for another reason, their unusual frankness of language and characterization. As shocking as the coarse soldiers' language of *What Price Glory?* was, its unromanticized psychology was even more revolutionary; and the other two plays' depictions of sexual passions and unashamed violations of conventional morality were both hailed and deplored. This was the decade in which Freudian psychology became a subject of interest in America; and if an earlier generation's contribution to dramatic realism lay mainly in finding new complexities to moral and social issues, the 1920s saw an increasing interest in dramatizing the darker complexities of human psychology.

In some cases, of course, this new psychologizing was trivial, merely adding a thin Freudian gloss to a conventional murder mystery or drama of marital problems. But at its best the combination of Freudian psychology and dramatic realism could produce chillingly accurate depictions of characters and situations hitherto ignored or only glanced at by American drama. In George Kelly's *Craig's Wife* (1925) a cold and neurotic woman openly admits that she married for economic and social power rather than love. She defines her success by her elegant house, which she compulsively keeps in pristine order, screening out anything that could taint its perfection. When her husband finally realizes the extent of her obsession and leaves her, the pathetic woman is still tidying the picture-perfect living room that is all she has in life. Sidney Howard's *The Silver Cord* (1926) presents an even more disturbed woman, a mother so neurotically attached to her grown sons that she treats everything from their careers to their women as romantic rivals. She almost succeeds in destroying one son's marriage, defeated only by a wife more determined than she, and does end her other son's engagement, reducing him to infantile dependence on her.

The new psychological depth was not just a matter of presenting neurotic monsters on stage. Even a comparatively minor play such as *Dancing Mothers* (1924) by Edgar Selwyn and Edmund Goulding, about a wife who tries to reform her straying husband by acting wild herself, could gain resonances by showing that the self-indulgent and self-centred perceive themselves as normal, and cannot be changed overnight by simple stage conventions. And even comedy could occasionally support some psychological realism; the domineering mother of *Mrs Partridge Presents* (1925), by Mary Kennedy and Ruth Hawthorne, is not significantly different from the monster in *The Silver Cord*, and only her children's success in rebelling makes the play comic.

Yet another form of realism is represented by Elmer Rice's *Street Scene* (1929), a nearly plotless slice-of-life drama set on the sidewalk and front steps of a working-class New York City apartment building. In the course of two days we watch residents and neighbours go in and out, look out their windows, pause to chat or gossip on the steps and generally just carry out the very ordinary non-events of life:

> MRS FIORENTINO   Good evening, Mrs Jones.
>
> MRS JONES (*stopping beneath Mrs Fiorentino's window*)   Good evenin', Mrs F. Well, I hope it's hot enough for you.
>
> MRS FIORENTINO   Ain't it joost awful? When I was through with the dishes, you could take my clothes and joost wring them out.
>
> MRS JONES   Me too. I ain't got a dry stitch on me . . . . (*As Olga Olsen comes up the cellar stairs*) Good evenin', Mrs Olsen. Awful hot, ain't it?
>
> MRS OLSEN   Yust awful. Mrs Forentiner, my hoosban' say vill you put de garbage on de doomvaider?
>
> MRS FIORENTINO   Oh, sure, sure! I didn't hear him vistle. Don't go 'vay, Mrs Jones . . . . (*Willie Maurrant, a disorderly boy of twelve, appears at the left on roller skates.*)
>
> WILLIE (*raising his head and bawling*)   Hey, Ma!
>
> MRS JONES   If you want your mother, why don't you go upstairs, instead o' yellin' like that?
>
> WILLIE (*without paying the slightest attention to her, bawls louder*) Hey, Ma!

The bulk of the play is made up of scenes like this, pointless except that their depiction of uneventful reality is the whole point. In addition to the six families in this building and their visitors, the play calls for more than fifty passers-by, each briefly individualized by costume or manner, and for the continuous background sounds of the city – a carefully choreographed and orchestrated evocation of reality in whose context a skeletal plot of adultery and murder seems out of place. One is more likely to remember and believe in the smaller events and subsidiary characters: the young couple who are drunk and loving at midnight but bitter and abusive at dawn, the man who buys ice cream cones for everyone, the carefree children who do not understand the shame of being evicted. *Street Scene* builds on the innovation of Eugene O'Neill's *Glencairn* plays in presenting the facts of life as dramatic and interesting in themselves, and anticipates the Depression-era plays of Clifford Odets in using the domestic setting to suggest the larger world outside.

Comedy

Much nineteenth-century American comedy played on the idea of the artless American triumphing over the sophisticated Englishman or Bostonian, and variants on that convention survived into the new century in such plays as Booth Tarkington's *Clarence* (1919) and Don Marquis's *The Old Soak* (1922). The twentieth-century variant pitted old-fashioned values against new-fangled manners and morality, usually in a romantic setting, as in Langdon Mitchell's *The New York Idea* (1906), in which a divorced couple remain friendly and eventually remarry, shocking everyone but their equally sophisticated friends. Salisbury Field's *Wedding Bells* (1919) and Philip Barry's *Philadelphia Story* (1939) are among its direct descendants. A formula popular in the 1920s pitted young lovers against their more conservative parents; Anne Nichols's *Abie's Irish Rose* (1922), whose title says all that is necessary about its mix of romantic and ethnic humour, exploited the possibilities of the formula successfully enough to run for almost a decade. There was comparatively little pure slapstick or physical humour, that being the speciality of film comedians; and strikingly absent from the American tradition, with rare exceptions, was the quick-under-the-bed-it's-my-husband bedroom farce of the Feydeau school. As a result, there was little exploration of comedy's anarchic or critical potential in the American drama of this period – or, indeed, of any period except briefly in the 1960s. While audiences in the commercial Broadway theatre were surprisingly supportive of challenging serious drama, they came to comedies for relaxation and escape, and could be confident of leaving with their values and assumptions unshaken.

The two best-regarded comic playwrights of the period were George S. Kaufman and Philip Barry. Kaufman, usually writing with a collaborator, specialized in the satire of generally easy targets. *Dulcy* (1921, written with Marc Connelly) pokes gentle fun at a well-meaning but scatter-brained society matron, while *To The Ladies!* (1922, with Connelly) satirizes big business by having a clever wife guide her dull husband to a promotion. *Merton of the Movies* (1922, with Connelly), *The Butter and Egg Man* (1925), and *June Moon* (1929, with Ring Lardner) mock, respectively, Hollywood, Broadway and pop music. Many of Kaufman's plays are adaptations of short stories or developments of his collaborators' ideas, with his contribution being the comic structure and dialogue, paring the action to the bone and providing the fast-paced gags, wisecracks and clever repartee that gave the plays a knowing modern air. His only rivals in this particular genre were Ben Hecht and Charles MacArthur, who collaborated on two classic farces, *The Front Page* (1928), about unscrupulous newspapermen, and *Twentieth Century* (1928), about a Hollywood producer trying to seduce and sign an actress in the course of a train journey.

The overwhelming majority of Philip Barry's twenty-one plays were not humorous, but the overwhelming majority of those were failures, so it is on a handful of successful comedies that his reputation rests. And on that basis – on two plays in particular – Barry is recognized as the

American master of sophisticated drawing-room comedy. While Kauf-man specialized in frenetic action and snappy repartee, Barry's was more a comedy of character and idea, with a philosophical and moral core beneath the light veneer. All his comedies are set in the world of the well-to-do; all see conventional morality and the business ethic as the enemy of the individual, especially the artistically inclined; all celebrate the instinct to violate convention, while keeping that rebellion well within the bounds of comedy. In *You and I* (1923) a sympathetic father, a frustrated artist himself, subsidizes his talented son's studies so that he can have both art and marriage; in *The Youngest* (1924) a young writer triumphs over his business-oriented family; in *Paris Bound* (1927) a self-consciously 'modern' couple find conventional morality difficult to escape. Typically with Barry, the humour in these plays lies not so much in single lines as in the twists of plot and the reactions of the conventional characters to the unconventional; and there is always an undisguised but controlled element of sentiment and seriousness, particularly in the recognition that happiness is a rare thing, to be grasped at in whatever form it takes.

It was with *Holiday* (1928) that Barry first found the perfect balance of these elements. The story itself is trivial and even contrived: a success-ful young businessman shocks his fiancée and her father by declaring his contempt for business values and his plan to make only enough money to allow himself to take a few years off to enjoy himself. These unconventional impulses are shared by the fiancée's ugly-duckling sister, and the play bides its time while the right couple discover each other. In the interim we get to watch the idle rich at play in the world of beautiful clothes, champagne suppers and sophisticated dialogue, while we enjoy the effect even mild rebellion has on the stuffy, cheer the growing independence of the sister, and finally delight in the plot twists that end one romance and start another. Determined to make his mark as a serious dramatist, Barry would not find the same comic success until *The Philadelphia Story* eleven years later.

Alternatives to realism

Although hindsight recognizes the beginnings of twentieth-century American drama in the most realistic plays, particularly those exploring social issues or psychological complexities, it would not have been quite so clear to contemporary audiences that this was the direction the drama was going to take. One of the most critically respected dramatists of the first two decades of the century, for example, was the now almost-forgotten Percy MacKaye, whose plays ranged in style from pseudo-Sha-kespearean verse tragedy to grand semi-operatic masques and pageants. MacKaye, whose father, Steele MacKaye, had been a master of nine-teenth-century spectacle melodrama, inherited a sense of theatricality.and ambitiousness, which in his case took the form of poetic dialogue, classi-cal and mythical subjects, and spectacular staging. He experimented in almost every non-realistic mode – Shakespearean-style verse tragedy and comedy, Greek-style tragedy, pastoral American romance, *commedia dell'arte* – before turning his hand to pageants and community dramas, very large-scale outdoor performances on grand themes, often involving whole communities in their casts. A Massachusetts production of *The Canterbury Pilgrims* (1903) had a cast of 1500, and *St Louis, a Civic Mas-que* (1914) had 7500 principals, chorus members and extras on its vast playing area. Other titles – *Washington, The Man Who Made Us* (1916), *The Roll Call, a Masque of the Red Cross* (1918) – indicate both the grand subjects and the extra-dramatic mission of these pageants, dedicated as much to communal involvement and celebration as to literature.

MacKaye was not alone in any of these styles. Verse dramas, classical tragedies and pageant plays made up a small but respected and note-worthy part of the American dramatic repertoire in the early years of the century, and some contemporary critics thought they saw the future of American drama in these ambitious modes rather than in the quieter realistic plays. Meanwhile, other writers looked to other non-realistic forms. The social and political agendas of some little theatre groups led to clumsy attempts at allegorical and agitprop plays, while some more commercial writers continued to find vitality in historical and costume melodramas. Edward Knoblock's *Kismet* (1911), an Arabian Nights tale, was a big hit; and through the first thirty years of the century virtually every Broadway season had at least one exotic melodrama set in a Chinese opium den, one swashbuckler set in eighteenth-century France, one romantic adventure involving Mexican bandits, one biblical parable or epic, one pseudo-Shakespearean verse play, and so on.

European influences began to be felt in the American drama in the early 1920s, as the plays of Strindberg, Capek, Pirandello and the Ger-man expressionists and epic dramatists were read and produced in America. The Broadway season of 1922–23, for example, included pro-ductions of Capek's *R.U.R.* and *The Insect Comedy*, Pirandello's *Six Characters in Search of an Author*, Meinhard and Bernauer's 'fantastic melodrama' *Johannes Kreisler*, Claudel's *The Tidings Brought to Mary*, An-dreyev's *Anathema*, and Ibsen's *Peer Gynt*, along with the Moscow Art Theatre's repertoire of Gorky and Chekhov, providing a particularly intense but by no means unique seminar in European drama. American experiments, particularly in expressionism and its offshoots – dream, memory, flashback and fantasy plays – were a staple of the 1920s, rarely accounting for more than a handful of plays a season but never absent.

As early as 1924 Kaufman and Connelly were able to use the form comically in *Beggar on Horseback*, in which a young musician has a nightmare vision of what a conventional job and marriage would be like for him; though the play's satire is primarily aimed at the business world, the audience could not see the joke if they were not familiar with expressionism and the parodic ways in which Kaufman and Connelly use it.

One of the most successful American expressionist plays is *The Adding Machine* (1923) by Elmer Rice, who had already broken new theatrical ground nine years earlier in *On Trial* (1914), the first appearance of the now-familiar device of using courtroom testimony to lead into flashbacks re-enacting the events leading up to the crime. Although Rice denied having read any European expressionist plays, he used many of the same techniques in *The Adding Machine* to portray visually and aurally, not objective reality, but reality as perceived and experienced by his central character, the identityless clerk Mr Zero. While early scenes only hint that something other than external reality is being presented, the play clearly moves into Zero's mind when his boss announces that he is to be replaced by an adding machine:

> *Soft music is heard — the sound of the mechanical player of a distant merry-go-round. The part of the floor upon which the desks and stools are standing begins to revolve.. . . . The platform is revolving rapidly now. Zero and the Boss face each other. They are entirely motionless save for the Boss's jaws, which open and close incessantly. But the words are inaudible. The music swells and swells. To it is added every offstage effect of the theater: the wind, the waves, the galloping horses, the locomotive whistle. . . . For an instant there is a flash of red and then everything is plunged into blackness.*

What has happened, we shall later learn, is that Zero has killed the boss, but we don't see that; in the expressionist manner we see and hear what goes on inside Zero rather than outside. Later, at Zero's trial, he pours out the emptiness of his life in an extended stream-of-consciousness monologue that is clearly more a depiction of his internal mental breakdown than of the external situation. The second half of the play, showing Zero's execution and afterlife, is completely stylized and unrealistic.

The Adding Machine's expressionism is not merely a technical experiment; Rice uses it as some of his contemporaries used realism, to dramatize his central character's psychology. Zero is so broken in mind and spirit that he cannot enjoy heaven, choosing to spend eternity serving a cosmic adding machine. The play includes some overt commentary on mankind's regression to 'a waste product, a slave to a contraption of steel and iron', but its theatricality is stronger than its politics; by taking us inside Zero, Rice gives us a direct experience of his loss of dignity and humanity.

Another alternative to realism during the 1920s was the folk play – a term describing the content or effect, and not suggesting a communal or non-literary creation. Though sometimes ostensibly realistic in the tradition of local colour drama, many of these plays used music, dance and other production elements to produce a dream-like or mythical effect. It was a function of the American social situation of the period that plays about southern blacks were likely to carry almost automatic associations of religious music, superstition and childlike fantasy, and two of the most successful folk plays were written by white authors about black characters.

Dorothy and DuBose Heyward's *Porgy* (1927), most familiar as the source of George Gershwin's opera *Porgy and Bess*, is a romantic fable of a crippled beggar's love for a whore. The play is almost as filled with music as the opera, either in the form of spirituals or of accompaniment to stage effects. It is clear, for example, that the end of Act One, a funeral service filled with singing, is meant to affect the audience on more than a merely realistic level:

> *The beautiful old spiritual beats triumphantly through the narrow room, steadily gaining in speed. Serena is the first to leap to her feet and begin to 'shout.' One by one, as the spirit moves them, the Negroes follow her example till they are all on their feet, swaying, shuffling, clapping their hands. . . . 'Allelujahs' and cries of 'yes, Lord,' are interjected into the singing. And the rhythm swells till the old walls seem to rock and surge with the sweep of it.*

Later a storm scene is orchestrated as a blend of wind and rain sounds outside and spiritual singing inside. To some extent scenes like these are merely local colour, attempts to capture the atmosphere of this unfamiliar and somewhat exotic culture. But *Porgy* is not, as some local-colour plays were, merely theatrical anthropology. For the play to work – for the love story to be more than pathetic or ludicrous, and for Porgy's search for Bess as the play ends to be felt as a noble romantic quest – the audience must relate to *Porgy* as to a romance or folk tale. The musical and staging effects, along with the melodramatic plot twists and even the racial stereotypes, are designed to induce the suspension of disbelief.

Marc Connelly's *The Green Pastures* (1930) is a *faux-naif* retelling of the bible from the supposed point of view of an uneducated southern black child translating the tales into the world of his experience. Thus all the characters are black, heaven is a continual fish fry occasionally interrupted for spiritual singing, and 'De Lawd' has the appearance and manner of an imposing country preacher. The world of the Old Testament is conflated into modern black America: the Flood is inspired by God's unpleasant encounter with some crap-shooters; Moses must deal with the Sublime Order of Princes of the House of Pharaoh, Home

Chapter; and Babylon is a flashy New Orleans night club. Only the discovery that some men have found through suffering the ability to love and forgive reunites De Lawd with his creation:

> GOD   Through *sufferin'*, he said.
> GABRIEL   Yes, Lawd.
> GOD   I'm tryin to find it, too. It's awful impo'tant. It's awful impo'tant to all de people on my earth. Did he mean dat even God must suffer? . . . (*In the distance a voice cries.*)
> THE VOICE   Oh, look at him! Oh, look, dey goin' to make him carry it up dat high hill! Dey goin' to nail him to it! . . . (*God rises and murmurs 'Yes!' as if in recognition . . . All of the angels burst into 'Hallelujah, King Jesus.' God continues to smile . . .*)

If one puts aside what is now likely to be seen as implicit racism in the play's patronizing picture of blacks, then the play's charm, humour and emotional power are apparent. *The Green Pastures* proves that the sophisticated tools of non-realistic drama can transport a play and an audience to a world of childlike faith and imagination, producing effects the naturalistic drama could not.

Eugene O'Neill: the experimental plays

The one dramatist who was most active and most successful in exploring alternatives to realism in the 1920s was Eugene O'Neill. Despite his beginnings in realistic drama, or perhaps because of them, O'Neill had already begun to turn away from realism by the time he wrote *Desire Under the Elms*. That play's conscious striving towards tragedy was one sign of O'Neill's dissatisfaction with the limits of realism; he spent the decade and beyond experimenting with almost every possible theatrical style and device: expressionism (*The Emperor Jones, The Hairy Ape*), fantasy and dream sequences (*The Emperor Jones, The Fountain*), Greek tragedy (*Mourning Becomes Electra*), symbolic sets or lighting (*The Hairy Ape, Welded, All God's Chillun Got Wings*), masks (*The Great God Brown, Lazarus Laughed, Days Without End*), spoken thoughts (*Welded, Strange Interlude, Dynamo*), pageant-like epic staging and spectacle (*Marco Millions, Lazarus Laughed*). *All God's Chillun, The Fountain, The Great God Brown, Marco Millions* and *Strange Interlude* all cover fictional periods of twenty years or more, while *Mourning Becomes Electra* (a trilogy), *Marco Millions* (written as two plays, though cut for production) and *Strange Interlude*

(5½ hours) test the outer limits of playing time.

O'Neill was not experimenting for experiment's sake. He was driven during this period by a basic dissatisfaction with the limitations of conventional theatre. Every alternative he tried was essentially a stretching device, an attempt to make the drama as a literary form hold more, express more, cover more, go deeper, or show more of reality than it had been asked to show before, and more than O'Neill felt realism could capture. Before discussing the individual plays, then, it may be useful to summarize briefly the nature of the philosophical, metaphysical and psychological weight he was asking the drama to carry.

Any discussion of O'Neill's ideas must begin with the fatalism and sense of doom already apparent in his early plays. With rare exceptions, O'Neill's characters are trapped by some internal or external condition that limits their possibilities and frustrates their desires. In various plays this fate will take the form of biology (*The Emperor Jones*), economics (*The Hairy Ape*), social conditioning (*All God's Chillun*), individual limitations of mind (*Mourning Becomes Electra*) or spirit (*The Great God Brown, Marco Millions*), and metaphysics (*Strange Interlude*). In some cases the purpose of the play is to demonstrate the lack of freedom; in others, to explain its causes or to explore its effects. The assumption that life is defined by painful and inescapable limits is never far from the centre of O'Neill's work.

O'Neill once wrote half-seriously that the key to understanding all his works was to remember that he had been raised as an Irish Catholic. To him that meant an inheritance of guilt, repression and an instinctively pessimistic view of life – an inheritance he rejected as an adult but then spent his life fighting against while never completely escaping. His plays are filled with characters whose lives are desiccated and darkened by their religion, or who, like Anna in *Anna Christie* or the Tyrone family of *Long Day's Journey into Night*, are trapped in a conviction of guilt and unworthiness. These and other plays also illustrate O'Neill's rebellion against life-negating religion; *The Great God Brown, Strange Interlude, Lazarus Laughed, Dynamo* and *Days Without End* focus on characters who either succeed or fail in finding a life-affirming religious faith.

O'Neill was one of the most intellectual and well-read of all American dramatists, and the products of his thoughts and reading found their way into his plays. As a playwright he was directly influenced, at least briefly, by Strindberg and the German expressionists. As a thinker and analyst of reality he was strongly affected by his reading of Nietzsche, Jung and Freud, among others. From Nietzsche O'Neill took the view of life as a struggle between two contradictory forces: the instinctive, sensual, life-affirming Dionysian and the rational, inhibiting, life-denying Apollonian. Repeatedly in his plays, particularly in the 1920s, he dramatizes the conflict between these two forces, which exist both cosmically and internally, either as a struggle between characters (*Desire Under the Elms*), between individuals and social forces (*Mourning Becomes Electra*) or within the individual (*The Great God Brown*). O'Neill's sympathy, like Nietzsche's, was with the Dionysian impulse, and in *The Fountain* and *Lazarus Laughed* he attempts to celebrate the imagined triumph of life-affirmation. But far more often he recognizes the inevitable supremacy of the Apollonian as life-affirming characters are dragged under by the power of reason, convention and death.

In the work of the age's leading psychologists O'Neill found modern scientific explanations for the trapped, doomed quality he sensed in the human experience. Freud, after all, demonstrated that adults have virtually no free will, being almost inescapably the products of influences and traumas in their childhood. His explorations in the area of sex helped explain why that presumably life-affirming force so often turned against man. In several plays O'Neill gives his characters textbook Freudian neuroses, like the Oedipal complexes of Eben in *Desire Under the Elms* and Orin in *Mourning Becomes Electra*. In the latter play Freudian psychology is offered as a modern dramatic equivalent for the Fates and Furies of Greek tragedy, and elsewhere it is used to give verisimilitude to O'Neill's fatalism. O'Neill took from Jung the concept of racial memory – thoughts and instincts inherited biologically from ancient ancestors and still colouring and shaping our lives. The concept appears most overtly in *The Emperor Jones*, but it is also there in all the plays in which characters are driven by needs defined as inherently human rather than individual.

It should be obvious, even from this brief summary, that there are many parallels and connections among these various influences. The concept of inescapable fate runs through all of them; Catholicism and Apollonian life-denial are almost alternative terms for the same thing to O'Neill; and religious guilt, failed Dionysian impulses and Freudian sexual complexes offer non-contradictory explanations for the same observable behaviour. Philosophy, science and O'Neill's own instinctive sense of life reinforced and validated each other; and the burden he asked his plays to bear was not only to dramatize the truths he saw, but to provide one or more of these explanations. Indeed, O'Neill was inclined to mix his metaphors and offer more than one explanation at a time, sometimes to the detriment of a play's coherence. And, of course, like any dramatist, he wanted each time to tell a story that engaged an audience's emotions.

This, then, is some of the weight O'Neill was asking the drama as a literary form to carry. It is a greater burden than any previous American dramatist had put on the genre, and perhaps more than had been asked of it by anyone since the Renaissance. Even if all of O'Neill's plays had been failures, this demand alone would give him an important place in the history of American literature, for leading the drama, and other playwrights, towards a greater seriousness and artistic ambitiousness. And since he was asking such a young and relatively untried genre to carry such weight, it is not surprising that he felt the need to redefine its conventions and stretch its definitions to make it capable of the task.

O'Neill's non-realistic plays of the 1920s can be divided into two groups, not according to style, since virtually every play introduced new techniques and devices that were dropped after one experiment, but by the general thematic impulse that drove them. In keeping with O'Neill's need to explore the full depth of the fate-driven human experience, many of the plays look inward, employing one non-realistic technique or another to bring his characters' inner experience on stage. Meanwhile, the same desire to create works of stature that inspired his early forays into tragedy led him in other plays to reach outward to subjects whose importance could be measured by their epic size and scope. These two impulses were not mutually exclusive, and in fact the one play in which they come together most successfully, *Strange Interlude*, is probably O'Neill's most successful experiment of the decade.

Although there were hints of non-realistic experiment in the visionary sequence of *Where the Cross is Made* and the rudimentary symbolism of *Beyond the Horizon*, O'Neill's first big step into new forms came with *The Emperor Jones* (1920), the first of his inward-looking expressionist plays. *The Emperor Jones* shows the disintegration of an American black man who has used his sophistication to conquer the superstitious natives of a West Indian island. When a rebellion threatens, Jones escapes into the jungle, only to be met by a series of visions beginning with 'little formless fears' and going backward in his memory (a murder he committed, a chain gang) to other 'memories' that can only be racial (a slave auction, a slave ship), and finally to a nightmarish encounter with an African witch doctor and a crocodile god. Accompanying this backward movement are other symbols of Jones's internal collapse – the progressive stripping-away of his clothes until he is reduced to a loin cloth; the incessant beating of native drums, starting at normal heartbeat rate and gradually increasing in speed and volume; and the incremental reduction of the playing space as he moves to smaller and smaller clearings in the forest.

The Emperor Jones is about the essential human reality that lies behind any façade of civilization, and the impossibility of escaping it. In this case, the sophisticated black man, no matter how superior to the natives he considers himself, cannot escape his inheritance of primitive instinct and belief, which ultimately destroys him. The play is likely to offend modern sensibilities through its implicit racism, but certainly O'Neill chose a black man primarily because his story is so effectively dramatizable; it would be difficult to find as clear a set of symbols of historical regression for a white character. Jones's fall, like Icarus's, is a metaphor for the inability of any man to escape the limits imposed on him by the human condition. The expressionistic devices O'Neill employs make us experience this fall from within the character, and thus recognize a common truth, rather than allowing us the luxury of distance and dissociation.

In *The Hairy Ape* (1922), O'Neill's expressionism is more direct. Dropping the device of visions and dreams, he presents external reality in distortions that expose essence rather than surface. The subject of the play is at least two-fold: the social criticism of a capitalist world that not only lives off the labourer but dispossesses him, and the spiritual and psychological effects of losing one's sense of place and value. Yank, a stoker on an ocean liner, is first seen in the cramped, cage-like crew's quarters that reduce the men to stooping and moving about like apes, and in the stokehole in which they feed the monstrous furnaces. Despite the dehumanizing surroundings, Yank sees himself as triumphant man, source of the energies that move the world, until a chance encounter with a wraith-like rich girl from above decks makes him suddenly aware of a world of power that excludes him, and fills him with the raging determination to reassert his importance. Adventures in New York City – encountering the rich, who do not acknowledge his existence; being arrested; attempting to join the socialist IWW and being rejected as a spy – lead Yank to the realization that not only is he not at the centre of power, but he has no any real place in the human world. He finds more to empathize with in a zoo gorilla:

> So yuh're what she seen when she looked at me, de white-faced tart! I was you to her, get me? On'y outa de cage – broke out – free to moider her, see? Sure! Dat's what she tought. She wasn't wise dat I was in a cage, too – worser'n yours. . . .Yuh don't belong wit 'em and you know it. But me, I belong wit 'em – but I don't, see?

In his confused identification with the ape, Yank sets him free, only to have the animal's embrace kill him.

The play's method throughout is symbolic and expressionistic: the sets and stage directions of the scenes on board ship emphasize the workers' trapped, dehumanized condition, while contrasting their obvious vitality to the enervated rich above. The rich New Yorkers are puppet-like automatons, lifeless compared to Yank but invulnerable to his enraged attacks. Jewellery in shop windows is attached to over-sized price tags blinking their figures in electric lights, while prison is a row of cells receding into infinity. Both the imbalances of capitalism and Yank's disorientation at discovering that his energy is exactly the thing that disqualifies him from human society are thus presented as he experiences them, for us to experience with him.

Welded (1924), *All God's Chillun Got Wings* (1924) and *Desire Under the Elms* (1924) are essentially realistic plays in which O'Neill still strove to depict internal experience through non-realistic devices. *Welded* uses touches of expressionism and symbolism to explore a Strindbergan marriage: the couple are isolated from the rest of reality by spotlights, and join in a crucifixion pose at the end. *All God's Chillun* shows a doomed inter-racial marriage and dramatizes the inescapability of the husband's blackness by having a photograph and an African mask symbolically grow larger from scene to scene, while the room they are in seems to shrink. As shown earlier, *Desire Under the Elms* makes symbolic use of the stones and walls of the Cabot farm, while invoking both Freudian and Nietzschean explanations of the characters' passions.

For the most part, O'Neill's plays thus far use non-realistic devices intermittently or as supplements to conventional storytelling. In *The Great God Brown* (1926) he takes the leap of making the violations of convention central to the communication of his themes. The play is, characteristically, about several things at once. On one level it is an overt depiction and discussion of the Apollonian/Dionysian division of experience and its effects on man; on another it is a study of the gap, often ironic and sometimes tragic, between public face and private identity; on yet another it is an exploration of the female essence, the images by which women define themselves and are defined by men; and somewhere around the edges of all this it is an attack on the dehumanizing power of the business ethic. O'Neill's primary device for presenting these multiple themes is the use of masks. Each of the major characters in *The Great God Brown* wears a mask of his or her own face, representing the image seen by others, but removes it in private moments to let us see the real person beneath. As the play progresses, mask and face may grow further apart, so that we see truths about the character to which others are blind; at times the others, accustomed to a character's mask, cannot recognize the bare face. At a key moment in the play one character puts on another's mask and is accepted as the other person by everyone else.

At the centre of the play are two men, the successful but shallow William Brown and the tormented artist Dion Anthony, the one damning himself by settling for too little, the other destroying himself in his search for intense experience, both seeking comfort from the same two women. Dion represents the Dionysian impulse and Brown the Apollonian, and neither alone is sufficient, as Brown admits by taking Dion's mask when he dies and spending the second half of the play alternating between the two personalities. Compounding and to some degree confusing the central theatrical imagery of the play are other symbolic languages, some of them reaching more towards epic scope than psychological and spiritual insight. O'Neill calls for every set to resemble a courtroom, producing the almost subliminal impression of characters on trial for the manner in which they are leading their lives. One woman, identified symbolically with both the Virgin Mary and the redemptive female character in *Faust*, becomes a demonstration of Christianity's failure when she cannot save either of the men; and the other is presented as an instinctively pagan earth-mother who comforts each of the men as they are dying, with the Nietzschean assurance that the pain of life is the prelude to an eternal joy. And O'Neill expects his audience to be able to read subtle and significant character developments in every small alteration of a face or mask. Nevertheless, *The Great God Brown* was O'Neill's greatest commercial success up to that point; and despite the occasional murkiness of theme and symbol, audiences could see and appreciate that the play was addressing the tragic combination of torment and glory in the fully lived and fully self-conscious life, and that it was stretching the theatrical vocabulary to find new ways of expressing new thoughts.

O'Neill's epic impulse is best represented by *Lazarus Laughed* (1928), a play so huge in scope and so theatrically demanding that it has never received a full professional production. O'Neill takes up the story of the man Jesus raised from the dead where the bible leaves off, imagining Lazarus so transformed by his experience that he preaches a gospel based on the denial of death:

> Laugh! Laugh with me! Death is dead! Fear is no more!
> There is only life! There is only laughter!

With messianic and almost magical power, Lazarus inspires a cult of laughers-at-death, freed from fear through laughter and revelry. The play follows him through his progressive encounters with Jews, Greeks, Romans, finally the Emperor Tiberius. Each of the central scenes has almost the same outline, as initial scepticism or hostility is overcome by the irresistible power of Lazarus's preaching and laughter, and his converts join in orgiastic singing and dancing.

Lazarus Laughed is the culmination of O'Neill's fascination with Nietzsche, and is therefore significant despite its theatrical failure. This time O'Neill is dealing not so much with Nietzsche's Dionysian/Apollonian contrast as with the celebration of the god in man. Lazarus's gospel comes straight out of *Also Sprach Zarathustra*, insisting that if we recognize that man himself is God, then there can be nothing greater for him to fear. But that freedom carries new obligations with it, as Lazarus reminds the weak: 'That is your tragedy! You forget! You forget the God in you! You wish to forget! Remembrance would imply the high duty to live as a son of God – generously! – with love! – with pride! – with laughter! This is too glorious a victory for you, too terrible a loneliness!'

This, once again, is the sense of man's limitations that is inescapable for O'Neill: however he may wish to celebrate a Nietzschean godhead, his own instincts recognize that all but the sainted few are unable to rise above their human bonds. Lazarus's followers all revert to sobriety and fear of death when he leaves them; and Tiberius and Caligula, fearing

Lazarus more than they love him, have him put to death. Although Lazarus dies with laughter and the reassuring 'Fear not, Caligula! There is no death!', the last words are those of the despairing Caligula: 'All the same, I killed him and I proved there is death! (*Immediately overcome by remorse, groveling and beating himself*) Fool! Madman! Forgive me, Lazarus! Men forget!'

What makes *Lazarus Laughed* unstageable is O'Neill's determination to express this grandiose and ultimately tragic statement in grandiose terms. The script calls for a number of elaborate processions and spectacles and for a cast of 420, with as many as 100 characters on stage at one time. Moreover,

> All of these people are masked in accordance with the following scheme:
> There are seven periods of life shown: Boyhood (or Girlhood), Youth,
> [etc.] . . .; and each of these periods is represented by seven different
> masks of general types of character as follows: The Simple, Ignorant; the
> Happy, Eager; the Self-Tortured, Introspective; [etc.]. . . . Thus in
> each crowd . . . there are forty-nine different combinations of period and
> type. Each type has a distinct predominant color for its costumes.

Clearly this is in the realm of closet drama; even if O'Neill's vision were stageable, the information and impressions he is trying to communicate are beyond an audience's ability to absorb. Nevertheless, one can say in defence of *Lazarus Laughed* that O'Neill is trying to say something very large that almost justifies the package.

O'Neill had previously ventured into the realm of epic theatre with *The Fountain* (1925) and *Marco Millions* (1928). *The Fountain*, his story of Ponce de Leon and the search for the fountain of youth, spans twenty-two years and two continents, includes in its cast both Christopher Columbus and a symbolic beauty suggestive of Dante's Beatrice, and has as its theme nothing less than the essential unity of all religions and human experiences. As sometimes happens in O'Neill's more ambitious plays, the various strands and themes mingle to the detriment of the play's coherence and clarity. In the central scene his hero has a vision in which figures representing Buddhism, Islam, Christianity and the American Indian religion join together; age and youth are united; and Beatriz, the daughter of his lost love, is transfigured in an eternal flame. The symbolism is murky, and even his interpretation of it is more allusive than clarifying: 'Fountain of Eternity, Thou are the All in One, the One in all – the Eternal Becoming which is Beauty!' It is clear, though, that O'Neill is reaching for images of all-absorbing unity to communicate a somewhat oriental sense of an eternal flow that incorporates youth and age, life and death, man and nature. The final act of the play shows the effect of this vision on Juan: when the real Beatriz goes off with a young idealist, he sees his own youth repeated in an eternal cycle, and dies in peace.

Like *Lazarus Laughed*, *Marco Millions* is so grand in sweep as to be virtually unproducible as written: it was composed as two plays running for six hours, and was heavily cut by O'Neill at the demand of his producers. *Marco Millions* is built on a central satiric irony: the merchant and explorer Marco Polo travels from Venice through all the rich and exotic cultures of Asia; he lives for more than fifteen years in the court of the great Kaan of China, a philosopher-king who repeatedly attempts to engage him in religious and metaphysical discussion; and he is loved by the Kaan's daughter – and Marco, whose imagination cannot extend beyond commerce and the amassing of money, is totally unaffected by any of this. It takes little interpretation to see that the play is an attack on American materialism; O'Neill makes the connection explicit in a final stage direction:

> *The play is over. The lights come up brilliantly in the theatre. In an aisle seat in the first row a man rises, conceals a yawn in his palm. . . . In fact, it is none other than Marco Polo himself, looking a bit sleepy. . . . Arrived in the lobby his face begins to clear of all disturbing memories of what had happened on the stage . . . . His car, a luxurious limousine, draws up at the curb. . . and Marco Polo, with a satisfied sigh at the sheer comfort of it all, resumes his life.*

The satiric point of *Marco Millions* is a legitimate one, and the conception of Marco Polo as the quintessential American businessman is clever. What makes the play unmistakably part of O'Neill's experiments of the 1920s is his assumption that the irony requires an enormous gap between the reality Marco experiences and his limited perception of it. O'Neill repeatedly calls for overwhelming stage spectacles, such as the grand court of the Kaan, filled with warriors, musicians, courtiers, concubines and elaborate sets, just to make Marco's blindness all the more obvious: '*Marco stands, a sample case in each hand, bewildered and dazzled.*' In the end, though, *Marco Millions* is a mountain labouring to bring forth a mouse; unlike *Lazarus Laughed*, its ideas, however good, simply do not need or justify the size and weight of the production. If O'Neill was stretching the boundaries of the theatrical medium, he clearly reached one set of limits in these outward-looking plays: epic scope and sheer numbers were not the way to make the drama carry the burden he wanted.

The epic and psychological/spiritual impulses come together in *Strange Interlude* (1928), the most successful of O'Neill's plays of the 1920s, both artistically and commercially. The play covers twenty-five years and attempts a cosmic definition of humanity's relationship to God, but also uses all of O'Neill's Freudian knowledge and sense of fate to explore his characters' psychology and emotions. It is not a complete triumph; its extreme length and the extreme verbosity generated by its central technical device make it rather heavy going for most audiences. Still, in it he comes closest to the goal he had been striving for throughout the decade: stretching the medium so that it could carry greater dramatic and philosophical weight, while still producing an effective piece of theatre.

O'Neill avoids some of the diffuseness of the epic plays by limiting himself to a small group of characters in a domestic situation. Nina Leeds, mourning her war hero fiancé, marries his friend Sam Evans in the in hope of having a son to name after the dead Gordon. When she learns that hereditary insanity in Sam's family makes a child impossible, she turns to Dr Ned Darrell to father her son. As more than two decades pass, Sam dies, young Gordon grows up, and Ned finally breaks free, leaving Nina with the sexless and avuncular family friend Charlie Marsden. What gives this relatively simple story its depth, and the play its length, is a technical innovation designed to take us further into the characters than realism could. In *Strange Interlude* we hear each character's thoughts as well as his words, and a simple scene is thus textured by levels of passion, irony and insight that are not apparent on the surface. Here, for example, is the first meeting of Ned and Charlie (The ellipses are all O'Neill's, indicating pauses; some stage directions have been omitted).

MARSDEN (*thinking sneeringly*) Amusing, these young doctors! . . . perspire with the effort to appear cool! . . . writing a prescription . . . cough medicine for the corpse, perhaps! . . . good-looking? . . . more or less . . . attractive to women, I dare say . . .

DARRELL Here, Sam. Run along up the street and get this filled.

EVANS Sure. Glad of the chance for a walk. (*He goes out, rear.*)

DARRELL (*turning to Marsden*) It's for Nina. She's got to get some sleep tonight.

This Marsden doesn't like me . . . that's evident . . . but he interests me . . . read his books . . . wanted to know his bearing on Nina's case . . . his novels just well-written surface . . . no depth, no digging underneath . . . why? . . . has the talent but doesn't dare . . . afraid he'll meet himself somewhere . . . one of those poor devils who spend their lives trying not to discover which sex they belong to! . . .

MARSDEN Giving me the fishy, diagnosing eye they practice at medical school . . . like freshmen from Ioway cultivating broad A's at Harvard! . . . what is his specialty? . . . neurologist, I think . . . I hope not psychiatrist . . . a lot to account for, Herr Freud! . . . punishment to fit his crimes, be forced to listen eternally during breakfast while innumerable plain ones tell him dreams about snakes . . . pah, what an

> easy cure-all! . . . sex the philosopher's stone . . . 'O
> Oedipus, O my king! The world is adopting you!'

Here, in an essentially minor scene, the spoken thoughts tell us volumes about the characters, including insights that will reverberate ironically later. More significant than their insights into each other (though both are right: Ned's professionalism is an affectation and Charlie is sexless) is what each man exposes about himself: the mask of superiority Charlie uses to cover his inadequacy and fear of self-exposure, and the scientific detachment Ned will be unable to maintain under Nina's influence. The technique proves to be quite versatile, allowing not only this sort of insight and irony, but also moments of high drama, as in Nina's seduction of Ned, which begins with both maintaining a mask of scientific detachment, speaking in the third person, only to have the internalized passions overpower the restraints of speech:

> NINA   Ned does not love her – but he used to like her and, I
> think, desire her. Does he now, Doctor?
> DARRELL   Does he? . . . who is he? . . . he is Ned! . . .
> Ned is I! . . . I desire her! . . . I desire happiness! . . .
> But, Madame, I must confess the Ned you are speaking of is I,
> and I am Ned.
> NINA   And I am Nina, who wants her baby. I should be so grate-
> ful, Ned. I should be so humbly grateful.
> DARRELL   Yes – yes, Nina – yes – for your happiness – in that spirit!
> I shall be happy for a while! . . .

The centre of the play is Nina's relationship with the men in her life, and her attempt to control her own fate by controlling them. But the elaborate construct of husband, lover, son and friend she creates must constantly be maintained. Ned cannot be dismissed once he has served his biological function, but must be kept in thrall to her sexual power. Sam must be protected from the knowledge of his inadequacy, if only because his loyalty to the first Gordon has earned him the courtesy. Young Gordon must be shaped into the ideal form of his namesake, so that his mother can define herself through his glory. And even Charlie must be kept on a loose rein, as a tie to the simpler and safer past. But the child is never really hers, having a closer spiritual affinity to the man he thinks is his father; the husband is a burden; the lover constantly struggles to escape; and the passionless friend wins her in the end only because the struggle of life has worn her out, and his emptiness seems like a safe harbour.

So, once again, O'Neill is dramatizing the limits of man's – or, here, woman's – control over her fate. Nina is one of the strongest and most determined characters O'Neill had created up to this point; she is fully self-conscious and aware of her desire to shape the world to meet her needs; she spends twenty-five years in continuous and inventive stratagems to achieve her goals. And in the end she must not only acknowledge failure but give up the struggle in exhaustion. Her understanding of the struggle is, appropriately, expressed in sexual terms. Early in the play she tells Charlie, 'The mistake began when God was created in a male image . . . . We should have imagined life as created in the birth-pain of God the Mother.' Throughout the play she draws strength from her identification with this female God, but in the end she must acknowledge a force larger than hers that mocks her attempts to create and control her fate: 'Yes, our lives are merely strange dark interludes in the electrical display of God the Father!'

O'Neill would make only a few more attempts at new forms. His final play of the decade, *Dynamo* (1929), borrows an image from Henry Adams's philosophical autobiography *The Education of Henry Adams*, as O'Neill offers the electrical dynamo as the defining icon of the twentieth century, with his central character led to worship and ultimately sacrifice himself to the spirit of electricity. Thematically, *Dynamo* recalls elements of earlier plays: the conflation of Oedipal love, romantic love and religion in *Desire Under the Elms*, the search for a maternal saviour in *The Great God Brown*, the hunger for a new religion in *The Fountain* and *Lazarus Laughed*. But it is forced and clumsy – the scenes of Reuben Light worshipping his dynamo goddess are embarrassing when not comic, and O'Neill's perennial weakness for purple passions and purple prose (perhaps noticed, even if not pointed out, in some of the passages quoted earlier) is particularly apparent.

It is *Strange Interlude* that is the climax of O'Neill's stylistic experiments of the 1920s; and perhaps only with hindsight is it so strikingly apparent that, despite its epic scope and stylistic innovations, it is essentially a domestic melodrama. O'Neill was not giving up his artistic ambitions or the demands he was making on the drama as a literary form, but we can see in *Strange Interlude* the beginnings of a discovery that would generate his greatest plays: that he could say and do everything he wanted to through the mode of domestic realism.

In summary, then, the first thirty years of the century saw the American drama reborn as a serious literary form. Beginning with a tentative realism that resembled the naturalism of turn-of-the-century American novelists, dramatists discovered that their plays could acknowledge the existence of social and moral issues that did not have pat answers. Later generations of playwrights, finding audiences receptive to this new seriousness, shifted the focus from the theoretical to the personal, combining contemporary discoveries in psychology with the stage's ability to reflect reality, to present more fully rounded and fully explored characters than the American drama had previously supported. Indeed, in such works as Eugene O'Neill's early sea plays, Susan Glaspell's depictions of the female experience, and Elmer Rice's *Street Scene*, the convincing and insightful reflection of reality was a satisfying end in itself, without the need of thesis or social comment.

But realism was not the only mode being explored by artistically ambitious American dramatists, nor was it clearly the dominant mode. With its focus on the specific and its surface similarities to the shallower plays of the nineteenth century, it seemed to some writers and critics a limited and inflexible form. Some of the most ambitious, if not necessarily the most successful plays of the first thirty years of the century were experiments in forms that seemed inherently or potentially grander in scope than simple realism. Following the lead of European experimenters and staking out new stylistic and technical ground of their own, O'Neill and others redefined the boundaries of the medium, finding new artistic vocabularies with which to address new subjects. It was an exciting period of exploration during which even unsuccessful experiments were valuable in helping the theatrical community to discover what various styles of drama could and could not do.

By 1930, then, what had been merely an unpretentious medium of popular entertainment had become a vital art form that was still in the process of discovering its own potential. In any given year, the overwhelming majority of new plays were conventional potboilers of one sort or another, as was true in every art. But the possibility existed, as it really had not in the nineteenth century, for serious artistic work to be done in the dramatic mode. The next generation of American dramatists would explore that possibility even further, in the process discovering the American drama's native and natural voice.

Chapter 3
1930-1945: Reality and Realism

The 'plot' of Chapter 2 was the discovery by serious American writers that the drama was an amenable vehicle for their artistic ambitions, and the free-wheeling experiments in various styles and forms that ensued. The plot of this third chapter is two-fold: the irresistible intrusion of external reality into the world of literature, and the discovery that one of the many dramatic modes playwrights had experimented with in the first decades of the century was far more useful and natural to the American drama than any of the others.

The fifteen years covered in this chapter saw two extraordinary historical events – a decade-long worldwide economic depression, followed by a world war. It may be difficult for younger readers to understand how all-pervading and life-altering these events were. The Great Depression of the 1930s was not merely a matter of a stock market crash and an increase in unemployment. It was the cause of financial strain on almost every family in America, and directly affected and altered lives in ways that might not immediately be thought of as economic. Career choices were made or altered, dreams were abandoned, marriages were cancelled, crimes were committed, religious faith was lost or found – millions of people's lives were irreversibly altered by the economy.

There were also political and philosophical consequences. Whatever perspective hindsight has allowed since then, at the time the Depression did not seem like a natural, if extreme, part of a business cycle that would eventually correct itself. It had a cataclysmic, end-of-the-world quality that could be interpreted as the irreversible failure of capitalism and breakdown of the American economy. And that belief, or even suspicion, could lead to larger social and moral uncertainty. Was the American Dream – the belief that this was a land of opportunity in which hard work and talent would inevitably be rewarded – being proved invalid? If that national promise was being broken, what of the others – brotherhood, the Melting Pot, democracy? Not since the Civil War had the continued existence of America as a concept been so threatened. These were not the idle musings of philosophers; it was neither accident nor disloyalty that led a generation of young idealists to consider socialism or even Soviet-style communism as an alternative to an apparently dying system.

It is a simple measure of the importance and pervasiveness of this new reality that it became a recurring subject in the American drama, which had hitherto not been particularly quick to deal with historical events; even the First World War had appeared in only a handful of plays, and reflections of the social reality of the 1920s were generally limited to jokes about flappers and wild youth in escapist comedies. Alongside this discovery of new subject matter occurred a stylistic evolution. While some playwrights of the 1930s continued the experiments in dramatic form and method that had characterized the previous decade, a clearly discernible mainstream developed. By the end of the period covered in this chapter there could be no question that the dominant, natural voice of American drama was realism – realistic, contemporary, middle-class, domestic melodrama or comedy.

Each of those words was defined in the first chapter. At this point it is worth reiterating that the development was both technical and substantive. Domestic realism, which had shown itself capable of illuminating individual experience through psychological analysis, had seemed to Eugene O'Neill and some of his contemporaries ill-suited to the depiction of whole cultures or the exploration of metaphysical questions. The discovery by Clifford Odets and others that the great national traumas of the Depression and the war could be dramatized through their effects on a small group of people in a domestic setting meant that American dramatists did not have to wrestle with epic theatre or other non-realistic modes, but could present their observations in a theatrical form familiar to their audiences. Even more significant, however, was the cultural assumption that made the technical discovery possible: that the domestic experience, and not the financial statistics or mass movements, *was* the real story of the Depression or the war. A later generation of American dramatists, led by Tennessee Williams, would carry this assumption even further, recognizing that a group of people interacting in their personal, private ways could not only draw a picture of the world outside that was affecting those personal lives, but could have an inherent dramatic power and importance without need of a larger context. But for the dramatists of the 1930s the first step was a significant and exciting discovery in itself.

And it was indeed a discovery, made gradually and collectively, in the same erratic, unplanned manner as other developments in American dramatic history. The emergence of a dominant dramatic style was not the creation of a conscious 'school' or artistic movement. Such self-conscious direction or manipulation is actually quite rare in any of the arts in America; and, in fact, what little artistic doctrine existed in the 1930s – that influenced by the Communist Party – specifically rejected domestic drama, demanding literature about the masses. And, despite a growing consensus, some significant playwrights of the period, seeing that domestic realism had limitations as well as potentials, rejected the mode and continued to experiment in non-realistic styles. What happened in the 1930s was a legitimate evolution of the art form, as the experiments of the 1920s led writers, individually and collectively, to discoveries about what worked best in the theatre, and then to discoveries of what could be done within the dramatic mode most of them chose.

Drama of the Depression: Clifford Odets

One of the first playwrights to attempt to deal with the Depression in domestic terms was Elmer Rice, whose *We, the People* (1933) is an episodic panorama of domestic scenes reflecting the effects of the economy on more than forty characters. The central plot, about a family whose members must each give up a dream because of the Depression, is only the skeleton on which are hung scenes representative of the times: an immigrant who explains how empty the American Dream seems to the poor; a farm family broken by the economy; factory owners and bankers, oblivious to the suffering around them, buying fine art and politicians. The play ends with a public meeting at which characters from these various worlds give a series of speeches openly criticizing America for having lost its political, moral and economic way. *We, the People* is least successful on its domestic level, since Rice's attempt to include as many different examples of injustice as he can fit into the play reduces it to a series of sketches, too brief to allow any real empathy or identification by the audience, and almost of necessity drawn in the broadest black-and-white terms. By resorting to open speechifying in the final scene, and frequently before that, Rice implicitly admits a failure to dramatize his message. Still, the basic insight is an important one: the stories to be told about the Depression are set in people's kitchens and living rooms.

Clifford Odets borrowed the basic structure of *We, the People* two years later in *Waiting for Lefty* (1935), giving the episodes more of a focus by incorporating them in a frame plot. At a taxi-drivers' union meeting, with the theatre audience taking the role of the membership, various speakers address the question of a strike, their speeches fading into dramatizations of the events that have brought them to this juncture: a doctor victimized by anti-Semitism is reduced to driving a cab, another driver realizes that he can't afford to marry his girl, and so on. Episodes back in the union hall include the unmasking of a company spy in the audience and the climactic news that the union leader Lefty has been murdered, leading to the unanimous vote to strike.

Much that could be said in criticism of *We, the People* is equally true of *Waiting for Lefty*. The episodic structure allows little more than broadly sketched characterizations and almost forces the characters into undramatically overt statements of Odets's messages. Still, the union hall frame excuses much of this by presenting each scene openly as a vignette rather than as part of a continuous dramatic action, while the political speeches of the frame scenes are justified by the dramatic premise of a strike meeting. In other words, *Waiting for Lefty* defines itself as a kind of play that will operate in brief sketches and broad emotional effects, and audiences can relate to it on that level; at particularly successful performances the audience would rise and join in the final strike call.

Moreover, while the villainous characters tend towards caricature, the sympathetic figures are given some reality by the simple device of making them politically naive. Thus, for example, a wife nagging at her husband to fight for more money and dignity does not consciously spout Party doctrine; her motives are domestic, and she finds her way to politically correct insights and language by instinct and accident:

> I know this – your boss is making suckers outa you boys every minute. Yes, and suckers out of all the wives and the poor innocent kids who'll grow up with crooked spines and sick bones. Sure, I see it in the papers, how good orange juice is for kids. But damnit our kids get colds one on top of the other. They look like little ghosts. Betty never saw a grapefruit. I took her to the store last week and she pointed to a stack of grapefruits. 'What's that!' she said. My God, Joe – the world is supposed to be for all of us.

Waiting for Lefty represents an important advance over *We, the People*, not just in dramatic structure, but in the discovery that large political issues could not only be presented in domestic settings, but they could be expressed through characters thinking and speaking in domestic terms. The episodic structure of *We, the People* and *Waiting for Lefty* was used in some subsequent plays, notably the *Living Newspaper* series, but the logical next step was to maintain this method in a full-length, dramatically integrated domestic play.

Odets achieved this in his next and best play, *Awake and Sing!* (1935), which is on its surface merely the unremarkable domestic life of a New York City Jewish family. Father Myron Berger is a nonentity, and the family is ruled by mother Bessie, who coolly marries her pregnant daughter Hennie off to an innocent neighbour and as cold-bloodedly breaks up her son Ralph's romance with a poor girl who might be a drain on the family's finances. Grandfather Jake, an ineffectual socialist, falls or jumps from the roof, leaving his insurance money and ideals to Ralph, and Hennie deserts husband and baby to run away with the war veteran and minor gangster Moe Axelrod.

As the Bergers' lives seem frozen by the Depression, Odets lets us realize gradually that they are all honourably attempting to function in the ways they have been taught, but that they are living in a world in which the rules have changed. Myron believes in the American Dream, as expressed in quotations from his childhood hero Teddy Roosevelt, but he can do no more to achieve it than fantasize impotently about winning contests. Jake dreams of a better world, but cannot get beyond such platitudes as 'Life shouldn't be printed on dollar bills', and the books he bequeaths to Ralph have not been read. Ralph and Hennie want nothing more than what their culture has taught them young people should want – love, pleasure, the right to dream of a future – and are lost because they cannot have it.

Moe and Bessie are particularly victimized because their attempts to function do actual harm to themselves and others. Moe fought for his country and lost a leg in the process; he deals with the pain by adopting a persona of cynical realism and a determination to beat the system as the ultimate entrepreneur, a criminal. But his racketeering is stalled at the level of cheating Myron out of a couple of dollars on a bet, and his wise-guy mask leaves him unable to express his sincere feelings for Hennie in any other terms but 'I got a yen for her and I don't mean a Chinee coin'. In an important speech late in the play, Odets lets Bessie make it clear that she never acts out of malice or selfishness, but out of duty as she sees it:

> Ralphie, I worked too hard all my years to be treated like dirt
> . . . . Did I ever play a game of cards like Mrs Marcus? Or was
> Bessie Berger's children always the cleanest on the block?! Here
> I'm not only the mother, but also the father. . . . If I didn't
> worry about the family who would?

But this commitment to what she understands to be her moral obligation turns Bessie into the villain of the play, forcing Hennie into marriage, breaking up Ralph's romance, and later trying to steal Jake's insurance money.

Everyone is doing what they're supposed to do, and it isn't working. The economic collapse has changed the world so that all the old values and models for behaviour – responsibility, ambition, patriotism, the American Dream – are useless or actively dangerous. At the end of the play Ralph is inspired to the socialist cause by Jake's death, but his call to arms is clearly not Odets's solution. Ralph's socialism is as vague and utopian as his grandfather's ('Maybe we'll fix it so life won't be printed on dollar bills.'), with not much more promise of changing the world, and the play equates it with Hennie's decision to run off with Moe. The only thing – and thus the important thing – that her hedonism and Ralph's idealism have in common is a break with the values and patterns of their past. *Awake and Sing!* is not a call towards any specific path, but a call to any path that leads away from what the play has depicted as the deadly models of a dying culture.

After a brief detour into simple political drama with *Till the Day I Die* (1935), about the struggles of German communists against the Nazis, Odets spent the rest of the decade exploring the double discoveries that the most effective medium for discussing the Depression and the real stories to be discussed lay in domestic realism. *Paradise Lost* (1935) presents another family in its living room. Leo Gordon is cheated by his business partner; one son is tempted into a robbery during which he is killed; another succumbs to a debilitating illness; and a daughter sinks into near-madness when she and her fiancé cannot afford to marry. And yet these somewhat sensational events are not really the focus of the play. Long before the Gordons lose their money they have lost their moral and spiritual direction, their faith in themselves and the world around them. Watching his world disintegrate, Leo cries to his wife, 'What is happening here? Once we were all together and life was good.' When the financial crash finally reaches the Gordons it is almost anticlimactic; as the socialist Mr Pike points out, with all the attention paid to the economic Depression, 'No one talks about the depression of the modern man's spirit, of his inability to lead a full and human life.'

And here *Paradise Lost* parts company with *Awake and Sing!* because Odets does not put the blame for this malaise on the dead American culture, but on a temporary dislocation from what was best in the American culture. At the end of the play Leo Gordon rediscovers his belief in the American Dream and is moved to a climactic assertion of his faith:

> No! There is more to life than this! . . . Oh, if you could only see with me the greatness of men. . . . Yes, I want to see that new world. I want to kiss all those future men and women. . . . Oh, yes, I tell you the whole world is for men to possess. Heartbreak and terror are not the heritage of mankind! The world is beautiful.

Leo's vision may be as nebulous and Utopian as Ralph Berger's, but that is not the point. Just as the important thing for Ralph was to break with the past and set out on a new path – *any* new path – Leo's salvation comes from his regaining the ability to dream *any* dream. On one level *Paradise Lost* contradicts *Awake and Sing!* by embracing the values of the past rather than rejecting them; on another level it simply goes far beyond the earlier play, by seeing that the real Depression is spiritual rather than economic.

Golden Boy (1937), Odets's next and commercially most successful play, shifts the focus back towards the economic, while still speaking in personal terms. The central metaphor of a musician who becomes a prizefighter to earn a living clearly points an accusing finger at a world that forces a man to give up the most important part of himself in order to survive; the key to Joe's progress as a fighter is the development of his killer instinct, and the boy who could say 'There's no war in music' ends the play by killing an opponent in the ring. Underlining the importance of this personal cost, some of the background action is taken up with the buying and selling of shares in Joe's contract until the question can be unironically asked, 'How much does Joe own of himself?'

Odets reinforces his political point by carefully keeping any of his characters from functioning as simple villains. Joe's manager, the gangster who buys into his contract, and the girl who serves as bait to lure him away from his family are all shown to be victims of the Depression, so that the worst that can be said of them is that they are doing what they must in order to survive. The girl falls in love with Joe and, like Ralph Berger and Leo Gordon before her, is allowed a Utopian vision: 'Somewhere there must be happy boys and girls who can teach us the way of life! We'll find some city where poverty's no shame – where music is no crime – where there's no war in the streets – where a man is glad to be himself, to live and make his woman herself!' But this time Odets denies the validity of that hope. When Joe and Lorna run off together they are killed in an automobile accident. It is possible to interpret their deaths as suicide, indicating their realization that Lorna's fantasy is unattainable in life, or as a simple accident, suggesting a cruelly ironic God. Most likely, however, since Joe's fast car has been carefully identified with his growing commitment to boxing, is the conclusion that death is the inevitable extension of the self-destructive process Joe was forced to choose in his search for economic security.

Golden Boy is something of a throwback for Odets, his last play to focus on the economic effects of the Depression. His next play follows more directly the lead of *Paradise Lost* in finding deeper domestic and psychological losses that have little to do with the national economy. Ben Stark, the central character of *Rocket to the Moon* (1938), is a fairly successful dentist, and the important secondary figure of his father-in-law is actually rich; reminders that the country is still in the Depression are limited to background characters and passing comments. The centre of the play is both men's relationship to Ben's receptionist Cleo, an insecure, uneducated but intensely vital girl whose unformed quality is a large part of her attraction. Unhappy in his marriage, Ben has an affair with Cleo. Lonely in his riches, Mr Prince offers her a marriage of mutual exploitation, his money and worldly experience in exchange for her youth and passion.

The effect that Cleo has on both men is to make them aware of the spiritual emptiness of their lives. This feeling of inadequacy or incompleteness, resembling the 'depression of the spirit' that was the focus of *Paradise Lost*, is the true subject of the play, and is exposed in all the characters, even Ben's shrewish wife. More significantly, it is also there in Cleo, and is the force that drives her determination to live life more fully than the others. At the play's climax, when the men press her to choose between them, she astonishes both by choosing herself instead. When Mr Prince asks what she has to lose by choosing, she replies, 'Everything that's me'.

> I want a love that uses me, that needs me. Don't you think there's a world of joyful men and women? Must all men live afraid to laugh and sing? Can't we sing at work and love our work? It's getting late to play at life; I want to *live* it. Something has to feel real for me, more than both of you.

So once again Odets ends a play with a Utopian vision, but once again it is clouded by doubt. Cleo may just have the energy and courage to wrest her self-fulfilment from life, but Ben's sad little hope that he, too, has made a life-altering discovery is much less convincing: 'For years I sat here, taking things for granted, my wife, everything. Then just for an hour my life was in a spotlight. . . . I saw myself clearly, realized who and what I was. Isn't that a beginning? Isn't it?' The play's title refers specifically to the ability to break out of a spiritual inertia (Mr Prince to Ben: 'Why don't you suddenly ride away, an airplane, a boat! Take a rocket to the moon! Explode!'), but in Ben's case, at least, such an awakening is as unattainable a fantasy as space travel.

Other realists

Realistic plays about ordinary people coping with the Depression were a staple of the 1930s, with as many as half the serious new American plays in a Broadway season meeting this description. Few of these were noteworthy on their own merits; even Odets could not make a domestic story dramatically effective when its real subject was not larger than the specific anecdote. *Night Music* (1940), the romance of a boy and girl adrift in New York, does not succeed in evoking larger meanings, even though repeated references are made to the economic environment that constrains the lovers; and *Clash By Night* (1941) amounts to little more than its plot of a straying wife whose husband murders her lover. Domestic realism in itself was not the point; the important discovery of the 1930s was domestic realism as a means of depicting a larger reality.

Sidney Kingsley's *Dead End* (1935) uses the unlikely but striking setting of a New York City street on which a luxury apartment house stands next to a slum tenement to dramatize the seemingly unresolvable injustices of the Depression. Its central characters include a crippled and unemployed architect, a neighbourhood girl who has moved from tenement to apartment by becoming a rich man's mistress, a gangster who risks arrest for a sentimental visit to his mother and his old girlfriend, and the teenage boys of the slums. The girl loves the architect but leaves because she cannot accept a life of poverty; the gangster, after discovering that his old sweetheart is a whore and his mother curses him, is killed in a shoot-out with the police; and one of the boys is arrested and sent to a reformatory. Much of *Dead End*'s power comes from its *Street Scene*-like naturalistic depiction of the ordinary events of the day, particularly the activities of the boys, who wander aimlessly from innocent games to robbery and violence. But Kingsley shows how every facet of life on this street is shaped by the Depression, from the gangster's choice of crime – 'What da hell did yuh tink I wuz gonna do? Hang around dis dump waitin' fer Santa Claus tuh take care a me, fer Chris' sake' – to the girl's choice of lovers – 'I've known what it means to scrimp and worry and never be sure from one minute to the next. I've had enough of that.' – to the emptiness of the boys' days and hopelessness of their futures.

The Depression was not the only subject for realistic drama in the 1930s. Some writers used realism as an end in itself, in equivalents of the local colour plays of thirty years earlier: Louis Weitzenkorn's *Five Star Final* (1930) and Sidney Kingsley's *Men in White* (1933) both set melodramatic plots against almost documentary backgrounds, respectively a newspaper office and a hospital. Such private-lives-of-the-great plays as Robert E. Sherwood's *Abe Lincoln in Illinois* (1938), E. P. Conkle's *Prologue to Glory* (1938) and Sidney Kingsley's *The Patriots* (1943) employ domestic realism as a history lesson, betraying the unspoken assumption that the significant truths about America's cultural heroes are the domestic ones.

For other writers domestic realism could be the vehicle for presenting a world view not in itself particularly realistic. Robert E. Sherwood's *The Petrified Forest* (1935) and William Saroyan's *The Time of Your Life* (1939) are idealistic romances of different sorts that gain credibility by being presented realistically. Sherwood puts a wandering philosopher, a romantic young girl and a gangster into the same room and lets their unlikely conjunction dramatize the value of the fulfilled life and the capacity for the chivalric gesture, as the writer and gangster, doomed and spiritually lost, conspire to give the girl the future they can't have. Saroyan offers an openly sentimental and romantic picture of life as it might be if most men were inherently good and life rewarded them accordingly, celebrating the small adventures of the regulars in a friendly San Francisco bar:

> *The atmosphere is now one of warm, natural, American ease; every man*
> *innocent and good; each doing what he believes he should do, or what he*
> *must do. There is a deep American naivete and faith in the behavior of*
> *each person . . . . Each man is following his destiny as he feels it*
> *should be followed; or is abandoning it as he feels it must, by now, be*
> *abandoned; or is forgetting it for the moment as he feels he should forget it.*

The plot of *The Time of Your Life* is less significant than the milieu; like Sherwood, Saroyan uses dramatic realism to present his characters and their world as real, solid and ordinary, so that his rosy-coloured view of life becomes at least temporarily convincing.

Lillian Hellman's second and best play, *The Little Foxes* (1939), uses domestic melodrama as historical allegory. (Hellman's 1934 play *The Children's Hour*, about the tragedies caused by a malicious schoolgirl's lies, has a simple moral purpose, though some indecision about whether to focus on the sensational events or their psychological effects weakens it.) Set in the American South in 1900, *The Little Foxes* is the story of the Hubbard family, two brothers and a sister who have risen through skilful and ruthless business dealings to displace the old southern aristocracy in their town. Given an opportunity to become truly rich, they stop at nothing – theft, blackmail, double-crossing, murder – to succeed. The play works theatrically on its surface level of intrigue and betrayal, but it gains deeper resonances as Hellman repeatedly identifies the Hubbards as the spirit of the New South of the twentieth century, fated by historical inevitability to displace the Old South while still retaining a regional identity that distinguishes it from the commercial and industrial North. They explain this to their northern partner-to-be:

> MARSHALL   It's very remarkable how you Southern aristocrats
>   have kept together. Kept together and kept what belonged to
>   you.
> BEN   You misunderstood, sir. Southern aristocrats have *not* kept
>   together and have *not* kept what belonged to them. . . .
>   Because the Southern aristocrat can adapt himself to nothing
>   . . . . *Our* grandfather and *our* father learned the new ways
>   and learned how to make them pay.

And the play dramatizes this, characterizing the New South represented by the Hubbards as a mix of cold-blooded avarice and unhypocritical commitment to some higher values; at the end, when Regina cheats her brothers out of the lion's share of the new deal, Ben has the grace to accept with some philosophical resignation:

> I'm not discouraged. The century's turning, the world is open.
> Open for people like you and me. Ready for us, waiting for us.

> After all this is just the beginning. There are hundreds of
> Hubbards sitting in rooms like this throughout the country. All
> their names aren't Hubbard, but they are all Hubbards and they
> will own this country some day. We'll get along.

The play does not celebrate the Hubbards, nor does it leave them unam-
biguously triumphant. Regina's husband and daughter suggest a third,
more moral stage in the development of the southern culture that is not
yet strong enough to displace the Hubbards but is gathering its forces. As
an historical allegory, *The Little Foxes* offers an explanation of how and
why the South changed with the new century, and also a balanced
evaluation of the costs and benefits of that change, all within the boundaries of a theatrically effective realistic domestic drama.

Plays of the Second World War

The Second World War affected every element of American life just as
fully as the Depression had, so it may seem odd that it was not reflected
as extensively in the drama. Of many possible explanations the simplest
is probably that the war was more naturally the province of films, which
could depict scenes of battle more realistically and effectively. While
each Broadway season during the war saw three or four battlefield plays,
virtually all were commercial and artistic failures. As with the subjects
that had concerned the dramatists and audiences of the 1930s, the war
story would be told on stage, when it was told at all, through small
personal dramas.

   A significant subgenre of pre-war and wartime plays uses domestic,
personal stories to symbolize a national awakening or to invoke a call to
moral arms; Lillian Hellman's *Watch on the Rhine* (1941) is one of the
most effective of this group. On its surface it is an adventure story in a
domestic setting: an American woman long resident in Europe returns to
her mother's home with her German husband, an anti-Nazi under-
ground fighter whose life is endangered by the spying of a Romanian
guest in the house; the husband is eventually forced to kill the spy in
order to be able to return to Europe to continue his work. But, while
the surface drama is about the freedom-fighter, the play's subtext is centred on the Americans, the wife's mother and brother. Their story is one
of awakening to the horrors and high stakes of the drama the Europeans
are living, and of discovering in themselves the moral strength to share
that commitment. Hellman never patronizes these characters; from the
start they are shown to be open, gracious and honourable. But they are

innocents just by virtue of being Americans, and the European characters, good and evil, are inclined to dismiss them as irrelevant. It comes as something of a surprise to everyone that they handle each new revelation as well as they do; and by the end, while they are still not as dangerously involved as the freedom-fighter, they have risen to the task of supporting him as much as they can, and to the knowledge that more will be asked of them in the future. On this level, then, *Watch on the Rhine* is an allegory of America's late discovery of the fascist menace, and a statement of faith in the nation's ability to react heroically once its eyes have been opened.

This is the pattern for the most successful wartime drama, very localized and personal stories that take on larger resonances through representativeness or implicit allegory. Similar in structure to *Watch on the Rhine* are Robert E. Sherwood's *Idiot's Delight* (1936) in which an American entertainer in Europe is politicized; Maxwell Anderson's *Key Largo* (1939), in which a fight against American gangsters is presented as a microcosm of the European struggle; Anderson's *Candle in the Wind* (1941), whose American heroine works to free her French lover from the Nazis, suggesting an America drawn into the European conflict only by its emotions but discovering an unexpected capacity for political and moral commitment; and Lillian Hellman's *The Searching Wind* (1944), in which a shallow American couple who spent the twenty years before the war in Europe must now face the judgement of their soldier son that they helped cause the war they did not help prevent. In *Tomorrow the World* (1943), by James Gow and Arnaud d'Usseau, an American family takes in a German orphan only to discover that the boy is a fervent Nazi, and the domestic adventure dramatizes both the American realization of the high stakes of the war and the faith that the German people can somehow be separated from their fascist ideology.

A cluster of plays of the 'plucky little Finland' type presents European civilians somehow fitting heroism into their daily lives: Robert E. Sherwood's *There Shall Be No Night* (1940), John Steinbeck's *The Moon is Down* (1942), Dan James's *Winter Soldiers* (1942). When actual soldiers do appear, they are likely to be off the battlefield: Paul Osborn's dramatization of John Hersey's novel *A Bell for Adano* (1944) shows an American major trying to establish democracy in a liberated Italian town, and being liberated in spirit by the townspeople; John Patrick's *The Hasty Heart* (1945) is set in a military hospital, as an international mix of soldiers work to befriend and soften an unlikable Scot who is dying; in Arthur Laurents's *Home of the Brave* (1945) a psychosomatically paralysed soldier is helped to realize that there is no guilt in being glad to have survived a battle in which his friend was killed. Each of these plays implicitly declares through its domestic focus that the real story lies in the personal experiences occasioned by the war, rather than in the war itself.

Alternatives to realism: Maxwell Anderson

Not every play of the 1930s was set in someone's living room. But most of the alternative modes of the 1920s had fallen by the wayside. Gone were the exotic melodramas – the Chinese opium dens, Mexican bandits and French swashbucklers. Expressionist plays, dream plays, open allegories and biblical parables virtually disappeared from the stage, and the very few that were produced were all failures. None of Eugene O'Neill's experiments in form in the 1920s bore fruit beyond the O'Neill plays themselves, as even he abandoned each alternative style after trying it. The few significant dramatic experiments of the 1930s were new responses to the limitations of domestic realism.

The dominance of domestic realism as a dramatic mode proved how flexible and effective in conveying an author's psychological, social and moral visions it was. Despite this striking effectiveness and the ease with which it seemed to adapt to various uses, domestic realism had its limitations. One problem of the genre which was noticed by contemporaries was that, when used as a reflection of larger issues, it implicitly went beyond realism to naturalism. That is, any playwrights who dealt with economic, social or moral forces by dramatizing their effect on individuals were accepting the same assumptions that had driven such nineteenth- and early twentieth-century novelists as Norris and Dreiser: they implicitly defined life as a struggle between the individual and the larger forces that made up his environment, and they implicitly conceded that the environment was stronger. Seen from this perspective, many plays of the 1930s seem to admit defeat for humanity before they begin: the characters of Lillian Hellman's *The Children's Hour* or Sidney Kingsley's *Dead End*, for example, have no chance against the social forces they fight, while the few of Clifford Odets's characters who have happy endings do so only through Utopian visions that the plays do not show them actually achieving.

One dramatist who reacted against this limitation was Maxwell Anderson. He began his career as a realist, with *What Price Glory*, and continued to write occasional realistic plays into the 1950s, but in the 1930s he became the modern American drama's foremost (almost by default) writer of verse tragedies in the Elizabethan mode. Anderson's break with convention, then, is not merely a matter of his writing in an unobtrusively irregular blank verse. Like O'Neill a decade earlier he was reaching towards tragedy, which is more than a literary mode, but a vision of the human condition incompatible with the implicit naturalism of his contemporaries.

However one chooses to define tragedy, a few characteristics are inescapable. Tragedy presumes a more exalted, consciously heroic picture of humanity than does melodrama; a character to whom a tragedy can occur is virtually by definition extraordinary. To the Greeks the tragic hero fell at least in part because his stature threatened the gods; to Shakespeare it was because the depth of his character and passions, and the extent of his virtues and vices, were too great for the earth to hold. Thus tragedy is anti-naturalistic; in the battle between man and the environment, tragedy is at least willing to raise the possibility that man could win. The tragic hero's defeat is ultimately at his own hands, as some inner flaw, division, conflict or excess brings him down; and the magnitude of that internal struggle is itself part of the tragic writer's exalted picture of humanity.

Thus, while another writer of the period might have presented the life of Elizabeth I of England as a domestic drama, emphasizing the ordinariness and universality of the private story, Anderson in *Elizabeth the Queen* (1930) presents a tragedy. He focuses on events late in Elizabeth's life, involving her love for the Earl of Essex. (Like any historical dramatist, Anderson is not too tightly bound by facts; the Elizabeth–Essex romance is more in the province of myth than history, and the key final meeting of the two after Essex's arrest never happened.) Falsely accused of treason, Essex recognizes in himself the capacity for treason, and accepts his death rather than pleading for mercy. Thus it is he, rather than Elizabeth, who is tempted by personal virtues and weaknesses to over-reach himself and thus bring on his inevitable destruction; and it is he who learns from the experience, achieves some self-recognition, and is changed for the better before his death. But Anderson is not a follower of the 'tragic flaw' school of tragedy. Essex is not a good man brought down by one small but fatal weakness such as vanity or ambition. Rather, like Shakespeare, Anderson sees that in certain contexts a man's virtues can become tragically self-destructive, that only the great are tempted to go too far. The qualities that doom Essex are those that make him great, as Elizabeth recognizes:

> You are young and strangely winning and strangely sweet.
> My heart goes out to you wherever you are.
> And something in me has drawn you. But this same thing
> That draws us together hurts and blinds us until
> We strike at one another. This has gone on
> A long while. It grows worse with the years. It will end badly.

If Essex is the traditional tragic hero in the play, brought down by the incompatibility of his greatness with the world around him, but granted the self-awareness to die a better man than he had lived, then Elizabeth is tragic in a more modern sense. Hers is the experience of making hard choices and then having to live with them, knowing that she has brought unending pain on herself by her decision. Like some of Shakespeare's heroes, she is forced to choose between her passions as an individual and her obligations as a ruler, voluntarily closing off some integral part of herself: 'he who would rule must be / Quite friendless, without mercy, without love.' But it is not until the final moments of the play that she fully realizes the price she is paying:

> Oh, then I'm old, I'm old!
> I could be young with you, but now I'm old.
> I know now how it will be without you. The sun
> Will be empty and circle round an empty earth . . .
> And I will be queen of emptiness and death.
> [ellipses Anderson's]

It is very much a modern sensibility that suggests that the one who lives may suffer more than the one who dies, and that a tragic heroism lies in choosing a path of pain.

Anderson's use of dramatic verse is skilful and impressive. The Queen's speech just quoted, for example, moves seamlessly from the uncensored and very dramatic outburst of the first line, through the simple statements of the next two lines, to the evocative imagery of the last two. Anderson never achieves, and rarely attempts, the linguistic complexity and density of Shakespeare, but he is able to use the occasional well-placed image or poetic device to intensify a moment or to underline a thought. At other times the verse is barely noticeable, merely a more regularly rhythmic prose, keeping the play from sounding too exotic or self-conscious.

Like most writers drawn to the story of *Mary of Scotland* (1933), Anderson sees the centre of her myth in the contrast and conflict with Elizabeth of England; and like most writers he does not resist the impulse to violate history by building his play around a face-to-face encounter between the two women who actually never met. In Anderson's version of the contrast Elizabeth is cold, intellectual and intensely political, and Mary sincere, naive and personally charming; the conflict is not so much between two queens as between a queen and a woman. In their climactic meeting Mary makes the mistake of greeting Elizabeth as a sister, 'a woman like myself, fearing as I do, / With the little dark fears of a woman,' only to be assured by Elizabeth that her power comes from having dehumanized herself: 'It's thus if you would rule; / Give up good faith, the word that goes with the heart, / The heart that clings where it loves.' And here Mary reaches the recognition of her failure – 'Oh, I'm to blame in this, too! / I should have seen your hand!' – and of her victory:

> MARY   Still, STILL I win! I have been
>   A woman, and I have loved as a woman loves,

> Lost as a woman loses. I have borne a son,
> And he will rule Scotland – and England. You have no heir!
> A devil has no children.
> ELIZABETH   By God, you shall suffer
> For this, but slowly.
> MARY   And that I can do. A woman
> Can do that.

Mary will die as a woman, true to herself and tragically defeated only because the world of Elizabeth cannot support such a person. And Elizabeth, as in the earlier play, will triumph in the world's terms but live on with the recognition of her private defeat.

Winterset (1935) faces the challenge of applying this poetic style and tragic vision to a contemporary story, with mixed results. It seems on its surface to have much in common with the realistic melodramas of the Depression: its setting is a riverside slum alley much like the set of Kingsley's *Dead End*, and its characters are the barely surviving poor. But Anderson's interest in *Winterset*, as in his other poetic plays, is in his characters' inner torments, not their conflict with the world outside. Thirteen years before the opening of the play a man was falsely convicted of a murder, and three men now converge on a witness to the killing: the convicted man's son Mio, trying to clear his father's name; the actual murderer, determined to prevent a reopening of the case; and the judge, driven mad by the fear that he might have collaborated in an injustice. The play is built around obsessions: the murderer's damns him; the judge's drives him mad; and Mio's, which at first seems to be an ennobling quest, is revealed as a spirit-destroying prison resistant to the healing power of a woman's love:

> When I first saw you,
> not a half-hour ago, I heard myself saying,
> this is the face that launches ships for me –
> and if I owned a dream – yes, half a dream –
> we'd share it. But I have no dream.

The climax comes, then, not with Mio's death, but a few moments earlier, as the woman's simple faith leads him to the light:

> MIO   Miriamne, if you love me
> teach me a treason to what I am, and have been,
> till I learn to live like a man! I think I'm waking
> from a long trauma of hate and fear and death
> that's hemmed me from my birth – and glimpse a life
> to be lived in hope. . . .
> MIRIAMNE   He would have forgiven.
> MIO   He?
> MIRIAMNE   Your father.

MIO   Yes. . . .
   Then there's no more to say – I've groped long enough
   through this everglades of old revenges – here
   the road ends. – Miriamne, Miriamne,
   the iron I wore so long – it's eaten through
   and fallen from me.

Anderson tries to give tragic stature to this small story of redemptive but doomed love by surrounding it with the discussion of philosophical and metaphysical questions, but the attempt is misguided and the philosophy and metaphysics the weakest parts of the play. *Winterset* is most successful on the small, personal scale that Anderson's instinct towards tragedy seems to have mistrusted.

The remainder of Anderson's verse plays are less interesting. *Valley Forge* (1934) is notable for depicting a George Washington almost unprecedented in American drama, not the cardboard saint of tradition but a three-dimensional figure capable of rage and despair as well as idealism. The play makes no attempt at tragedy, being satisfied to use the power of verse to celebrate the common soldiers who were the true heroes of the American Revolution. *The Wingless Victory* (1936), a retelling of the Medea myth in American terms, wavers uncertainly between being an attack on intolerance and a tragedy based on its effects. *The Masque of Kings* (1937), Anderson's version of the Meyerling story, is too much a replay of *Mary of Scotland* to be satisfying, with Crown Prince Rudolph a Mary-like idealist and his father the Elizabeth figure. In *High Tor* (1937), the ghosts of seventeenth-century Dutch sailors interact with a modern American idealist and some low-comic criminals; Anderson tries to capture the tone of *A Midsummer Night's Dream*, in which high romance and low comedy can co-exist, but the play is an uneasy blend of romance, satire, fantasy, thesis drama and slapstick. *Key Largo* (1939), Anderson's drama of the battlefield deserter who finds the chance to redeem himself by standing up to a gangster, suffers from the same clashes of style and tone that weakened *Winterset*, as the author, evidently not trusting the inherent power of his domestic story, weighs it down with excess poetry and philosophy. His one post-war verse play, *Anne of the Thousand Days* (1948), is actually two-thirds prose, and again seems a return to old thoughts and patterns, with Anne Boleyn presented as an Essex-like tragic hero, instinctively passionate and ambitious, but less skilled at the cold-blooded games of power than her enemies.

In the end, the results of Anderson's experiment proved ambiguous. Without question, poetic drama was a viable medium, and at least a few of his verse plays were artistic successes. But Anderson's own later plays discovered nothing further in the alternative medium, and even receded from the new artistic ground staked out by his first explorations, proving most successful as domestic stories that might just as well have been written in prose. *Elizabeth the Queen*, *Mary of Scotland* and *Winterset* closed the same doors they opened by showing the limits as well as the possibilities of verse tragedy, and there seemed no place to go once the point had been made. Anderson himself returned to prose; and the few verse plays written in America in the years to come were more likely to be by poets trying their hands at drama (e.g. Archibald MacLeish and Robert Lowell) than by dramatists drawn to poetry.

On the other hand, Anderson's dissatisfaction with the prosaic language and naturalistic world view of much of American drama of the 1930s was a legitimate criticism of a real limitation of the realistic genre, and it is noteworthy that the next generation of essentially realistic writers would expand the definitions of realism beyond that limitation. The discovery that the evocative language and tools of poetry could be incorporated into a richer, heightened version of realistic prose would be one of the major contributions of Tennessee Williams; and while some dramatists, notably Arthur Miller, would continue to look at domestic situations as the exemplifications of larger social forces, Williams and others in the 1940s and 1950s would, following Anderson's lead, find the value of such stories in the human interactions and adventures themselves.

Alternatives to realism: Thornton Wilder

The decade's other important stylistic non-conformist was, like Anderson, a conscious rebel against the limitations of domestic realism. To Thornton Wilder a play that was set too firmly in a specific time and place forsook the drama's ability to be universal, and a play that emphasized too assertively the realness of its setting lost the drama's ability to evoke a sense of magic and mystery. Moreover, like Anderson, Wilder had a greater interest and faith in the value of the individual adventure for its own sake than in its utility as a vehicle for political and social comment. Where Anderson's method for escaping the limitations of realism was to step into the clearly artificial through verse, Wilder's was to engage the audience's attention and imagination through the openly theatrical; where Anderson celebrated the value of the individual by raising him to tragic stature, Wilder sought out and illuminated the wonders of the most ordinary lives.

Until the mid-1930s Wilder was known primarily as a novelist, although he had published two volumes of short plays, *The Angel that Troubled the Waters* (1928) and *The Long Christmas Dinner* (1931). The second collection includes three plays that define the shape and purpose of Wilder's break with realism. In 'The Long Christmas Dinner' time is accelerated so that a single family dinner encapsulates the events of ninety years. Characters age and develop; some excuse themselves from the table to die, their seats filled by younger replacements; and the table talk describes the changes in the family's fortunes and surroundings as the years pass. 'The Happy Journey to Trenton and Camden' is assertively about nothing more than that: a family of four drives across New Jersey for a visit. In addition to condensing the several-hour trip into less than half an hour of playing time, Wilder focuses our attention by stripping away almost all distracting externals. The car consists of four plain chairs on a bare stage, the passing scenery is reflected only in the family's comments on it, and all secondary roles are played by a Stage Manager who also moves the few props. The small pleasures and adventures of the trip thus become remarkable because the play's unusual technique isolates them for appreciation. The third of Wilder's short experiments is the most ambitious. Like 'The Happy Journey', 'Pullman Car Hiawatha' has a Stage Manager, who marks the outline of a railroad car in chalk on the bare stage and cues the actors to carry on the chairs that will represent their berths and compartments. This Stage Manager is more obtrusive than the other, addressing the audience, controlling the action, instructing the passengers to let us hear first their small talk and then their private thoughts, and interrupting to call on a parade of allegorical figures who provide us with 'its position geographically, meteorologically, astronomically, theologically considered'.

The double time scale of 'Dinner' and the parade of allegorical figures in 'Hiawatha' would reappear in *The Skin of Our Teeth*, both of them in more sophisticated forms. The bare stage and minimal props, and the resulting focus on the universality of the human adventure, anticipate *Our Town*, as do the narrative and directorial figure of the Stage Manager, the impulse to bracket the dramatized event in its cosmic context, and even some specific language, including a reference to a town called Grover's Corners and a dead woman's farewell to the world.

Our Town (1938) is one of the best-known and most beloved of American plays. Its quiet story of the value of ordinary lives, told in a highly sophisticated style that has the deceptive appearance of simplicity, and its unashamed appeal to open and honest sentimentality make it perhaps the most accessible of great plays, and a staple of the amateur and student theatre repertoires. On its surface it is the story of thirteen years in the lives of a handful of small-town people; just below its surface it is a celebration of the holiness of the ordinary; and skilfully hidden by Wilder's art it is a carefully constructed exercise in non-realistic theatrical method.

Our Town opens in 1901 in the fictional small town of Grover's Corners, New Hampshire, where teenagers George Gibbs and Emily Webb are neighbours and school friends. Three years later we attend their wedding, and nine years later Emily's funeral. The play's central message is that we require no tragic heroes or allegorical interpretations to make

ordinary life significant, because the simple and mundane facts are themselves almost too precious and extraordinary for us to absorb and appreciate;
and the specialness of the ordinary is affirmed repeatedly throughout the
play. Act One ends with news from George's younger sister Rebecca:

> I never told you about that letter Jane Crofut got from her minis-
> ter when she was sick. He wrote Jane a letter and on the en-
> velope the address was like this: It said: Jane Crofut; The Crofut
> Farm; Grover's Corners; Sutton County; New Hampshire;
> United States of America. . . . But listen, it's not finished: the
> United States of America; Continent of North America; Western
> Hemisphere; the Earth; the Solar System; the Universe; the Mind
> of God. . . . And the postman brought it just the same.

However tiny, however insignificant, however lost in the hugeness of
the universe, Jane Crofut can still be found, and is still worth finding.
Later, Wilder interrupts the preparations for the wedding to go back to
the moment when George and Emily fell in love, only to discover that
lives are not changed by grand dramatic events, but by moments so tiny
and fleeting that they cannot be pinned down. All we can see is the
moment the couple realize that the other moment has just passed:

> GEORGE   Emily, if I *do* improve and make a big change . . .
>   would you be. . . I mean: *could* you be . . .
> EMILY   I. . . I am now; I always have been.
> GEORGE   So I guess this is an important talk we've been having.
>   [Ellipses Wilder's]

Two technical devices overtly announce the play's departure from the
conventions of dramatic realism, and less obviously help the play to
achieve the ends Wilder felt realism could not. The first is the almost
complete absence of scenery or stage props. As in 'The Happy Journey'
and 'Pullman Car Hiawatha', plain tables and chairs are used to imply all
the other furnishings in the rooms around them, while most hand props
are mimed by the actors. At the end of Act One, in the play's most
famous visual effect, George and Emily sit on top of two ladders on a
bare stage, creating the impression of their two houses and the upstairs
windows through which they call to each other. Thus, as in the earlier
plays, Wilder makes the ordinary significant simply by focusing on it in
an unexpected way: when all we are allowed to see is a mother prepar-
ing breakfast and sending her children off to school, or a teenage boy
puzzling over his algebra homework, or a girl wondering if she is pretty
– each of these without even sets or scenery to distract us – then we can
look at each of these afresh, and find the beauty in them.

The second break with realism is the use of a Stage Manager even more intrusive than the one in 'Pullman Car Hiawatha'. He provides continuity, background information and overt commentary, as in his Act Two salute to wives and mothers:

> I don't have to point out to the women in my audience that those ladies they see before them, both those ladies cooked three meals a day – one of 'em for twenty years, the other for forty – and no summer vacation. They brought up two children apiece; washed; cleaned the house, – and *never a nervous breakdown*.

He plays a variety of minor roles, and frequently interrupts and directs the action to control the flow and time scheme of the play. It is he who allows the dead Emily to revisit a day from her childhood before leaving the earth, and who counsels her on her return; and it is he who reminds us at all times that what we are watching *is* a play, an invented reality distinct from the one we inhabit, and that he can move back and forth between the two at will. He can also move backwards and forwards in time, and Wilder uses this magic to emphasize the play's pastoral and nostalgic atmosphere: 'Along here's a row of stores. Hitching posts and horse blocks in front of them. First automobile's going to come along in about five years.'

The play's emotional climax comes when the dead Emily insists on her right to relive a day from her past, a morning scene very similar to the one that opened the first act. She discovers that it is too painful to experience again:

> I can't. I can't go on. It goes so fast. We don't have time to look at one another. I didn't realize. So all that was going on and we never noticed. Take me back – up the hill – to my grave. But first: Wait! One more look.
> Good-by, Good-by, world. Good-by, Grover's Corners . . .
> Mama and Papa. Good-by to clocks ticking . . . and Mama's sunflowers. And food and coffee. And new-ironed dresses and hot baths . . . and sleeping and waking up. Oh, earth, you're too wonderful for anybody to realize you.
>   [Ellipses Wilder's]

She asks the Stage Manager if any humans ever realize the preciousness of life. He answers, 'No. The saints and poets, maybe – they do some.' The purpose of the play, of course, is to number the audience among the exceptions.

Wilder's next play, *The Merchant of Yonkers* (1938), is a light farce loosely based on a nineteenth-century Austrian play about the clerks of an intimidating provincial shopkeeper, who steal a day off to go to the big city. Wilder adds the character of the local marriage broker, who encourages the boys in their liberation and catches the shopkeeper for herself. (A 1954 revision, *The Matchmaker*, was the basis for the very successful 1964 musical *Hello, Dolly!*) The play's enthusiastic employment of the artificialities of farce reflects Wilder's delight in open theatricality; and Wilder reaffirms his celebration of the simple pleasures of life, as the cold merchant is gradually humanized and the boys learn to appreciate both the value of adventure and the comfort of the safe and familiar.

The Skin of Our Teeth (1942) is a complex allegory saved from pretentiousness by an ironic attitude towards its own ideas and methods; almost everything Wilder says and does in the play is immediately made the subject of a joke, demystifying both philosophy and dramaturgy – this at the apparently acceptable cost of an ironic distance that prevents the degree of identification and emotional involvement that makes *Our Town* so powerful. It purports to be about a typical American couple who live in New Jersey with their children and maid. But Mr and Mrs Antrobus are also Adam and Eve after the fall, and also Noah and his wife, and also embodiments of the spirit of man and womankind from the cave days to the present, and also the actor and actress playing these roles; and Wilder breezily mixes these metaphors with no apparent concern for consistency. In Act One, Mr Antrobus returns home from a busy day at the office, where he has invented the wheel, the alphabet and the multiplication table, to discover that his family is threatened by approaching glaciers. In Act Two he addresses a convention of the Ancient and Honorable Order of Mammals before escaping from a sudden flood with some of the other delegates and their wives. In Act Three he returns from a world war against an enemy led by his son Henry (né Cain) and prepares to start up the work of civilization again.

The reassurance implied by the title, that humanity can and will survive anything, if only barely, must have been particularly welcome to its wartime audiences: despite moments of weakness, lapses of faith, and everything that an unpredictable cosmos can throw at them, Mr Antrobus's inventiveness and Mrs Antrobus's domesticity carry them through. Indeed, we are shown that survival and progress are a matter of instinct as much as conscious determination; even the wavering and sceptical maid Sabina is ultimately incapable of giving up: 'All right, I'll go on just out of *habit*, but I won't believe in it.' In each act of the play Mr Antrobus has a moment of despair or back-sliding from which he is able to rouse himself just in time: the inventor of the wheel is broken by the news that Henry-Cain has been throwing stones again until Mrs Antrobus's faith revives his spirits; the conventioneer is seduced by bathing beauty Sabina and ready to leave his wife, but her commitment to the family wins him back just in time for them to board the Ark; the war veteran's encounter with the unrepentant Henry again depletes his reserves of hope until he reminds himself that 'I have never forgotten for long at a time that living is a struggle. I know that every good and excellent thing in the world stands moment by moment on the razor-edge of danger and must be fought for. . . . All I ask is the chance to build new worlds and God has always given us that.'

Added to the play's anachronisms and mixed metaphors is its constant assertion of itself as a play. The actress playing Sabina repeatedly revolts against her part – 'I hate this play and every word in it' – and the lines she is forced to speak – 'I don't understand a word of this play.' These interruptions are startling and funny, disarm any audience suspicion that the play is over their heads, and in fact encourage the audience, who are rarely as confused as the actress claims to be. They are also used seriously; in Act Two the Sabina actress refuses to play the seduction scene 'Because there are some lines in that scene that would hurt some people's feelings and I don't think the theatre is a place where people's feelings ought to be hurt.' There's a joke there, about the popular belief that the theatre should be nothing but light entertainment, but also the opportunity to talk directly about the scene's implications. Sabina also interrupts the climactic scene between Mr Antrobus and Henry because last night the actors got carried away and actually fought; in the brief psychodrama that follows, the two actors find flaws in their offstage personalities that parallel and underline their characters' moral failings. And the play ends with a theatrical trick that is both joke and summing up: the action restarts with Sabina's opening lines, which she interrupts to address the audience: 'This is where you came in. We have to go on for ages and ages yet. You go home. The end of this play isn't written yet.'

Thornton Wilder's place in American drama, like Maxwell Anderson's, is an ambiguous one. There can be no question that *Our Town* is a play of major stature, one of a small handful of American dramatic masterpieces. But, as breaks with the mainstream of realistic drama, Wilder's formal and theatrical experiments proved to be as much dead ends as were Anderson's verse tragedies: he proved without question that they could be done, and done effectively; and, that having been proved, there oddly seemed little point in his or anyone else's doing them again.

And yet, like Anderson, Wilder did expose some of the failings of domestic realism as practised in the 1930s. In particular, he spoke of a hunger for more exploitation of the theatre's potential for imaginative magic, and also for consideration of domestic lives for purposes other than social or moral comment. *The Skin of Our Teeth* says that domestic melodrama, freed from the constraints of place- and time-specific social comment, can speak of the essential human condition, while *Our Town* insists that the domestic world is of interest and importance in itself. Two highly significant changes would be seen in the mainstream domestic drama of the 1940s and 1950s – a movement from political to psychological and spiritual subjects, and a loosening of the bounds of realism to allow the occasional dream sequence or expressionist effect. While neither of these can be traced directly to Wilder's example – just as the increasingly evocative and poetic prose cannot be said to come directly from Anderson, – in each case the later developments were manifestations of the same impulse to stretch the dramatic form that inspired Anderson and Wilder.

Eugene O'Neill

As he had in the previous decade, Eugene O'Neill spent the 1930s following his own drummer, paying little heed to what was going on in the mainstream or alternative drama around him. Only three new O'Neill plays were staged in the 1930s, each, characteristically, completely different in style from the others and from the string of stylistic experiments that had preceded them.

Mourning Becomes Electra (1931) is a trilogy based on the *Oresteia* of Aeschylus. On its surface, it is a domestic melodrama set just after the American Civil War, with none of the overt violations of realism that characterized O'Neill's plays of the 1920s. But it is significantly different from the domestic plays of O'Neill's contemporaries in more than its length (a total of thirteen acts, meant to be performed in a single night). Finding modern equivalents of the ancient Greek sense of Fate in a combination of mythical allusions, American Puritanism and Freudian psychology, O'Neill reaches in *Mourning Becomes Electra* for the stature and power of classical tragedy.

Aeschylus's trilogy traces the effects on the royal house of Atreus of a curse invoked by Atreus's brother Thyestes. Aeschylus joins the story at the end of the Trojan War, as Agamemnon, son of Atreus, is murdered by his wife Clytemnestra and her lover Aegisthus, son of Thyestes. In the second play Agamemnon's son Orestes, spurred by his sister Electra, avenges his father by killing the murderers; and in the third Orestes is haunted by the avenging Furies until the Olympian deities Apollo and Athena rescue him. O'Neill translates the story and characters bodily into an American setting. Following Sophocles and other writers, he focuses on Electra more than Orestes, but otherwise he makes few significant changes in the basic situation: General Ezra Mannon returns from the Civil War to be murdered by his wife Christine and her lover Adam Brant, Ezra's cousin. Lavinia Mannon (Electra) moves her brother Orin (Orestes) to kill Brant, after which Christine commits suicide. Driven mad by guilt, Orin kills himself; and Lavinia accepts the inescapability of the Mannon curse, withdrawing from the world to live out her days in the family mansion. The parallels to Aeschylus are open, with the title, the names (Ezra Mannon/Agamemnon), the set (the Mannon mansion is described as resembling the *skene* of Greek tragedy), and the use of a chorus of townspeople calling attention to them.

The power of Aeschylus's tragedy comes from three central sources: the concept of an inevitable Fate in the form of the curse, which separates the descendants of Atreus from the rest of humanity and marks them for pain and doom; the violations of profound taboos in the string of crimes and counter-crimes, particularly Orestes' matricide; and the allegory of a redeeming cultural evolution in the Olympian gods' defeat of the Furies. O'Neill's trilogy does not include the third of those elements, since he offers no escape or redemption for the Mannons, but he does reach for the dramatic power of the first two; and his biggest challenge in *Mourning Becomes Electra* was to find substitutes for Aeschylus's Fate and cultural taboos that would have an equivalent effect on twentieth-century American audiences.

In place of the curse O'Neill creates a Mannon temperament, a concentration of pride, intense passion barely held in check by Puritan repression, and susceptibility to feelings of guilt. The chorus's reaction to Christine's first appearance is that 'There's somethin' queer lookin' about her face. . . . Secret lookin' – 's if it was a mask she'd put on. That's the Mannon look. They all has it.' Each member of the family is described at some point as wearing a version of Christine's cold, emotionless mask: Ezra Mannon's voice '*has a hollow repressed quality, as if he were continually withholding emotion from it,*' and he admits in a weak moment that 'Something queer in me keeps me mum about the things I'd like most to say – keeps me hiding the things I'd like to show. Something keeps me sitting numb in my own heart – like a statue of a dead man in a town square.' The Mannons are not emotionless, but the only emotions that can break through their masks are the strongest, and those are likely to be warped by the strain. Disagreements of any sort instantly evoke intense, murderous hatred; uncertainties turn into panic or madness; regret becomes unbearable guilt. Their shared pain from this constant swing between emotional deadness and frighteningly uncontrollable passion is betrayed by their shared fantasy of escape to a South Sea island of natural, unperverted emotion. Orin and Lavinia do go to that island between the second and third plays, and Lavinia does find a shameless romantic and sexual abandon there, only to discover on her return that her experience and change are seen as depraved and sinful. Love, like other emotions, is only permitted to the Mannons in a pathologically intense and corrupted form.

As part of his modern image of Fate, and as an equivalent of the deeply frightening archetypal crimes of the *Oresteia*, O'Neill invokes Freudian sexual psychology, making the Mannon family a tangle of warped and uncontrolled sexual conflicts. The most centrally and explicitly presented are the Oedipal and Electra complexes of Orin and

Lavinia. Lavinia idolizes her father, rejects any suggestion of similarity to her mother (although O'Neill stresses that it is there), and is Christine's rival for each of the men: 'You've tried to become the wife of your father and the mother of Orin!' Orin not only has an unresolved Oedipal conflict – referring to Brant, he says, 'If I had been he I would have done what he did! I would have loved her as he loved her – and killed Father too – for her sake!' – but he is encouraged in it by Christine's excessive need for him: 'I feel you are really – my flesh and blood! She isn't! She is your father's! You're a part of me!' Though speeches such as these suffer from being a little too explicitly spelled out, the Freudian complexes do have the effect of exposing culture-threatening forces that can affect an audience with the emotional power of Aeschylus's mythic taboos. And, when seen as part of the more intricate and sophisticated Mannon temperament O'Neill has created, they do contribute to a sense of fatal forces beyond the control of the doomed characters.

Mourning Becomes Electra is as successful as one could imagine a modern version of a Greek tragedy to be. But, like the neo-Elizabethan tragedies of Maxwell Anderson or, indeed, most of O'Neill's other experiments, it is also a dead end. In proving that it can be done O'Neill also seems to have proved that this is as successfully as it can be done, leaving no room for any further exploration of the subgenre. It is worth noting that, its length and classical echoes aside, *Mourning Becomes Electra* is on its surface a realistic domestic melodrama. Perhaps unconsciously, O'Neill was discovering in his own terms what his contemporaries were discovering in theirs, that domestic realism was more adaptable to his ambitious visions than he had previously realized. O'Neill would certainly retain his tragic sense and his inclination to embody it in drama, and when he returned to that impulse near the end of his career, he would find shape for it entirely within the bounds of domestic realism.

O'Neill's next play, *Ah, Wilderness!* (1933), stands out even in the context of a career in which no two plays seemed to have been written in the same style. It is O'Neill's only comedy, with a tone and content that specifically deny the dark vision of human guilt and limitation that is O'Neill's hallmark – an elegiac, nostalgic piece set in an innocent small-town America of 1906 that probably never existed, in which an adolescent boy's rebellious fling amounts to little more than getting painfully drunk, and all evils are merely easily-rectified misunderstandings. It is almost as if O'Neill chose, as an act of will, to pretend he believed in everything that he disbelieved about life, and to write a play in that spirit. *Ah, Wilderness!* is pleasantly entertaining, in part because it is so bland and conventional; were it not by O'Neill there would be little to say about it, and what there is to say makes it of interest as a footnote to other plays rather than for its own merits. In particular, this is one of the first O'Neill's plays since some of the early one-acts to be drawn directly from his own life, though in a highly fictionalized and romanticized way; and it invites comparison with the later *Long Day's Journey into Night*, both for its similarities – the self-portraits have a similar ironic distance – and differences – the later play presents a far darker vision of the family and the world it inhabits.

Days Without End (1933) was intended as the second play of a trilogy on the theme of man's search for faith that began with *Dynamo*, but its failure led O'Neill to leave the third play unwritten. The hero of *Days Without End*, John Loving, is a man whose loss of faith has led to the disintegration of his personality, a condition O'Neill dramatizes by dividing the character between two actors, the good but weak John and the bitter and evil Loving. Only John and the audience see Loving, who wears a mask of John's face in a cynical sneer, but the other characters hear both figures as if they were one man speaking. *Days Without End* seems at times to be made up of leftovers from earlier O'Neill plays: the mask and divided personality from *The Great God Brown*, the desperate search for faith from *Dynamo*, the internal debates from *Strange Interlude*, with other echoes of *Lazarus Laughed* and *Welded*, and anticipations of *Long Day's Journey*. The play is clumsy in writing and construction, and O'Neill may have sensed that his experiments with expressionism and other non-realistic techniques had run their course; it would be thirteen years before his next play, which would mark a radical change in dramatic style, was produced.

Comedy

If one of the functions of drama is to reflect and illuminate the world of reality to its inhabitants, certainly another is to distract them from it; and it is not surprising that the majority of comedies produced during the Depression and war years either ignore the harsher facts of life, actively deny them, or deny their importance. Several distinct subgenres of comedy can be discerned in this period, and virtually all of them pretend that there is nothing more serious in life than whether or not a particular pair of attractive young lovers find each other.

Many comedies of the 1930s are virtually indistinguishable from similar plays of the preceding decade. Working with a new collaborator, Moss Hart, George S. Kaufman continued his practice of satirizing easy targets with fast-paced wit and humourous dialogue. *Once in a Lifetime* (1930) skewers Hollywood with many of the same jokes as the Kaufman–Connelly *Merton of the Movies* of eight years earlier, as does Samuel and Bella Spewack's Hollywood satire *Boy Meets Girl* (1935). Other successful comedies that might well have been written in any other decade include A. E. Thomas's *No More Ladies* (1934), about the wife who wins back her straying husband by pretending a dalliance of her own, and Kaufman and Hart's *George Washington Slept Here* (1940), about the predictable tribulations of a city man who buys a run-down country house.

Also similar to earlier plays are the 1930s versions of 'beautiful people' drawing-room comedies in the Noel Coward manner, whose only dramatic question is which rich and witty man will end up with which rich and witty woman. Essentially the same basic plot generates such plays as S.N. Behrman's *Brief Moment* (1931), in which a weak millionaire marries a poor girl who quickly makes a man of him; Philip Barry's *The Animal Kingdom* (1932), in which the man marries a conventional girl who emasculates him, but returns to his Bohemian mistress and happiness; and Samson Raphaelson's *Accent on Youth* (1934), in which a devoted secretary rejuvenates a middle-aged playwright. The best of this group alters the formula with a switch of genders: in Philip Barry's classic *The Philadelphia Story* (1939), icy heiress Tracy Lord is unforgiving of any imperfections in others, be they her ex-husband Dex's irresponsibility or her father's extra-marital straying, until an innocent slip of her own humanizes her and she finds happiness in remarriage to Dex. As with the other plays of this subgenre, the pleasure for the audience is provided, in almost equal parts, by witty banter, a slight touch of non-conformity, the inevitable pairing of the right couple, and a parade of expensive-looking costumes on elegant sets; characteristically, Barry adds just enough sentiment and emotional depth to give his variant a warmth many of the others lack.

Different in style, but appealing to the same how-the-other-half-lives escapism, is Kaufman and Hart's *The Man Who Came to Dinner* (1939) about curmudgeonly media celebrity Sheridan Whiteside, who breaks his leg on a speaking tour and becomes the involuntary houseguest of an Ohio family. He completely disrupts his hosts' lives with a steady stream of imperious demands and shameless insults ('My great-aunt Jennifer ate a whole box of candy every day of her life. She lived to be a hundred and two, and when she had been dead three days she looked better than you do now.'). Probably most theatre-goers were aware that the main character and his show business friends were based on real-life celebrities of the day; they certainly were titillated by a peep into a world in which names like Cary Grant, H. G. Wells, Lord and Lady Astor, and more than fifty others were dropped in casual conversation.

If the drawing-room comedies allowed the audience to imagine a world untouched by the Depression or the rumblings of war, another group encouraged the fantasy that life could somehow go its benign way in spite of outside events. Kaufman and Hart's *You Can't Take It With You* (1936) presents the eccentric Sycamore family: Grandpa quit work thirty-five years ago because he was not having any fun; his daughter writes unfinished plays and paints unfinished portraits; her husband manufactures fireworks in the cellar; and various friends and acquaintances add to the disorganized happiness. The one relatively ordinary member of the family loves an ordinary boy, and the plot turns on a disastrous meeting of the Sycamores and the boy's staid parents which threatens the romance until Grandpa's wisdom can begin to loosen up the in-laws-to-be. The faith that Grandpa's dinner table prayer expresses –

> Well, Sir, we've been getting along pretty good for quite a while
> now, and we're certainly much obliged. Remember, all we ask
> is just to go along and be happy in our own sort of way. Of
> course we want to keep our health, but as far as anything else is
> concerned, we'll leave it to You.

– is the fantasy the play allows the audience to enjoy for two hours: that love, tolerance and innocent eccentricity make the cold fact of the Depression irrelevant, and that the world is ultimately a good place in which only good things happen to good people.

The same fantasy of a loving providence watching over the innocent colours such comedies as James Hagan's *One Sunday Afternoon* (1933) and Maxwell Anderson's *The Star-Wagon* (1937), both of which allow their heroes to relive their lives and discover how satisfying they are. It is there in Paul Osborn's *On Borrowed Time* (1938), in which Death is magically trapped in a tree until the old man he has come for decides he is ready to go; and in Osborn's *Morning's at Seven* (1939), about four elderly sisters and their families, whose lives include problems no greater than wondering if a forty-year-old son will finally marry. It lies beneath *My Sister Eileen* (1940), the dramatization by Joseph Fields and Jerome Chodorov of Ruth McKenney's short stories about two naive Ohio girls who come to New York and find nothing harsher than romance, jobs and friendly neighbours. It infuses Joseph Kesselring's *Arsenic and Old Lace* (1941), in which a pair of little old ladies blithely murder lonely old men and let their mad brother, who thinks he's Teddy Roosevelt, bury them in the Panama Canal he's digging in the cellar. And it is certainly there in Mary Chase's *Harvey* (1944), about a gently potty man whose best friend is a six foot tall invisible rabbit. The same wilful blindness to reality may explain the popularity for several years of plays about the innocent adventures and small calamities in the lives of teenagers. Clifford Goldsmith's *What a Life* (1938), Chodorov and Fields's *Junior Miss* (1941), F. Hugh Herbert's *Kiss and Tell* (1943), and Norman Krasna's *Dear Ruth* (1944) all implicitly pretend that life holds no greater dangers than the school bully and no deeper emotions than puppy love. The subtext of all these comedies is the pretense that the more unpleasant facts of the outside world are not really there.

One effective escape from the unpleasantness of the present is a retreat into the past, and it is probably not coincidental that the most successful comedy of the 1940s is set in the 1880s. *Life With Father* (1939), drawn from the stories of Clarence Day by Howard Lindsay and Russel Crouse, celebrates an innocent past in which gruff and domineering father could easily be manipulated by his wife and children and the most dramatic event in their lives was his somewhat-delayed baptism. Much the same spirit permeates John Van Druten's *I Remember Mama* (1944), from Kathryn Forbes' stories of growing up in a Norwegian family in San Francisco, and the more acerbic *The Late George Apley* (1944) by John P. Marquand and George S. Kaufman from Marquand's novel: though the Boston Brahmin father in that play does turn his son into a stuffy duplicate of himself, the distance of history blunts any satire or suggestion that all is not for the best in this best of all possible worlds.

Still, a few comic writers of this period managed to acknowledge the world outside or the possibility of emotions deeper than love at first sight. S.N. Behrman gave the drawing room subgenre some additional weight by adding a bittersweet, elegiac tone in *Biography* (1932) and *End of Summer* (1936). In the first, a Bohemian artist writing her kiss-and-tell autobiography realizes it could harm an old lover; forced to recognize, perhaps for the first time, that her actions affect others, she destroys the manuscript and ends the play a deeper character than she began. *End of Summer* has a similar spirit, as an aging social butterfly comes to realize, and accept with some grace, the fact of her own inconsequentiality.

Other Behrman plays make a point of searching for comedy in the face of reality rather than through the denial of it. *Rain From Heaven* (1934) would be a typical drawing room comedy, even to the extent of being set in an English country house, were it not that the two men the heroine must choose between are an apolitical adventurer and a Jewish anti-Nazi fighter, so that scenes of typically brittle wit alternate with serious political and moral debates. In *No Time for Comedy* (1939), a Noel Coward-like playwright cannot bring himself to write drawing-room comedies in the face of the horrors of war, and the play reaches a comic resolution without pretending that the world outside its boundaries is also harmless and comic. Behrman is one of the very few wartime comic writers to acknowledge a reality harsher than the fact that Washington DC had a civilian housing shortage (the comic basis of Joseph Fields's 1942 comedy *The Doughgirls*) or that soldiers are attracted to pretty girls (John Van Druten's 1943 *The Voice of the Turtle* among others). In *Jacobowsky and the Colonel* (1944), adapted from a play by Franz Werfel, Behrman follows a desperate but resourceful Polish Jew as he stays one step ahead of the advancing Nazis in France.

It is striking how very few other comic plays in this fifteen-year period attempt a little extra depth of emotion, characterization or reality. Kaufman and Hart's *Merrily We Roll Along* (1934) traces the moral and artistic decline of a writer who sells out for success, but it is more notable for its narrative trick of telling the story in reverse chronology, starting with the writer's corruption and working back to ironic scenes of youthful idealism. Robert E. Sherwood's *Idiot's Delight* (1936), mentioned earlier in this chapter, would be a conventional light romance between sophisticated Americans in Europe were it not set on the eve of war, with the protagonists learning the importance and dangers of political commitment from the Europeans around them. Clare Boothe's *The Women* (1936) looks at first like a typical beautiful-people comedy, with the gimmick of an all-female cast only serving to permit lots of elegant gowns and catty repartee, but it confounds the conventions of the genre by presenting what should be a figure of fun, a deceived wife, as deeply unhappy. *Stage Door* (1936), by Edna Ferber and George S. Kaufman, is a sentimental celebration of the dreams and dedication of would-be actresses in a theatrical boarding house, but it offers a passing glimpse of reality when one of the girls kills herself, showing the toll that poverty and constant rejection can take.

By 1930, then, it was clear that drama in America had become a significant art form, capable of supporting ambitious literary intentions, both serious and comic, while still meeting its social function as a source of entertainment. Ironically, the theatrical style in which the twentieth-century drama had been reborn – realism – had begun to seem limited and limiting to some of the most ambitious playwrights, and Eugene O'Neill and others had rejected it in their search for other modes through which they might be able to dramatize subjects and artistic visions that earlier generations of playwrights would never have attempted. In this context, the fifteen years covered in this chapter represent an important turning point, the return to dominance of domestic realism with the realization by playwrights that it was capable of much more than had been asked of it previously.

The harsh and inescapable external reality of the 1930s demanded dramatic consideration in a way that the more benign 1920s had not, and the major discovery by Clifford Odets and other socially aware playwrights of the period was that the largest political and social issues could best be dramatized through their reflection in a domestic situation. This led in turn to the further perception that almost any large subject – social, philosophical, moral – could be addressed successfully in the same manner, and not only because realism was a more flexible and adaptable mode than it had previously seemed. Something in the instinctively democratic American perspective recognized that the important thing to be said about any large subject was the way it affected the lives of ordinary people, and thus the American drama found its native and natural voice in domestic realism.

Domestic realism was not infinitely adaptable, of course, nor had all its potential yet been realized; and the alternative styles of Maxwell Anderson and Thornton Wilder, and continued strivings of Eugene O'Neill, were generated by a legitimate reaction against some of the dominant style's apparent limitations. But the important discovery had been made: experiments in alternative styles such as expressionism were simply unnecessary. The occasional variation notwithstanding, the drama and dramatists of the Depression and war years made it clear that the typical American play was going to be set in someone's living room. The next step would be further exploration of just how rich a dramatic setting that could be.

Chapter 4
1945-1960: The Zenith of the Broadway Theatre

The era of Williams and Miller

The period covered in the preceding chapter saw the American drama finding its natural voice in domestic realism, and the exploration of some of the potential scope and power of that mode, particularly its ability to deal with large social, political and moral issues. In the fifteen years following the Second World War the next generation of American dramatists built on these discoveries, and on the psychological dramas of earlier writers, to carry the Broadway-based American theatre to its highest accomplishments. This period produced the greatest plays of America's greatest playwrights: the early works of Arthur Miller and Tennessee Williams, and the late and posthumous works of Eugene O'Neill. It was a golden age for Broadway in other ways as well, featuring the highest achievements of the musical theatre, most notably in the collaborations of Richard Rodgers and Oscar Hammerstein; the introduction and development of 'Method' acting; and the creative and illuminating accomplishments of such directors as Elia Kazan and Jose Quintero.

In one important way the drama of the 1950s turned away from the direction set in the 1930s. Although some playwrights, notably Arthur Miller, continued to address social and political issues by dramatizing their effect on the everyday domestic lives of ordinary people, others, led by Tennessee Williams (and anticipated by O'Neill), returned to the focus on psychological exploration that had been the concern of the realistic dramatists of the 1920s. Now, however, the concentration was not so much on explaining abnormal behaviour through Freudian analysis, as George Kelly, for example, had done in *Craig's Wife*, but on expressing and illuminating the emotions that lay beneath both normal and abnormal behaviour. Not the least of Method acting's contributions to the theatre was its making playwrights and audiences as well as actors aware of 'subtext', the emotional drama going on beneath the most mundane of conversations. For some of the best American dramatists of the 1950s and thereafter, the subject to be dramatized was their characters' spiritual and psychic adventure, what it felt like to be alive and trying to cope in the middle of the twentieth century.

More often than not, what they discovered was that it felt rather frightening, that even their most successfully functioning characters were actually being driven by feelings of inadequacy or inability to cope with the ordinary pains and pressures of life. Plays that dramatized this insight could give the audience a sort of comfort, in the demonstration that such insecurities were not individual failings but part of the human condition. Plays that showed realistically uncertain characters coping with or triumphing over their fears provided encouragement and inspiration. So the function and capacity of domestic realism was expanded once again, to include a spiritual content and purpose, in plays that not only explained or argued, but actually offered counsel, consolation and reassurance.

Just as the American drama of the 1920s was dominated by the figure of Eugene O'Neill and the drama of the 1930s given shape and focus in the plays of Clifford Odets, the mid-century drama can be defined by the work of, in this case, two dominant figures. (As always, Eugene O'Neill, though towering over the others, stood apart from them, with little effect on his contemporaries.) There is a difference, however, and it is not just a matter of number. O'Neill was without question the best and most ambitious American dramatist of the 1920s, but he was not a part of whatever mainstream there was. Odets helped to discover and shape the mainstream dramatic mode of his decade and after, but that is clearer in hindsight than it was at the time, when he seemed to be just one talented writer among many. The 1945–60 period was clearly dominated by its two leading dramatists; virtually every serious American play of the time functioned within artistic boundaries defined by the plays of Tennessee Williams and Arthur Miller.

It may be useful, therefore, to start with an overview and some generalizations, before looking closely at each writer. Williams and Miller had strikingly parallel careers. In each case some early writing led to an inauspicious New York debut: Miller's first Broadway play lasted four performances while Williams's closed out of town. Each followed with a second play that declared him to be a writer of importance, and with a third that would prove to be the finest play of his career. They went on to write some of the best American plays of the 1950s, and both ended their periods of greatest accomplishment in the early 1960s.

Beyond the parallels and the excellence of the individual plays, Williams and Miller had clearly developed dramatic styles and concerns that between them delimited both the manner and the matter of mid-century American drama. Following the lead of the previous decades, both wrote predominantly in the mode of contemporary, realistic domestic melodrama. But both helped to stretch that style a little through the introduction of symbolic or expressionistic elements that did not break or weaken the overall sense of realism. Miller followed in the direction begun by Herne and Crothers at the start of the century, and refined by Odets and the other realists of the 1930s, by using domestic stories to reflect larger political or moral issues. Williams, perhaps moved by an impulse parallel to those that led Maxwell Anderson and Thornton Wilder to other styles, helped to move domestic realism beyond this political focus towards its new function of illuminating psychological and emotional forces within his characters. Miller repeatedly took as his subject the ordinary person placed under extraordinary pressure by his society and either destroyed by it or triumphant over it; Williams wrote of extraordinary people, frequently the freaks and misfits of humanity, trying to survive the ordinary pressures of life emotionally and spiritually. Thus Miller's plays were, in effect, vertical in their thrust, celebrating the potential for stature and greatness in the Common Man (Miller's phrase), while Williams's were horizontal, speaking of the common humanity shared by the normal and abnormal. And while Miller, in keeping with his social agenda, strove for a style of clarity and direct statement, Williams brought the instincts of a poet to the drama, speaking and allowing his characters to speak in the language of symbols, emotionalism and rhetorical flourishes.

Miller and Williams were thus not merely the outstanding American dramatists of the period. Almost all their contemporaries also wrote predominantly in the mode of domestic realism, and chose as their subjects either the social/political or the psychological/spiritual. It would be tempting, therefore, to label each of them as being of 'the school of Miller' or 'the school of Williams' were the concept of such 'schools' simply not native to the American drama. While there are isolated cases of direct influence (Odets on Miller, Williams on Albee), what happened in the 1950s was as unplanned as what had happened in previous decades: individual writers followed their own muses, and their cumulative experience, along with audience response, gave a shape to the drama of the period. In this case, the styles and concerns of Arthur Miller and Tennessee Williams mark the ends of a very short continuum on which virtually every other serious American play of the 1950s can be placed, and thus define their age in a way that O'Neill and Odets did not define theirs.

Arthur Miller

Arthur Miller's first success, *All My Sons* (1947), introduces themes that would run through his work: the inescapable drive for economic success and public approval, the conflict between competing moralities, the temptation to do the wrong thing for the right reasons, and the identification of the political and economic system as the culpable cause of these torments and dilemmas. Its central character, Joe Keller, manufactured defective aircraft engines that killed some pilots during the war, but can come no closer to a confession than the assertion that he did what was necessary to support and protect his family, until the discovery that his son killed himself in shame leads him to recognize the higher moral obligation implied by the play's title. The play is told entirely in domestic terms: its fictional centre is the question of whether Joe's surviving son Chris should marry his dead brother's fiancée. The revelations about the past, and the direct discussion of the moral questions, come out in the course of resolving the family conflict; and Miller is scrupulously fair in presenting both the characterizations and the terms of the debate. Though Joe Keller is in the wrong, he is not the heartless capitalist of leftist propaganda, but a little man trying to do what seems to him to be the right thing:

> KELLER   I could live on a quarter a day myself, but I got a
>   family, so I . . .
> MOTHER   Joe, Joe . . . it don't excuse it that you did it for the
>   family.
> KELLER   It's got to excuse it!
> MOTHER   There's something bigger than the family to him.
> KELLER   Nothin' is bigger!
>   [Ellipses Miller's]

And while Chris is in the right, he has an unattractive element of self-righteousness in common with some of Miller's other 'correct' characters, and he is shown to be motivated more by his own psychological need for a world that makes moral sense than by any special purity of soul:

> Everything was being destroyed [in the war], see, but it seemed
> to me that one new thing was being made. A kind of responsi-
> bility. Man for man. . . . And then I came home and it was in-
> credible. . . . Because nobody was changed at all. It seemed to
> make suckers out of a lot of guys. I felt wrong to be alive.

Chris *is* right, for whatever reason, and the discovery that the pilots Joe killed were his responsibility as much as his own sons leads to Joe's suicide. Miller has no doubt that Joe Keller is in the wrong for defining his moral accountability so narrowly and locally, and for losing sight of his connection to the larger human family. But the final moral judgement of the play is not Chris's 'There's a universe outside and you're responsible to it.' The play pities Joe Keller more than it condemns him.

It recognizes the sincerity of his values, inadequate as they were, and directs the blame at a world that would turn a man's love for his family into a crime and force him to choose between conflicting moral imperatives.

The same condemnation of an economic and social system that precipitates individual tragedy is the generating force behind *Death of a Salesman* (1949), Miller's best play and one of the finest and most important plays by any American dramatist. *Death of a Salesman* is the story of a small man driven to madness and despair by his inability to succeed economically in a system that seems to guarantee success; it is an exposé of the dark and dangerous side of the American Dream. To dramatize his hero's internal experience and focus attention on his spiritual and mental collapse, Miller inserts an expressionistic element in his essentially realistic play, as Willy Loman repeatedly withdraws into memories of the past and into imagined conversations with his brother Ben, his symbol of success. Thus, much of the play is internal; in key scenes it is not reality that we see, but reality as experienced, remembered or imagined by a man for whom reality is too frightening to face directly. Willy is a hard-working travelling salesman who has always tried to believe that he was more successful than he actually was. No longer able to keep up the pretence and yet unable to give up his dream, he puts all his hopes in one last fantasy of success for his son Biff, who tries to make his father recognize and accept their parallel failures. Determined to affirm his faith that Biff could succeed if he only had the starting capital Willy's insurance would provide, Willy kills himself.

Willy's life is defined by his absolute faith that success, measured in economic terms, is available almost without effort to those who deserve it, 'Because the man who makes an appearance in the business world, the man who creates personal interest, is the man who gets ahead. Be liked and you will never want.' The problem with that definition of how the world operates is that reality does not support it; Willy and Biff are well-liked and unsuccessful while their neighbours Charley and Bernard are unimpressive drudges who succeed. So Willy must work harder and harder to sustain his conviction that economic triumph is available to him and his sons, and to deny a reality that threatens that faith: thus the increasing withdrawal into the past, and thus a continuing conflict with Biff, who is slowly escaping the dream. Ultimately the preservation of the fantasy is more important to Willy than his own life, and he dies to affirm it.

The source of Willy's fantasy is so obvious that Miller does not even have to identify it. It is the American Dream – the cultural doctrine that America is by definition the land of opportunity, the place where any boy can grow up to be President, the place where success is a birthright waiting to be claimed, 'and that's the wonder, the wonder of this country, that a man can end with diamonds here on the basis of being liked'. Willy Loman's own experience proves that the dream is false: success is in fact not guaranteed to the well-liked, or even to the hard-working. But that is not the American Dream's greatest lie. The inevitable corollary to the belief that success is available to everyone is the conclusion that failure can only be the fault of the individual. Despite his growing realization that he does not want what the world calls success, Biff can only call himself a worthless failure for not achieving it. The possibility that Willy was simply not fated to be rich, or that he took the wrong route to it, is beyond Willy's comprehension. If they have not grasped the bounty that the American Dream insists is just lying there waiting for them, they must not be good enough, and that conclusion is so frightening to Willy that he will die rather than consider it. Even worse, the American Dream is exclusive; it will not allow its believers to acknowledge or even imagine alternative definitions of value or accomplishment. Willy has a loving wife, a supportive friend, and sons who try, within their limits, to love him. He enjoys looking at nature and working with his hands. But Willy cannot see the value in these things; the only definition of success available to him is measured in dollars, and in numbers that are always beyond his reach.

There are many resonances to Miller's choice of a salesman as the archetypal American, ranging from a reflection of the materialism that engulfed America in the post-war economic boom to the irony that Willy himself has been 'sold' the fantasies that trap him. One effect that the play underlines is the denial of any blame or criticism of Willy's blind faith in the American Dream; the fault is in no way his for believing what his culture gives him no option but to believe. A salesman's life is by its very nature constructed entirely of faith and fantasy: he trades the promise of delivery for the promise of payment. As Charley says at Willy's grave, 'Willy was a salesman. And for a salesman, there is no rock bottom to the life. . . . A salesman is got to dream, boy. It comes with the territory.' Even at the end of the play Biff (and only Biff; his brother reaffirms his commitment to Willy's doctrine) will only say of Willy, 'He had the wrong dreams,' acknowledging the possibility of alternative definitions of success and personal value, but not condemning his father for needing a dream.

The tragedy of Willy's commitment to his dream is highlighted by the contrast to his son, who painfully achieves a partial release never available to his father. The memory scenes show Biff being indoctrinated into Willy's creed, and as an adult he remains trapped by it. Early in the play Biff tells his brother about his recent experiences in the American West:

> This farm I work on, it's spring there now, see? And they've got about fifteen new colts. There's nothing more inspiring or – beautiful than the sight of a mare and a new colt. And it's cool there

now, see? Texas is cool now, and it's spring. And whenever spring
comes to where I am, I suddenly get the feeling, my God. . . .

It is obvious where that sentence wants to go; the logical continuation
is something like ' . . . life is wonderful'. But that insight is not open
to Biff:

> . . . I suddenly get the feeling, my God, I'm not gettin' any-
> where! What the hell am I doing, playing around with horses,
> twenty-eight dollars a week! I'm thirty-four years old, I oughta be
> makin' my future.

A moment earlier Biff had confessed, as if it was a personal failing, 'I
don't know – what I'm supposed to want.'

And yet Biff does escape his father's fate by choosing reality over the
fantasy. A flashback shows the young Biff discovering his father with
another woman and turning against him. Most critics agree that this is
the weakest element in the play, offering an overly simplistic Freudian
explanation for Biff's break from Willy. Fortunately Miller does not rely
too heavily on this moment, instead identifying Biff's escape with a per-
ceptual leap beyond the ability of anyone else in the family:

> I stopped in the middle of that building and I saw – the sky. I
> saw the things that I love in this world. The work and the food
> and time to sit and smoke . . . . Why am I trying to become
> what I don't want to be? What am I doing in an office, making a
> contemptuous, begging fool of myself, when all I want is out
> there, waiting for me the minute I say I know who I am!

The power of the dream is so strong that Biff cannot fully escape it; the
only liberation Miller allows Biff is what feels to him like the painful
acceptance of his own inadequacy. Biff never sees that Willy's doctrine is
false, merely that it is not for him. He still judges himself a failure, but
he accepts that failure, gives up the futile struggle, and looks for his
fulfilment elsewhere, in the personal satisfaction of 'the things that I love
in this world'.

Much ink has been spilled over the question of whether *Death of a
Salesman* is a tragedy, a question raised by Miller himself in his extensive
writings and interviews about the play. Certainly it has few of the characteristics of classical or Shakespearean tragedy. Miller's own justification
for applying the label is based on the play's socio-political statement; he
argues that, just as classical tragedy implicitly accused the gods of unfairly
denying the tragic hero his full stature, *Death of a Salesman* points the
accusing finger at the life- and dignity-destroying aspects of American
culture. But few readers or theatre-goers are likely to share that

specialized definition of tragedy. If the story of Willy Loman inspires pity and fear, it is in its personal and human level – in the way the fall of this unheroic little man reminds us of our own fragile mortality, and in Miller's success in convincing us that the pain and death of any human being is tragic. As Willy's wife says, in the play's most powerful lines,

> Willy Loman never made a lot of money. His name was never in the paper. He's not the finest character that ever lived. But he's a human being, and a terrible thing is happening to him. So attention must be paid. He's not to be allowed to fall into his grave like an old dog. Attention, attention must be finally paid to such a person.

Miller's next play, an adaptation of Henrik Ibsen's *An Enemy of the People* (1950), was not a commercial success, but it can be seen as an important prelude to the play that would follow, *The Crucible*. Ibsen's account of a doctor who insists on publicizing scientific findings that endanger his town's economy is complex and even ambivalent, but ultimately asserts the absoluteness of truth. Miller's adaptation changes the terms of the debate from a matter of true and false to a conflict of deeply held beliefs, and thus shifts the moral centre of the play to the individual's right and duty to follow his conscience even in the face of an overwhelmingly opposing social consensus.

Since that theme, to be further explored and affirmed in *The Crucible*, had very specific topical implications in 1950, a brief reminder of the historical context may be in order. Soon after the end of the Second World War, one part of America's politically conservative movement became deeply afraid of Communist Russia, and particularly of the prospect of Soviet espionage and subversion within the United States. This fear was not totally unfounded, of course, and the discovery of Soviet spies and agents, along with the exploitation of the issue by some politicians, fuelled the anxiety until it extended to almost every level of American society. The phenomenon, and the hysterical patriotic fervour it generated, are most strongly associated with the name of one of the first politicians to capitalize on the issue, Senator Joseph McCarthy, though in fact it was the Un-American Activities Committee of the House of Representatives, along with a number of self-appointed citizens' groups, that did most to spread the hysteria.

At its most extreme, this panic led to the suspicion of anyone whose patriotism was not absolutely unchallengeable – in particular, to anyone who had ever done anything that could be interpreted as un-American. Unfortunately that definition covered a large percentage of Americans who had come of age during the Depression and had joined, supported or at least agreed with some innocent cause which was now retroactively tainted because the Communists had also supported it. Careers and lives were destroyed because of petitions signed or meetings attended twenty years earlier; and the only defence that Congress or the civilian patriotic organizations would accept was abject confession and cooperation in the investigation of others. Miller himself was called before the House Un-American Activities Committee later in the decade, as were many of his friends and theatrical associates; like some and unlike others, he refused to name anyone else for the Committee to investigate, and was convicted of contempt of Congress.

In this light, Miller's version of *An Enemy of the People* is not merely an abstract speculation on the nature and power of truth, but a directly political assertion of the democratic right to freedom of belief. The issue is not whether Stockmann is correct, as it is in Ibsen, but whether the mere fact that his opinion is unpopular – indeed, is perceived as a threat to society – is sufficient cause to suppress it and to require him to repudiate it. Where Ibsen's Stockmann stands firm in his conviction that he is right, Miller's stands for his right to his convictions. Stockmann's final speech, which most translators give as some variant of 'The strongest man in the world is the man who stands alone', becomes in Miller's adaptation less a theoretical aphorism and more an acknowledgement of the price to be paid for freedom of conscience: 'We're the strongest people in the world and the strong must learn to be lonely!'

In *The Crucible* (1953) Miller addresses the subject as directly as the times would allow, through an easily decipherable analogy to the witch-hunt hysteria of colonial America. The play touches on every element of McCarthyism: how a legitimate cultural fear is exploited by those to whom such exploitation gives power; how innocent people can be suspected on minimal, manufactured or non-existent evidence; how growing hysteria can make suspicion tantamount to proof; and how well-meaning citizens and even public officials are unable to resist the self-perpetuating process or the deviousness of those manipulating it. The whole procedure, from tainted accusers to show trials and hypocritical offers of mercy in return for new names, is dramatized in a way that makes both its obscenity and its modern parallels clear. This encounter between the judges and a townsman charging an accuser with personal motives could easily have come from a congressional hearing of the 1950s:

> GILES   If Jacobs hangs for a witch he forfeit up his property –
> that's law! And there is none but Putnam with the coin to buy
> so great a piece. This man is killing his neighbors for their land!
> DANFORTH   But proof, sir, proof.
> GILES, *pointing at his deposition* The proof is there! I have it from
> an honest man who heard Putnam say it! The day his daughter
> cried out on Jacobs, he said she'd given him a fair gift of land.
> HATHORNE   And the name of this man? . . . The man that
> gave you this information.

GILES, *hesitates, then* Why, I – I cannot give you his name.
HATHORNE   And why not?
GILES, *hesitates, then bursts out* You know well why not! He'll lay
   in jail if I give his name! . . .
DANFORTH   In that case, I have no choice but to arrest you for
   contempt of this court.

Remarkably, given the very specific contemporary phenomenon that
generated *The Crucible*, the passage of time has not seriously dated it.
Some of Miller's righteous indignation does seem strident and over-
stated when the opposition is no longer a real and present danger, but
that loss is balanced by an increased awareness of his main character's
spiritual struggle, which is not tied to the topical allusions. When John
Proctor's wife is named by a girl who lusts after John, his attempt to
expose the accuser results in his own arrest. Tempted to save himself by
confessing, John decides that honour requires his death. On this level his
story has Kafkaesque overtones: just as some of the weaker victims of
the witch hunt come to believe in their own guilt because it is asserted
so repeatedly, John is led to examine his life in the light of the accusations and to realize that, if he is innocent of witchcraft, he is not without other guilt. Confession of his adultery with the accuser begins his
spiritual self-evaluation, which leads to the belief that even his execution
for witchcraft would be unearned, since he would be dying in the company of the truly innocent.

So Miller shows that the witch hunters were right in an ironic way
they could not have guessed: where there is suspicion there *is* guilt, but
only because the true accuser is within. The human spirit must eventually be honest with itself, and what it finds when it is ready for self-
examination is a profound sense of unworthiness. Yet that impulse to be
unsparing is not just self-condemning but the means to salvation because,
once acknowledged, it can be relied on as a guide to truth. John signs
his confession because he believes himself too guilty to die with honour,
but he recants when he realizes that his life would be more of a theft
from the innocent than his death: 'Beguile me not! I blacken all of them
when this is nailed to the church the very day they hang for silence!'

Again and again for Miller the key and the metaphor for self-
discovery and self-acceptance is the individual's ability to name himself.
Joe Keller insisted in *All My Sons* that 'I'm his father and he's my son,
and if there's something bigger than that I'll put a bullet in my head'
only to discover that those labels were insufficient. Biff Loman cried
'What am I doing . . . when all I want is out there, waiting for me the
minute I say I know who I am!' and Eddie Carbone in *A View From the
Bridge* will define the loss of his honour and self-respect in terms of the
loss of his name. For John Proctor the final realization is triggered by the
demand that his signed confession be displayed in public; he refuses

'Because it is my name! Because I cannot have another in my life! . . . How may I live without my name? I have given you my soul; leave me my name!' This discovery of his core of identity, his basic self that cannot be denied or found unworthy, enables Proctor to reject the lie of a confession and affirm both his readiness and his right to die.

Miller's next Broadway production, in 1955, was a double bill. *A Memory of Two Mondays* is a simple and realistic slice-of-life in an automobile parts warehouse, as observed by a college student temporarily working there. Its quiet social commentary lies in the sad irony that the boy sees the unpleasant working conditions and limited lives of his co-workers without realizing that such deprivations are an inevitable part of their social and economic caste – a caste he does not quite perceive because he is in the process of escaping from it. The companion piece, *A View From the Bridge*, came to have an independent life when Miller expanded it into two acts for the first London production in 1956; it is that longer version, whose major differences are the abandonment of awkward blank verse in favour of essentially the same dialogue printed as prose, and the addition of background action and detail, that is usually published and revived.

Much more than *Death of a Salesman*, *A View From the Bridge* represents a conscious attempt at classical tragedy. Like Eugene O'Neill in *Mourning Becomes Electra*, Miller uses Freudian psychology as a modern equivalent of inescapable fate, to give a tragic stature and intensity to the story of Eddie Carbone, whose love for his niece approaches the incestuous. When the girl falls in love with a cousin smuggled into the country, Eddie is driven to violate one of his culture's greatest taboos by reporting the alien to the immigration authorities; unable to admit his guilt, he dies defending himself against the charge. The dramatic centre of the play thus lies in Eddie's inner torment, and if the subject matter suggests a comparison to Shakespeare's *Othello*, a closer resemblance is to *Macbeth*, with the weak man driven by his internal demons ever deeper into his own damnation, while experiencing the additional agony of helplessly watching it happen to him.

But Miller's commitment to realism almost cripples the play, since it is essential to his conception of Eddie's character that he be unable to acknowledge, much less verbalize, what is happening to him. The nearest Eddie can come to expressing his feelings is to deny them – 'That's what you think of me – that I would have such a thought?' – and the treachery of informing is so beyond his capacity for self-awareness that he must fight to the death to deny having done it. So the burden of exposition and insight into Eddie's disintegration falls on other characters, particularly his wife Beatrice and the lawyer Alfieri. It is Beatrice who must, in two particularly clumsy scenes, confront Eddie with the complaint that he has stopped sleeping with her, and instruct Catherine to stop walking around in her slip, just to bring the sexual tensions in the household to the audience's attention. And it is Alfieri, in his role as chorus-narrator, who must repeatedly intrude on the realistic action with such self-consciously portentous statements as 'Eddie Carbone had never expected to have a destiny', and 'His eyes were like tunnels; my first thought was that he had committed a crime . . . but soon I saw it was only a passion that had moved into his body, like a stranger'. As this external commentary begins to become oppressive, the voice of an author insisting on the significance of his material rather than dramatizing it, it is ultimately self-defeating and unconvincing. The fact that Alfieri keeps telling us how meaningful Eddie Carbone's tragedy is almost forces the audience to resist the quiet pathos and horror inherent in the story.

A *View From the Bridge* was Miller's last play for eight years, and *After the Fall* in 1964 would represent a shift in his focus and style. His contribution in the 1940s and 1950s, aside from the merits of the plays themselves, was the reaffirmation and extension of the discoveries made by Clifford Odets and Lillian Hellman in the 1930s: that domestic realism could address such diverse and ambitious subjects as private morality, public policy, tragic destiny and the American Dream. Repeatedly he takes his protagonists and even tragic heroes from the ranks of the ordinary, affirming the very American concept that such people are worthy of attention. Never far from the focus of his study is the individual's relationship to the larger social and political community, and the evils that result from violation of the implicit social contract, either by the individual (*All My Sons*, *A View From the Bridge*) or by the society (*Death of a Salesman*, *The Crucible*). If there is a prosaic and sometimes preachy quality to his writing, that is almost inevitable, given the degree to which the plays are thesis-driven.

It is not accidental that Miller's critical and popular reputation is even greater outside the United States than within. Because they address social, moral and political issues in terms of their effect on ordinary Americans, his plays seem particularly and specifically American to foreigners, and are welcomed as accurate and evocative depictions of the American experience. But even American audiences can respond to that quality in Miller's plays; an important part of the continuing power of *Death of a Salesman*, *The Crucible* and the others is that they help to explain America, as a culture, to itself.

Tennessee Williams

In contrast to Arthur Miller, Tennessee Williams is an almost completely non-political writer. In fact, more than any other American dramatist, he helped move domestic realism beyond its accomplishment of reflecting large political and social issues through their effect on the domestic setting, and into the final stage of its evolution, the exploration of the emotional burdens of ordinary life. Though Williams might not have seen it this way, he and many of his contemporaries were returning to the modern American drama's roots, in the plays of Herne and Crothers that were the first to acknowledge that life was coloured by problems with no simple solutions. Playwrights of the 1920s had sought to explain the behaviour in such a world through Freudian analysis; the implicit question being answered in such plays as Kelly's *Craig's Wife* or O'Neill's *Desire Under the Elms* was 'Why did this happen?' For Williams, and increasingly for other American dramatists, the real question was 'What did it feel like to have this happen?' American plays began again to look inward rather than outward, as characters in the privacy of their domestic setting exposed their very private pains and joys. If Miller and others in the tradition of Odets were attempting to explain a culture to itself, Williams was exploring the workings of the human spirit and psyche.

And, in almost every case, the fragile and deeply wounded spirit and psyche. For much of his career Williams's popular reputation was as a sensationalist, with characters in various plays guilty of (or victims of) murder, rape, castration, cannibalism, alcoholism, promiscuity, homosexuality, and other shocking violations of moral and social norms. But these elements are not gratuitous in his plays. Like many other southern writers, Williams was drawn to extreme and even gothically bizarre stories and characters because he found in the fringes of acceptable human behaviour clearly dramatizable examples of universal experience. In Williams's eyes, everyday life is for most people an almost Sisyphean labour, the burden of a cold and threatening world borne by a lonely and self-doubting individual. His recurring themes are loneliness and insecurity, the fear of not being up to the task of living, and the grasping at any sustenance for the labour or distraction from the pain. Dramatizing this vision through explicitly melodramatic stories serves a double purpose: it underlines and clarifies the insights through intensity; and it also leads the audience to recognize the emotional experience they share with the characters, and thus to feel more sympathy and charity for those driven to aberrant behaviour.

One can find the seeds of many of Williams's later themes and characters in the volume of early one-act plays published in 1945 as *27 Wagons Full of Cotton*. Two patterns recur: the spiritual or emotional crippling of characters unable to cope with a cold and frightening world – a young man paralysed by the process of moving away from home in 'The Long Goodbye,' a weak-witted and weak-willed woman helplessly facing a summer of daily rapes in '27 Wagons Full of Cotton' – and the impulse of others to escape into a mythologized past – a whore fighting to retain the fantasy of an aristocratic heritage in 'The Lady of Larkspur Lotion', a travelling salesman regretting the good old days in 'The Last of My Solid Gold Watches', a mad spinster turning a brief encounter of twenty years ago into a dream lover in 'Portrait of a Madonna'. One sees unmistakably in these plays the sensibility that would create Amanda Wingfield, Blanche DuBois, Brick Pollitt, Chance Wayne and Williams's other victims of life.

Williams's first Broadway-bound play, *Battle of Angels* (1940) closed during its out-of-town previews; it would reappear in revised form as *Orpheus Descending* in 1957. His second attempt, *The Glass Menagerie* (1945) was much more successful, and announced Williams as an important new voice, not least because it stretched the boundaries of domestic realism in promising ways. Williams's method in *The Glass Menagerie* is as different from the realism of Odets and Miller as his purpose is. The central action of the play is, for the most part, a conventional domestic story, but it is filtered through the sensibility of a poet. Tom Wingfield, the narrator, defines the play's mode in his opening speech: 'The play is memory. Being a memory play, it is dimly lighted, it is sentimental, it is not realistic.' The non-realistic elements in *The Glass Menagerie* lie in the richly poetic language, the undisguised verbal and physical symbols, and above all the operative mode of suggestion – of allowing glimpses into thought processes and emotions that are too evanescent to be analysed or explicated logically. Williams does not violate realism as thoroughly or continuously as, say, O'Neill did in his expressionistic plays. But by presenting his domestic story as emotionally coloured memory he gives it the quality of a reality beyond mere verisimilitude. As Tom says in the play's opening lines,

> Yes, I have tricks in my pocket, I have things up my sleeve. But I
> am the very opposite of a stage magician. He gives you illusion
> that has the appearance of truth. I give you truth in the pleasant
> disguise of illusion.

The Glass Menagerie is about the Wingfield family, living in genteel semi-poverty in Depression era St Louis. Mother Amanda is a former southern belle inclined to live in the memories and values of her past; daughter Laura, hampered by a limp and an overpowering shyness, retreats from the world into her collection of glass animals; son Tom is trapped in a stifling job and aches to leave home, but Amanda insists that he first supply a man to care for Laura in his absence. The acquaintance Tom brings to dinner actually begins to bring Laura out of her shell, but the news that he is already engaged dashes any fantasies of romance. The play is narrated by Tom in the present, perhaps ten years after the dramatized action, and his relation to the story he is telling is a significant part of the play's subject.

In content as well as style, *The Glass Menagerie* is essentially different from the plays of Arthur Miller. It has virtually no larger political, social or moral agenda: though Tom as narrator repeatedly refers to the Depression and the warfare in Europe, it is always as things outside the play and separated from it, and Tom calls Jim 'an emissary from a world of reality that we were somehow set apart from'. The focus is on these three characters, on the internal qualities that created their shared adventure and on its effects on them. Williams presents all three members of the Wingfield family as unable to function in the world of reality, and presents that inability as a virtue more than a handicap. The characterizations and the play's symbolic language repeatedly identify Amanda's faded gentility and Laura's fragility as special qualities to be treasured and protected. Amanda's memories, even at their most foolish, have an evocative beauty; see, for example, her aria on jonquils in Scene Six. Laura is repeatedly labelled as special and precious rather than inadequate, through such symbols as the botanical hothouse in which she spends her days; the glass animals, particularly the unicorn; and Jim's nickname for her, 'Blue Roses'. Williams makes it clear that the cost of successfully functioning in the real world, if that were at all possible, would be the loss of everything that is special about these characters: the only glass animal Jim can take back to reality with him is the broken unicorn that is 'just like all the other horses'. The result is that, rather than rejecting Amanda and Laura as misfits, we come to cherish them as beautiful alternatives to the ordinary and to be grateful that they have found an environment in which, like the hothouse flowers, they can be protected and nourished. Some people are simply not equipped to deal with reality, says the play, and that may well be an indictment of reality.

So seductive and evocative is the alternative reality of Amanda and Laura that it is easy to forget that the central action of *The Glass Menagerie* is not the story being related but the relation itself; the reality of the play is Tom the sailor a decade later, reliving his past. His story is one of failing to recognize that his mother and sister were spiritually better off where he left them, and that he himself was more at home with them than he could be in the world of wars and depressions he keeps trying to convince himself is the real one.

> I traveled around a great deal. The cities swept about me like dead leaves. . . . I would have stopped, but I was pursued by something. . . .
> Perhaps I am walking along a street at night, in some strange city, before I have found companions. I pass the lighted window of a shop where perfume is sold. The window is filled with pieces of colored glass, tiny transparent bottles in delicate colors, like bits of a shattered rainbow.
> Then all at once my sister touches my shoulder. . . . Oh, Laura, Laura, I tried to leave you behind me, but I am more faithful than I intended to be!

Like that other tale-telling seaman, Coleridge's Ancient Mariner, Tom is driven by a sense of guilt, more for being untrue to himself than for deserting his mother and sister. And in the play's final moment he remains untrue to himself, trying to convince himself, in the face of all the evidence of the play, that the only reality is the one outside, and thus dooming himself to further torment: 'I reach for a cigarette, I cross the street, I run to the movies or a bar. I buy a drink, I speak to the nearest stranger – anything that can blow your candles out! – for nowadays the world is lit by lightning!'

A Streetcar Named Desire (1947) is without question Williams's best play, and shares with Miller's Death of a Salesman and O'Neill's Long Day's Journey into Night the very top rank of American drama. On its surface it is a simple, fairly sensational melodrama: frayed southern aristocrat Blanche DuBois visits her sister Stella in New Orleans and finds her married to the crude, intensely physical Stanley Kowalski. Shocked by Stella's new life, Blanche tries to take her away from it, but we gradually learn that Blanche is not as pure as she pretends and that she is struggling desperately to retain her emotional and mental equilibrium. The failure of her romance with Stanley's friend Mitch, and a violent and sexual confrontation with Stanley, finally break her; and the play ends with Blanche being led off to an asylum while Stanley and Stella remain together.

The emotional spine of the play is the decline and fall of Blanche DuBois, who enters the play in a state of physical and emotional exhaustion, and fights a tragically losing battle against insanity. She is a rich and complex character (one of the greatest acting roles in American theatre; Stanley Kowalski is another), made up of contradictory elements that she cannot reconcile. The last representative of an elegant southern aristocracy, she is committed to the values and moral imperatives of her class, values which the play gradually exposes as corrupted and barren. By nature unable to deal with reality, she escapes into a world of ideals; recognizing her own fragility, she desperately tries to make intimate contact with those who seem abler, confessing, in her final line of the play, 'I have always depended on the kindness of strangers.' When she is finally driven by her disastrous encounter with Stanley into the protective fantasies of psychosis, the play mourns her loss as well as the loss of the beauty and idealism she tried so hard to represent.

If the play's emotional centre is in Blanche's tragic experience, it is philosophically centred on Stella. Structurally, A Streetcar Named Desire resembles a medieval morality play, with Stella – and thus the audience – being pulled in two directions and having to choose between her tempters. Blanche stands for idealism, culture, purity, and the love of beauty, but also for falsehood, fantasy, weakness and the rejection of unpleasant reality. She is associated through verbal and physical symbols with whiteness, soft colours, a lost and romanticized past, cleanliness, art and the zodiacal virgin; and also with death, sterility, and debased or perverted sexuality. Stanley is essentially physical and sexual: *'Animal joy in his being is implicit in all his movements and attitudes. Since earliest manhood the center of his life has been pleasure with women. . . . Branching out from this complete and satisfying center are all the auxiliary channels of his life.'* He enters the play like a caveman, tossing Stella a package from the butcher with the cry of 'Meat!' His tastes are elemental and crude, and his manner brusque and violent, especially when he feels threatened. He is symbolically associated with Capricorn, gaudy colours and raw sexuality.

On this semi-allegorical level the play seems to be offering a choice between the higher and lower aspects of the human potential, and Stella – and thus the play – chooses Stanley over Blanche. It is important to see that Stella does *choose* Stanley. Blanche's report of being raped by Stanley shocks her, and she elects to believe that it is the fantasy of a broken mind. Blanche's mind *is* broken, but Stella would send her to the asylum sane rather than face the consequences of the truth; as she explains to her neighbour, 'I couldn't believe her story and go on living with Stanley.' And her friend approves of her decision: 'Don't ever believe it. Life has to go on.'

What justifies Stella's shocking choice is Williams's perception of the stakes. When Stella confesses to Blanche that she cannot bear life without Stanley – 'I can hardly stand it when he is away for a night. . . . When he's away for a week I nearly go wild! . . . And when he comes back I cry on his lap like a baby.' – she exposes an insecurity of her own that cannot be blamed on the values that handicap Blanche. When Stella temporarily flees to the neighbours after Stanley has hit her, Stanley cries desperately for her to return, in a scene of almost mythic power, and she does, recognizing the depth of his need for her. And when Mitch, stumbling towards romance, expresses himself in less than cavalier terms – 'You need somebody. And I need somebody, too. Could it be – you and me, Blanche?' – Williams demonstrates that Blanche is not the only one who finds that the task of living and coping demands the very utmost of her resources. In a world in which such insecurity is the norm, psychic and spiritual survival cannot be taken for granted. And however attractive may be the values of purity, culture and idealism for which Blanche stands, her own downfall demonstrates that they actively interfere with the ability to cope and function. Even before that is evident, Williams shows that Blanche has nothing to offer Stella; she can only make demands on her – demands of guilt, of moral obligation, and of desperation:

> Maybe we are a long way from being made in God's image, but Stella – my sister – there has been *some* progress since then! Such things as art – as poetry and music – such kinds of new light have come into the world since then! In some kinds of people some

tenderer feelings have had some little beginning! That we have
got to make *grow*! And *cling* to, and hold as our flag! In this dark
march towards whatever it is we're approaching. . . . *Don't –
don't hang back with the brutes!*
     [Ellipses Williams's]

What Blanche actually represents in the play's allegory are the human
values and attributes that are life-draining rather than life-supporting, and
they demonstrably do not work. Stanley, and the aspects of humanity
that he represents, may be primitive and ugly, but they are eminently
equipped to deal with reality. As he would frequently through his career,
Williams uses sex as a metaphor for both vitality and spiritual sustenance:
Stella explains that 'there are things that happen between a man and a
woman in the dark – that sort of make everything else seem – unimport-
ant'. In that context, Stanley's boast about having taken Stella from the
house with white columns to the land of coloured lights becomes a valid
claim to have saved her life. Williams can regret that the world is such
that the Stanleys survive and the Blanches do not, but the most valuable
counsel he can offer is to accept that fact and to choose life over death.
     Williams's other plays of this period vary considerably in quality and
commercial success. *Cat on a Hot Tin Roof* (1955) and *The Night of the
Iguana* (1961), while not quite as overpowering as *Streetcar*, show him at
the top of his talent. *Summer and Smoke* (1948), *Suddenly Last Summer*
(1958) and *Sweet Bird of Youth* (1959) are flawed but effective. *The Rose
Tattoo* (1951) and *Period of Adjustment* (1960) strive for less than the
others and are less noteworthy; and *Camino Real* (1953) and *Orpheus
Descending* (1957) are too basically flawed to succeed. The determining
factor in each case is, to a great extent, Williams's success in balancing
his impulse towards the poetic and symbolic with his need to ground the
plays in a solid and humanly believable reality. Strikingly, the more successful his plays are as domestic realism, the more successful they are as
poetry, allegory or universal statement.
     Cat on a Hot Tin Roof (1955) is Williams at his near-best, with a
strong, slightly sensationalistic domestic story dramatically effective for its
own sake while also offering psychological insights and moral judgements. Like *Streetcar*, *Cat* has a double focus: Big Daddy Pollitt's need to
decide which son to leave his plantation to, the successful but unloved
Gooper or the loved but alcoholic Brick; and Maggie's fight to save her
marriage to Brick. The who-will-inherit plot resembles the Blanche–
Stanley conflict in forcing a choice on the audience – in this case between practical considerations, which clearly favour Gooper, and matters
of empathy and morality, which favour Brick. Big Daddy is a Falstaffian
figure, hugely and vulgarly alive. His one great hatred is of mendacity;
he defines himself by his ability to deal with the truth, and has contempt
for those who cannot. In this, Brick is his natural heir; he and Maggie

share that hatred and that commitment to life, and part of the play's
hope for Brick lies in the faith that those qualities are so integral to his
nature that they cannot have been completely destroyed by his spiritual
and psychological decline. So when Big Daddy decides in his favour,
Williams is arguing that spiritual affinity is more important than practical
concerns, while reaffirming his conviction that an enthusiastic immersion
in life is to be celebrated and rewarded.

But, just as the *Streetcar* audience is more involved with Blanche's
experience than with the play's metaphysics, any *Cat* audience will find
the play in the emotional journeys of Maggie and Brick rather than in
the question of inheritance. Brick, like Blanche, is trapped in a morality
of purity that he cannot live up to, in his case an extremely limited
definition of masculinity that forced him to reject his best friend. It is
almost irrelevant whether Skipper or Brick actually had homosexual in-
clinations; for both, anything less than being a 'real man' was suspect,
and neither could live with the suspicion. Skipper killed himself and
Brick withdrew from the sexual arena; the trauma he is forced to go
through during the play is not so much the acknowledgement of his role
in Skipper's death as the acknowledgement of his own fears. He does
not withdraw again from the truths he faces – indeed, he affirms his
opposition to mendacity and his respect for his father by telling Big
Daddy the truth about his health – and the play offers some hope of his
recovery in this commitment to reality.

Maggie the Cat's story is also one of self-discovery and self-acceptance.
She begins the play in almost manic desperation – much of Act One is
an almost uninterrupted monologue, and the play's title is a symbol of
nervous energy. She announces her determination to fight for the estate
and for Brick's love, but also confesses that this struggle threatens her
sense of herself. She thinks of herself as weak and feminine, and is
frightened by what having to fight is doing to her: 'I've gone through
this – *hideous!* – *transformation*, become – *hard! Frantic!*' But the truth is
that Maggie is not inherently weak – she is, after all, Big Daddy's heir –
and her spiritual adventure in the play is the process of recognizing and
accepting this redefinition. At first she resists, instinctively separating herself from the role she is playing:

> *When she opens her eyes again, what she sees is the long oval mirror and
> she rushes straight to it, stares into it with a grimace and says: 'Who are
> you' – Then she crouches a little and answers herself in a different voice
> which is high, thin, mocking: 'I am Maggie the Cat!'*

But by the end of Act One she has integrated the new Maggie into her
sense of self: 'I don't know why people have to pretend to be good,
nobody's good . . . but I'm honest! . . . *I'm alive!* Maggie the cat is –
alive! I am alive, alive! I am alive!' At the end of the play she has not only

accepted the new definition of herself but also its implications for her marriage: 'Brick, I used to think that you were stronger than me and I didn't want to be overpowered by you. But now, since you've taken to liquor – you know what? – I guess it's bad, but now I'm stronger than you and I can love you more truly!'

That last passage comes from the 'original' Act Three of the play, as opposed to the 'Broadway Version', which requires some comment. Most editions of the play include two third acts, along with Williams's explanation that the first was the script he delivered to his director at the start of production, and the second represents changes he was advised to make – briefly, to soften Maggie, to bring Big Daddy back for another scene, and to offer more signs of Brick's spiritual recovery after the trauma of Act Two. All three were based on theatrical rather than literary considerations: the absence of the high-energy Big Daddy would make the last act anticlimactic, for example. Williams acquiesced in these changes, but chose to print his original text along with the revision when the play was published. It is worth noting that no new play has ever opened with exactly the same script the author first delivered to the producers; large and small changes are made before and during rehearsals as the needs of performance become clear. But, with rare exceptions, the published text is always the opening night text, and earlier versions are discarded with the notes and rough drafts. So the only unusual thing about the *Cat* text is not that there were revisions but that Williams saved his original version and published it. (Williams actually made a third version for a 1974 revival and published it in 1975; essentially it attaches the original ending to the Broadway act.)

We shall stretch the chronological boundaries of this chapter to include *The Night of the Iguana* (1961), since it deals with some of the same themes as *Streetcar* and *Cat*, and with some of the same power. *Iguana* does have a notable structural difference, in building towards an open, almost Shavian discussion of its issues; the minimal plot of the play clearly exists just to get two carefully delineated and contrasting characters to the same place so that they can meet and debate. The Reverend T. Lawrence Shannon, former minister reduced to leading third-rate guided tours of Mexico and in the process of one of his regularly scheduled nervous breakdowns, resembles Brick Pollitt of *Cat* and Chance Wayne of *Sweet Bird of Youth* in his self-destructive determination to deal with the world on his own ideal terms, without capitulation to its impurity. Hannah Jelkes is Amanda, Blanche and Alma Winemiller of *Summer and Smoke* reborn, but with one new and essential distinction: she has the strength and means to function in reality without being broken by it. The subject of their discussion is the question that drives virtually all of Williams's plays: how can the sensitive person survive the pain of existence?

For Shannon, the mere act of living is almost overpoweringly difficult

- 'It's horrible how you got to bluff and keep bluffing even when hollering "Help!" is all you're up to.' The earthy Maxine Faulk offers a sexual and financial partnership that she sees as an acceptable compromise with reality, but Shannon rejects that option as a capitulation to the world's corruption. Hannah dismisses his pride as pointless vanity, and insists that it is possible to engage the challenge of living. She rejects a moral or emotional fastidiousness that would lead one to spurn any source of assistance: 'Endurance is something that spooks and blue devils respect. And they respect all the tricks that panicky people use to outlast and outwit their panic. . . . Anything, everything, that we take to give them the slip, and so to keep on going. . . . '

> SHANNON   You mean that I'm stuck here for good? Winding up
> with the . . . inconsolable widow?
> HANNAH   We all wind up with something or with someone, and
> if it's someone instead of just something, we're lucky, perhaps
> . . . unusually lucky.   [Ellipses Williams's]

The second-level plays of this period all reaffirm Williams's sympathy for those who find the task of living almost beyond their strength. He feels a particular affinity for the most sensitive, the Blanches and Bricks who commit themselves, however self-destructively, to their ideals, and yet he is forced to admire those with the courage to immerse themselves in life despite the pain; and he has the intellectual courage to recognize that neither way is easy, and that compromise and very modest victories may be all that are available. *Summer and Smoke* (1948) offers a milder version of the Blanche–Stanley choice and concludes, as *Streetcar* did, that life, in whatever form it takes, is preferable to the avoidance of life. Operating in broad strokes, as in *Streetcar*, he presents Alma Winemiller and John Buchanan as extreme opposites, she the sexually repressed daughter of a minister, and he a self-destructive Byronic hero. Much of the first half of the play is devoted to demonstrating their excesses: his whoring, drinking and gambling; her poetry circle and nervous attacks. Each of them is identified with a physical symbol, Alma with the statue of an angel and John with a medical chart of the human body. But the play is more concerned with their human story than with their allegorical significance; Williams is not presenting the clash of opposing forces as in *Streetcar*, but is dramatizing the dangers of the partial and unintegrated personality. In a key scene John forces Alma to examine the anatomical chart, demanding that she acknowledge that the sexual organs and their needs are part of being human, while she insists that life includes a spiritual dimension not to be found in a map of the body.

Each of them has been living a half-life, Alma driven to neurosis by the repression of her physical side, John reduced to self-disgust by his rejection of the spiritual. Thus, when the play brings them together again after a separation, only to discover that they have exchanged positions, she ready to accept her sexuality and he hungry for something deeper, Williams can regret the mistiming and still accept the alternative each finds. John chooses marriage to an ordinary girl whose main attraction is that she will not offer excesses of either body or soul, while Alma becomes a fallen woman, picking up strangers in the park. And for each the ending, while not the happiest imaginable, is offered by Williams as the happiest available. Once again, by starting from the assumption that life is a painful and lonely experience, Williams reaches the conclusion that any form of comfort is better than none. The weakest aspect of *Summer and Smoke* is its symbolism, which is awkwardly imposed on the human story. Perhaps sensing this, Williams wrote an alternative version of the play, *The Eccentricities of a Nightingale*, which was not staged until 1964; it cuts much of the symbolism and reduces the extremes of characterization, and the resulting quietly domestic play of mismatching and mistiming is in some ways more successful than the original, although it loses the larger resonances about the necessity of integrating soul and body.

Suddenly Last Summer (1958) is one of Williams's most gothic plays, and suffers somewhat from its excessive dependence on sensationalism, but at its core it is another exploration of one of Williams's recurring themes: the self-destructive danger of too great a commitment to purity. Its centre is the life and death of Sebastian Venable, whose extreme asceticism is a cover for homosexuality and whose death is the result of a cannibalistic attack by starving beggars. The dominant images of the play are of violent nature – a jungle-like garden, the attacks of birds on sea-turtles, a rape, the cannibalism – and of an imperfect purity built on the denial of nature – Sebastian's white suit and empty notebook, his pretence of asexuality, his mother's refusal to admit the truth of his life and death. Williams paints Sebastian somewhat more darkly than he did Blanche and Brick, recognizing that the search for purity, especially for the artist, can be selfish and cruel; and that uncharacteristic lack of sympathy gives an unpleasant tone to this reminder of the fate of those who would deny their connection to an impure and unforgiving world.

Williams's two images of the purist, the cruelly selfish artist and the helpless victim of life, reappear in *Sweet Bird of Youth* (1959), in which an aging gigolo tries vainly to hang on to symbols of his youthful purity. The sensationalistic plot turns on violence, political corruption, alcohol and drug abuse, sex for hire, racism, venereal disease, castration and hints of incest; and, as in *Suddenly Last Summer*, the gothic elements threaten to overwhelm the human story. But as in *Suddenly Last Summer* and, in a much more controlled way, *Streetcar*, Williams is using these symbols of violence and depravity to define the stakes of the game, to give a sense of the frightening and actively hostile world in which his characters must live out their adventures. Chance Wayne and his current patron Alexandra Del Lago are both fighting against the inevitable reality of time and their own moral and physical corruption. But she survives with the instinctive selfishness and strength of the egoist, while Chance, who never had any identity except his youth and sexuality, must go the way of Blanche DuBois, accepting fate with the passivity of the born victim: 'Whatever happens to me's already happened.' It is clear that, while Williams can admire the monstrous energy of Alexandra Del Lago as he did Stanley Kowalski, his sympathies are with the doomed Chance Wayne. The final line of the play is spoken by Chance directly to the audience: 'I don't ask for your pity, but just for your understanding – not even that – no. Just for your recognition of me in you, and the enemy, time, in us all.' In its bathos that may be the worst curtain line ever written by a great playwright, but its intent is clear: it is Chance's experience as a victim of life that Williams sees as universal, and that he wants to prepare the audience to face.

This discussion of Williams's second-level plays may have already given a hint as to the limits of his talent. It is certainly no criticism of any writer that he stakes out a particular aspect of the human experience and explores and re-explores it from slightly varying perspectives in his works. Williams's weaknesses were elsewhere – ironically in the area of his greatest strength, his poetic instincts and powers. At his best, Williams brought the sensibility and tools of a poet to the theatre more effectively than any other American dramatist, but he had to keep them under tight control or he would stray into distracting and obscuring excess. During his peak years he was usually able to anchor each play in a domestic realism solid enough that the imagery and poetic devices could resonate outwards without danger. But if he did not keep a very tight rein on these elements, they drew attention to themselves and away from the small and specific human story at the core of each of his plays. To the extent that *Suddenly Last Summer* is a play about cannibalism and not about the pain of living in a cruel reality, it fails; to the extent that the symbolism in *Summer and Smoke* seems imposed on a story that functions satisfactorily without it, it weakens the play. A playwright without a poet's instincts could not have written *The Glass Menagerie* or *A Streetcar Named Desire*, but throughout his career Williams would wrestle with the impulse to go too far.

Orpheus Descending (1957) demonstrates what happened when Williams was not in absolute control: an over-ambitiousness and over-complexity of symbolic and thematic intent that swamp the story and cripple its power to affect us on the human level. As the title makes clear, Williams intends mythic resonances for the play about an itinerant musician, Val Xavier, who comes to a southern town and stirs up the loneliness of the women and the enmity of their men. But the intended parallel to Orpheus, murky to begin with, is compounded with Christian imagery identifying Val with Christ, mystic themes invoked by the

presence of an Indian Conjure Man, Williams's familiar symbolic identification of sex and life, and a variety of stray and disconnected symbols.
All these levels of meaning, along with an excess of self-consciously
poetic language, overwhelm a play whose potential strength would have
been where Williams's strength always is, in the simply human story of
lonely and frightened people reaching for anyone or anything that could
ease their pain. Val is allowed some of the purest expressions of this
experience in all of Williams: 'We're all of us sentenced to solitary con-
finement inside our own skins, for life!' and

> What does anyone wait for? For something to happen, for any-
> thing to happen, to make things make more sense. . . . Does
> everything stop because you don't get the answer? No, it goes
> right on as if the answer was given, day comes after day and night
> comes after night, and you're still waiting. . . .

But *Orpheus Descending* is just too symbolically and metaphysically clut-
tered to allow this human story to emerge.

Even less successful is *Camino Real* (1953) an openly symbolic and
allegorical play without any anchor in domestic realism: a group of romantic characters drawn from literature (Don Quixote, Marguerite Gau-
tier), history (Byron, Casanova) and myth (Kilroy) inhabit a decadent
and inhospitable world that sneers at their values. The play's themes – a
plea for compassion for the romantics wounded by an uncaring world,
and a call for such victims to be true to their ideals and not surrender to
despair – are all but lost when there is no recognizable human reality
under the confused dramaturgy and symbolic excess. *The Rose Tattoo*
(1951) and *Period of Adjustment* (1960) are minor comedies, both recognizing the spirit-crippling power of loneliness and withdrawal from life,
and both offering immersion in sexuality as a life-affirming solution. *The
Rose Tattoo* has an infectiously joyous air, not least in what seems almost
like a self-parodying excess of symbols in the ubiquitous roses: rose tat-
toos, rose oil, a rose silk shirt, the names Rosario and Rosa delle Rose,
and the flowers themselves. *Period of Adjustment* is quieter in tone and
somewhat less successful, neither brainlessly funny enough to work on
the level of empty romantic comedy nor developed enough to treat
successfully the familiar Williams themes it hints at.

Williams continued to write new plays after 1961, but *The Night of
the Iguana* was his last artistic or commercial success. Soon afterwards he
went into a personal and artistic decline, triggered by the death of his
longtime companion and exacerbated by alcohol, drugs and nervous
breakdowns, from which he never recovered; the second half of his
career would be marked by exactly the loss of control over his talents
that had marred some of the early plays, producing a series of unfocused
and overwritten failures. So the years and plays between *The Glass Menagerie*

and *The Night of the Iguana* represent Williams's major contribution. They include some of the best plays in the American repertoire, and some of the most challenging roles for actors and actresses. Williams stretched the boundaries of domestic realism by approaching it with the instincts of a poet, making it support verbal and physical symbolism and a heightened, image-filled poetic prose. At the same time he reaffirmed its power as the native American dramatic form, by demonstrating that the dramatization of domestic events could illuminate the spiritual and emotional struggles of characters with an authenticity that made even the most bizarre convincingly human. His recurring observation – that ordinary, unheroic life was overwhelmingly challenging and painful for many people – proved to be such a powerful insight into the mid-century American experience that it was taken up by other writers, and came to be the dominant subject of the serious drama. Even more than Arthur Miller, whose work was really the culmination of earlier movements, Tennessee Williams redefined and reshaped the American drama in the 1950s.

William Inge

The one new dramatist of the 1950s who comes closest to being in the same league as Miller and Williams is William Inge, a protegé of Tennessee Williams's whose plays suggest a kind of domesticated Williams: sensitive and sympathetic studies of lonely and frightened people, but without the poetry or sensationalism of Williams. In each of his major plays Inge writes of small, ordinary people leading small, ordinary lives and frustrated by their inability to fulfil their romantic dreams. While he occasionally allows his characters a hope of happiness, he is more likely to offer them nothing more than the peace that comes from the resigned acceptance of their small, ordinary fates.

Come Back, Little Sheba (1950) is the story of a married couple, Doc and Lola, who have long since lost the romance and dreams of their youth, and are held together by little more than habit and practical need. Much of the first half of the play is given over to the exposition and demonstration of the many disappointments that make up their lives; even their dog Little Sheba ran away, and Lola's mourning turns Sheba into a symbol of all the other lost possibilities and hopes. Doc catalogues their disappointments and concludes, 'But we don't have any of those things. So what! We gotta keep on living, don't we? I can't stop just 'cause I made a few mistakes. I gotta keep goin' . . . somehow.' [Ellipses Inge's] The rest of the play is really about that 'somehow', as Lola and Doc try to keep going. Their successes, and even their efforts, are not consistent, and Inge does nothing to imply that Doc and Lola are extraordinary in any way; they are not even particularly attractive. Yet their unremarkable pains are real pains, and the task of coping with life, even on this level, is a heroic one. In the final scene Lola tells Doc of a dream in which she saw Little Sheba dead, and the play ends with their response:

> LOLA   I don't think Little Sheba's ever coming back, Doc. I'm
>   not going to call her any more.
> DOC   Not much point in it Baby. I guess she's gone for good.
> LOLA   I'll fix your eggs.

Lola and Doc do not change radically for the better as a result of their losses; nor do they kill themselves in despair; nor do they find new fantasies to build their hopes on. They go on, somehow. And Inge makes that seem remarkable.

Picnic (1953) shows another group of small-town midwestern characters forced to face the impossibility of their dreams and to make their peace with reality. In a plot situation that resembles Williams's *Orpheus Descending* but with none of that play's pretensions to symbolism, a handsome young drifter shakes up a neighbourhood of women, reminding them of half-forgotten fantasies and frustrations, and then leaves with the girl who has fallen in love with him. The end of the play, with Madge following Hal into an unknown future, has all the trappings of fairy-tale romance, the sort of happy ending that requires that the audience not ask what will happen next. But Inge raises the question, and makes it clear that Madge faces it, too:

> FLO   He's no good. He'll never be able to support you. When
>   he does have a job, he'll spend all his money on booze. After a
>   while, there'll be other women.
> MADGE   I've thought of all those things.

Madge and Hal are prepared to settle for considerably less than perfection because it is the best option available; they are not running towards a guaranteed happy ending but away from a guaranteed unhappiness. In the subplot a spinster schoolteacher willingly demeans herself by begging and finally trapping a man into marrying her; she does not love him and realizes he does not love her, but the alternative is unbearable. Each character in the play comes to recognize that the slim possibility of happiness is better than nothing – indeed, that something different, even if equally unhappy, is preferable to the unhappiness you know.

Inge shares with Tennessee Williams this conviction that no source of comfort, however fragile or ephemeral, should be disdained in a frightening and inhospitable world. It reappears in his next play, *Bus Stop* (1955), whose veneer of light romantic comedy only partially hides the recognition that life is lonely and any human contact is better than none. Bo, a simple cowboy, has abducted the saloon singer Cherie in the naive faith that if he loves her she must love him. The basic romantic convention on which that plot is built makes its happy ending inevitable, but Inge colours and surrounds the central action with reminders that the stakes are less happily-ever-after than anything-ever-after. Both Bo and Cherie are allowed quiet moments of reflection in which they realize that the lives they are leading are lonely and unpromising, and both readjust their expectations for the future accordingly. The small stories that surround the central action all serve to emphasize that Bo and Cherie's romance, even if imperfect, is better than most people get; the proprietor of the bus stop, for example, settles for brief sexual liaisons with the drivers. And the play ends, not with Bo and Cherie's triumphal ride into the sunset, but with Bo's friend, who has been left behind, discovering that the restaurant is closing and he has no place to go:

> GRACE   Then I'm sorry, mister, but you're just left out in the cold.
> VIRGIL   Well . . . that's what happens to some people.
> [Ellipses Inge's]

The Dark at the Top of the Stairs (1957), set in 1920s Oklahoma, is the story of Rubin and Cora Flood, whose basic differences almost destroy their marriage until both realize how much they need the other's support to face the pains and fears of life. The significance of the title is explained by ten-year-old Sonny, who is afraid to go upstairs to bed alone: 'You can't see what's in front of you. And it might be something awful.' At that point in the play his mother offers to go upstairs with him; in the final scene Rubin goes up first to light the way for Cora. The play thus continues Inge's exploration of the insecurities and fears of inadequacy that he, like Williams, sees as central to the twentieth-century American experience, and his analysis of the limited options open to ordinary people and the need to find – and settle for – imperfect solutions to inescapable problems. As in *Picnic* and *Bus Stop*, Inge surrounds the main characters with thematically supportive subplots, but somewhat less effectively, as the complexity of the secondary material threatens to upset the play's balance: the unhappy schoolboy and sexually frustrated sister whose lives teach Cora that her unhappiness is not unique actually take up more of the play's attention than Rubin does, and the complicated Oedipal relationship between Cora and Sonny seems grafted onto the play rather than integral to it. Apparently Inge was losing control of his craft; although he continued to write plays through the 1960s, this was his last commercial and artistic success.

Other new dramatists of the 1940s and 1950s

Miller and Williams (and, in a different way, Eugene O'Neill) so dominated the serious American drama mid-century that only a few other writers stand out, either for a body of notable work or for individual plays of special merit or importance. A survey of the Broadway seasons of 1945–1960 finds, even among the hits, a large number of one-play playwrights or genre plays that succeeded because they were that year's version of some type of play that Broadway always requires. That some were better than others is almost incidental to their effectiveness; each was at least skilfully assembled and better than any unsuccessful rivals, and met the audience hunger for that particular type of melodrama.

It is not surprising, for example, that the Second World War was followed by a string of plays set in the war or in the post-war experiences of returning soldiers; Miller's *All My Sons* fits partially in the latter category. Among the more interesting on their own merits are Arthur Laurents' *Home of the Brave* (1945), about a soldier dealing with the guilt of survival; Thomas Heggen and Joshua Logan's *Mr Roberts* (1948), a sentimental comedy about the Navy; William Wister Haines's *Command Decision* (1947), about Air Force officers making difficult choices in battle; *Stalag 17* (1951), by Donald Bevin and Edmund Trzcinski, a comedy in the unlikely setting of a prison camp; and Alfred Hayes's *The Girl on the Via Flaminia* (1954), in which an American soldier in post-war Rome learns that occupying forces can unwittingly injure and humiliate their hosts.

Another recurring subgenre is made up of dramatizations of fiction, history, biography and other non-dramatic sources: Ruth and Augustus Goetz's *The Heiress* (1947), from Henry James's *Washington Square*; William Archibald's *The Innocents* (1950), from James's *The Turn of the Screw*; *The Diary of Anne Frank* (1955), dramatized by Frances Goodrich and Albert Hackett; Ketti Frings's adaptation of Thomas Wolfe's *Look Homeward, Angel* (1957); Dore Schary's biography of Franklin Roosevelt, *Sunrise of Campobello* (1958); and William Gibson's drama of the youth of Helen Keller, *The Miracle Worker* (1959). Each of these plays is constructed with considerable theatrical skill, though their very nature keeps them subservient to their source material.

Among the other new dramatists of this period, Robert Anderson resembles Inge – and thus, by extension, Williams – in addressing the private unhappiness of life's victims and offering the counsel that no source of comfort or consolation should be disdained because it is imperfect. In his first Broadway success, *Tea and Sympathy* (1953), a prep schoolboy is suspected of being homosexual just because he is unusually sensitive, and the only person to offer him any sympathy is the unhappy wife of one of the schoolmasters. At the final curtain, with the oft-quoted (and parodied) line, 'Years from now – when you talk about this – and you will! – be kind', she offers herself to him sexually, both out of her own loneliness and as a way of reassuring the boy he is normal. Some critics have attempted to read *Tea and Sympathy* politically, as an attack on the mob hysteria and fear of the different that constituted McCarthyism. But Anderson's story is the personal one: of Tom, confused by the attacks and, in his innocence, almost convinced they are valid; of Bill, whose marital problems have the same roots as his compulsion to persecute the boy; and of Laura, whose sympathy for Tom's pain springs from her own unhappiness. The play does cheat a little to achieve its ends, making the villains all evil and the imminent sexual act unequivocally pure; while Anderson does not pretend that Laura's giving herself to Tom will be more than a very temporary interruption to her unhappiness, he does imply that the event will resolve all the boy's problems.

A similar quality might be said to mar *Silent Night, Lonely Night* (1959), about two unhappy people – her marriage is collapsing, his wife is insane – who allow themselves the comfort of a one-night affair. Anderson's point is that even an immoral act can be justified by its power to provide solace, but he does unfairly weigh the argument in his favour by setting the play on Christmas Eve, thus implicitly blessing the sin, and by rewarding both characters the next morning, her with a reconciliation with her husband, him with news of his wife's partial improvement. Like Inge, Anderson is sometimes charged with philosophical cowardice for pretending that complex problems have simple solutions, when he is really saying that even partial and imperfect solutions must be embraced gratefully when the alternative is unassuaged pain. And, like Inge, he is sometimes accused of introducing salacious material just for titillation, without facing its moral or psychological implications. But the moral simplifications that defang his shocking subjects are the very things that make the plays accessible to a mainstream audience, allowing it to see past the shock to the author's empathy for his main characters.

Lorraine Hansberry's *A Raisin in the Sun* (1959) is noteworthy both for its quality and for being the first play by a black woman to be staged on Broadway. The play's central action, about a black inner-city family who resist the attempts by racists to keep them from moving into a white neighbourhood, is actually not its moral centre. (It is noteworthy that the basic plot does not really depend on race; the Youngers might as easily be Italians, Irish, Jews or any group unwelcome in a restricted neighbourhood.) Its real insight is into a unique tragedy of black family life in America: that generations of racism have damaged the spirit of the men, forcing the women to assume responsibilities that only further the men's emasculation. The mother of this family has the power, and is always aware of her need to wield it without damaging the dignity of her adult son. She makes a point of giving him control of the family's money, even at the risk of his losing it:

> There ain't nothing worth holding on to, money, dreams, nothing else – if it means – if it means it's going to destroy my boy . . . . It ain't much, but it's all I got in the world and I'm putting it in your hands. I'm telling you to be the head of the family from now on like you supposed to be.

When he does lose it, the danger to his manhood is greater than the financial setback, and his mother calls on the other women in the family to help save his soul: 'What you tell him a minute ago? That he wasn't a man? Yes? You give him up for me? You done wrote his epitaph too – like the rest of the world? Well, who gave you the privilege?' They help him to find in himself the strength to reject the racists; and when the white man turns to the mother for help he gets only a joyful abdication of power: 'My son said we was going to move and there ain't nothing left for me to say.' The enduring power of *A Raisin in the Sun* lies more in its picture of the Youngers' domestic relations than in their encounter with racism.

Paddy Chayefsky began his career writing for television and ended it writing for film, and had his greatest successes (*Marty, Network*) in those media. But his stage plays of the 1950s offer an urban, Jewish complement to those of Inge and Anderson in telling small stories of small people with affection and respect. In *Middle of the Night* (1956) a middle-aged widower and a younger married woman fall in love, shocking family and friends on both sides; and the couple themselves begin to doubt their right to defy conventional mores. As Inge or Anderson probably would, Chayefsky allows his lovers to choose an imperfect happiness over a guaranteed unhappiness. Whether these ordinary people will have an ordinary chance at a future is treated with an unpatronizing respect for the reality of their emotions. In *The Tenth Man* (1959) the elderly members of a small Jewish congregation attempt an exorcism on a schizophrenic girl, and actually affect the dead-spirited young man they recruited to help in the ritual; with renewed faith and capacity for love, he proposes to her. Unfortunately a string of easy and patronizing jokes at the expense of the bored and confused old men almost overpowers the human story of the damaged young people reaching towards each other. In his later plays Chayefsky turned to a more intellectual, issue-oriented mode that proved more successful on film than on stage.

Between writing films and musical comedies Arthur Laurents offered several object lessons in the value of accepting imperfection in an imperfect world. *Home of the Brave*, in which a soldier forgives himself for what he took to be cowardice, has already been mentioned. In *The Time of the Cuckoo* (1952) an American woman in Venice has a brief romance with an Italian shopkeeper but is shocked by his moral casualness; she realizes too late that the price of her high moral standards is the loss of what would have been at worst a pleasant adventure. *A Clearing in the Woods* (1957), one of the very few non-realistic plays of the decade, confronts a woman with several girls and women who she realizes are herself at earlier ages. They help her see that her unhappiness has been caused by a perfectionism that led her to label each of them a failure; and by embracing them she learns to accept herself.

In a small but steady stream of plays by writers from other genres who were trying their hands at drama, Carson McCullers's *The Member of the Wedding* (1950) stands out as a sensitive portrait of a girl at the cusp of adolescence. Twelve-year-old Frankie vacillates between cuddling in the lap of her black maid and fantasizing about joining her brother and his bride on their honeymoon, between playing with her six-year-old cousin and discovering boys her own age. Her pre-teen angst, philosophizing and self-dramatizations are all treated with a respect that is not blind to their silliness. Archibald MacLeish's *J.B.* (1958) is a retelling of the Job story in modern terms, with J.B. a smug businessman who not only retains his simple faith in God through his ordeals, but develops humility and the capacity for love. MacLeish almost buries this modernization in additional and distracting symbolism, but the novelty of what was virtually the only verse play of the decade attracted and held audiences.

Eugene O'Neill

After *Days Without End* in 1933, Eugene O'Neill did not have another new play produced until *The Iceman Cometh* in 1946, and only one more (*A Moon for the Misbegotten*, 1947) before his death in 1953. But, although the last twenty years of his life were marked by extended periods in which physical and mental ailments kept him from writing, he was not as idle as the production record would seem to indicate. During this period he worked on a large number of uncompleted plays, most notably an eleven play cycle with the umbrella title 'A Tale of Possessors, Self-Dispossessed', in which he planned to follow a family through the two centuries of American history. He also planned a second cycle of eight one-act plays with the group title 'By Way of Obit', completed the somewhat autobiographical *Long Day's Journey into Night*, and had notes or outlines for other plays.

But O'Neill did not finish many of these projects, destroyed most of his notes and manuscripts, and ordered that *Long Day's Journey* be with-held from publication and production until twenty-five years after his death, to avoid embarrassment to his family. His widow overrode that request, and allowed the play to be published in 1956, and to be pro-duced in Stockholm (in gratitude for O'Neill's having been awarded the Nobel Prize in 1936) and New York that same year. Meanwhile, a successful Off-Broadway revival of *The Iceman Cometh* in 1956 had re-awakened interest in O'Neill, and gradually three more posthumous plays appeared: *A Touch of the Poet*, the only completed play of the 'Possessors' cycle (Stockholm 1957, New York 1958); *Hughie*, the only play from the one-act cycle (Stockholm 1958, New York 1964); and *More Stately Mansions*, a second play in the 'Possessors' cycle, surviving only in an overlong draft which had to be heavily cut for production (Stockholm 1962, New York 1967).

The last six plays have two extraordinary things in common. First, while they are not all of equal quality, as a group they are as superior to O'Neill's plays of the 1920s as those plays were to their contemporaries – which is to say that the most successful of them – certainly *Iceman*, *Moon* and *Long Day's Journey* – are among the very best plays ever writ-ten in America. Second, they contain none of O'Neill's characteristic experiments in technique, but are simple narratives of families or friends in the setting of their homes. After a lifetime of trying and discarding every dramatic and theatrical style he could adapt or invent in his at-tempt to stretch the genre and make it able to carry the weight and breadth of his concerns, O'Neill returned in his final masterpieces to the most conventional of forms. Perhaps the greatest artistic discovery of his life was that he could say what he wanted to say through domestic realism.

The Iceman Cometh is set in a cheap New York saloon populated by failures whose only activities are drinking until they pass out and com-forting themselves with fantasies ('pipe dreams') of some day regaining their proper place in society. A friend talks them into actually looking for the job or contacting a friend as they had always promised, and shows no surprise when they all return in defeat, assuring them that admitting their worthlessness will free them to enjoy failure without guilt. In explaining how the process worked for him, he discovers an unbearable truth and retreats into the belief that he has gone mad. The others pretend to have been humouring him, and revert happily to their pipe dreams.

The play is about the need for fantasy – in particular, the ego-comforting fantasy that we are essentially better than we may appear to be at the moment – without which humanity cannot bear the pain of reality. The general tone of the first act, before Hickey's arrival, is of a contented, functioning community; as Larry Slade (one of the drunks, whose protective fantasy is that he does not care about life, but is just observing it with amusement) explains, 'To hell with the truth! . . . The lie of a pipe dream is what gives life to the whole misbegotten mad lot of us.' Larry calls it the Tomorrow Movement, since the pretence that each of them will achieve something tomorrow makes it easier to live with the failure of today. It is easy to miss the vitality and cameraderie in the first act because the sordid and debased quality of the drunks' lives dominates our impressions. We notice it most when Hickey's campaign puts a damper on the party atmosphere, turning the friends against each other, driving them away from company to hide in solitude, and even depriving them of the solace of drunkenness. Larry identifies the change in the air: 'I'm damned sure he's brought death here with him. I feel the cold touch of it on him.'

Pipe dreams mean life and truth means death – one character kills himself after losing his fantasy – because the human animal is simply not equipped to deal directly with reality. The purest evidence of this is Hickey's own case. Hickey is honestly confused that the others do not find peace, and is compelled to tell his story, to show them how they should be reacting. What he wants to explain is that he gave up the fantasy that he would reform, and then killed his wife to save her from the pain of watching his surrender. But O'Neill makes brilliant use of a psychological insight he would also exploit in *Long Day's Journey*: that if a character talks long enough he will eventually say something he did not intend to say:

> Anyway, she forgave me. The same way she forgave me every
> time I'd turn up after a periodical drunk. You all know what I'd
> be like at the end of one. You've seen me. Like something lying
> in the gutter that no alley cat would lower itself to drag in –
> something they threw out of the D.T. ward in Bellevue along
> with the garbage, something that ought to be dead and isn't! . . .
> There's a limit to the guilt you can feel and the forgiveness and
> the pity you can take! You have to begin blaming someone else,
> too.

The momentum of his self-exposure brings him to the night of the killing: 'I remember I heard myself speaking to her, as if it was something I'd always wanted to say: "Well, you know what you can do with your pipe dream now, you damned bitch!" '

The failure of the others to find peace in surrender to reality as Hickey did is explained: that is not what happened to him. He did not kill the pipe dream; he killed a nagging wife, and then *created* the pipe dream that he had done it out of love. The truth about himself – that he was capable of such hate – was unbearable, and he built the whole fictional construct about giving up pipe dreams and finding peace, to protect himself from that truth. And O'Neill lets us watch him do it again: 'No!

That's a lie! I never said – ! Good God, I couldn't have said that! If I did, I'd gone insane!' Harry Hope senses that if Hickey was crazy, the others can then pretend that they were just humouring him, and thus did not really fail. Hickey realizes this: 'Now, Governor! Up to your old tricks, eh? I see what you're driving at, but I can't let you get away with – Yes, Harry, of course, I've been out of my mind ever since! All the time I've been here! You saw I was insane, didn't you?' Before our eyes, Hickey leaps into a new pipe dream, knowing full well that it is false, because it is easier to handle that contradiction than to face the truth. And the others (except for Larry, who lives with the truth and awaits the release of death) embrace Harry's fiction, rediscovering the community, the happiness and even the kick in the booze.

The return to realism in *The Iceman Cometh* marks a startling change from O'Neill's earlier styles, but there is a continuity of themes. The inherent limitation in the human capacity for dealing with reality that O'Neill discovers in this play is related to similar limits – of fate, genetics or psychology – that he had dramatized in such plays as *The Emperor Jones* and *Mourning Becomes Electra*. The important difference is in the tone of the play. There is an implied forgiveness offered to the audience: no one should feel guilty about relying on psychological and spiritual crutches if life is impossible without them. *The Iceman Cometh* does not bewail the fact that humanity needs pipe dreams to survive; it celebrates the good fortune that, needing such dreams, man also has the capacity to find and maintain them.

A Moon for the Misbegotten was actually written after *Long Day's Journey into Night*, though it was produced first, and is a kind of sequel to it, picking up one of the characters a decade later. The self-hating alcoholic James Tyrone, Jr enjoys the company of sluttish Josie Hogan, but Josie, who is actually a virgin and who loves him, realizes that he needs comforting more than sex, and gives up an opportunity to take him to bed. On its surface, then, the play is a simple and sentimental love story; its power and its stature come from the depth of its psychological insights and from the wealth of compassion those insights inspire. In this play O'Neill eschews all the metaphysical and psychological theses – tragic Fate, the Dionysian–Apollonian conflict, Freudian determinism, etc. – that generated his early plays, and dramatizes directly the painful process of living. Like most cynics, Jim Tyrone is an idealist and romantic at heart, and cannot forgive himself for his failure to live up to his own standards. He is defined by an emptiness of spirit, 'like a dead man walking slow behind his own coffin', interrupted only by flashes of self-loathing – 'You better watch your step. It might work – and then think of how disgusted you'd feel, with me lying beside you, probably snoring, as you watched the dawn come.'

O'Neill has not changed so much since *The Emperor Jones* and *Mourning Becomes Electra* that he thinks people can triumph over their limitations.

But he now feels that they can gain some peace by forgiving themselves for those limitations, and he shows this happening to Jim Tyrone. As Jim and Josie sit and drink together in the moonlight, he can speak openly about his crimes, notably his drunkenness and whoring during his mother's last illness and after her death. That the behaviour he describes is clearly a matter of weakness or even normal response to grief, not depravity, is no comfort; he can only condemn himself for it, and condemn himself further for exposing Josie to it. Josie's unselfish love enables her to give Jim what he cannot give himself: 'I'm proud you came to me as the one in the world you know loves you enough to understand and forgive – and I do forgive! . . . As *she* forgives, do you hear me! As *she* loves and understands and forgives!' He awakes the next morning, after sleeping in her maternal arms, 'Sort of at peace with myself and this lousy life – as if all my sins had been forgiven.' She, and the play, realize that this forgiveness is not a panacea. He remains dead in spirit, but at least he is freed from self-torment, and she prays only that he will be spared another relapse: 'May you have your wish and die in your sleep soon, Jim, darling. May you rest forever in forgiveness and peace.'

Josie also comes to a self-acceptance. She begins the play trapped in the role of bawdy slut, which is really a mask to cover her feelings of unworthiness – 'I'm an ugly overgrown lump of a woman, and the men that want me are no better than stupid bulls.' – but ends the play in peace, having sacrificed her one chance for romance, but appreciating the value of her capacity for giving. *A Moon for the Misbegotten* shares with *The Iceman Cometh* and, indeed, all of O'Neill's final plays this theme and tone of forgiveness. In *Iceman* O'Neill offered the audience a release from guilt by showing that some dependencies are part of the human condition, and not the result of individual inadequacy. In *Moon* he dramatizes how desperately important the capacity for self-forgiveness is, and offers the reassurance that such mercy, and the peace it provides, are available.

If there is such a thing as the single greatest American play, it is almost certainly *Long Day's Journey into Night*. In this unflinchingly probing exploration of what it is like to be human, O'Neill exposes some of the most frightening truths about what we do to ourselves and each other, and then probes even deeper to find, in the horrors themselves, the means of surviving the horrors. That he does so in a work that was a personal torment for him to write must increase the play's stature and our admiration for its accomplishment. *Long Day's Journey into Night* is a fictional portrayal of O'Neill's own family: miserly father, morphine-addicted mother, alcoholic and self-pitying sons. The Long Day of the play sees two crises: Mary, who has been off her drug for some time, starts taking it again; and the family learns that Edmund has consumption and must be hospitalized. Old grievances come to the surface with the new pains, and recriminations and accusations of blame are traded among the four members of the family. At the end of the play, with Mary lost in her drugged fantasies and the men paralysed by drunkenness, it seems impossible that the sun will ever rise again.

The first aspect of the play to note and then move beyond is the autobiographical element. The Tyrones are unquestionably based on the O'Neills, but one of the accomplishments of the play is O'Neill's transformation of the raw material of his life into something more. On the simplest level, he makes important changes in the characters, so they may better serve his symbolic and thematic purposes: Edmund is far more of an unformed adolescent than Eugene O'Neill was at that point in his life, for example; and the author conceals the fact that Mary O'Neill eventually overcame her addiction. More significantly, there is much more to the play than the telling of its story. The real importance of the autobiographical element is the fact that O'Neill had the courage and ability to take material that must have been painful for him to work with, to find a basis for hope and consolation in its apparently unbroken darkness, and to offer those gifts to the world through his art.

On the surface, there seems to be little basis for hope and consolation in the experience of the Tyrones. As a sunny day is darkened first by fog and then by night, we discover a network of sins committed by the Tyrones against each other. The father's miserliness and unsettled actor's life led to Mary's addiction and kept her from recovery; his constant criticism of Jamie alienated and embittered him; and his penny-pinching now threatens Edmund's life. Mary's addiction tortures all the men, as her repeated reminders of the sacrifices she made to marry Tyrone condemn him, and her obvious preference for Edmund contributes to Jamie's bitterness and Edmund's extended adolescence. Jamie actually killed a third son, by infecting him with measles, and has deliberately corrupted Edmund out of jealousy; and his dissipation and open antagonism are a continual source of pain to his parents. Edmund's birth led to Mary's addiction; his illness contributes to her relapse; his innocence is an affront to Jamie; and his petulance and self-pity impose guilt on all of them.

O'Neill offers no hope that these outrages could have been avoided, or that mutual atrocities are not inherent in man's fate. In fact, *Long Day's Journey* asserts more emphatically than any of his plays since *Mourning Becomes Electra* his lifelong conviction that human life is limited and controlled by forces outside our control. But, as he did in *The Iceman Cometh*, O'Neill forces fatalism to yield up a grain of reassurance. For one thing, the very complexity of the network of crimes relieves any one person from unique guilt. Exactly who, for example, is responsible for Mary's addiction? At various times the play blames the quack doctor, for first giving her morphine; Tyrone, for being too cheap to get a good doctor; Edmund, for being born; Eugene, for dying; Jamie, for killing Eugene; the parents, for preferring Eugene and inspiring Jamie's jealousy; Mary, for having an addictive personality; and so on, up to and including the economic forces of fifty years ago that led Tyrone's father to abandon his family. A similar list of causes could be assembled for every other offence in the play – Jamie's bitterness, Mary's relapse, etc. – leading inevitably to the sense that when responsibility is spread as widely as this no great burden of guilt can rest on any one person.

Even further, O'Neill recognizes that many of the crimes his characters have committed against each other were intended to be acts of love. Tyrone did not take Mary on the road with him to degrade her, but because he loved her too much to leave her behind. The end product was her degradation, but O'Neill makes us distinguish between intent and result. Mary does not baby Edmund to encourage his weaknesses, but because he is her baby. In the last act Jamie tries to warn Edmund against himself, but what slips out is a vicious expression of his resentment that he immediately regrets. It is a tragic fact of human interaction that sometimes an act or word of love gets inexplicably transformed in transit, and reaches its recipient as an attack. O'Neill cannot explain why that happens, and certainly cannot offer any means of preventing it. But he can help his audience to recognize that it does happen, and to learn to look past the received hate and honour the intended love; as Mary begs Tyrone, 'James! We've loved each other! We always will! Let's remember only that, and not try to understand what we cannot understand, or help things that cannot be helped – the things life has done to us we cannot excuse or explain.'

The grammar of that last phrase is significant, and is repeated elsewhere in the play (Tyrone: 'life had me where it wanted me'). In *Long Day's Journey*, O'Neill offers a psychological model that replaces free will with the limits imposed on a person by the events of his past. The Tyrones do not choose to behave as they do; they cannot help it, because their past experience has programmed them to behave this way. Tyrone is not miserly out of conscious malice; indeed, in his most self-aware moments he actually tries to be generous. But the extreme poverty of his youth warped him in a way he cannot reverse. In the last act he tells Edmund about his childhood, and then tries to fight his programming: 'If I took this state farm sanatorium for a good bargain, you'll have to forgive me . . . . You can choose any place you like! Never mind what it costs! Any place I can afford. Any place you like – within reason.'

The sad comedy of that reversal is repeated by each of the characters throughout the play, as they demonstrate O'Neill's thesis that even the occasional attempts at free will are doomed by this internal fate. O'Neill dramatizes this pattern most brilliantly in the last act, which contains some of his finest dramaturgy and dialogue. In a series of uncharacteristically eloquent and poetic speeches, the usually prosaic O'Neill allows each of the men to realize a truth about himself and then shows that each of them is unable to change in spite of the insight. Edmund admits that he doesn't have the poetic talent he wishes for, but then lapses into the bathetic imagery and posing he has just rejected. Jamie breaks through his wise-cracking persona to warn his brother against himself, but then returns to his viciously cynical mode. Tyrone talks about how his lust for money destroyed his talent as an actor, reaching the sorrowful conclusion that 'I'd be willing to have no home but the poorhouse in my old age if I could look back now on having been the fine artist I might have been.' But at the very moment that he is saying those words he is unscrewing light bulbs to save pennies.

How does a denial of free will offer any basis for hope? A recurring trope in the play, repeated at least ten times, usually by Mary, is some variant of 'It's not your fault':

> It's wrong to blame your brother. He can't help being what the past has made him. Any more than your father can. Or you. Or I.

If the psychological model O'Neill offers in this play is correct – if indeed we cannot control our actions – then, as O'Neill argued in *Iceman*, we cannot be held culpable for them. O'Neill is not saying that real crimes are not committed and real pain felt. He sees, however, that there is a second level of pain, built on guilt or recrimination, that piles additional torments onto the first level. He is too much of a fatalist to believe that the first level – the actual wounds we cause to each other, intentionally or not – can be avoided. But the second level can be. The same dark facts of reality that limit and pervert our attempts to be loving and moral are the reason we should forgive ourselves for our failures. Unlike the characters in *A Moon for the Misbegotten*, the Tyrones never achieve self-forgiveness, and that is why this play ends so very darkly. But the author has learned to view them with (in the words of his dedication of the play to his wife) 'pity and understanding and forgiveness;' and he offers the gift of that ability to the world.

A Touch of the Poet, the only surviving completed play from the proposed eleven-play cycle, is a slight digression in what was to be the saga of the Harford family, here kept mainly offstage; some of the play's secondary themes, notably the conflict between idealism and money-making, were evidently more important to the cycle as a whole than to this play. The focus here is on Con Melody, an army officer reduced to tavernkeeper, and on his daughter Sara's romance with Simon Harford; and the strongest themes are those that tie this play to *The Iceman Cometh* – the paradoxically life-giving nature of fantasy – and *A Moon for the Misbegotten* – the deep satisfaction women can find in unselfish love. Con Melody is a ridiculous figure, the village tavern owner whose cronies play up to his eccentricities just to cadge drinks. But O'Neill goes to great lengths to establish that there is also something imposing about this self-styled Byronic hero; like the pipe dreams of the bums in *The Iceman Cometh*, the persona of Major Melody is a self-delusion, but one that makes Con's disappointing life worth living, and gives him a vitality and dignity that reality cannot. Sara, who thought she had nothing but contempt for the fantasy, surprises herself with the depth of her disappointment when it is destroyed. Unlike the *Iceman* characters, Con will survive without his pipe dream, and on at least one level his life may be improved by its loss; he is finally able to look at his wife as his equal and tell her he loves her. But a glory has gone out of the man, and O'Neill leaves the audience wondering whether truth is really preferable to fantasy.

Although O'Neill's last two plays were not staged in America until after 1960, it seems appropriate to discuss them along with the other posthumous works. The one-act play *Hughie* is built on a rambling monologue by Erie Smith, small-time gambler, to the night clerk of his hotel, who responds only enough to indicate that he is really lost in his own thoughts. Erie reminisces about the previous night clerk, Hughie, who had lived vicariously through Erie's tales of the fast life, and whose appreciation had given Erie the confidence to keep going; since Hughie's death Erie has been on a losing streak. The clerk finally hears some of what is being said, and the play ends with the sense that he will replace Hughie as Erie's audience and ego-booster. Again there are echoes of *The Iceman Cometh* in the suggestion that fantasy can be more satisfying than reality (for the two clerks) and even a prop to support one through reality (for Erie). It is a slight piece, little more than a footnote to *Iceman* and *Touch of a Poet*, but it shows one direction O'Neill's exploration of realism was taking him, towards the exposure of inner experience through small talk.

It is difficult to analyse the final posthumous play, *More Stately Mansions*, very thoroughly, since it exists only in an unedited draft that is five times the length of an ordinary play. The two produced texts (Stockholm 1962 and New York 1967) and the published text represent different selections and ordering of scenes and speeches by different editors, none of them including more than half the manuscript. So one can only indicate some of the things O'Neill was considering putting into the play, without knowing for certain which would have survived his editing. The three texts have the same outline: Sara Melody has married Simon Harford, and competes with his mother Deborah for his love. The play is a series of power games, with the women occasionally uniting to manipulate Simon, and then splitting to fight over him. The struggle eventually takes its toll on Simon, who is in danger of losing his mind; and the women then outdo each other in sacrificing to save him, Sara giving up her ambitions while Deborah deliberately chooses insanity to free him from her spell.

The conflict between business and romanticism, with the dangers inherent in both, was evidently going to be the continuing theme of the cycle. But *More Stately Mansions* has other concerns as well, some of them, harkening back to much earlier periods in O'Neill's work. Simon Harford's disintegrating personality recalls *The Great God Brown*; the separation of woman into mother and whore, and then the confusion of the two, echoes both *Desire Under the Elms* and *Mourning Becomes Electra*; there is even a scene of spoken thoughts in the manner of *Strange Interlude*. In performance, the strongest aspect of the play is likely to be the domestic situation, with its horrifying picture of the power politics of marriage and family, filled with sudden reversals and shifting allegiances. Deborah Harford's conscious flirtation with insanity is also fascinating, and her deliberate entry into the summer house, which has been established as the place where she will go mad, is a powerful image of sacrifice. Still, the play cannot escape looking like the unformed and unwieldy draft that it is, and cannot be analysed or judged as a finished work.

Throughout his career O'Neill stood apart from the mainstream of American drama, not being influenced by what was being written around him and not having much direct influence on other dramatists, except by setting high standards. And yet the history of his career resembles that of the American drama as a whole, starting with small plays of psychological realism, moving through an extended period of stylistic experiment, and then returning to domestic melodrama, this time with the confidence that the conventional genre was far stronger and more flexible than it had seemed. He – and the American drama as a whole – also moved from overtly thesis-driven plays to those that at least give the impression of being generated by character, and from studies in such large subjects as Race and Fate to examinations of the psychological and spiritual experience of everyday life. And in his late masterpieces, all written before the major plays of Tennessee Williams and his contemporaries, he anticipated the discovery that the true calling of the mid-twentieth-century American dramatist lay in offering some hope and consolation to those for whom everyday life was a painful challenge.

Other older dramatists

Several playwrights whose careers began in the 1920s and 1930s remained active into the 1950s, though it is notable that few of them had more than one or two successes, which suggests that the public and the genre had moved beyond them. Maxwell Anderson, for example, attempted one more verse play, a couple of historical costume dramas, a musical and a domestic melodrama, and had his biggest hit with a popular adaptation of a suspense novel. *Anne of the Thousand Days* (1948) reaches for tragedy in presenting Anne Boleyn as an admirably intelligent and self-reliant figure tempted to abuse her power, but actually functions on a less heroic level, suggesting the ironic fate of an amateur politician defeated by those far more skilled at the game. The central question of *Joan of Lorraine* (1946) is whether Joan should have compromised her idealism to the inevitability of working with imperfect human associates. Anderson applies the question to the world war that had just ended, presenting Joan's story as a play being rehearsed by modern actors, who debate its interpretation. In *Barefoot in Athens* (1951), Anderson characterizes Socrates as a simple believer in democracy whose countrymen are unfortunately not as wise as he hopes; there are overtones of McCarthyism in his fate, and Anderson seems uncertain whether society's persecution of its inconvenient idealists is to be celebrated or deplored. *Bad Seed* (1954), an adaptation of a novel by William March about a murderous little girl who covers her complete lack of morality with a veneer of innocence, is the not negligible accomplishment of a proficient technician able to make a slight piece work in theatrical terms.

Lillian Hellman's post-war plays show her moving from the social commentary mode of the 1930s to psychological studies more typical of the 1950s – or, in other words, from the Arthur Miller end of the continuum towards the Tennessee Williams end. *Another Part of the Forest* (1946) returns to the characters of *The Little Foxes*, dramatizing events twenty years before the earlier play in which Ben blackmails his father into giving him control of the family business. It thus fills in some of the background to *The Little Foxes*, in particular the curiously friendly competition between Ben and Regina in the other play, both by showing one of their first clashes and by more explicitly identifying the qualities that they share and that they bemusedly recognize and appreciate in each other. But the play stands on its own as a fascinating study in familial politics and infighting, and as a chilling demonstration of the triumph of the ruthless and devious over the simple or the merely ruthless. Indeed, the biggest weakness of this play is that it does so very successfully what Hellman had already done so very successfully; except for the added insights into some of the characters, *Another Part of the Forest* is essentially a remake of *The Little Foxes* without the resonance of historical allegory.

The Autumn Garden (1951) is a much quieter play with overtones of Chekhov, as a group of old friends are led by the tactless comments of an outsider to recognize how completely they have wasted their lives. The discoveries serve no purpose, as they also understand that their inertia is too ingrained to alter; all that will happen is that they will now be more consciously aware of their own unhappiness, though an ironic resignation to the inevitable can temper and soften the regrets of age. As in Chekhov, very little actually happens, and much of that is offstage; life is not made of melodramatic climaxes, but of the gradual discovery that we are who we are, for better or worse. *Toys in the Attic* (1960) is a somewhat darker psychological study, as spinster sisters are so threatened by their brother's good fortune that they sabotage it to bring him back under their control. The plot involves incest, miscegenation, violence, neurosis and failure in a New Orleans setting, so a comparison to Tennessee Williams is inescapable; like Williams, Hellman is exploring the bargains and compromises people make with life in order to achieve something like happiness, and is interested in aberrant psychology primarily for what it can illuminate about normal life. But *Toys in the Attic* is unmistakably by the author of *The Little Foxes* as well, in its focus on the irresistible power of obsession and in an ironic distance that lets Hellman see that victories are sometimes Pyrrhic; an important secondary theme of the play is the danger of getting what you think you want.

Clifford Odets also turned from social criticism to psychological study after one last play of the earlier mode. Odets had spent much of the previous decade in Hollywood, and there are autobiographical overtones to his anger in *The Big Knife* (1949) at its corrupting seductiveness, but the Hollywood of *The Big Knife* is ultimately a metaphor for America and the drive for economic success, much like the boxing ring in *Golden Boy*. In both plays Odets shows that something must be sold to obtain a lot of money, and that is usually one's sense of self; this play's equivalent of Joe's violin is Charlie Castle's real name, which the studio made him change. *The Big Knife* is a weaker play than *Golden Boy*, in part because Odets's personal anger interferes with its focus, in part because it lacks the context of the Depression to establish universality. In the same Broadway season Arthur Miller offered Willy Loman as an example of the dangers of the American Dream, and Odets's Hollywood star proved harder to feel sorry for than the failed salesman.

Perhaps realizing that the time for plays like *The Big Knife* had passed, Odets turned to a more domestic analysis of relationships and psychological needs, combined with elements of the whodunit, in *The Country Girl* (1950). When a director casts a faded and alcoholic actor in a play, he is led to believe that the actor's dependent wife caused his downfall, and tries to keep her from interfering with the comeback. He ultimately learns that the opposite is true; the actor is self-destructive, and his wife's support is the only thing that has kept him going. At the centre of the play is an analysis of the politics of marriage, particularly the way in which the stronger party's willingness to serve the needs of the weaker actually puts the weaker in control. Another of Odets's observations is the human need for simple and schematic definitions, and the degree to which such definitions limit our perceptions. Because he wants a world made up of villains and victims, the director eagerly misinterprets all the wife's behaviour to make it fit his model; much of the play's theatrical power comes from the fact that we also misinterpret events and motives through much of its length. Odets's last play, *The Flowering Peach* (1954), is a retelling of the Noah story meant as an allegory of the modern conflict between faith and rationality, but defeated by stereotypical characterizations and weak jokes that are ineffective when not actually offensive. Despite the commercial success of *The Country Girl*, Odets remains a playwright – arguably *the* American playwright – of the 1930s.

Similarly Sidney Kingsley's one post-war success is not enough to move him out of his earlier place in history. *Detective Story* (1949) shares with Kingsley's earlier *Men in White* and *Dead End* an almost documentary background, this time of a police station, full of the routine comings and goings of officers and criminals. In the foreground is Detective McLeod, a man with an unequivocal sense of morality and a blind hatred of evildoers. When he discovers that his own wife has a tainted past, not even love can modify his absolute standards. He rejects her and, in torment, lets an escaping prisoner kill him. McLeod's drama implies a message about the need to balance morality with charity, but Kingsley does not press the generalization, focusing instead on the detective's psychological and spiritual pain.

Comedy

Although some of the important comic dramatists of previous decades – Kaufman, Behrman, Lindsay and Crouse – continued writing into the 1950s, none of them dominated the decade, nor did any newcomers. Broadway comedy at mid-century had evolved into a polished and somewhat homogenized commodity that could virtually be manufactured by formula, and an individual play's fortune was more likely to be a matter of how skilfully it resembled other successes than how original it was. A few subgenres, virtually blueprints for the construction of a comedy, account for most of the comedies, successful or not, of the fifteen-year period.

Not surprisingly, most comedies had an element of romance built into the plot, many relying on a comic staple that goes back at least as far as Shakespeare's *Much Ado About Nothing*, the couple who spend most of the play fighting until they finally realize what the audience has seen from the start, that they are in love. In Elmer Rice's *Dream Girl* (1945) the title character, escaping into various romantic fantasies, keeps fighting off the jocular cynic who eventually wins her. In Garson Kanin's *Born Yesterday* (1946) an uncouth businessman hires a reporter to give his dumb blonde girlfriend some class, and teacher and student spar through the play. Other romantic comedies let small plot complications loom large as temporary threats to a happy ending; the hero of Norman Krasna's *John Loves Mary* (1947) is a soldier who went through a marriage of form to help a friend's English girlfriend come to America and now must stall his eager fiancée until he can get a divorce. Still others built their suspense on whether the couple could avoid getting together: in George Axelrod's *The Seven Year Itch* (1952) and *Will Success Spoil Rock Hunter?* (1955) and Leslie Stevens's *The Marriage-Go-Round* (1958) the hero must resist the temptations of a desirable woman seemingly determined to seduce him.

Satire was fairly rare in Broadway comedy, and when it did appear it was usually directed at safe targets: government or military bureaucracy, stuffy businessmen, television, etc. Among the comedies that dared to suggest that the American military was not a thoroughly efficient and logically run operation, the strongest is the adaptation by Thomas Heggen and Joshua Logan of Heggen's book *Mr Roberts* (1948), about the crew of a Navy supply ship resisting the authority of their mad captain; it stands out also as one of the few comedies of the period to successfully mix low humour and sentimentality. In John Patrick's *The Teahouse of the August Moon* (1953, from the novel by Vern Sneider), soldiers trying to Americanize an Okinawan village find themselves going native instead; and in Ira Levin's *No Time for Sergeants* (1955, from the novel by Mac Hyman), a bumbling hillbilly is drafted into the Air Force, much to the regret of the Air Force.

The pattern of *No Time for Sergeants*, in which the innocent little person manages to wreak havoc on a mighty institution just by doing what comes naturally, worked just as well in other contexts. The dumb blonde in *Born Yesterday* ruins her sugar daddy's dishonest deals by applying the basic civics she learned from her tutor. *Life With Mother* (1948), Howard Lindsay and Russel Crouse's sequel to their 1930s hit, shows Mother once again manipulating Father simply by assuming she is in the right. In Samuel Spewack's *Two Blind Mice* (1949), two little old ladies run an obscure federal agency forgotten by the government and use the confusion and gullibility of the bureaucracy to keep from being shut down. In *The Solid Gold Cadillac* (1953), by Howard Teichmann and George S. Kaufman, another little old lady asks an innocent question at a stockholders' meeting and ends up running the company. Less innocently, the heroine of William Marchant's *The Desk Set* (1955) foils a corporate attempt to computerize her office by proving smarter than the computer.

Another recurring subgroup is made up of plays built around a magnetic and unorthodox character who deliberately and comically shakes up the conventional world. In Robert E. McEnroe's *The Silver Whistle* (1948) a vagabond philosopher challenges the demeaning routine of an old folks' home and rejuvenates its inhabitants. In S. N. Behrman's *Jane* (1952, from a Somerset Maugham short story), a plain-speaking country cousin plays the games of sophisticated society more skilfully than those born to it. In Gore Vidal's *Visit to a Small Planet* (1957) an uninhibited man from outer space causes trouble in Washington just for the fun of it. The hero of *The Pleasure of His Company* (1958), by Samuel Taylor and Cornelia Otis Skinner, is a charming socialite who returns from banishment on the eve of his daughter's wedding, determined to save her from a conventional life. The archetype of this pattern is *Auntie Mame* (1956), Jerome Lawrence and Robert E. Lee's adaptation of Patrick Dennis's novel about the life-loving and aggressively eccentric woman who drags her nephew through several lifetimes' worth of comic escapades with the rallying cry, 'Life is a banquet, and most poor sons-of-bitches are *starving* to death!'

With hindsight we can see that the Broadway theatre of the 1950s was the goal that the American drama had been moving towards for half a century. It was the full flowering of realistic contemporary domestic melodrama, a mode that proved itself to be the natural medium for the expression of the American experience in drama, by adapting to the very different styles and demands of Arthur Miller, Tennessee Williams and Eugene O'Neill. The important discovery of the previous generation, that realistic domestic stories could be used to reflect and comment on the world outside the living room, provided Miller with the dramatic tools for questioning the nature of the American Dream and the American system more acutely than any previous playwright; and such plays as *Death of a Salesman* and *The Crucible*, by showing how the injustices and failures of the system threatened the individual's sense of self, turned political and social theory into very human drama. Williams, starting from a sympathy for the outcasts and misfits of society, used domestic realism to present their experience with an intimacy that led audiences to recognize a shared humanity, and thus guided audiences to the recognition of their own feelings of inadequacy and failure, painful discoveries for which Williams then offered counsel and reassurance. O'Neill's career proved a microcosm of the history of the American drama as a whole, as he returned after years of experimentation to the domestic realism he had rejected in the 1920s and found that realistic plays with a domestic setting could carry the weight of his profound psychological and philosophical insights.

Even more striking than the divergence of these three leading playwrights, and the many second-level writers around them, is their convergence. Not only could the social critic, the poet and the philosopher all use variants of the same dramatic style, but they reached variants of the same dramatic statement. The Miller who argues in *Death of a Salesman* that failure in the world's terms is not necessarily a mark of personal inadequacy, the Williams who shows in *A Streetcar Named Desire* that everyone experiences life as painful and difficult, and the O'Neill who dramatizes in *Long Day's Journey into Night* his belief that our crimes against ourselves and others are not our fault, are ultimately offering the same gift of absolution and forgiveness.

The best plays of these three writers are the best American plays ever; and, along with their second best, and the best plays of secondary writers such as Inge and Hansberry, make up a body of work as yet unmatched in any other decade of the century. It might also be said that the American drama finally found its true subject in this period, in the realization that a significant portion of the audience found the task of day-to-day living an overpowering one, and was prepared to turn to the theatre for guidance and reassurance. The challenge of providing that almost religious service would continue to engage American dramatists for the rest of the century.

Chapter 5
1960–1975: The Post-Broadway Era

For most of the first half of the twentieth century the terms 'American theatre' and 'Broadway' were essentially synonymous, the commercial theatre centre of New York City being virtually the sole source of new American plays, and theatrical activity throughout the rest of the continent consisting of little more than revivals or touring productions of Broadway hits. As explained in the first chapter, this situation began to change around 1950, with the birth of a fringe or alternative theatre community within New York, and the establishment of the first resident professional theatres in other cities. Both Off-Broadway and the regional theatres began by staging classics and Broadway revivals, but both turned to new American plays in the early 1960s. Within a few years, as Off-Broadway and regional theatres became more established, the fringe moved outwards, creating an Off Off-Broadway of experimental companies in New York, and alternative theatres in cities around the country, all specializing in new work. Very quickly the lines dividing these theatrical worlds began to fade: by the 1970s a new young playwright might have his first play produced Off Off-Broadway, his second in Los Angeles or Chicago, and his third on Broadway; or he might make the same journey in reverse. Established Broadway dramatists were produced Off-Broadway or in regional theatres, while regional or Off Off-Broadway hits transferred to Broadway for commercial runs. The historical background of this chapter is the extraordinary expansion of the American theatre: as early as 1960 in New York, and by the late 1960s elsewhere in the country, new American plays were produced outside the realm of Broadway in unprecedented numbers, adding new dramatists and new points of view to the American dramatic repertory.

By its very nature, the expanded theatrical arena encouraged new experiments in form and content. In part because of the younger and more sophisticated audiences of the alternative theatres; in part a result of the discovery of challenging new European dramatists such as Samuel Beckett, Eugene Ionesco and Jean Genet, and a revival of interest in Bertolt Brecht; in part out of rebellion against the commercial theatre of

Arthur Miller and Tennessee Williams; and in part because the essentially non-commercial alternative theatres could more afford to take chances more than Broadway could – for these reasons and perhaps just because any art form that achieves its maturity invites challenge, some new dramatists of the 1960s rejected domestic realism and sought to expand the stylistic vocabulary of the American drama. The surprising result of this new experimentation would not become clear for another decade or so; at the time the 1960s resembled the 1920s as young playwrights, convinced that their new ideas or perspectives required new forms beyond the domestic realism of Miller and Williams, attempted to discover what else the drama could do.

This volume is not primarily a theatrical history, and generally has not discussed changes in acting or staging methods. Still, it is worth noting that a small but significant part of the alternative theatre movement, particularly in the late 1960s, was devoted to experiments in production and performance styles that had some effect on the literature of the theatre. Companies such as the Open Theatre and the Performance Group in New York, the Odyssey Theatre in Los Angeles, the Firehouse Theatre in Minneapolis, and the Living Theatre in self-imposed European exile shared an impulse to move away from author- and text-dominated drama to develop new forms. Along with other companies and directors, they treated a script as only the starting point for theatrical invention, relying extensively on improvisation and borrowing freely from such allied arts as mime, dance and religious ritual. Often their final product bore only a slight resemblance to the original text, while in some cases they dispensed with the playwright by composing the work communally, or reduced the author to the role of a scribe who recorded the final product of the group creation.

However anti-textual these approaches were, some playwrights found them amenable. Jean-Claude van Itallie and Megan Terry, for example, worked closely with the Open Theatre; and Sam Shepard and Lanford Wilson were strongly influenced by the company's style. In particular, all these writers found the company's rehearsal exercises, and the skills they developed in the performers, supportive of their own experiments in play construction and character development. In one such exercise, 'Transformation', actors playing a scene would be ordered suddenly to switch roles, jump to a different play, become animals, or otherwise make instant changes in the reality they were portraying. The purpose of the exercise was to stimulate the performers' imaginations and powers of concentration, as they created fully realized characterizations instantly. For the playwrights it provided a liberation from extended exposition and mood-setting, offered new and efficient means of characterization, and allowed for a cinematic structure of short scenes flowing or jumping into one another.

In *Interview*, one of the playlets of van Itallie's *America Hurrah* (1966), a number of disconnected scenes and events are tied together thematically through sudden juxtaposition, and the play is full of such stage directions as

> The remaining actors return to the stage to play various people on Fourteenth Street: ladies shopping, a panhandler, a man in a sandwich board, . . . and so on. . . . Each time they approach the audience, they do so as a different character. The actor will need to find the essential vocal and physical mannerisms of each character, play them, and drop them immediately to assume another character.

In a programme note van Itallie credits the original company with helping to shape his text through their rehearsal improvisations.

For *The Serpent* (1968), the Open Theatre explored improvisations on the theme of Creation for several months before van Itallie came in to observe and to combine the results of their work with material of his own in a final text, a series of scenes and interludes dramatizing or responding to the story of Adam and Eve. Enactments of the Temptation, the Fall and the murder of Abel alternate with symbolic stagings of the 'begat' genealogies of Genesis, the assassination of President John Kennedy, and the emptiness of twentieth-century life. The general style is non-realistic, incorporating mime, stylized and ritualistic movement, and distortions of time and space: the assassination is turned into a living newsreel film, which is re-run forward and backward, in slow motion and frame-by-frame, to capture the horrible fascination of the moment; and the genealogy is accompanied by the group miming of intercourse and birth. The governing idea of the play is that events precede the understanding of them, with humanity running a constant race to catch up to the implications of its own past.

Megan Terry's *Viet Rock* (1966) was also developed through improvisations which Terry moulded into a script. Earlier Terry had used Transformation as the structural basis for such plays as *Keep Tightly Closed in a Cool Dry Place* (1965), in which three prisoners act out their tensions by playing various roles, and *Calm Down Mother* (1965), in which three actresses portray the many aspects of woman. Lanford Wilson used Transformations in several early plays, to let a small cast fill the stage with characters, and to produce a cinematic flow of short scenes. Sam Shepard's characteristic juggling of reality levels and dramatic metaphors in such plays as *Action* and *The Tooth of Crime*, and his extensive use of magic, music and ritual also owe a great deal to the theatrical experiments he observed Off Off-Broadway. Though the fashion for improvisation, communal creation and de-emphasis of the text waned in the early 1970s, some of the techniques developed for acting and staging purposes have become staples of contemporary play construction.

Meanwhile, although the distinction between Broadway and the newer branches of the American theatre would begin to fade in the 1970s, it remained sharp in the 1960s; and it was still possible to identify individual playwrights as Broadway or non-Broadway, Edward Albee being one of the very few to move definitively from the alternative to the mainstream. On the other hand, no differences ever really developed among the kinds of plays written for the various alternative theatrical settings; and there was no clear distinction between, say, Chicago or Los Angeles playwrights and Off Off-Broadway playwrights, since in many cases they were the same people. In the absence of useful geographical divisions, it may be more profitable to classify the non-Broadway writers by genres and types of play; and here the distinction made in the previous chapter between the 'schools' of Tennessee Williams and Arthur Miller can still be of use. Many young writers of the 1960s followed the path of Williams and Inge, using the drama to explore and illuminate psychological states, particularly the burdens borne by those for whom day-to-day living was a difficult task. Others, in the very politicized national atmosphere of this decade, addressed social and political issues either directly or, in the tradition of Odets and Miller, by dramatizing their impact on the domestic lives of ordinary people; a significant offshoot of this group is made up of black playwrights dramatizing the black American experience to make moral and political statements.

Psychological and existential plays

One of the first original Off-Broadway hits was Jack Gelber's *The Connection* (1959), about heroin addicts idly waiting for their dealer. Gelber's fictional premise is a play-and-film-within-the-play in which actual addicts have been cast while a documentary film crew records their performance. As the 'actors' wander from or argue with the script, the supposed playwright, producer and film-makers are repeatedly drawn into the action, allowing Gelber to examine not only the nature of the heroin community but its connections to and impact on the 'straight' society. The addicts experience life as shapeless and disordered, something they must improvise their way through without a guide (as reflected by the presence on stage of jazz musicians who break into improvisations at seemingly random moments in the play), and from which heroin offers an escape. The straight characters sense the same frightening emptiness in existence, but frantically invent forms and labels to protect themselves from this realization. Thus the playwright and producer repeatedly insist that what we are watching is fiction, existing within a safely controllable frame, even though the addicts continually break through the frame; thus they constantly try to impose logic and meaning on the action, even when the addicts reject their definitions. Eventually the playwright confesses the inadequacy of his defences by joining the addicts and shooting up, allowing the play to wander shapelessly to its end.

The comic side of early Off-Broadway drama is best represented by Edward Albee's *The American Dream*, discussed later, and by Arthur Kopit's Dadaesque *Oh Dad, Poor Dad, Mamma's Hung You in the Closet and I'm Feelin' So Sad* (1962). Fabulously rich Madame Rosepettle travels the world, indulging herself in vengeance against everything she despises or resents, and dragging behind her – along with her husband's body, a talking fish and two giant venus fly-traps – her grown son Jonathan, whom she calls by whatever name comes first to mind, and whom she keeps in a state of arrested childhood to protect him from the world's corruptions. But Jonathan falls prey to the sexually voracious Rosalie, their bedroom encounter interrupted by the corpse of his father, which falls on them from its place in the closet. Jonathan panics and kills Rosalie, leading to the play's curtain line, when Madame Rosepettle returns:

> *Robinson!* I went to lie down and I stepped on your father! I lay
> down and I lay on some girl. Robinson, there is a woman on my
> bed and I do believe she's stopped breathing. What is more,
> you've buried her under your fabulous collection of stamps, coins,
> and books. I ask you, Robinson. As a mother to a son I ask you.
> *What is the meaning of this?*

From its title to its punchline, *Oh Dad* announces itself as a parody of absurd drama, or at least of the public's perception of plays that don't seem to follow traditional rules of dramaturgy. But behind the jokes is a view of life akin to that of Gelber and Tennessee Williams. Both Jonathan and his mother find the world frightening and hostile. Madame Rosepettle responds by attacking, making herself strong enough to shape her environment to her design, while Jonathan has no such resources and is left waving at a passing airplane in the futile attempt to make the universe acknowledge his existence.

A number of other Off-Broadway comedies touch on this basic existential insecurity, though generally without Kopit's bravura; in fact, their authors seem slightly disconcerted by their own insights, hurriedly retreating from them into easy and irrelevant jokes. In Bruce Jay Friedman's *Scuba Duba* (1967), a man whose wife has left him for a black lover finds himself adrift in a world of sexual freedom, psychiatric mumbo-jumbo and his own racist fantasies, and is unable to cope; in Friedman's *Steambath* (1970), death is a Turkish bath and God its Puerto Rican janitor, and the new arrival who tries to talk his way out comes to understand how empty and meaningless his life was. In Terrence McNally's *Next* (1969) a 48-year-old man called up by his draft board also tries to argue his way out and also gives up when he realizes how little he is fighting for. Elaine May's *Adaptation* (1969) presents life as a nightmarish TV game show that is impossible to win.

Paul Zindel's *The Effect of Gamma Rays on Man-in-the-Moon Marigolds* (Houston 1965) mixes black comedy with a domestic melodrama of survival in the face of despair. A neurotic and depressive mother and her disturbed and unhappy teenage daughters are barely able to cope with life's disappointments, but one girl's involvement in a school science project is her first tiny step towards self-acceptance and confidence. Zindel maintains a careful balance between light and dark: depending on whether one identifies more with daughter or mother, the ending is either optimistic or a futile fantasy of hope in the face of an overwhelmingly antagonistic universe.

The best of this genre is John Guare's *The House of Blue Leaves* (1971), mixing slapstick farce with pathos while demonstrating that coping with life is just beyond the ability of the ordinary person. A would-be songwriter saddled with an insane but sadly sweet wife plans an escape to Hollywood until a series of unlikely events somehow involving three nuns, a mad bomber, a deaf starlet and the Pope brings an end to his fantasies. In a mix of love, pity and desperation he kills his wife, and is left to face the world with no dreams at all. As with the other emptiness-of-life comedies, Guare seems vaguely embarrassed by his insight and his sympathy for his troubled characters, and hides his seriousness behind the mask of a *farceur*.

A similar mixture of tones characterizes Mart Crowley's *The Boys in the Band* (1968), one of the first commercially successful American plays to deal openly and sympathetically with homosexuality. A group of New York homosexuals, ranging from the very straight-acting Hank to the wildly effeminate Emory, gather at Michael's for a party, but the arrival of a (presumably) heterosexual friend of the host turns the revelry sour. Driven by his own insecurity, Michael is determined to prove that his friend is also gay, and forces everyone to play a self-exposing game that only ends in humiliating all of them, affirming the outsider's straightness, and revealing the depth of Michael's anguish. The image of homosexuals as self-hating neurotics may no longer be acceptable, but at the time Crowley's sympathetic presentation of them as feeling recognizable human pains, along with his salute to the courage with which they mask their insecurities with inventive humour, was a strong blow against current prejudices.

Edward Albee: the Off-Broadway plays

Of the many writers whose plays appeared in the first flourish of new Off-Broadway drama − from, say, 1958 to 1965 − some proved less interesting than novelty made them seem at first, some turned out to have only one play in them, some left the theatre for other callings. Among those who did produce one or more works of lasting interest, either for their inherent merits or as representatives of the time, only a very few were able or inclined to graduate from the fringe to the mainstream theatre. Most notable among these was Edward Albee, whose move to Broadway helped establish him as the dominant serious American dramatist of the 1960s.

Albee's first produced play, *The Zoo Story* (Berlin, 1959; New York, 1960), is essentially an extended monologue by a young New Yorker so alienated that any contact with another being, however one-sided or incomplete, is a relief:

> A person has to have some way of dealing with SOMETHING. If
> not with people . . . if not with people . . . SOMETHING.
> With a bed, with a cockroach, with a mirror . . . no, that's too
> hard, that's one of the last steps. With a cockroach, with a . . .
> with a . . . with a carpet, a roll of toilet paper . . . no, not
> that, either . . . that's a mirror, too; always check bleeding. You
> see how hard it is to find things? [. . .] with . . . some day,
> with people.   [All but bracketed ellipses Albee's]

He chooses a conventional man he meets in the park to be his first attempt at human contact, but is unable to move his listener sufficiently by merely telling his story. Desperate for reassurance of his existence and his ability to affect another, he starts a knife fight and impales himself on his opponent's blade, dying with thanks for this ultimate proof: 'I came unto you and you have comforted me.'

The effect of this eloquent but tragically alienated character on the American theatre was of the same sort, if not the same magnitude, as the effect of John Osborne's Jimmy Porter on the British theatre. This was a new voice which had not been heard before in the drama but which was instantly recognizable as authentic, representing the experience of a hitherto ignored or unnoticed portion of the population. On the basis of a one-act play Albee was hailed as an important new writer and looked to for new insights into contemporary American life, an assignment he soon implicitly accepted.

After two brief and minor works, *The Sandbox* (1960), in which a dying woman meets a friendly Angel of Death, and *Fam and Yam* (1960), about the disconcerting effect of a young playwright (evidently Albee) on an older one (evidently Inge), Albee turned to an analysis of American racism in *The Death of Bessie Smith* (Berlin, 1960; New York, 1961), based on the traditional story that blues singer Bessie Smith died because she was refused admission to a white hospital after an automobile crash. Albee's central character is the admitting nurse at the hospital to which Bessie's driver brought her after being turned away elsewhere, and the bulk of the play precedes the arrival of the body. In the Nurse's bitter interactions with other characters, Albee shows how the emptiness of her life has produced a frustration and resentment for which racism is merely a convenient outlet. The climax of the play is not Bessie's death, but the Nurse's explosion a moment before it:

> I am *sick*. I am sick of everything in this hot, stupid, fly-ridden *world*. I am sick of the disparity between things as they are, and as they should be! [. . .] I am sick of going to bed and I am sick of waking up. . . . I am tired . . . I am tired of the truth . . . and I am tired of lying about the truth . . . I am tired of my skin . . . I WANT OUT!
> [All but bracketed ellipses Albee's]

This kind of pain must be avenged on somebody, and blacks are as convenient a scapegoat as any.

The American Dream (1961) is a darkly comic piece that combines echoes of Ionesco's *Bald Soprano* (in such toying with language as the extended discussion about whether a hat is wheat or beige coloured, and in the cartoonishly exaggerated characters) with a chilling condemnation of American values. On one level, then, the play is in the tradition of Arthur Miller's *Death of a Salesman*, using a domestic story, however unrealistically presented, to comment on the society outside the living room. But, where Miller condemned the American Dream for being impossible to achieve, Albee caustically depicts its dehumanizing success. Presenting what is implicitly a typical American family – selfish and catty Mommy, emasculated and almost invisible Daddy and wise-cracking Grandma – Albee satirizes and condemns a hollowness in American values that is not the result of inadequacy but of deliberate choice. Themselves almost totally inhuman, having withdrawn into a self-absorption from which they stir themselves only with great difficulty – it takes Daddy several pages to gather up the energy and determination to answer the doorbell – Mommy and Daddy *want* to be empty. Their comical abuse of language is not the result of linguistic incompetence, but a concerted effort to free themselves from the human obligations implied by communication. Grandma explains what happened to the child they once adopted in terms that explicitly identify misused words with acts of inhumanity:

> GRANDMA   One night, it cried its heart out. . . . Then it
> turned out it only had eyes for its Daddy.
> MRS BARKER   For its Daddy! Why, any self-respecting woman
> would have gouged those eyes right out of its head.
> GRANDMA   Well, she did. . . . But *then*, it began to develop an
> interest in its you-know-what.
> MRS BARKER   In its you-know-what! Well! I hope they cut its
> hands off at the wrists!
> GRANDMA   Well, yes, they did that eventually. But first, they cut
> off its you-know-what. . . . And then, as it got bigger, they
> found out all sorts of things about it, like: it didn't have a head
> on its shoulders, it had no guts, it was spineless, its feet were
> made of clay . . . .

The Young Man who appears at the end of the play is the twin of
the unsatisfactory baby, who has been sympathetically affected by his
brother's mutilation:

> Once . . . it was as if all at once my heart . . . became numb
> . . . almost as though I . . . almost as though . . . just like
> that . . . it had been wrenched from my body . . . and from
> that time I have been unable to love. Once . . . I was asleep at
> the time . . . I awoke, and my eyes were burning. And since
> that time I have been unable to see anything, *anything*, with pity,
> with affection . . . with anything but . . . cool disinterest
> [. . .] there are more losses, but it all comes down to this: I no
> longer have the capacity to feel anything.
>   [All but bracketed ellipses Albee's]

Grandma recognizes immediately that this Young Man will satisfy
Mommy and Daddy as his brother never did, because he is the American Dream. Mommy and Daddy did not mutilate their child to punish
it, but to turn it into this; and the baby's only failure was in dying before
it achieved the perfection of its brother. Mid-century America is characterized by an emptiness of spirit that requires emptiness around it, says
Albee. A culture with waning values is not backsliding from what it
really wants to be; it is actively striving for its complete loss of values,
and will celebrate beautiful deadness as the achievement of all its desires.
The artistic and commercial success of *The American Dream* prompted
Albee's move to Broadway, where he became the predominant representative of the new generation of playwrights in the mainstream theatre;
his Broadway plays will be discussed later in this chapter.

Sam Shepard: the early plays

Sam Shepard and Lanford Wilson, the two writers who would be recognized in the late 1970s as the leading American playwrights of their generation, both began Off Off-Broadway in the mid-1960s. Shepard wrote more than twenty-five plays between 1964 and 1975; not all of them were artistically successful, but the freedom provided by the non-commercial fringe theatre allowed him an extended apprenticeship during which he honed his craft and discovered his strengths. Shepard's earliest plays are almost spontaneous outpourings, rarely edited or rewritten after the first burst of inspiration. Almost inevitably, they are uneven and inconsistent, with radical shifts of character, tone and even dramatic mode – e.g., realism changing suddenly to expressionism or allegory and back again. (Shepard may have been influenced by the actors' exercise called Transformation, then popular in experimental theatre groups; see the discussion of experimental theatre earlier in this chapter.) Some are so personal that they almost require biographical footnotes: for example, *The Holy Ghostly* (1969), in which a son rejects and kills his father, is filled with extraneous details relevant only if one knows that the characters are based on Shepard and his father. Others make use of a private symbolism whose exact meanings are never explained: cowboys, rock musicians and supernatural monsters wander through his plays, often completely out of context, while in other plays characters suddenly become eloquent on such arcane subjects as urban planning (*Fourteen Hundred Thousand*, 1966) or dermatology (*La Tourista*, 1967).

If, at their weakest, these early short plays are so personal in reference and symbolic vocabulary as to be almost unintelligible, at their best they have a seemingly improvised jazz-like rhythm that carries them theatrically, along with visual images of undeniable power, if unclear meaning, and self-contained speeches of instant characterization and convincing psychology. And if the plays are rarely linear and consistent enough to be said to make statements, some assumptions and observations about psychology, metaphysics and even morality do recur. One repeated theme is the need of the individual to create himself in a world that gives him no particular identity to start with. In such plays as *Cowboys* (1964), *Melodrama Play* (1967), *The Unseen Hand* (1969) and *Action* (London, 1974), characters repeatedly experiment with alternative identities and behaviours, trying to find something that will be 'real' to them. In *Action*, the purest but unfortunately least comprehensible presentation of this idea, four people at a Christmas dinner go through a series of seemingly unmotivated and unrelated behaviours, randomly dancing, telling stories, breaking furniture or busying themselves in incongruous domestic rituals. The play defies interpretation unless one takes special note of the fact that it opens with the line, 'I'm looking forward to my life', and closes with 'I had no idea what the world was. I had no idea how I got there or why or who did it. I had no references for this.' And midway through, one character says, '*quietly to himself*',

> Just because we're surrounded by four walls and a roof doesn't mean anything. It's still dangerous. The chances of something happening are just as great. Anything could happen. . . . You hunt for a way of being with everyone. A way of finding how to behave. You find out what's expected of you. You act yourself out.

Evidently what Shepard intends is a vision of humanity experimenting with identities and modes of conduct in an undirected and unguided attempt at self-definition, but in performance this theme is far less evident than it is on the page.

Slightly clearer are the plays in which invented identity is part of a process of escape, as characters for whom the world is too frightening or unpleasant try to create an alternative reality they can control. In *Chicago* (1965) Stu is unable to deal with the fact that his girl is leaving him, so he sits in a bathtub and pretends to be at the beach, describing his fantasy in elaborate detail to block out the reality. The characters in *Icarus's Mother* (1965) are oddly bothered by a passing airplane, and invent fictions about it, imagining its pilot and pretending to signal him. What they are doing, evidently, is mythologizing the source of their fear in order to domesticate and defang it. As happens in several Shepard plays, the fantasies actually displace reality; after they pretend the plane has crashed it really does, leaving them frightened by their power.

Something similar occurs in *Red Cross* (1966), in which three characters take turns exorcizing their fears through elaborately detailed fantasies until one of the stories seems to come true, causing the speaker's head to bleed – a visualization, perhaps, of the 1960s phrase, 'It blew his mind.' Indeed, one of the moral judgements Shepard implies in these early plays is that in some situations withdrawing from reality is dangerous or irresponsible. Among the very few characters towards whom he shows some anger or contempt are the father in *The Holy Ghostly* (1969), who lives entirely in a romanticized past; the revolutionary in *Shaved Splits* (1970), whose self-indulgent fantasies are equated with pornography; and the girl in *Cowboy Mouth* (1971), who uses her sexual power to try to force a man into her fantasy. On the other hand, Shepard makes no judgement of the condemned man in *Killer's Head* (1975), whose final thoughts in the electric chair are mercifully about the mundane pleasures of his ranch.

Another recurring element in the early plays is Shepard's conviction that the supernatural exists in the real world, in the form of magic, mysticism, religion or folklore; and that failure to acknowledge or respect its existence is perilous. The characters in *Icarus's Mother* and *Red Cross* are punished for toying with powers they hardly realized they had. In *Back Bog Beast Bait* (1971) a mythical two-headed swamp monster is proved to exist, and those who denied it are transformed into animals for their apostasy. The couple in *Cowboy Mouth* dream of a 'rock-and-roll savior,' and only interrupt their fantasy to torment a restaurant delivery man with the misfortune to be wearing a lobster costume. So they are unprepared when the lobsterman, in a symbolic evolutionary leap, cracks his shell and steps out as the rock superman; and, unappreciated, he is left to attempt suicide at the end. In *Mad Dog Blues* (1971) a rock singer and a drug-dealer somehow conjure up Marlene Dietrich, Mae West, Captain Kidd, Paul Bunyan and other characters from history and fable, who join them in a farcical search for a buried treasure that proves to be of less value than the comfort found in communion with these mythic figures.

In Shepard's eyes, alienation from the spiritual goes hand in hand with alienation from the past, and another of his implicit moral judgements, which would become very important in his later plays, is that a culture dissociated from its past is in serious danger. In *Fourteen Hundred Thousand* (Minneapolis, 1966) the emptiness of a couple building a bookcase for books they won't read is identified symbolically with the replacement of country villages by dehumanizing cities. In *La Tourista* (1967) an American in Mexico is repeatedly overpowered and displaced by figures from richer native traditions until he sees himself as Frankenstein's monster, an obscene parody of the human beings the others are. In *The Unseen Hand* (1969) a rebellious slave from a mechanized and regimented planet comes to earth for help in his revolution. He turns first to a trio of nineteenth-century Western gunslingers, whom he magically resurrects, but it is the unashamed patriotism of a high school cheerleader –

> I love Azusa! I love the foothills and the drive in movies and the
> bowling alleys and the football games and the drag races and the
> girls and the donut shop and the High School . . . and the
> YMCA and the Glee Club and the basketball games and the sock
> hop . . . and the county fair and peanut butter and jelly sand-
> wiches and the High School band and going steady . . . and my
> Mom, I love my Mom most of all.

– that proves to be the key to his liberation by reminding him of his own cultural heritage.

These themes come together in *Operation Sidewinder* (1970), whose rather convoluted and melodramatic plot involves black revolutionaries, renegade Indians, a sightseeing housewife and a giant rattlesnake which is actually an experimental Air Force computer designed to contact UFOs. The Indians recognize the snake as the foretold sign of the apocalypse, and use it in a ritual that enables them to escape from earth just as the Third World War is about to begin. In this play Shepard finds almost every facet of American society – the military and the counter-culture, black revolutionaries and the white middle class – inadequate because of materialism and alienation from spiritual values, while the Indians' religion has a stronger appreciation of truth than the white man's science.

Shepard remains challenging and difficult in his best play of this period, *The Tooth of Crime* (London, 1972), in which he freely mixes theatrical metaphors and even invents a new language for his characters. At the core of his plot is the cowboy movie staple of the aging gunslinger challenged by a younger sharp-shooter. But Shepard's Hoss and Crow are also an established rock star and the unknown musician threatening his popularity with a new style, a teen gang leader and a gypsy loner, a veteran automobile racer and a talented unknown, a Mafia godfather and a freelance hit-man, a champion boxer and his challenger, and pawns in an intergalactic game manipulated by unseen 'Keepers'. Shepard conjures up these images interchangeably and without explanation, in the faith that their accumulated evocative power will outweigh any confusion they cause.

In each of these definitions, Hoss is the aging establishment figure, strengthened by his knowledge of his art's history and traditions, but weakened by the cushioned inactivity of success. Crow is the self-sufficient loner, with no knowledge beyond his own limited experience and no sense of community with past or present, but with the totally amoral freedom to act that such alienation brings. At the play's centre is their inevitable duel, which takes the form of imposing alternative realities on each other. Crow attacks with images of failure designed to reduce Hoss to snivelling surrender:

> The dumb kid. The loser. The runt. The mutt. The shame kid
> . . . . Catch ya' with yer pants down. Whip ya' with a belt . .
> . . Hidin' dirty pictures. Hide 'em from his Ma. Hide 'em from
> his Pa . . . . Just gimme some head boy. Just get down on your
> knees. Gimme some blow boy . . . . Get down! Get down!

Hoss parries with images of Crow's lack of musical roots:

> Yeah, well I hear about all that kinda 'lectric machine gun music.
> . . . Fast fingers don't mean they hold magic. . . . You ain't
> come inside the South. You ain't even opened the door. The
> brass band contain yo' world a million times over. . . . You lost
> the barrelhouse, you lost the honkey-tonk.

The young man wins, his shallowness giving him the flexibility to de-throne the champ. He happily offers to teach Hoss how to be like him, wiping away all his personal history and cultural roots and programming him with a new, deliberately empty identity, but the new persona is too much of a leap for Hoss –

> Mean and tough and cool. Untouchable. A true killer. . . . No hesitation. Beyond pride or modesty. . . . Holds no grudge. No blame. No guilt. . . . Passed beyond tears. Beyond ache for the world. Pitiless. Indifferent and riding a state of grace. It ain't me! IT AIN'T ME! IT AIN'T ME! IT AIN'T ME!!

– and he both accepts defeat and reaffirms his own identity by killing himself with a stylishness Crow can only envy. There is a lot going on in *The Tooth of Crime*, but at its core is a view of the world similar to Tennessee Williams's in *A Streetcar Named Desire* or Edward Albee's in *Who's Afraid of Virginia Woolf?* Hoss, like Blanche DuBois, represents the world of the past, with its rich history and accomplishments, and with its weaknesses. Crow, like Stanley Kowalski, is the wave of the future, crude and shallow and strong. Like Williams, Shepard acknowledges sadly that Crow is destined to win out; unlike Williams, he has no grudging admiration for this raw power, sharing Hoss's view that dissoci-ation from one's humanity is the equivalent of death.

Later in the 1970s Shepard would gradually move away from this style of mixed metaphors and sudden shifts in dramatic mode towards something more closely approaching domestic realism; and it is tempting to read *Geography of a Horse Dreamer* (London, 1974) biographically. Cody, who can foretell the outcome of horse races in his dreams, is held prisoner by gamblers. He is in a slump, no longer able to predict win-ners, until he shifts to greyhound racing, where his dreams once again prove profitable. A number of allusions identify Cody as a symbol of the artist exploited by commerce, so the play may be Shepard's acknow-ledgement of his own need to find a new artistic course. The biographi-cal interpretation is not essential, however, since the play includes others of Shepard's familiar concerns. Several of his plays of the period (*Cowboy Mouth, The Tooth of Crime, Angel City, Suicide in B^b*) deal openly or symbolically with artists, labelling the artistic impulse as somehow magi-cal. Cody is also identified with the old West and his captors with the city, and he is saved at the end by his cowboy brothers, so the play reiterates Shepard's idealization of the American past and his rejection of a present that does not respect it.

Lanford Wilson: the early plays

Like Sam Shepard, Lanford Wilson reached his full powers as a dramatist in the 1970s and 1980s; and like Shepard he used the freedom of the Off Off-Broadway theatre of the 1960s to explore themes and styles on his way to finding his true voice. Wilson's earliest plays are essentially character studies, using monologues and minimal interactions to provide insight into his generally unhappy characters. In · So Long at the Fair (1963), an untalented would-be artist copes weakly with a seductive girl and the likelihood that he will settle into an ordinary life. In The Bottle Harp (1963), a boy from Nebraska visits his New York sister and decides to stay so they can comfort each other in their loneliness. Home Free! (1964) presents an incestuous brother and sister hiding from reality in a private world peopled by fantasy characters. In Ludlow Fair (1965) a woman talks at length about her melodramatic sexual past to her room-mate, who then speaks of her own empty and sexless life. A seemingly ordinary man in Days Ahead (1965) slowly betrays his madness in a monologue.

The best of this early group is The Madness of Lady Bright (1964). Leslie Bright, an aging homosexual, sits in his New York City room on a hot summer's night, trying to find some distraction from his isolation. In what is essentially an extended monologue, with an actor and actress playing minor choric roles, he ranges from despair to campy humour and back again, reminiscing about past lovers and fighting the awareness of his aging, loneliness and growing desperation ('Can't you see I'm going insane alone in my room, in my hot lonely room? Can't you see I'm losing my mind? I don't want to be the way I am.'). Finally he succumbs to all three in a wail of pain:

> I am young tonight. I will never be old. I have all my faculties tonight. . . . I am beautiful. I am happy! . . . I grow tired easily. *I grow brittle and I break. I'm losing my mind, you know. Everyone knows when they lose their mind. But I'm so lonely!* . . . Just take me home, please; take me home, please. Take me home now. Take me home. *Please take me home.* . . . TAKE ME HOME, SOME-ONE! TAKE ME HOME!

This play, like most of the others, is strikingly unjudgemental. With one or two notable exceptions, Wilson is generally charitable and sympathetic towards his unhappy characters.

While most of these plays are fairly conventional in form, except for their reliance on monologue, Wilson was also experimenting with non-linear and non-realistic modes. Like Sam Shepard, he was impressed by the then-popular rehearsal exercise in which actors practised jumping instantly from one scene and characterization into another; and in *Balm in Gilead* (1965), *This is the Rill Speaking* (1965), *The Rimers of Eldritch* (1966), and a few other short plays, he juxtaposes and overlaps very short scenes, sometimes out of chronological order, to create a musical or cinematic flow rather than a simple narrative. *Balm in Gilead* is set in an all-night New York coffee shop frequented by whores, drunks, addicts and other dregs of society. There is virtually no plot – one character is killed in a soured drug deal – but Wilson's purpose is to capture the milieu rather than to tell a story. His primary tool is overlapping dialogue, with several inconsequential things happening simultaneously:

> TIG   You know in Egypt they had salves and things that could cure anything.
> DARLENE   That's better than those other two creeps were acting. Did you see them?
> JOE   They're just high. They're okay usually.
> TIG   Cancer even! It says so.
> ERNESTO   Show me where, you can't.
> TIG   It does.
> DARLENE   Why are you waiting for ten o'clock?
> TIG   Hey, John; you ever read the Bible?
> JOE   I'm meeting someone.
> JOHN   What?
> TIG   The Bible, stupid.
> JOE   Like a business deal. A transaction.

If that's confusing to read, isolate three conversations, between Tig and Ernesto, Joe and Darlene, and Tig and John. This is actually a fairly simple passage, ignoring most of the more than thirty characters. Wilson also attempts stage equivalents of familiar cinematic effects: occasional freeze-frames and pin-spots focusing our attention on one character; the equivalent of background music and voice-overs by some choric figures; and a counterpart to the movies' use of slow motion in death scenes, as the moment of Joe's murder is repeated three times. *Balm in Gilead* is not really successful – there is too much going on at once, to too little apparent purpose, for the play to be clear in performance. Wilson would later learn how to moderate this chaos and use it to great effect in such plays as *The Hot l Baltimore* and *5th of July*.

In *The Rimers of Eldritch* Wilson employs a montage of short, disconnected scenes along with some of the cinematic effects of *Balm in Gilead* to capture the hypocrisies and ironies that hide behind the pastoral image of small-town America. The people of Eldritch guard their dark secrets with the same fervour with which they gossip about each others', coating everything with a frosty and hypocritical piety. At the centre of the plot is a murder trial; Nelly Windrod killed the town character, Skelly, when he seemed to be raping crippled teenager Eva Jackson. She is acquitted although we learn, and many in the town know, that Skelly was actually trying to save Eva from Robert Conklin, the real rapist. Wilson offers brief, almost subliminal excerpts of the trial early in the play, returning to it with longer excerpts, including the verdict, before finally showing the perjured testimony of Eva and Robert at the end. Meanwhile, in one subplot the happy news of an upcoming wedding is followed by revelations of the hidden violence and deceit that led to it, while another subplot shows a harmless romance destroyed by gossip; in each case the effect of witnessing events out of chronological order is to emphasize the corrosive power of the town's hypocrisy.

Almost uniquely in Wilson's canon, *The Rimers of Eldritch* is a play written in anger. Eldritch is so corrupted that it has no place for ordinary, healthy emotions and behaviour, or even for harmlessly illicit activity. What could have been an innocent romance between Eva and Robert can only find expression in rape. The fact that Cora sleeps with a younger man damns her as a whore and foils her attempts to expose the truth about Skelly's death. Skelly himself is a harmless old coot reduced to peeping in windows because the town has declared him untouchable. Nelly Windrod abuses her senile mother; Peck Johnson beats his daughter; Patsy Johnson forces an innocent boy to marry her. And through it all, the preacher and the townspeople mutter empty homilies. In his other plays Wilson generally paints an idealistic, pastoral picture of the inherent virtues of small-town America, but here he uncovers all its darkest secrets in an unrelenting assault.

Wilson also wrote more conventionally structured plays during this period. *Lemon Sky* (Buffalo 1970) is the young playwright's obligatory autobiographical play: a young man from the Midwest visits his estranged father and the father's new family in California. He embraces this household as the family he never had, but father and son slowly disappoint each other, and the son is left, some years later, still trying to pinpoint exactly what went wrong. Two essentially unoriginal plays are excellently crafted models of their genres. *The Great Nebula in Orion* (Manchester 1971) retells the old story of college room-mates meeting after some years and confessing, in the course of a drunken afternoon, how empty their lives are; Wilson enlivens the cliches and leavens the bathos by allowing each of the women a series of bitchy asides to the audience. And *Ikke, Ikke, Nye, Nye, Nye* (New Haven 1972) is a sex farce in which an obscene caller cannot handle actually being alone with a willing woman until he telephones her from another room, to the excitement and satisfaction of both.

Wilson's best play of this period is *The Hot l Baltimore* (1973). In a run-down residential hotel (symbolized by the title, a neon sign with one letter burned out), a group of society's discards and outcasts live in an unjudgemental and mutually supportive community. As happy and colourful prostitutes pass the time between clients, and residents tease and joke with each other, almost no actual plot takes place. The night clerk silently loves one of the whores; another whore leaves to move in with her pimp; a young man looks for record of his grandfather but gives up the search; and a couple of transients split up, one remaining to join the family. The play makes use of some of the techniques of *Balm in Gilead* – plotlessness, simultaneous and overlapping conversations, an imprecise and flexible time flow – in a much more controlled and successful way.

On one level *The Hot l Baltimore* is a very light-hearted version of Eugene O'Neill's *The Iceman Cometh*, leading us to re-evaluate what might at first seem an unattractive group of characters and to celebrate their fortune in having this nurturing and purifying environment. In this fantasy world the whores are delightfully bawdy, like April, or essentially innocent, like The Girl. Crotchety old Mr Morse is teased but protected; dotty old Millie is respected as a source of wisdom; Bill's chivalric adoration of The Girl is pure and beautiful; and ecstasy, in the form of a pizza eaten in the bathtub, is available with a phone call. As in *The Iceman Cometh*, this island of refuge from the judgements of the world is threatened, making our appreciation of it more intense. The scheduled demolition of the hotel is part of a larger pattern, a general rejection by American culture of the values and beauties of the past. The Girl mourns the decay of the hotel in the same spirit as her anger at the decline of the railroads, as a renunciation by a cold and practical present of a beautiful and gracious past. Wilson extends the symbolic meaning of the hotel to include all that is or was glorious about America, turning The Girl's attempt to guess Paul's home town into a kind of incantation ('Denver. Amarillo. Wichita. Oklahoma City. Salt Lake City. . . . ') and finally generalizing:

> GIRL Baltimore used to be one of the most beautiful cities in America.
> APRIL Every city in America used to be one of the most beautiful cities in America.

Everything that goes wrong in the play is caused by a short-sighted rejection of the past in the name of an empty future. Paul Granger's missing grandfather only went on the road because Paul's parents wouldn't let him live with them, and Paul foolishly gives up the search through hotel records because 'I got things to do'. Suzy leaves what she admits is her family for the false promises of a pimp. The transient Jackie justifies stealing from Mr Morse because she is young and he is old; and when her dream of a farm in Utah is shattered she abandons her brother as an unwanted burden and runs away. The others protect him from that realization and welcome him into their family, reminding us again at the end of the play how valuable this refuge from the uncaring modern world is. Earlier plays such as *Lady Bright* and *The Rill* had hinted at this reverence for the fading past, but *The Hot l Baltimore* marks the discovery of what would become a recurring theme of Wilson's mature work.

This sense of loss recurs in *The Mound Builders* (1975), set near an ancient Indian village in southern Illinois. Archaeologists trying to beat a dam project that will flood their dig come up against a local resident who anticipates the prosperity the dam will bring; when they use a conservation law against him, he wrecks the site, killing himself and one of the scientists, and rendering the research useless. Part of the play's point lies in the sad irony that these scientists searching for knowledge of the human past have so little awareness of the human character that they cannot see the effect their perfidy will have. But there is a broader and sadder message. Early in the play someone tries to explain why the Indians built mounds: 'Every society reaches the point where they build mounds. . . . For an accomplishment, honey, to bring me closer to Elysium; to leave something behind me for my grandchildren to marvel at. To say I'd built something!' That impulse to leave one's mark on the world, to defeat time and mortality, is universal. The Indians built mounds; Chad dreams of resort hotels; and the scientists fantasize about foundation grants and their pictures on the cover of *Newsweek*. And in every case the attempt at immortality is doomed. The mounds, the archaeological treasures, even the bodies of Chad and Dan are covered by the inexorably rising waters of the lake. Nothing is learned and nothing is saved. As the Aztec poet quoted by one character understood: 'This earth is only lent to us. / We shall have to leave our fine work. / We shall have to leave our beautiful flowers. / That is why I am sad as I sing for the sun.'

Political and social plays

The 1960s were a time of multiple political and social upheavals in America: the Civil Rights campaign (evolving later into the Black Pride and Black Power movements), the sexual revolution, the youth/drugs/rock-and-roll generation gap, the hippies, the anti-war movement, etc. Inevitably some of these subjects, and the social tensions they generated, found their way into the drama of the period. Since alternative theatre writers and audiences were, on the whole, young and liberal, their plays are generally critical of the status quo and sympathetic to the forces of change. Those dramatists who do take what might loosely be called the conservative position are often also critical of the present, calling for a return to the values or modes of the past. A very few are able to avoid taking sides, instead exploring with objectivity or sympathy the effects of the social and political changes on their characters.

To some extent, the distinction between these playwrights, who follow in the tradition of Odets and Miller by addressing social issues through domestic drama, and those already discussed, who focused on their characters' psychological and spiritual crises, is an imprecise one. Some of the plays discussed elsewhere in this chapter – for example, Albee's *The American Dream* and *Who's Afraid of Virginia Woolf?* and Wilson's *The Rimers of Eldritch* and *The Hot l Baltimore* – have a social/political content, openly or implicitly indicting contemporary American culture as the source of the insecurity and pain that is their focus. Many plays of the period, however, are primarily about the larger issues, using the individual stories as representative or metaphor. In Israel Horovitz's *Line* (1967), for example, a group of people use intimidation, trickery and sex as they jockey for position in a waiting line, clearly a symbol of the struggle for success in a capitalist society that only rewards the ruthless. Horovitz's *The Indian Wants the Bronx* (1968) and *The Primary English Class* (1975) address the racism just below the surface of American culture: an East Indian lost in New York City is tormented and brutalized by a pair of young hooligans, for no other reason than that he is an outsider and thus fair game; and a teacher's inability to communicate with her students leads her to a violent outburst that betrays the xenophobic core beneath the very thin veneer of liberalism.

Terrence McNally's *Where Has Tommy Flowers Gone?* (New Haven 1971) is a character study of a child of the 1950s adrift in the 1960s, with no connection to anything beyond the icons of television and popular culture, and nothing to moderate his demand for instant gratification of every passing impulse. Like the characters in Albee's *American Dream* and Horovitz's *Line* he has not fallen away from the highest values of American culture but completely fulfilled them, and the play eventually recoils in horror at the world that created this amoral monster. In Jason Miller's *That Championship Season* (1972), the many mutual betrayals of a group of supposed friends are shown to be the direct result of the lesson they learned from their basketball coach twenty years earlier, to play dirty and win at any cost; athletic achievement reflects the American success ethic, and the men's moral and spiritual decay is an inevitable product of blind adherence to it.

Taking an approach closer to that of Albee's *Virginia Woolf*, Robert Patrick's *Kennedy's Children* (1973) portrays the emotionally wounded victims of a corrupted culture. In a series of parallel monologues, five characters who were shaped by the idealistic dreams of the early 1960s – a Vietnam veteran, a political activist, etc. – show how they have been maimed by the failure of the rest of the decade to live up to its promises. Each speaker's frame of reference is limited, even trivial, but each one's suffering is real; and by the play's end the sheer quantity of pain on stage is overwhelming. This is the true legacy of the 1960s, the play says: not the dreams or the hopes, but the disappointments, and a generation broken in mind and spirit. Jean-Claude van Itallie's *America Hurrah*, an evening of three one-act plays, also condemns the spiritual emptiness of the 1960s. In *Interview*, the demeaning rituals of a job interview lead to more nightmarish examples of American impersonality and disregard for the individual, while *TV* depicts the artificial emotions of television drama as more meaningful than a desiccated reality. In *Motel* van Itallie relates spiritual bankruptcy to aesthetic barbarianism, concluding that a culture without taste will create humans without humanity, and dramatizes that dehumanization by peopling the stage with actors encased in larger-than-life papier-mâché dolls; while a motel owner proudly describes the vulgar furnishings of a characterless room, her guests wantonly vandalize and destroy it.

In *Indians* (London 1968; Washington 1969), Arthur Kopit analyses the American psyche through the symbolic figure of 'Buffalo Bill' Cody, an actual frontier hero who later became a showman. Kopit shows Bill discovering to his horror that his Wild West Show actually contributes to the destruction of his Indian friends, by giving white America a distorted view of the cowboys-and-Indians world which then becomes the basis for national policy. Like some plays already mentioned, *Indians* is implicitly about Vietnam, showing how American myth-making, particularly the need to see ourselves as the 'good guys,' inevitably distorts our perception of other cultures; and offering in Bill Cody, the essentially good man who does the wrong thing for the right reasons and then does not have the moral courage or the ability to reverse himself, a not wholly unsympathetic portrait of President Lyndon Johnson.

The Vietnam War, on the battlefield and in its effects back home, was the single most significant social and political fact in American life in the late 1960s and early 1970s, and some dramatists did not disguise their criticisms of it in metaphor. Megan Terry's *Viet Rock* is a phantasmagorical picture of the war's atrocities, with scenes of basic training and battle combined with attacks on politicians who ignore all criticism in a blindly patriotic fervour. Barbara Garson's *MacBird* (1967) is a cheerfully libellous Shakespearean pastiche casting President Lyndon Johnson as Macbeth, who engineers the assassination of 'John Ken O'Dunc' and carries on the war to protect his power against the slain king's brother Robert. Kenneth H. Brown's *The Brig* (1963) is more broadly anti-military, overpowering the audience with a high-volume depiction of the incessant humiliation and brutality of military discipline.

David Rabe

The one American dramatist who most successfully captured the story of the Vietnam War is David Rabe; in three independent but complementary plays – *The Basic Training of Pavlo Hummel* (1971), *Sticks and Bones* (1971) and *Streamers* (New Haven 1976) – Rabe addresses horrors not normally thought of as part of a war story and thus illuminates the central fact of this particular war: that not all the casualties and atrocities were on the battlefield. Like Brecht's *Man is Man*, which it resembles in outline, *Pavlo Hummel* shows the transformation of a hapless young man into an ideal soldier. But there are two bitter differences: the intended end product is not a fighting machine, as in Brecht, but a dead body; and Pavlo does not passively allow himself to be changed, but races eagerly to his destruction.

In Rabe's eyes, the Army preys on weak, insecure adolescents and turns them into well-trained cannon fodder by offering the sense of identity, home and manhood the young men lack:

> NOW YOU ARE TRAINEES, ALL YOU PEOPLE, AND YOU LISTEN
> UP. I ASK YOU WHAT IS YOUR FIRST NAMES, YOU TELL ME
> 'TRAINEES'! . . . AND YOU LIVE IN THE ARMY OF THE UNITED
> STATES OF AMERICA. . . . WITH BALLS BETWEEN YOU LEGS! YOU
> HAVE BALLS! NO SLITS!

The Army thus promises everything an American boy is conditioned to want and to fear he does not have, and it lies. Pavlo is turned into a soldier but still cannot find friends or impress girls or avoid being wounded in battle. Vietnam is not a place of manhood, but a place where you haggle with whores over pennies and where the wounded beg to die. Pavlo is killed in a drunken fight, no closer to the secret of manhood than he was as a civilian, and with just the barest awareness that this irrelevant and pointless death, not heroic triumph, was what he was trained for. Something unhealthy in the American psyche confuses personal worth with victory in battle, Rabe charges, and something evil in the American system exploits that confusion to feed its cannon and fill its body bags.

Rabe brings the war home in *Sticks and Bones*, in the form of a blinded and guilt-ridden veteran who alternately mopes about, tries unsuccessfully to communicate the horrors he witnessed, and lashes out in rage at the offensive ignorance of those who were not there. But the play is not so much about him as about his family; and by naming his characters Ozzie, Harriet, David and Ricky, after the all-American family of a 1950s television series, Rabe makes them symbolic of the whole nation. David's family cannot or will not accept the horrible truths he brings home from the war – Harriet reacts to his pain by offering him fudge, and Rick works very hard at acting as if nothing is wrong – and the depth of their need to deny is the play's real subject. The presence in their home of a son who is imperfect, who has killed and still seems capable of killing, who has loved a woman of an alien race, calls into question every assumption by which they define their family and themselves. Rather than answer or even acknowledge those questions they reject the questioner; the play ends with the family killing David. His attempt to share his experience with those at home, his very presence as a reminder of the war, threatens an entire way of life, and to defend that way of life the family, and the nation, will do things that debase everything they are meant to represent.

Streamers, the strongest of the three plays, is written in sympathy rather than anger. Without pointing an accusing finger anywhere, Rabe depicts the horror of a war that seems to have become a self-perpetuating natural force. In an army camp in America several young soldiers await reassignment, possibly to Vietnam. Each has his own small neuroses. Roger, an educated black man, seems lost between his roots and his class. Ritchie a homosexual, keeps the others off balance by joking so much about his gayness that they do not know whether to believe him. Billy, who may be a repressed homosexual, is holding some emotional tension under tenuous check. Carlyle, an uneducated black, treats everything with the suspicion that street life has taught him. The play's title is macabre military slang for a snarled parachute hanging uselessly above a man plunging to his death, as described by an older soldier:

> This guy with his chute goin' straight up above him in a streamer . . . . He looks right at me. Then he looks up in the air at the chute, then down at the ground . . . . He started going like this. (*Cokes reaches desperately upward with both hands and begins to claw at the sky while his legs pump up and down.*) Like he was gonna climb right up the air.

That, of course, is the central image of the play. Each of the young men feels himself being pulled towards death by forces out of his control, and each is slowly going mad under the pressure. Roger has had one breakdown already, and spends the play trying to make himself invisible through perfect soldiering and practised ordinariness. Billy denies and represses, insisting that Ritchie cannot be gay, and compulsively washing and polishing everything in sight. Ritchie's fear and loneliness force him to be ever more overt in his appeals for sexual comfort. And Carlyle, exhausted by trying to apply street logic to an inherently illogical situation, is driven to angry rebellion. Finally there is violence – barely motivated and almost accidental – and death – random and irrelevant

– leaving the survivors with more confusion and tension to be unable to cope with. The play barely mentions Vietnam, but the war defines the lives of these characters, just as it did for every American male of draft age for more than a decade; the question was never *whether* it would affect their lives disastrously, but only *when*.

Black dramatists

The Civil Rights movement of the early 1960s, and the Black Pride and Black Power movements that evolved from it later in the decade, changed the lives of black Americans more than anything since the Civil War. The heightened self-awareness that came from these changes demanded artistic expression; and Off-Broadway and its equivalents around the country, with their educated and liberal audiences, proved more receptive to black playwrights than the commercial theatre had ever been. Some writers used the opportunity to vent their anger at racism, others to express hope for the future, still others to examine the nature of the black experience and its effect on individual black Americans.

In LeRoi Jones's *Dutchman* (1964) a middle-class black man is accosted by a seductive white woman who taunts him for denying his blackness until he reacts in rage, at which point she calmly murders him and prepares to begin again with another victim. Jones's despairing view of the possibilities of racial harmony is voiced in Clay's angry outburst, which stresses the fact that hatred of whites is *the* single defining element in black psychology: 'You don't know anything except what's there for you to see. An act. Lies. Device. Not the pure heart, the pumping black heart. You don't ever know that. And I sit here, in this buttoned-up suit, to keep myself from cutting all your throats. I mean wantonly.' The only thing that keeps blacks from wanton murder, he says, is their fear of that unlimited passion within them; they have not learned the white trick of hating calmly, and so the whole race consciously chooses to make itself neurotic by repressing and displacing its anger. This insight makes Lula's earlier taunting newly frightening; we see now that it was calculated to produce the anger that would justify her killing him. Murderous racial hatred is the defining emotion in whites as well as blacks, says Jones, the only difference being that whites have found ways of rationalizing and living with their genocidal impulses that blacks have not yet mastered. There can be no hope for racial harmony in these circumstances, only the prospect of war when blacks learn to kill as calmly as Lula.

Jones's *The Toilet* (1964) offers an alternative basis for the same conclusion, as a teenage gang leader takes part in an attack on an outsider whom he secretly loves. Race is barely mentioned in the play, though the victim is cast as white and the gang members as black, but this is clearly an allegory of race relations. There may be isolated individuals in any group who are capable of amity, Jones admits, but the social roles imposed on them will force them to act as enemies, whatever they feel. *The Slave* (1964) is set in the racial civil war of the near future, as the leader of the black forces explains to his white ex-wife that it hardly matters whether he is right or whether he particularly believes in his cause. The war, the destruction and the waste are foregone conclusions, and Jones can offer only resignation without even the comfort of outrage or anger.

The Slave was one of Jones's last plays for white audiences. Within a few years he left the theatre altogether, taking on the Muslim name of Amiri Baraka and devoting himself to social and political action. The few plays he wrote as Baraka were deliberately simplistic and one-sided propaganda works intended for theatrically unsophisticated black audiences. Like similar agitprop plays by other black writers of the period, they have little literary merit as measured by traditional standards – plots are mechanical and arbitrary, characters one-dimensional, and messages spelled out in overly simple and undramatic ways – but of course such judgements are unfair, since these playwrights were not trying to write traditionally literary drama. (Baraka himself follows the convention of retaining the name Jones on the earlier plays.)

.Not all black dramatists followed the lead of Amiri Baraka. Douglas Turner Ward was one of the very few to find humour in the black experience; in his double bill of *Happy Ending* and *Day of Absence* (1965) he reminds both black and white audiences that the current condition of blacks is not without its power and rewards. In *Happy Ending* a young black man is offended by what he takes to be his family's subservient grief at their white employers' divorce, only to learn they are really mourning the end of their systematic embezzling. In *Day of Absence* black performers in whiteface burlesque the confusion and dismay of a town of white southerners on the day all the blacks magically disappear and there is no one to cook the food, care for the children and do all the other menial jobs without which society collapses. Charlie L. Russell's *Five on the Black Hand Side* (1969) offers another essentially comic view by translating the civil rights movement into domestic terms, a downtrodden wife using sit-ins and picket lines to win concessions from her husband and finally to liberate his spirit.

But the same observation, that the rapid social changes of the 1960s were forcing even the most conservative and unpolitical blacks to redefine themselves, had serious and even frightening implications to other black writers. Charles Gordone's *No Place to be Somebody* (1969), about small-time criminals trying to make it big; *Ceremonies in Dark Old Men*

(1969) by Lonnie Elder III, about a family caught up in crime and revolution; and Joseph A. Walker's *The River Niger* (1972), about former gang members facing adulthood, all present black characters who find neither their old ways, the model of younger revolutionaries nor the imitation of white behaviour fully satisfactory. In each play at least one character dies while others are left to wrestle with the challenge of finding new identities, and the only reassurance any of the plays can offer is one that faintly echoes Clifford Odets in *Awake and Sing!*: the previous condition of blacks in America was a living death, so that any change will be for the better.

The black playwright who proved most successful in exploring and dramatizing the effects of the 1960s and 1970s on black Americans was Ed Bullins. Although he wrote a few 'revolutionary' plays in the manner of Amiri Baraka, his more characteristic plays focus on domestic life within the black community rather than on black–white relationships. Bullins is fascinated and disturbed by the very thin line that separates ordinary life in black America from sudden violence, despair or madness. Structurally, his plays are misleadingly loose and seemingly aimless in construction, wandering plotlessly through images of life in the urban ghetto until an abrupt and unexpected moment of violence not only accelerates the pace, but also forces a reappraisal of the earlier non-action as carrying in it the seeds of the sudden change.

In *Clara's Ole Man* (San Francisco 1965), a young black man spends an afternoon idly drinking and chatting with a girl he has just met and her mannish friend. Only when he repeats an overheard reference to 'Clara's ole man' does he realize that the women are lesbians; he is punished for his ignorance by being beaten up. In *Goin' a Buffalo* (1968), small-time criminals are sidetracked from their plans to leave town and start fresh by an unexpected quarrel and murder, and an outsider takes advantage of the confusion to steal both their money and their women. *In the Wine Time* (1968) is almost actionless through most of its length, merely depicting a poor black family in its daily routine of lounging, drinking, arguing and making up. When the boy of the family is attacked by a gang and his uncle is forced to kill to save him, we realize that ordinary ghetto life has crossed the line into dangerous anarchy and that these characters' lives had been moving inexorably towards some catastrophe from the start. A sequel, *In New England Winter* (1971), presents the uncle after he has left prison and joined with others planning a robbery. The personalities prove too different for the project to work, one man's obsessive order and meticulousness clashing with another's impulsiveness, and the play ends with a sudden fight and murder.

A recurring observation in Bullins's plays is that black Americans are often trapped more by the limits of their personalities and imaginations than by the external forces of racism. A central metaphor in *Goin' a Buffalo* is chess, a game that the gang members play in their idle moments; ironically they are unable in real life to plan several moves ahead or adjust their strategy when obstacles appear in their way. In *In the Wine Time* Cliff Dawson floats aimlessly through what he assumes is a life without possibilities, and as a result his life is altered by a decision he must make at the spur of the moment. Yet, as Cliff's relatively calm acceptance of his wife's infidelity in the sequel shows, this same limited vision can ironically save Bullins's characters from the despair that would come if they could fully appreciate the extent of their failures or losses. *The Taking of Miss Janie* (1975) explores this paradox by following a group of black and white characters from the late 1950s through the early 1970s, showing how they both fail to live up to their youthful dreams and adjust to that failure through compromise and rationalization. The central irony of the play is that none of the young people can imagine that their lives and identities will ever change, while from the perspective of the future none can see anything unpredictable in what actually happened. The same limitation that keeps them from imagining alternative futures saves them from the pain of imagining alternative pasts. On its surface the play seems to lament the lost idealism of the sixties, but it actually accepts the inevitable compromises, recognizing that they are more apparent to the observer than to the participants.

Broadway

Virtually all of the pre-war playwrights still writing in the 1960s ended their Broadway careers with anticlimactic disappointments: Sidney Kingsley's *Night Life* (1962), Lillian Hellman's *My Mother, My Father and Me* (1963), S. N. Behrman's *But For Whom Charlie* (1964). Even the younger writers of the 1950s had trouble in the new decade. A string of critical and commercial failures in the 1960s contributed to William Inge's suicide in 1973. A similar succession of failures led Paddy Chayevsky to desert the theatre for a more successful career in film. Lorraine Hansberry's only other completed play, *The Sign in Sidney Brustein's Window* (1964), closed three days after her death in 1965; and Robert Anderson's only hit was the relatively trivial *You Know I Can't Hear You When the Water's Running* (1967), four comic sketches with light hints of pathos. Even Tennessee Williams had an uninterrupted string of flops after 1962. Meanwhile, with more and more of the creative energy of the American theatre located beyond Broadway, only a very few new writers found their artistic home there; and the two most important new Broadway playwrights of the 1960s could hardly have been less alike. Edward Albee, the first dramatist from the alternative theatre to move successfully to Broadway, wrote complacency-challenging dramas about the emptiness of American culture and the uncertainties of human existence. Neil Simon, a former television joke writer, proved a master craftsman of light, unthreatening and highly entertaining comedies.

Edward Albee: the Broadway plays

Who's Afraid of Virginia Woolf? (1962), Albee's first Broadway production, is without question his best play, ranking just behind the very best of O'Neill, Williams and Miller in the American repertoire. It is the picture of a seemingly hellish marriage whose positive and supportive aspects we only gradually appreciate, as we understand how frightened and alienated the characters are, in an America similar to that of *The Zoo Story* and *The American Dream*. George and Martha (the names suggest an archetypal American couple) subject each other and another couple to a long liquor-filled night of humiliation and exposure, culminating in the revelation that their adult son is a fantasy they have maintained for twenty-one years to comfort themselves in the face of life's disappointments. Chastened by this exposure to a desperation far beyond their shallow experience, the other couple leave George and Martha to face the future without one of their most depended-on emotional crutches. The play has nothing to do with Virginia Woolf; its title, a parody of a song from a Disney cartoon, 'Who's Afraid of the Big Bad Wolf', begins as a characterizing device, identifying George and Martha as intellectual and verbal games-players, and later comes to symbolize the unnamed fears and insecurities of modern life.

Albee has three purposes in the play: to show that George and Martha's experience of life, like Jerry's in *The Zoo Story*, is dominated by an insecurity and alienation that make the task of coping with day-to-day disappointments overwhelming; to argue that their commitment to survival, even if the only means is degrading or abhorrent behaviour, is heroic; and, slightly peripherally, to expose the cause of this painful experience as a dehumanizing force in the American culture, similar to that revealed in *The American Dream*, and identified in this play with the second couple, Nick and Honey. The emphasis on depicting and celebrating characters who find daily life overwhelming puts Albee squarely in the tradition of Tennessee Williams, a debt Albee acknowledges in the play with brief allusions to *A Streetcar Named Desire*.

Throughout the play George and Martha let slip veiled or open admissions of their sense of weakness and failure, as in Martha's third-act confession of her need for him:

George who is good to me, and whom I revile; . . . who can
hold me, at night, so that it's warm, and whom I will bite so
there's blood; who keeps learning the games we play as quickly as
I can change the rules; who can make me happy and I do not
wish to be happy, and yes I do wish to be happy . . . . who has
made the hideous, the hurting, the insulting mistake of loving me
. . . who tolerates, which is intolerable; who is kind, which is
cruel; who understands, which is beyond comprehension.

Torn between fear of their inadequacy and refusal to avoid the struggle
for existence, they live lives defined by pain. George offers as a self-
description the declension 'Good, better, best, bested', and Martha
admits to the portrait of her father, 'I cry all the time too, Daddy. I cry
alllll the time; but deep inside, so no one can see me.'

Like many of Williams's characters and like Jerry in *The Zoo Story*,
George and Martha seem less bizarre when we interpret their behaviour
as reactions to a world that offers them no support. Their games are
attempts to cope with the pain, either as distraction – Martha calls them
'the refuge we take when the unreality of the world weighs too heavy
on our tiny heads' – or as a way of keeping themselves in shape for the
battle: George assures Nick, 'Martha and I are merely . . . exercising
. . . that's all . . . we're merely walking what's left of our wits.'
[Ellipses Albee's] A particularly skilful blow is likely to be met by con-
gratulations or mutual celebration, and they refuse to let each other relax
and coast: when George scores points off the completely outmatched
Nick and Honey, Martha's reaction is contempt for his 'pigmy hunting;'
and when George decides on the final battle over destroying the fantasy
son, he insists that Martha be at full strength to fight him.

If George and Martha must use every tool at their disposal to help
them fight the dehumanizing forces pitted against them, then the loss of
any tool must seriously endanger their struggle. The imaginary son com-
pensated for their sterility, helped to hold them together and gave them
a constant in their lives, but he has become a weapon they use against
each other, and therefore must be sacrificed. After the initial trauma
Martha accepts this judgement, and the play ends with them facing an
uncertain future with a bravery that consists of admitting their fear but
not turning back.

Albee forces us to recognize this immersion in life as heroic, particularly in contrast to the bland, evasive and ultimately cowardly Nick and
Honey, who consciously avoid the challenges of living. Nick keeps what
emotions he has under control, tries not to get involved in unpleasantness, and admits there is no passion in his marriage or in his pursuit of
Martha. Honey drinks until she passes out, decides not to remember
unpleasant things, and takes secret precautions to avoid having children.
They do not even have real identities: 'Nick' is the name used in the

stage directions, but it is never spoken in the play; and 'Honey' is merely his perfunctory endearment for her. Such lifelessness is not merely
evasion of responsibility; Albee sees it as a cause of the central couple's
pain. The main reason for setting the play in a university is the ease with
which the two men can be characterized by their specialities. In Act
One George defines the contrast in an extended mockery of Nick's
genetic research:

> It's very simple, Martha, this young man is working on a system
> whereby chromosomes can be altered.[. . .] We will have a
> race of men . . . test-tube-bred . . . incubator- born . . .
> superb and sublime.[. . .] But! Everyone will tend to be rather
> the same.[. . .] I suspect we will not have much music, much
> painting.[. . .] There will be a certain . . . loss of liberty.
> [. . .] Cultures and races will eventually vanish . . . the ants
> will take over the world.   [Unbracketed ellipses Albee's]

George's academic discipline symbolizes his commitment to life: 'And I,
naturally, am rather opposed to this. History, which is my field [. . .]
will lose its glorious variety and unpredictability.[. . .] the surprise,
the multiplexity, the sea-changing rhythm of . . . history, will be
eliminated. There will be order and constancy . . . and I am unalter-
ably opposed to it.' The force that causes life to be painful and difficult
for those committed to living it is the irresponsibility of those who attempt to find security by rejecting their humanity.

One important quality of Who's Afraid of Virginia Woolf? to which this
analysis has not done justice is its passion. George and Martha experience
and express extreme and uncensored emotions, and the play celebrates
those passions, good and bad, as part of the couple's commitment to the
challenge of living. Oddly, that passionate quality, which had also driven
The Zoo Story, begins to disappear in Albee's later plays, displaced by a
dry intellectuality that dooms some to failure and deprives even the most
successful of the theatrical power of the early plays. Tiny Alice (1964) is
the story of a religious man faced with what he has wanted all his life,
the opportunity to sacrifice himself to an impossibility that can only be
accepted through faith. But Albee presents this adventure as a series of
gratuitously mystifying puzzles and paradoxes, more an intellectual construct than a living drama. The mystery Julian is asked to worship is not
God but Alice, an essence who may be nothing more than a mouse in a
dollhouse, and who is represented by a woman named Alice who seduces him and then orders his death. The play ends with Julian's long
dying monologue, in which he either rambles incoherently or accepts
Alice as his God:

> How long wilt thou forget me, O Lord? Forever? How long wilt

thou hide thy face from me? [. . .] Oh, Alice, why hast *thou*
forsaken me? [. . .] Alice? . . . God? SOMEONE? Come to
Julian as he . . . ebbs. [. . .] Is that the humor? THE AB-
STRACT? . . . REAL? THE REST? . . . FALSE? It is what I have
wanted, have insisted on. Have nagged . . . for. [. . .] COME,
BRIDE! COME, GOD! [. . .] I accept thee, Alice, for thou art
come to me. God, Alice . . . I accept thy will.

> [Unbracketed ellipses Albee's]

What makes *Tiny Alice* difficult is Albee's conviction that what cannot
be understood through any means other than faith must be kept outside
the audience's understanding; he simply fails to make the story clear
much of the time. Meanwhile, the general air of mystification is maintained through secondary puzzles and red herrings, and through the
general refusal of any of the secondary characters to act in recognizably
human ways. Given its ambitions, it may be remarkable that *Tiny Alice* is
as nearly comprehensible as it is, but it certainly tests the outer limits of
a theatre audience's ability to grasp abstract ideas.

A Delicate Balance (1966) returns to some of the same concerns as
Who's Afraid of Virginia Woolf?, though in a considerably subdued manner. When friends unexpectedly demand refuge with Tobias and Agnes,
their presence disrupts the tenuous stability of the household, inspiring
alcoholic sister Claire to ever more outrageous conduct, and driving
daughter Julia to territorial hysteria. But it is their departure, when they
decide they are imposing, that finally panics Tobias, who cannot bear the
discovery that even the closest friendship has limits.

The title thus refers to the fragility of both social constructs and individual psychology. Agnes opens the play by entertaining herself with the
prospect of going mad, but Julia's leap from childish petulance to the
murderous defence of her turf, and Claire's from mildly anti-social to
aggressively bizarre behaviour, show how thin the line of sanity is. Even
more disturbingly, the carefully maintained balance of peace and civility
in the household, the preservation of the illusion of normality, is shown
to be very easily disrupted. The first half of *A Delicate Balance* has some
parallels to the opening of Eugene O'Neill's *The Iceman Cometh*, in that
an apparently diseased social milieu becomes somewhat more attractive
in retrospect when a disrupting influence produces something much
worse.

But more central than that, and tying this play to *Virginia Woolf*, is
the recognition that social constructs, family rituals and even aberrant
behaviour are defence mechanisms against an unnameable existential fear.
Claire's drinking, Julia's regularly scheduled returns to her childhood,
Agnes's reduction of every unpleasant thought to the level of abstract
intellectual speculation, and Tobias's constant placating and smoothing-
over of awkward moments are all ways of protecting themselves from

what Agnes calls a plague of communicable terror. As Claire reminds Tobias, whole lives can be built on the fantasy of order: 'We have our friends and guests for patterns, don't we? – known quantities. The drunks stay drunk; the Catholics go to Mass, the bounders bound. We can't have changes – throws the balance off . . . . Just think, Tobias, what would happen if the patterns changed: you wouldn't know where you stood.' For everyone there is the unbearable reality that an entire life must be constructed to blot out. For Tobias it is the possibility that no commitment is absolute and there is no promise one human can make to another that has no bounds. So, at the end of the play, when Harry and Edna decide that they have indeed imposed, their attempt to spare their friend the terror they carry actually brings it on.

The abstractly intellectual quality of Albee's later plays is seen in its purest form in *Box* and *Quotations from Chairman Mao Tse-Tung* (1968), an interrelated double bill sometimes called *Box-Mao-Box* because the first play is repeated at the end of the second. In *Box* we see only a hollow cube, while the recorded voice of a woman muses on its philosophical and moral implications. In *Mao* Mao Tse-Tung lectures on the class struggle, a Long-Winded Lady describes her fall overboard from an ocean liner, and an Old Woman recites a Robert Service-like poem about being rejected by her children in her old age. About midway through, the voice from *Box* joins the rotation of monologues, speaking a line or two from that play; at the end, the live actors are silent while the voice finishes her reprise.

The theme of both plays is cultural decay; the voice moves from an admiration of the workmanship of the box to a recognition that all standards are declining, and that we have gone beyond noticing the loss. The three monologues of the inner play demonstrate this decline through Mao's dependence on empty rhetoric, the Lady's self-centredness and the Old Woman's bathetic verse. But *Box-Mao-Box* is as much an intellectual exercise as a dramatic statement, a Beckett-like experiment in how little can be put on a stage and still have a play, and an attempt to structure the interlocking monologues musically. With *Tiny Alice* before it and *All Over* after, it represents Albee's furthest swing of the pendulum away from the passionate psychological realism of his early plays.

All Over (1971) is set in a more recognizable reality than *Box-Mao-Box*, but it is no less desiccated and lifeless. Its dramatic situation is in fact a deathwatch: an important man is dying, and his Wife, Mistress, Son, Daughter and Best Friend (who are given no other names) wait out his final moments. They show very little emotion; the few brief lapses, generally by the Son and Daughter, are treated as distasteful self-indulgences. Only at the very end does the Wife allow herself an open expression of grief – not for her husband's death, but for her lifetime of unhappiness. Like Honey in *Virginia Woolf* and Agnes in *A Delicate Balance* these characters distance themselves from experience to save themselves from the pain of having it. The difference is that Albee seems to approve, and to offer such deliberately chosen lifelessness as an acceptable model. That this seems to contradict everything his earlier plays stood for is a minor difficulty – authors have the right to change their minds. But a play full of characters repressing all emotions and keeping all interactions at a safe distance runs the risk of being as anaesthetized as they are; and the biggest problem with *All Over* is that it is dull.

In contrast to the dry plays that preceded it, *Seascape* (1975) is a charming and happy fable, using an entertaining bit of fantasy to make a positive if not particularly original statement. Nancy and Charlie, a middle-aged couple relaxing on a beach, encounter Sarah and Leslie, two human-size lizard-like amphibians who have chosen this moment to evolve out of the sea. After some comic shock on both sides, the new-comers prove to be very much like the humans, with middle-class amphibian values and parallel tensions in their marriage. But the introduction to life on shore involves discovering some painful new sensations, such as human emotions, and the lizards waver in their decision to evolve. Nancy and Charlie beg them not to go back into the sea, and the play ends with the humans' promise to help their new friends through their great adventure.

Sarah and Leslie are delightful characters, and their little break-throughs – learning to shake hands, marvelling at Nancy's breasts, experiencing sorrow for the first time – almost steal the show. But the fact that they do not appear until the end of Act One is a clue that the play is actually about Nancy and Charlie, the lizards' evolutionary leap a metaphor for the humans' uncertainty about what to do now that the main business of their lives seems completed. Charlie's commitment to helping the newcomers find their way is also his recognition that, for humans as well as lizards, the end of one stage in life is the cue to evolve into the next. *Seascape* is a small play, and one might even feel that Albee wasted a particularly clever invention on a fairly clichéd mess-age. But it makes its small point effectively, and with a liveliness and lightness of touch that had been missing from Albee's plays for over a decade.

Neil Simon

Neil Simon is, in commercial terms, the most successful dramatist in the American theatre, and probably in the history of the world. Beginning with his first Broadway success, *Come Blow Your Horn* (1961), he has turned out comedies at the rate of almost one a year; since most of these were successes, there has been hardly a season in thirty years without at least one Simon play – and sometimes as many as four – being performed on Broadway. And yet Simon has been accorded the least critical and academic study of any major American playwright, for a reason that says more about literary criticism than the plays. Literary analysts have never been comfortable with skilled craftsmen who make few if any pretensions to high art. Writers of detective novels, for example, may do what they do very well, but what they do is not what most literary critics are trained (or inclined) to analyse and judge. Much the same is true of the authors of stage comedy; criticism that presumes some value to the illumination of existential truths or the exploration of the deeper nuances of the human condition finds itself with little to say about writers who merely want to make the audience laugh, even if those writers are remarkably skilled at doing that.

The legitimate observation, for example, that almost none of Simon's early plays has more than a skeletal and mechanical plot must be accompanied by the recognition that the story lines are merely frameworks on which to hang comic situations and dialogue. Simon's general pattern is to juxtapose fairly simple opposites and then reconcile them or just enjoy the conflict. *Come Blow Your Horn* is about a boy who leaves home to move in with his playboy older brother. In *Barefoot in the Park* (1963) newlyweds go through a period of adjustment while his conservative nature gives way to her free-spiritedness. In *The Odd Couple* (1965) two divorced men rooming together prove to be comically incompatible. *The Star-Spangled Girl* (1966) brings two would-be revolutionary writers in contact with an all-American girl, with romance inevitably triumphing over politics. *The Sunshine Boys* (1972) reunites two feuding ex-vaudevillians and lets them renew their fighting. Other Simon plots of this period are about victims of their own limitations. *Plaza Suite* (1968) is three one-act portraits of middle-aged New Yorkers facing or denying the passage of time; *The Last of the Red-Hot Lovers* (1969) shows an unadventurous middle-aged man trying very unsuccessfully to commit adultery; and *The Prisoner of Second Avenue* (1971) watches a New Yorker being driven crazy by the comic pressures of city life. *The Good Doctor* (1973) is a collection of sketches adapted from Chekhov, generally of the small defeats of small people; *God's Favorite* (1974) is a modern-dress comic retelling of *Job*; and *The Gingerbread Lady* (1970), Simon's one serious play of the period, shows an alcoholic trying to recover.

A more legitimate criticism is that virtually none of these plays uses the implicit opportunity to explore character. The couple in *Barefoot in the Park*, for example, function as Beautiful Young People obviously fated to live Happily Ever After; the personality difference is not even introduced until midway through the play, after some earlier comic material has been exhausted, and is resolved without any soul-searching by either side. Only two of the early plays offer real psychological insights. In *The Odd Couple* prissy, meticulous Felix and aggressively sloppy Oscar may be static and somewhat one-dimensional characters, but their adventure rings true: two divorced men living together will recreate their failed marriages, each playing exactly the same infuriating role that drove his wife crazy, and each being driven crazy just like the wife he replaces. *The Sunshine Boys* recognizes that a partnership of fifty years is very much like a marriage, most dangerously threatened by petty exasperations rather than major incompatibilities, and ultimately surviving through a habit that is indistinguishable from love.

One reason why Simon's characters show little depth or individuality is that they all sound alike. At this stage in his career Simon was essentially a joke-writer, and his characters are all compulsively clever and wise-cracking; *The Gingerbread Lady* failed partly because the characters sound like they're making jokes even when they're being serious, and audiences were disoriented. Still, joke writing is an art, and so is the construction of a scene or a whole play built on jokes. Simon does not just throw a string of jokes together, but assembles them so that they feed on each other, the whole totalling more than the sum of the parts. Consider this exchange from the first scene of *The Odd Couple*:

> OSCAR Felix and Francis! They broke up! The entire marriage is
>   through . . . .
> SPEED After twelve years?
> VINNIE They were such a happy couple.
> MURRAY Twelve years doesn't mean you're a *happy* couple. It
>   just means you're a *long* couple.

The basic joke is in Vinnie's line, with its incongruity. It is a small joke, but Murray's repetition underlines it, and then his reversal tops it. Simon's plays are filled with such progressions, several small jokes producing more laughter together than they would alone. A related skill is the manipulation of running gags; each Simon play works inventive changes on a basic pattern, such as Oscar's exasperation in *The Odd Couple*.

Nevertheless, however impressive Simon's craft is, it is limited. It is no criticism of a comic writer to point out that he ultimately affirms conventional values, but Simon rarely even questions them, and there is no edge of danger in his early plays. The playboy in *Come Blow Your Horn* marries and settles down, thereby assuring us that his brother, after sowing some harmlessly wild oats, will do the same. The strangely Bohemian neighbour in *Barefoot in the Park* proves a perfect gentleman; the would-be lecher in *Last of the Red-Hot Lovers* is just too nice a guy to stray; and so on. The occasional attempts at seriousness or sentimentality, as in *The Gingerbread Lady*, are wooden or bathetic. Simon's milieu is middle-aged, middle-class New York, and he builds much of his humour on the familiarity of that world to his audience, citing currently fashionable brand names, for example, but he is lost when he strays too far from that territory; *The Star-Spangled Girl* does not work because he really doesn't know what young California rebels act and sound like. Not until the 1980s would Simon prove able to transcend these limitations.

On the other hand, if there is any doubt about Simon's supremacy in the limited realm of Broadway comedy, one need only consider the other successful comedies of the period, most of which do essentially the same things his do, though rarely with as much skill. Following in the tradition of the 1950s, the majority are built on the romance of a couple who spend the play either discovering the attraction that was obvious to us from the start or overcoming obstacles that usually turn out to be little more than misunderstandings. Among those that rise above the formula, through particularly witty dialogue or unexpected touches of characterization, are Jean Kerr's *Mary Mary* (1961), about an almost-divorced couple who rediscover their love just in time; Bill Manhoff's *The Owl and the Pussycat* (1964), about a stuffy author and a prostitute who evolve from feuding neighbours to lovers; Abe Burrows's *Cactus Flower* (1965, adapted from a French play), about a philandering dentist who involves his plain nurse in his subterfuges, only to have her blossom into a beauty and catch him in the end; Bob Randall's *6 Rms Riv Vu* (1972), about apartment-hunters who have a brief romance before returning to their spouses; and Bernard Slade's *Same Time, Next Year* (1975), about a couple whose affair consists of twenty once-a-year meetings.

Arthur Miller

When Arthur Miller returned to the theatre in 1964, after an absence of eight years, it was with a new subject and purpose. Where his earlier plays had all used domestic stories to raise and explore larger social and political issues, he was now to focus on the individual experiences themselves. His particular subject was guilt – or, rather, guiltiness: the sense of having failed some abstract or specific moral obligation and thus of having proved oneself inadequate or unworthy. To be sure, that subject was present in such early plays as *All My Sons* and *Death of a Salesman*, but as a means of criticizing the social situation that produced such feelings. Now Miller turned his attention to dramatizing the pain of feeling inadequate and to offering counsel and consolation to help alleviate that pain. In effect, then, he left the tradition of Odets to join the camp of

Williams, Inge and the later O'Neill. To the extent that such plays as *After the Fall* and *The Price* offer an explanation of life that frees the individual from unnecessary self-condemnation, they resemble both *The Night of the Iguana* and *Long Day's Journey into Night*.

In *After the Fall* (1964), Quentin faces his third marriage with the fear that his history makes him unworthy of the opportunity for happiness. He finds only failures and betrayals in his life, not only in his first two marriages but in his relations with friends and family, and in their relations with each other, so that he is convinced he has no right to impose himself on another victim. He finally realizes that such defects are part of the human condition, not his personal failing, and that hope for the future can be built on the ability to accept and forgive the inevitable lapses, and to carry on in spite of them. To dramatize this wholly internal experience, Miller uses a method even more expressionistic than the fantasy and memory sequences in *Death of a Salesman*: the fictional premise of *After the Fall* is that Quentin is talking to a friend represented by the audience, and the events he remembers are acted out on the stage behind him, Quentin moving back to join them and then returning to the conversation. Thus the bulk of the stage becomes a representation of Quentin's mind, with memories played out in various spaces as Quentin recalls them, and he is not always in complete control: some characters appear unbidden or through a chain of association to interrupt his talk. Through this device Miller can provide insights into Quentin's thinking that even he is not aware of, and thus keep us a step ahead of him in his discoveries.

Quentin is haunted until the final minutes of the play by the conviction that he is morally responsible for all the failed relationships in his life, but Miller shows that the guilt frequently lies elsewhere. Quentin's first wife Louise is neurotically jealous and unbending in her self-righteousness. His second wife Maggie, in her more than neurotic insecurity, makes ever-increasing demands Quentin cannot possibly meet (summed up in her simple requirement, 'Love me, and do what I tell you. And stop arguing.'), and yet he feels guilty for not meeting them. Quentin is so prepared to accept blame that he finds ways of condemning his innocence – 'Is it altogether good to be not guilty for what another does?' When a woman he has helped thanks him, he feels unworthy; when a friend's wife tries to seduce him, he feels ashamed for not even realizing what was happening; when he visits a concentration camp and recognizes the humanity of the builders, he fears that this empathy is proof of his baseness: 'I can easily see the perfectly normal contractors and their cigars, the carpenters, plumbers, . . . good fathers, devoted sons, grateful that someone else will die, not they, and how can one understand that, if one is innocent? If somewhere in one's soul there is no accomplice?'

A potential danger of the play is that Quentin's virtual lust for guiltiness and atonement – twice in the play he actually strikes crucifixion poses – will alienate the audience, but it is necessary for us to see the excesses of his self-condemnation before he does, so that we can be prepared for his climactic discovery. For theatrical reasons, Miller makes the realization come upon Quentin in a rush, beginning with the memory of his final quarrel with Maggie. To save himself from her madness, Quentin attacks her, and is once more almost drowned in guilt: 'What love, what wave of pity will ever reach this knowledge – I know how to kill?' The various betrayers and victims of the play gather on stage, and the concentration camp site is lit.

> Or is it possible – that this is not bizarre . . . to anyone? And I am not alone, and no man lives who would not rather be the sole survivor of this place than all its finest victims? What is the cure? [. . .] No, not love; I loved them all, all! And gave them willing to failure and to death that I might live, as they gave me and gave each other.

Some of the play's early detractors condemned Miller for excusing himself (i.e. Quentin) by putting the blame on everyone else, particularly Maggie, a character clearly based on his late wife Marilyn Monroe. But the accomplishment of *After the Fall* is that Miller offers Quentin a basis for self-forgiveness that does *not* transfer the guilt elsewhere, but rather provides a greater charity towards others. If, after the Fall, we are all imperfect, then perhaps we can accept and forgive our imperfections and build our lives on that foundation.

> To know, and even happily, that we meet unblessed; not in some garden of wax fruit and painted trees, that lie of Eden, but after, after the Fall.[. . .] And the wish to kill is never killed, but with some gift of courage one may look into its face when it appears, and with a stroke of love – as to an idiot in the house – forgive it; again and again . . . forever?

And if that sounds more like something O'Neill or Williams or Inge would say, *After the Fall* is further vindication of those writers' discovery that the most-needed gift of mid-century American drama was consolation and reassurance.

Miller's next play, *Incident at Vichy* (1964), offers little in the way of consolation, but it is, like *After the Fall*, an analysis of guilt and responsibility. In a group of Jews and other racial undesirables rounded up by the Gestapo in 1942 is an Austrian count, Von Berg, obviously arrested by mistake. The others, led by the Jewish psychiatrist Leduc, force Von Berg to recognize his complicity, if only passive, in the Nazi atrocities; and when Von Berg is given a pass to leave, he hands it to Leduc, staying to die in his place. On one level the play is a celebration of that inexplicable act, an affirmation of man's capacity for good set against the almost overwhelming contrary evidence of the Nazis. Beyond that, it is an analysis of social responsibility that recalls Miller's *All My Sons*. Von Berg, whose hatred of the Nazis never really extended beyond a distaste for their vulgarity, and who could overlook a cousin's participation in atrocities because he was of his class, is forced to recognize his larger obligation as Leduc makes him see that silence, even disgusted silence, is an acquiescence.

Had Miller written this play ten or twenty years earlier, its meanings would have stopped here, with Von Berg's discovery of his moral failure and his acceptance of responsibility and punishment. But *Incident at Vichy* is not really about Von Berg; it is about Leduc, whose experience raises issues larger even than Nazism and identifies guilts that even the seemingly just and innocent can bear. In the middle of the play Leduc tells a German officer that his life is worth more than the German's 'Because I am incapable of doing what you are doing. I am better for the world than you.' But when he later tries to convince Von Berg of his culpability, we sense, perhaps a few seconds before he does, the applicability of his words to himself: 'Jew is only the name we give to that stranger, that agony we cannot feel, that death we look at like a cold abstraction . . . the man whose death leaves you relieved that you are not him, despite your decency.'

So at the end of the play, when Leduc takes the pass and escapes, it is not Von Berg's fate that is meant to haunt us. By his own logic Leduc has declared himself the moral equivalent of the Nazis just by defining someone else's life as of less value than his own; and that he is passively accepting Von Berg's sacrifice is no more an excuse than Von Berg's allowing his cousin to do the dirty work for him. On this point, then, *Incident at Vichy* contradicts *After the Fall*: those who survive at the expense of others, or even those who accept the deaths of others as less tragic than their own would be, must carry a burden of responsibility and guilt for the rest of their lives; and the fact that this capacity for selfishness is universal does not make it forgivable.

The Price (1968) is more in the spirit of *After the Fall*, going beyond even forgiveness to offer the capacity for pride and a sense of accomplishment. The story is of two brothers, Victor and Walter Franz: when their father was ruined in the Depression Victor stayed to support him, giving up his chance for an education, while Walter went off to college and a lucrative medical practice. When they meet to sell their father's furniture, Victor presses the charge that Walter deserted them and ruined his life. His need to make sense of the past fuels his attack even more than the old resentments: an affirmation of his image of himself as victim of his brother's selfishness will at least give a shape to his wasted life. But Walter refuses to accept the role of villain, slowly forcing Victor to the realization that his father had manipulated him; in a powerful theatrical moment Walter points to the furniture and reminds Victor – and the audience – that the whole premise for their being in this room is the sale of these valuable pieces that could have been sold back then.

This discovery, which threatens to make Victor's whole life meaning-less, pushes him a step further into repressed memories. He knew his father was using him, but felt an obligation to remain loving and sup-portive: 'But you're brought up to believe in one another, you're filled full of that crap – you can't help trying to keep it going, that's all. I thought if I stuck with him, if he could see that somebody was still . . . I can't explain it; I wanted to . . . stop it from falling apart.' [ellipses Miller's] 'It won't work, Vic,' says Walter.

> Is it really that something fell apart? . . . What was here to fall apart? Was there ever any love here? When he needed her, she vomited. When you needed him, he laughed. What was unbear-able is not that it all fell apart, it was that there was never any-thing here . . . . It's that there was no love in this house. There was no loyalty. There was nothing here but a straight financial ar-rangement. That's what was unbearable. And you proceeded to wipe out what you saw.

This final revelation, which Walter thinks is an accusation, is actually the vindication of Victor's life that the play has been striving for. Earlier in the play Walter said people create themselves to escape the horror they fear most. The idea of a world without love was unbearable to Victor, and he denied it by making himself into a loving person. Without sup-port, without any precedent in his family, without even his conscious awareness, he created out of himself the capacity for love, sacrifice and service; and that is an explanation of himself he can live with.

Affirming the value of even modest human accomplishment is also the goal of Miller's next play, the somewhat less successful *The Creation of the World and Other Business* (1972), a partially comic retelling of the story of Adam and Eve in which God makes absolute and inexplicable moral demands while Lucifer promotes anarchy. In this vacuum Adam must find his moral values and his capacity for goodness within himself, and the play ends with his struggling to guide Cain towards repentance and Eve towards forgiveness. The play is crippled by Miller's obvious uneasiness with both allegory and comedy, but its generating idea is clearly of a piece with *The Price*: the reassurance that man has the capa-bility to create in himself the virtues and life-justifying qualities that the world outside does not provide him.

Tennessee Williams

The first two decades of Tennessee Williams's career represent an unmatched contribution to the American drama, not only in the individual plays but in the irreversible shift in the intention and effect of domestic realism, from the representation of larger issues to the exploration of the psychological and emotional burdens of everyday life. The second two decades of his career offer the much less happy picture of an artist with the misfortune to outlive his talent. Beginning in 1962, a series of personal crises and professional setbacks, exacerbated by alcohol and drug abuse, produced an artistic decline from which Williams never recovered. Although he continued to write for most of the next twenty years – it seemed to be a symptom of his emotional state that he felt compelled to produce new work even when craft and inspiration failed him – virtually all of his plays after *The Night of the Iguana* were artistic and commercial failures. (The following analysis will stretch the chronological boundaries of this chapter to include Williams's plays after 1975.)

His plays of this period are not significantly different in kind from those of the 1950s, and almost every one has one character or scene or speech that recalls Williams at his best. The otherwise undistinguished *The Mutilated* (1966), for example, includes a Christmas carol that is the purest Williams:

> I think the strange, the crazed, the queer
> Will have their holiday this year
> And for a while, A little while,
> There will be pity for the wild. . . .
> I think the mutilated will
> Be touched by hands that nearly heal,
> At night the agonized will feel
> A comfort that is nearly real. . . .
> I think for some uncertain reason
> Mercy will be shown this season
> To the wayward and deformed,
> To the lonely and misfit.

The generally moribund memory play *Vieux Carré* (1977) is enlivened by one of Williams's greatest comic characters, the mad landlady Mrs Wire; and some of the same grotesque comic energy appears in *The Gnadiges Fraulein* (1966) and *Kingdom of Earth* (1968). But one scene or speech or character does not make a play, and in every case the hint of Williams's earlier power either exists in a vacuum, unintegrated with the rest of the play, or lapses into excess. This speech from *The Milk Train*

Doesn't Stop Here Anymore (1963), for example, would not be out of place in *Streetcar* or *Summer and Smoke*:

> Have you ever seen how two little animals sleep together, a pair
> of kittens or puppies? All day they seem so secure in the house of
> their master, but at night, when they sleep, they don't seem sure
> of their owner's true care for them. Then they draw close
> together, they curl up against each other. . . . We're all of us
> living in a house we're not used to. . . . We have to creep close
> to each other and give those gentle little nudges with our paws
> and our muzzles before we can slip into – sleep and – rest for the
> next day's – playtime.

But it is completely out of place in *Milk Train*. Self-contained arias in the earlier plays – Blanche's 'Don't hang back with the brutes' speech in *Streetcar*, for example – were similarly self-conscious and even strained in their imagery and ideas, but they put into words impressions that the rest of their plays were dramatizing. But *Milk Train* is about the need for assistance in dying, not living; and that theme is never addressed with the poetic intensity Williams gives to this really irrelevant thought.

Another symptom of Williams's decline is the compulsive reworking of flawed material. Previously Williams was able to adapt and revise successfully: *Menagerie*, *Cat*, *Summer and Smoke* and *Iguana* were all based on earlier short stories; and *Eccentricities of a Nightingale* is a valid alternative version of *Summer and Smoke*. But now the tinkering proved fruitless. *Vieux Carré* recycles earlier autobiographical material with no advance in technique or insight, except for the depiction of Mrs Wire. *Milk Train* was produced in a preliminary version a year before its Broadway opening, revised for Broadway, revised again for the published text, and revised once again for a second Broadway production in 1964, with no significant improvement. *The Red Devil Battery Sign* closed out of town in 1975, was rewritten for a 1977 London production and revised again for publication in 1979. It seems to have begun as a play about conspiracy, the first version being set on the day of President Kennedy's assassination, but by the final version that element has been cut so clumsily that the central action, about a frightened woman's frantic romance with a dying musician, makes little sense.

One of Williams's biggest personal disappointments was the play variously known as *Out Cry* and *The Two-Character Play*, which he worked and reworked through at least five versions between 1967 and 1975 without conquering its basic flaw, which recalls the earlier *Camino Real*: the play operates in almost purely metaphoric terms, without the anchor in domestic realism that characterized his best work, and the result is too lifeless and fragile to hold an audience. A brother and sister acting team rehearse a play about an agoraphobic brother and sister, the distinctions between performers and roles gradually disappearing. The inner play, essentially an extended metaphor of madness and the capitulation to madness, is sensitively balanced by the extended metaphor of the outside play, which is of resisting madness and trying desperately to function in reality even when the capacity for coping has been exhausted. *Out Cry* is thus one of the purest expressions in the Williams canon of some of his recurring themes: the pain of existence, the feelings of inadequacy, and the seductive power of madness, along with Williams's admiration and affection for those who fight, even (or especially) if they lose. But its purity is its downfall. The characters in *Out Cry* have no reality as human beings; they are merely the voices speaking Williams's words. Samuel Beckett at his best could create living drama out of virtually disembodied voices, but that is beyond Williams's scope.

This play also exposes another, particularly sad symptom of Williams's decline, his growing inability to separate himself from his plays. There was never any question in his prime that some of his characters were projections of aspects of his own personality; and indeed a large part of the achievement of a Blanche or Brick was that Williams was able to transmute his own emotional experiences into fully realized dramatic creations. But in *Out Cry* the expressions of stage fright, the temptation to withdraw from the world rather than face its ridicule, and the compulsion to carry on in spite of waning powers are all clearly the author speaking, without translation into art. The same embarrassing self-exposure cripples *In the Bar of a Tokyo Hotel* (1969), whose secondary character of a painter in the midst of a mental and artistic breakdown (expressed in a style of unfinished sentences everyone in that play affects) is so obviously a self-portrait that he breaks the bounds of the play:

> I've understood the *intimacy* that should, that has to exist between
> the, the – painter and the – I! It! Now it turned to me, or I
> turned to it, no division between us at all any more! The one-
> ness, the! . . . There was always a sense of division till! Gone!
> Now absolute one-ness with! . . . This work is hard to confine
> to. . . . Always before I felt controllable limits, I.

And Scott and Zelda Fitzgerald in *Clothes for a Summer Hotel* (1980) are used as almost mythic examples of burnt-out artists who outlived their limited talents; that they are hardly-disguised projections of the author's own self-pity is obvious from the unsubtle ways Williams betrays his identification, repeatedly and pointlessly questioning Scott's heterosexuality, and once again making them speak for him more than themselves: 'The losses accumulated in my heart, the disenchantments steadily increased. . . . Wouldn't accept it. Romantics won't, you know . . . . I went back to the world of vision which was my only true home.'

Another form of falling-off of powers is evident in two plays of the

period which work as domestic melodramas though they have little new
to say, *Small Craft Warnings* (1972) and *A Lovely Sunday for Creve Coeur*
(1979). In the first, the denizens of a neighbourhood bar rearrange their
pairings and their lives, settling for the best options available; in the
second, a schoolteacher has her fantasies of romance and social advance-
ment destroyed, and accepts a less glamorous fate. What we have here,
in short, are two William Inge plays, about little people surviving little
disappointments and settling for little satisfactions. Both might in fact
have been more successful had Inge written them, without the awkward
attempts at poetry in the first and at grotesque humour in the second.

Williams spent the last twenty years of his life trying to say the same
sorts of things he had said in his best plays, using the same tools of
poetic imagery, grotesque humour, intense sympathy for human suffering, and frequently sensationalistic plots. It was not that he could not do
these things any more, but that he could not make them work. Even at
his most successful, he had been a dramatist of broad strokes and extreme images, but he was able to control his rich poetic imagination and
produce powerfully effective art. With the loss of that control, the plays
of his final period either seem empty compared to the emotional resonances of his great plays or approach self-parody in their undisciplined
excess. The poetry becomes disconnected and unmanageable, as in *Milk
Train*; the style becomes self-conscious and precious, as in *In the Bar*; the
characters and emotions become too personal, as in *Out Cry* and *Summer
Hotel*; the plot structure becomes disjointed, as in *Red Devil*; the plays
become either all symbol and no reality (*Out Cry*) or mere narrative
without resonance (*Vieux Carré*). At his peak Williams was a playwright
of unrivalled imagination and poetic power; we can see now that what
really made those great plays work was his ability to discipline, control
and shape the outpourings of his genius. The brilliance of Tennessee
Williams's masterpieces was always obvious; the particular nature of his
decline tells us to go back and appreciate their craftsmanship.

The period in the history of the American drama covered in this chapter
is less clear in definition than some of the others. Unlike the 1930s or
1950s it is not dominated by one writer or style; it seems, like the
1920s, to be more a period of transition or exploration. In retrospect,
one can see a clear and straight line from O'Neill's early experiments,
through Odets, to the triumphs of Miller and Williams. But, having
reached that zenith, the Broadway theatre seemed to be marking time;
of the Broadway playwrights of the 1950s, only Arthur Miller continued
to grow and produce effective new work in the 1960s. Meanwhile, the
face of the American theatre changed in the 1960s, inevitably producing
changes in the American drama. As new theatres welcomed new writers,
the dominance and homogeneity of Broadway-based drama was broken.
Inevitably, some of these new writers experimented with alternatives to

domestic realism, as O'Neill and others had done in the 1920s, and perhaps with the same motivation, the belief that the new statements and points-of-view they wanted to bring to the drama required new forms.

Still, as new and diverse as the playwrights of the 1960s were, what they had to say proved not all that different from what previous generations of dramatists had offered and previous generations of audiences had responded to. The social criticism of writers such as LeRoi Jones, David Rabe, Lanford Wilson and the Edward Albee of *The American Dream* and *Who's Afraid of Virginia Woolf?* stemmed from the same impulse that had driven Clifford Odets and Arthur Miller: the need to warn Americans against the failings and dangers inherent in their own culture. The existential pain dramatized by Albee in *The Zoo Story* and *Virginia Woolf*, by Jack Gelber in *The Connection*, by Sam Shepard in *Action* and *The Tooth of Crime*, and by many other playwrights treated in this chapter is not radically different from the loneliness and insecurity that were the continuing subject of Tennessee Williams and William Inge.

Moreover, despite the wide-ranging experiments in alternative styles, some of which proved particularly useful to the more radical new writers and would eventually affect the mainstream drama, the fact remains that the majority of the plays described in this chapter are set in someone's living room. It was noted in the preceding chapter that the artistic voyage of American drama before 1950 – from realism, through experiment, back to domestic realism – was replicated in the individual case of Eugene O'Neill. While it may not yet be wholly apparent, the next chapter will show that the same is true of the careers of Albee, Wilson, Shepard and many of their contemporaries. Having proved its effectiveness and versatility in the 1950s, domestic realism was challenged by a new generation of writers in the 1960s. It would withstand that challenge successfully in the following decade, confirming its power as the natural voice of American drama. Meanwhile, for the first time in more than half a century the terms 'Broadway' and 'American theatre' were not synonymous, and the range of American drama became broader, richer and more varied.

Chapter 6
1975–1990: A National Theatre

New theatres, new plays

By the mid-1970s Broadway's domination of the American theatre was decisively over. Off- and Off Off-Broadway theatres routinely produced six or more times as many shows as Broadway did each season; and the hundreds of professional theatres around the country together staged many more productions than all the New York City theatres put together. This imbalance was particularly extraordinary in the case of new American plays, which were simply no longer the domain of Broadway. For various reasons, including financial constraints as well as the artistic flourishing of other venues, by 1980 the Broadway repertoire was made up almost entirely of plays first produced elsewhere.

In some cases, to be sure, this was merely a modification of Broadway's old out-of-town-trial system, with a commercial producer placing a new script in a regional theatre for an inexpensive test run before bringing it to Broadway. But in the majority of cases new plays were produced independently in regional or fringe theatres, only attracting the attention of Broadway producers when their success suggested commercial potential. The originating theatres could then participate in any commercial profits, and the plays would benefit from the publicity and 'seal of approval' Broadway still had the power to bestow. One way or another, the best new American plays of this period usually did get New York productions eventually, but many bypassed Broadway.

This change in the theatrical balance of power had direct and indirect effects on the plays and playwrights themselves. First, there were many more opportunities for new plays to be produced. Even in its most active years the Broadway theatre had rarely introduced more than fifty new American plays a season; by the early 1980s the combination of regional and New York fringe theatres could easily produce six or eight times as many. It also meant an opportunity for greater variety. Having at least partly escaped the inhibiting shadow of high budgets and the need to show profits, regional and fringe theatres could be far more open than the commercial theatre to playwrights representing minority groups, addressing minority interests, dealing with uncommercial subjects or employing challenging and unconventional styles. Plays by women; plays by black, Hispanic and Asian dramatists; plays by and about the concerns of feminists, homosexuals and Vietnam veterans; plays reflecting regional subjects and cultures; plays in styles ranging from the mime/dance/ritual of performance artists to the most conventional domestic realism – for the first time in the twentieth century the American theatre had the capacity to stage such a broad representation of the American experience. Inevitably, many of these new plays and playwrights were unsuccessful or unimpressive, but the sheer quantity meant a greater opportunity for plays of merit or potential to be seen.

Another by-product of the new theatrical set-up was the chance for a new play to be staged several times, in several versions, on its way to its final form. Most regional theatres, and many New York companies, had new play workshops and staged readings of works-in-progress built into their structure. By the 1980s it was the rule rather than the exception for a playwright to see a new work performed in a workshop or staged reading, then in one or more full productions, and perhaps then a commercial New York staging, with the opportunity to revise and polish the script based on what was learned each time. August Wilson's *Joe Turner's Come and Gone*, for example, had workshop stagings at New Dramatists in New York in 1983 and 1984, a staged reading at the O'Neill Theatre Center in Connecticut in 1984, a full production by the Yale Repertory Company in 1986, and further productions in Boston, Seattle and Washington on its way to a Broadway run in 1988. (One minor problem generated by this pattern is deciding which date to assign to such plays; in this chapter the opening date of the production that corresponds most closely to the published text will be used.)

Despite the increased variety of voices, styles and subject matter represented by the new American drama of the 1970s and 1980s, a clear mainstream remained; and the discovery by previous generations of dramatists that the natural American dramatic mode was domestic realism was continually affirmed. Whatever the subject, however dominant the social or political agenda, however particular or unconventional the life experience being explored, the overwhelming majority of American dramatists continued to find that their concerns could best be dramatized through the everyday, personal experiences of ordinary characters. There were, to be sure, some noticeable alterations in this dominant mode; and two stylistic innovations in particular became so widespread and so generally accepted that they practically became absorbed into the definition of realism.

One was a general replacement of traditional act and scene structure by something considerably more fluid. While many dramatists continued to write thirty- or forty-minute scenes separated by closed curtains and set changes, many others wrote in five- or ten-minute units, with brief scenes flowing into each other or leaping over time and space in a cinematic way. Indeed, it is likely that film and television were the inspirations for this structure, with a generation of dramatists and audiences raised on those more fluid media able to absorb information offered in short bursts and to make the imaginative leaps from one to the next. (A somewhat more cynical way of looking at it would be that a generation raised on American commercial television could think only in ten-minute units.) But it is worth pointing out that Shakespeare did much the same thing, and this fluid structure may have been made possible, as Shakespeare's was, by the nature of the theatres in which the plays were performed. For various historical reasons, the majority of regional theatres had arena or thrust stages rather than the conventional proscenium stage, while many fringe companies, in New York and elsewhere, performed in converted spaces that were essentially bare rooms. These settings, along with the relative poverty of most companies, encouraged the use of bare stages or minimal, impressionistic sets; and these theatrical factors combined to allow and even encourage a more cinematic flow of scenes.

A second violation of traditional play structure that came to be familiar enough that it was hardly noticed was the breaking of the fictional frame to allow direct audience address by one or more characters. Of course this, too, had been done before, by Shakespeare among others, but always in plays that were consciously declaring themselves as nonrealistic through the device – Wilder's *The Skin of Our Teeth*, for example, or Williams's *The Glass Menagerie*. The difference now was that a character, frequently a narrator figure like Williams's Tom Wingfield, could step outside the play for a moment without seriously breaking the illusion; and the audience would not be disconcerted, but would experience the play as continuous and realistic. A play that combined these two innovations, such as Mark Medoff's *Children of a Lesser God* (Los Angeles 1979), would have been considered highly experimental thirty or forty years earlier, but fits comfortably within the expanded definition of realism.

So, with this expanded definition, it is possible to say that the dominant mode of American drama in the 1970s and 1980s remained the realistic, contemporary, middle-class domestic melodrama discovered by Odets and others in the 1930s and refined by Miller and Williams in the 1950s. Both Miller and Williams continued to write into this period, though Miller produced only a few new plays and Williams was in severe decline. (Williams's plays of the late 1970s were discussed in the previous chapter.) From the generation of the 1960s Edward Albee and Neil Simon continued to define the extreme boundaries of the commercial drama; and Sam Shepard and Lanford Wilson came into their full powers, fulfilling their early promise with mature works. The closer we come to the present, the more difficult it is to distinguish the major writers from the merely interesting or trendy, but David Mamet and August Wilson would seem to be unquestionably in the first category; and such others as A. R. Gurney, Beth Henley, David Henry Hwang, Terrence McNally, Marsha Norman and Wendy Wasserstein are certainly worthy of attention.

Arthur Miller

Miller's few plays of this period are an even mix of the predominantly social and thesis-driven drama of his early years and the psychological and spiritual explorations he had begun in the 1960s. *The Archbishop's Ceiling* (Washington 1977) is fully in the tradition of *The Crucible* in condemning an evil society for its crimes against individuals. Writers in an unnamed eastern European country must function with the suspicion, but not the certainty, that their rooms are bugged and that one or more of them may be government agents. So the most innocent conversations have multiple levels, as they perform for an audience that may or may not be there while simultaneously trying to be open and honest with each other. Deciphering the ambiguities of reality is not a theoretical puzzle for these characters; the society that controls their lives forbids them to live naturally. Every conscious moment must be spent in trying to interpret, decode and clarify not only each other's words and actions, but their own.

As in *The Crucible*, where false accusations led John Proctor to discover real guilt in himself, the constant monitoring of themselves and each other forces the characters of *The Archbishop's Ceiling* to face their private, unpolitical ambiguities and duplicities. The American visitor Adrian sincerely wants to help his friends, but he is writing a novel about them, and he and they can never be sure whether he is thinking of them as people or characters. Even if they are not spies, Marcus and Maya enjoy the small luxuries of officially approved writers, and cannot themselves be sure that the desire to retain those does not lead them to do the government's work unbidden. Here, even more than any acts of direct repression, are the social atrocities Miller condemns: first, the theft not only of privacy but of personality. It is not only in Adrian's novel that they will be fictionalized; when everyone must constantly play a role, no one can be himself. Even worse is the forced imposition of an awareness of one's own moral failures; being obliged every day to search out the truth about oneself, and thus every day to face oneself, is the most exquisite torture a diabolical state can impose.

The American Clock (1980) is an attempt at social epic, a history of the Depression of the 1930s in both national and personal terms, narrated through flashbacks by two survivors. Lee Baum's memories are all domestic, of his middle-class Jewish family's decline into genteel poverty, while Arthur Robertson, a financier who anticipated the crash and saved his riches, observes as society crumbles around him. Miller is clearly uncomfortable with the epic mode, and the play has some of the same flaws – a disjointed, episodic structure and scenes which are too obviously striving to be archetypal to have much reality – as *We, the People*, Elmer Rice's early attempt at reflecting an entire culture through domestic realism. But if the play's dramaturgy is clouded, its point of view is not, and Miller succeeds in stating a judgement of the Depression even if he fails to dramatize it. His premise is that, for all its destruction, the Depression ultimately affirmed and strengthened the American experiment. Baum and Robertson both repeatedly express their astonishment that the apparent breakdown of the system did not lead to revolution from the left or right, and find the explanation in a redefinition of the American Dream; seeing his mother as representative, Lee realizes that

> She was so like the country; money obsessed her but what she really longed for was some kind of height where she could stand and see out and around and breathe in the air of her own free life. With all her defeats she believed to the end that the world was meant to be better.

In an early version of the play Robertson reached a similar conclusion, which the London text gives to another character: 'Roosevelt gave them back their belief in the country. The government belonged to them again! . . . The return of that belief is what saved the United States, no more, no less!'

Miller's next plays are as different from these – and, indeed, most of his earlier work – as could be. The one-act *Elegy for a Lady* (New Haven, 1982) is a delicate study in intimate human relationships and a teasing exercise in ambiguity. An older man enters a women's shop to buy a gift for his somewhat younger lover, and enlists the help of the proprietress in making his selection. This involves some explanation of the relationship: although accepting him as her lover, the woman has maintained a certain independence and distance; now she is dying, and the man fears that too intimate a gift will violate her boundaries while one too impersonal will misrepresent his feelings. The proprietress, first guessing and then speaking with some confidence about the woman's feelings and thoughts, is able to reassure him that his lover understands his love and has been totally satisfied by the form their relationship took.

The power of the play comes from the mystical and dream-like tone that develops as the proprietress becomes progressively identified with the dying woman, speaking for her and allowing the man to speak to his lover through her. At first she merely sympathizes, but soon she is describing the woman's feelings with insight and authority, and then speaking for her:

> MAN   But her independence means more to her than any relationship, I think.
> PROPRIETRESS   How do you know? – You were the one who ordered her not to love you.

Eventually the two women blend into one, so it is not clear who is speaking or being addressed:

> PROPRIETRESS   I never condemn anyone; you know that . . . .
> MAN   That's your glory, but in some deepest part of you there has to be some touch of contempt.

And thus the proprietress's eventual assurance that he has not failed his lover and can honour her best by respecting her privacy provides the comfort that the man needs.

Miller invites speculation: has the proprietress had a similar experience and relationship in her life, that she has such insight into this one? Is she graciously offering herself as a surrogate, through whom the man can work out his feelings? Does she know the woman for whom she speaks so confidently, and does that mean she also knows this man who appears to be just a chance customer? Does he know her, so that he is slowly opening up to a friend, rather than to a stranger? Is this in fact the woman, with both parties delicately speaking in the third person to protect themselves from the painful reality of her dying? Or is this indeed a dream, a projection of the man's internal process of acceptance and resolution? This uncharacteristic excursion into ambiguity is completely successful, the various possibilities resonating against each other to deepen the emotional effect.

Its companion piece, *Some Kind of Love Story* (1982), has similar ambiguity, though without the same resonance and delicacy. A private detective has been questioning a prostitute about a murder for years; at each meeting she offers another tantalizing hint of what she knows, but if he pushes too hard she withdraws into schizophrenic fantasy. He has come to realize that she will never tell him everything, and even to suspect that she has no information of value and is just stringing him along to keep their relationship alive, but he also realizes that he has too much invested in the search, and in her, to give up. During the play she metes out one more clue, keeping him on the string, but bringing him no closer to the solution of the mystery or the resolution of the strange hold they have on each other. As the title makes clear, Miller is suggesting that this kind of mutual need and mutual exploitation has the effect, if not the familiar face, of love; and that both parties are getting more from the continued cat-and-mouse game than they could from the achievement of their ostensible goals. But these two characters are much less insightful and eloquent than the pair in *Elegy for a Lady*, and the play must operate in broader, cruder strokes that present the ambiguities in their feelings without evoking the feelings themselves.

The same imbalance exists in Miller's other double bill of the 1980s. *I Can't Remember Anything* (1987) is an affectionate but external picture of two elderly people, showing how the banes of old age – physical frailty, fading memory, alienation from friends and family – are blessedly accompanied by philosophical resolutions, quieted passions and a focus on the smallest and most immediate pleasures and pains: with every reduction of power comes a matching reduction of desire, so the loss is not felt and the quiet passage towards death is eased. It is a quiet, pleasant play, with the elegiac tone of *Elegy for a Lady*, if not its emotional depths. The second half of the bill, *Clara* (1987), is a much more ambitious play, an attempt to address moral and psychological issues akin to those of *The Crucible* and *After the Fall* in the context of this new intimate style Miller was exploring in the 1980s. A man whose daughter has been murdered is questioned by a sympathetic but determined detective who suspects that guilt for not protecting her has blocked the memory of the key suspect's name. But rather than releasing guilt, the questioning revives the man's faith in his daughter's essential goodness and his own. The play thus explores two familiar concerns of Miller's. The first is connection and responsibility, the need to recognize one's ties to and effects on others. As far back as *All My Sons* Miller saw dissociation as a moral lapse, and he introduces Albert Kroll as a man so cut off from humanity that he has difficulty carrying on a coherent conversation. Under Fine's relentless guidance, Kroll remembers the ways he helped to shape his daughter through his stories and behaviour, and accepts responsibility for the woman she became. The second and decisive step is the reaffirmation of one's own highest virtues. Like Victor in *The Price*, Kroll has lost sight of his own achievements, but as he remembers his former idealism, so different from his present acquiescence to minor corruption, he is gradually reintegrated with that purer self; and it is when he can embrace his younger self with joy that he can declare his love for his daughter and, incidentally, remember the name of the probable murderer.

These late plays provide a quietly satisfying if slightly uncharacteristic coda to Miller's long career. Certainly his most significant contributions to the American repertoire lie in his plays of the 1940s and 1950s, and in his reaffirmation that the American drama was able to address social and political issues without losing the power and immediacy of domestic realism. If in such later plays as *The Price* and these one-act sketches he acknowledges that small, personal epiphanies or accommodations are also of importance, and worthy of dramatic exploration, he does not deny his earlier work but supplements it. If the dramatists of the 1950s can be divided into the Miller and Williams camps, Miller alone lived long enough and evolved enough to write effective plays of both types.

Neil Simon

Having established himself as the pre-eminent craftsman of joke-filled urban comedy, Neil Simon continued to dominate that branch of the American drama through the 1980s. Such plays as *California Suite* (1976), *Chapter Two* (1977), *I Ought to Be in Pictures* (1980) and *Rumors* (1989) fit comfortably in the genre of *Barefoot in the Park*, confidently working minor variations on the formulas Simon mastered in the 1960s. Tentative steps beyond those limits, particularly in the direction of deeper characterization or more serious subjects, repeatedly produce the weakest moments in the plays. Well into the 1980s, then, it appeared that Simon was limited to excellence in a very narrow field – not just comedy, but the comedy of topical references, upper-middle-class New York City characters, and unpausing gags. But in 1983 Simon discovered a capacity for presenting real sentiment, believable characters and even social and historical insight, without wandering too far from the type of comedy that was his natural mode.

Brighton Beach Memoirs (1983) is a sentimental and semi-autobiographical comedy of life in Depression-era New York. Jack Jerome is overworked to the point of a heart attack trying to support his wife Kate and sons Stanley and Eugene, and Kate's widowed sister Blanche and her two daughters. In the course of a week there is a variety of large and small crises: Jack's heart attack, Blanche's failed first attempt at dating, fights between Kate and Blanche and between Blanche and her daughter Nora, Stanley's chagrin at losing his paycheck in a poker game. The story is narrated by Simon's fictional self, thirteen-year-old Eugene; and for virtually the first time in Simon's career the comedy is based on character rather than isolated jokes, the central comic figure being Eugene himself, caught between boyish enthusiasm for baseball and adolescent discovery of lust, and constantly feeling put upon for being the family errand boy and scapegoat. A typical joke, part of a furtive discus-

sion of sex with his older brother, has the rhythm of a standard Simon
two-liner:

> STANLEY   How horny can you get?
> EUGENE   I don't know. What's the highest score?

But that line is clearly Eugene's; he has his own voice, which is a function of his age, his precocious self-awareness, and the conflicting forces
pulling at him. This character may be a familiar one, but Simon gives
him a reality and individuality, and he provides a strong centre and point
of view for the play.

But the real strengths of the play, and innovations for Simon, lie in
the background characters, who are not only allowed to be real and
individual, but to feel actual, unmawkish emotions and to express them
dramatically. The central quarrel between Kate and Blanche is triggered
by a specific event, Blanche's failed date, but expands movingly and
believably as two lifetimes of repressed pain come to the surface:

> JACK   You want to get it out, Blanche, get it out! Tell her what
> it's like to live in a house that isn't yours. To have to depend
> on somebody else to put the food on your plate every night
> . . . . Tell her, Kate, what it is to be an older sister. To
> suddenly be the one who has to work and shoulder all the
> responsibilities and not be the one who gets the affection. . . .
> BLANCHE   I love you both very much. No matter what Kate says
> to me, I will never stop loving her. But I have to get out. If I
> don't do it now, I will lose whatever self-respect I have left.
> For people like us, sometimes the only thing we really own is
> our dignity.

'For people like us. . . . ' In this scene, in the earlier scene in which
Jack must painfully guide Stanley towards compromising his ideals in
order to keep his job, in Stanley's deep shame at realizing that the
boyish indiscretion of gambling becomes adult irresponsibility when his
contribution to the family income is involved, and in the later scene in
which Blanche fights to make contact with her alienated daughter, the
play rises above Simon comedy and indeed above comedy. *Brighton
Beach Memoirs* actually has less in common with Simon's previous work
than it has with the Depression-era plays of Clifford Odets. Like them it
uses the native American dramatic form of domestic realism, here tem-
pered with warm and unobtrusive humour, to depict a society in crisis
and transition, through its reflection in the everyday lives of ordinary
people.

A sequel, *Biloxi Blues* (1985), is not nearly as strong, but represents
a consolidation of Simon's new-found powers. It amounts to a very

conventional military comedy, with Eugene Jerome experiencing the adventures and misadventures of basic training, but if there is little new, there is also a clear escape from Simon's old vices. The characters have some individuality; the warm humour of Eugene's embarrassed visit to a whore is not spoiled by gratuitous jokes; and the climactic encounter between the rebellious soldier Epstein and the dedicated Sergeant Toomey resolves one of the play's few dramatic subplots satisfactorily. This may seem like faint praise, and indeed the play would hardly attract notice if written by someone else. But all these things had once been beyond Simon, and his casual competence here demonstrates that the superior *Brighton Beach Memoirs* was not a fluke.

(Biographical and psychological critics will note that the character of Arnold Epstein, a bitter New York City Jew whose experience of the army is of humiliation and anti-semitic prejudice, appears to represent a side of himself Simon was unwilling to put into Eugene. There is in fact a pattern of displacement running through all three Eugene Jerome plays. The wise and loving father who guides the Jerome family and supports his in-laws in *Brighton Beach Memoirs* was absent from the Simon family, who actually had to live with their relatives. And a key speech of anger at the father in *Broadway Bound*, a speech that clearly represents the author's feelings, is given to Stanley rather than Eugene.)

Broadway Bound (1986) picks up the story after the war. Stanley and Eugene, now aspiring comic writers, sell their first sketch to a radio programme, but discover that jokes drawn from their family life are painful to the loved ones being ridiculed. Their father leaves the family for his long-time mistress; their socialist grandfather rejects his daughter Blanche for marrying a rich man; and Eugene cajoles his mother into telling the story of the romantic highlight of her youth, the night she danced with movie star George Raft. Even more than *Brighton Beach Memoirs*, *Broadway Bound* is a melodrama with humour rather than a comedy with serious moments; Eugene's parents are not the comically squabbling couple of his radio sketch, but two mismatched and emotionally repressed people with the not-uncommon experience of having drifted apart. The play sympathizes more with Kate than with Jack, but it recognizes that her single-minded commitment to home and family has turned her, like Odets's Bessie Berger, into a repressive, life-draining figure from whom Jack can reasonably feel a need to escape.

It is that double perspective that gives Kate's scene of reminiscence such power, as she briefly becomes (and Eugene is allowed to see) the open, exciting girl she was before she chose to turn herself into a wife and mother. The same complexity is seen in the other characters: grandfather Ben rejects his rich daughter and lives apart from his wife in the name of his socialist principles, but it was he who taught his daughters how to be loving even in the face of rejection. Blanche wears her new prosperity with the same mix of pride and pain with which she wears her mink coat: 'It keeps out the cold, but it also stops my father from reaching out and holding me.' And even Simon's on-stage surrogate becomes more than merely an attractive narrator when his experiences shake him. Stanley's explosion of anger at Jack leads Eugene to realize his own emotional repression –

> I was the one who should have had the fight with him. Only I didn't know I was so angry. Like there's part of my head that makes me this nice, likeable, funny kid . . . and there's the other part, the part that writes, that's an angry, hostile real son of a bitch.   [Ellipses Simon's]

– just as Kate's exposure of her secret, romantic self both thrills and embarrasses him – 'Dancing with my mother was very scary. . . . And holding her like that and seeing her smile was too intimate for me to enjoy. Intimacy is a complex thing. You had to be careful who you shared it with.'

Lost in Yonkers (1991) is a return to more familiar Simon territory, as two precociously witty boys endure the comic frustrations of living with their tyrannical grandmother. But a subplot shows his new mastery of seriousness and psychological depth as the boys' mentally retarded aunt stands up against her mother and claims her measure of dignity and independence. The three Eugene Jerome plays, and *Lost in Yonkers* represent a significant advance for Neil Simon and a valuable contribution to the American repertory. Without departing too far from his strengths as a joke-writer and easy entertainer, he moves into the realm of Clifford Odets by dramatizing the social effects of first the Depression and then the post-war prosperity through their impact on the domestic lives of ordinary people, and into the realm of William Inge by sympathetically and respectfully observing these ordinary people as they make the small compromises and adjustments necessary for survival.

Meanwhile, with Simon continuing to define and dominate the realm of Broadway comedy, few new writers made much impression in this field. Larry Shue's farces provide a satisfying number of laughs in a totally unthreatening environment; in *The Nerd* (Milwaukee 1981) a man is tormented by an unbearably dull and boorish visitor he cannot get rid of, while *The Foreigner* (Milwaukee 1983) presents a man who tries to assure himself a quiet vacation by pretending not to understand English, only to discover that his deception elicits the solicitude and confidences of others. Some of Christopher Durang's plays have a benignly satiric tone: *A History of the American Film* (1978) takes its characters through parodies and pastiches of every classic film from *Intolerance* to *Dr Strangelove*, celebrating in the process the way in which films have guided and reflected American culture; and *Beyond Therapy* (1981), in which two neurotic lovers turn for help to their psychiatrists only to find them even crazier, pokes easy fun at easy targets. Other Durang plays are marked, and possibly marred, by a much darker tone: *Sister Mary Ignatius Explains It All for You* (1979) angrily satirizes a nun whose religion and values are restricted to the most repressive, irrational and life-denying elements of Catholicism; and *The Marriage of Bette and Boo* (1985) is a nightmarish account of the doomed marriage of two sadly trivial people, narrated by their son, who seems to feel that their neuroses and weaknesses were all deliberately adopted with the express purpose of warping him.

Edward Albee and other dramatists of the 1960s

Edward Albee's rate of production, like Arthur Miller's, slowed in the 1970s and 1980s, in his case through an admitted frustration with a theatre and audience that seemed unable to appreciate his work; his last commercial success was *A Delicate Balance* in 1966. The general trend of cold intellectuality and lack of dramatic vitality in his plays that was noticed in the last chapter continued to the point almost of self-parody, as Albee seemed more and more like an author talking to himself in a private vocabulary. *Listening* (British radio, 1976; Hartford, 1977) presents three people in the decaying garden of a mental hospital, two staff members and a patient who make fragmented and unsuccessful attempts to penetrate each other's self-absorption. The Man begs The Woman to acknowledge that they were once lovers; The Woman goes through the rituals necessary to break through The Girl's catatonic withdrawal; and The Girl, in her occasional lucid moments, must constantly interrupt the others' conversations to be heard. In the end The Girl slits her wrists and, although The Man is frightened, The Woman seemingly approves and allows her to die.

As early as *The American Dream* and *The Death of Bessie Smith* Albee had made the Miller-like judgement that self-absorption was immoral and could be murderous. But just as *All Over* seemed to be celebrating the emotionless, life-avoiding characters he had condemned in his earlier plays, so *Listening* seems to accept behaviour he had previously rejected. The play offers no particular sympathy to The Man, who seems most interested in making human contact with the others, and it makes no real criticism of their self-absorption. When The Man finally explodes and cries to The Woman, '*Reveal* yourself!' she replies, 'There is no revelation *in* me'; and a moment later her only response to The Girl's suicide attempt is an aesthetic approval: 'Done beautifully.' In *The Zoo Story* Albee presented the inability to communicate with others as tragic, and in such plays as *Virginia Woolf* and *A Delicate Balance* he stressed the human need for integration and involvement with others. But in *Listening* he seems to be postulating, without emotion, a view of human existence as so empty and without external value that self-referential detachment is an appropriate behaviour.

Oddly, a companion piece, *Counting the Ways* (London, 1976; Hartford, 1977), seems to take the opposite position, celebrating romantic love with a benign and comic awareness of its foibles and imperfections. Beginning when She asks He, 'Do you love me?' it is a series of sketches and blackouts presenting situations in which love may be called into question: in the midst of unsuccessful sex, after an argument, at a time of grief, while consulting flower petals, etc. Nothing really unpleasant is discovered, so the last scene, in which He finally asks if She loves him and She replies, 'I don't *know*. I *think* I do.' is a reassuring joke, suggesting the occasion for another round of considerations, not a negative. Albee labels the play 'A Vaudeville', and it functions as an occasionally thoughtful but never threatening light entertainment.

The Lady from Dubuque (1980) is Albee's most ambitious and significant play of the period, ultimately a failure of execution rather than of conception. A stranger appears in the home of a dying woman and claims to be her mother, here to help her through the process of dying. (The title refers to a comment made in the 1920s about the sophisticated magazine *The New Yorker*, that it was not edited for the archetypal midwesterner; Albee seems to use it to identify Elizabeth as the ultimate Other.) Whether she is meant to be the angel of death or just a guide along the way, the play has echoes of both Thornton Wilder's *Our Town* and Tennessee Williams's *The Milk Train Doesn't Stop Here Anymore* in the idea that dying is a weaning away from life that requires some assistance. But one of the problems of the play is that this process is never really dramatized; Jo's departure seems quick and easy, and is seen entirely from the outside, while her husband's feeling of desertion and exclusion is most strongly dramatized, even though the play keeps declaring it to be irrelevant: 'What does Sam know? Sam only knows what *Sam* needs. . . . And what about what Jo needs? What does what Sam needs have to do with that?'

There are other structural flaws to the play. Since the supernatural visitor does not appear until the very end of the first act, there is no clear focus to the first half, and the audience must spend Act Two recalling and reinterpreting earlier events while keeping up with the new action. Meanwhile, Elizabeth is so pointlessly and cruelly coy about her identity and mission through much of the second act that the audience is likely to turn against her before her role as comforter and guide is finally made clear, and thus to sympathize with Sam's outrage more than the play desires. The potential power of *The Lady from Dubuque* lies in its insight that death is a process the dying must be guided through, even at the cost of excluding the living. The failure of *The Lady from Dubuque* lies in the basic error, far too representative of Albee's later work, of presenting this as an intellectual concept rather than as the play's dramatic and emotional core.

The Man Who Had Three Arms (Chicago, 1982) is a failure of another sort: like some of Tennessee Williams's late plays, it seems to reflect an author unable to separate himself from his own creation. The play takes the form of a lecture by the title character, whose physical abnormality made him a celebrity until the third arm withered and the public lost interest in him; he is reduced now to being the substitute speaker on a minor lecture circuit, telling his story and venting his anger at the fickleness and cruelty of the world. (An Albee play titled *The Substitute Speaker* was repeatedly announced as in progress during the 1960s.) There are some small indications that Albee intended the play as a study in the harmful effects of celebrity on the celebrated, so that Himself's petulance, self-pity and lashing-out would be seen as signs of his spiritual decay. The problem is that Himself's story, of instant elevation to stardom on the basis of his curiosity value and just as instant rejection when he no longer continued to amuse, is very close to Albee's own experience; and Albee was never reticent about expressing his resentment towards the critics and audiences that forsook him after his early triumphs. In the absence of any effective distancing of the play's voice from its central character's, it must inevitably be experienced as Albee's own uncensored demand that the world apologize. Albee's few short plays since 1982 have been kept away from the commercial theatre and neither published nor revived after their brief runs, so, like Williams's late self-pitying works, *The Man Who Had Three Arms* makes an embarrassing coda to a career that began with such accomplishments.

Few other dramatists of the 1960s and early 1970s continued to produce work that fulfilled their early promise. Arthur Kopit's only important play after *Indians* is *Wings* (radio, 1977; New Haven, 1978): through a collage of distorted sounds and fragments of language and non-language, he captures the experience of a woman having and then recovering from a stroke; the rather static play is better suited to its original medium than to the stage. David Rabe proved to be a one-subject playwright with nothing to say after his three powerful Vietnam plays. *In the Boom Boom Room* (1974), an attempt to turn the sordid and pitiful life of a go-go dancer into a metaphor for the American spiritual condition, does not make the evocative connection; and *Hurlyburly* (1984), about a group of men whose treatment of each other and particularly of their women is marked by an infantile need for immediate gratification and a Mamet-like ability to convince themselves of their depth and sincerity, remains on the rather unattractive specific level, with no resonances at all.

Terrence McNally had turned from social commentary to simple farce in the early 1970s, and *It's Only a Play* (1985) seemed to continue that process, skewering the pretensions, despairs and hypocrisies at a Broadway opening night party with delightfully bitchy humour. But McNally's next two plays have more substance. *Frankie and Johnny in the Clair de Lune* (1987) is one of the best of a subgenre of plays about unconventional but deeply sincere lovers slowly breaking through the defences of emotionally wounded women, in what is something of a *leitmotif* in American drama of the 1970s and 1980s; others include Edward J. Moore's *The Sea Horse* (1974), Lanford Wilson's *Talley's Folly* (1979) and *Burn This* (1987), Mark Medoff's *Children of a Lesser God* (1979), William Mastrosimone's *The Woolgatherer* (1980), Gardner McKay's *Sea Marks* (1981), Sam Shepard's *Fool for Love* (1983), and John Patrick Shanley's *Danny and the Deep Blue Sea* (1984). We meet McNally's couple in the middle of the sexual act on their first date, and then watch as the man tries to change the tone of the evening from lust to love. At first she is incredulous, thinking he's just making ritual sweet talk; then annoyed, thinking he is patronizing her; then annoyed at the discovery that he is serious; then threatened by his unrelenting attack on her scepticism; then frightened by the exposure of her own loneliness and need for love; and finally won over. The play is alternately amusing, touching and emotionally disturbing but, like others of its type, it ultimately affirms the romantic fantasy that even in the twentieth century sincere, honest emotion, however unpoetically expressed, will eventually lead to happily-ever-after.

In *The Lisbon Traviata* (1989), McNally seduces us with a lovingly amused look at a harmless eccentricity, only to shock us later with the exposure of its underside. Stephen and Mendy are homosexual opera buffs of the sort that combine flamboyant, self-dramatizing displays of emotion with real obsessiveness, collecting obscure bootleg recordings of Maria Callas and delighting in their erudition in this very narrow field. But a first act of almost pure comedy is followed by the discovery that Stephen's lover Mike is leaving him for another man; Stephen's obsessive hobby is also a way of distancing himself from real life and real emotions, and Mike is willing to settle for a lesser man who will be emotionally present for him. The shock and pain almost draw Stephen back into reality, but in the end he is left alone with his music. *The Lisbon Traviata* had a particularly complex production history, beginning as only the first act, and going through several significant revisions afterwards; and McNally never really succeeded in integrating the two very different acts into one play. And yet, even as a loosely interrelated double bill of one comedy and one drama, it presents a sympathetic reminder that even the most apparently happy in the gay world can be lonely and frightened.

Lanford Wilson

Lanford Wilson's plays after 1975 build on the strengths he had discovered through his earlier experiments, particularly the ability to depict
the complex emotions and relationships of a group of characters through
a domestic realism given a lyrical tone by a musical and poetic use of
language. Wilson is something of an heir to Tennessee Williams in this
regard, though both his prose poetry and his view of life are generally
much more subdued and gentle. Themes introduced in such earlier plays
as *The Hot l Baltimore* are developed further, particularly Wilson's respect
for love and commitment in whatever form they take and his awareness
of the folly and danger of discarding the past.

5th of July (1978), one of Wilson's best plays, mixes humour and
sentiment in the Chekhovian mode of *The Hot l Baltimore* and *The
Mound Builders*, filling the stage with characters each of whom is following his own agenda, and finding that the most dramatic effects come
from small commitments and betrayals. Kenneth Talley, legless Vietnam
veteran, has returned to his family estate in Missouri with the plan of
selling it and moving on. Also in residence are his lover Jed, his sister
June and her precocious daughter Shirley, and his eccentric Aunt Sally.
They are visited by Ken's former student friends John and Gwen, who
may buy the house to convert into a recording studio for Gwen's as-yet-
imaginary career as a singer. Each of these characters is the centre of his
or her own drama: June is sorting out her unresolved sexual tensions
with John; John is cold-bloodedly exploiting his rich wife; Gwen is in
the overdue process of discovering an identity and purpose for herself,
somewhat in parallel with Shirley; and so on. Wilson keeps all these
individual stories going and makes it clear that none of the characters
would admit to being a background figure in someone else's drama,
while still guiding our focus onto Ken. His desire to sell the house is a
symptom of a central void in his character, the inability to accept
responsibility for his own life and the fear of commitment to anything
because it may not be perfect; June accuses him of being 'the
only person I know who can say "I'm not involved" in forty-five
languages'.

Ken's experience in the play is the slow acceptance of his need to
stop drifting and define himself, and of his need for, and ability to rely
on, Jed's love and support. Each of the characters and subplots is able to
serve him in this process. From his anger at John's perfidy he discovers
his ability to feel a commitment to his values; from Sally he learns the
strength of character that is his inheritance; in Gwen and Shirley's comic
attempts at self-definition he sees challenges being faced without the fear
of being ridiculous. And when he falls down and Jed is there instantly to

protect and help him, he accepts his dependence with the security that it will not be exploited.

Wilson confirms Ken's discoveries with several evocative symbols and images. The garden Jed is planting is a commitment that will take years to complete, and the lost species of rose he has rediscovered proves the Talley land a source of life and hope. Aunt Sally scatters her dead husband's ashes in the rose garden, offering the future nourishment from the past. Ken himself recognizes that the mildly scatological myth told by Gwen's musician, in which Eskimos die because their meat is spoiled, is wrong: 'Don't choke on it, don't turn up your nose, swallow it and live, baby.' And it is he who reads the end of a student's science fiction story:

> After they had explored all the suns in the universe, and all the planets of all the suns, they realized that there was no other life in the universe, and that they were alone. And they were very happy, because then they knew it was up to them to become all the things they had imagined they would find.

That the task of becoming yourself is a precious opportunity rather than a burden is a very positive statement for a play about cripples and misfits to make; that the strength to meet this challenge can come from the past and from an unjudgemental acceptance of support in any form is an addition particularly characteristic of Wilson.

The Aunt Sally of *5th of July* and the husband whose ashes she scattered are the subjects of *Talley's Folly* (1979): in a boathouse on the Talley estate in 1944, Matt Friedman courts Sally Talley, and the two emotionally damaged people discover that their common neuroses and fears paradoxically seem to guarantee their happiness. Matt opens the play by asking the audience for its support in his quest for Sally's heart – 'If everything goes well for me tonight, this should be a waltz, one-two-three, one-two-three; a no-holds-barred romantic story, and since I'm not a romantic type, I'm going to need the whole valentine here to help me' – and from then on this little play pretends to be no more than the small, sweet love story it is. It fits comfortably in the context of Wilson's other work in both its quiet poetry and its conviction that in a sometimes cruel world the less-than-perfect is not to be disdained as a refuge.

In *Angels Fall* (1982) Wilson uses an openly artificial device, an accident at a uranium mine, to bring a disparate group of characters into the same place so they can react to each other: a priest, an Indian doctor, a professor recovering from a nervous breakdown, and a rich woman and her lover-protégé. In the course of an afternoon they each slowly emerge from their self-absorption to recognize similarities to the others, and to rediscover their own strengths through the comparisons. Niles's breakdown came when he realized that he did not believe the absolute judgements on which his books and lectures were based, and Father

Doherty recognizes this as a loss of faith. The tennis player Zappy's hypochondria and pre-tournament nerves are a trivial and comic counterpart to Don's fear that Indian health problems are too great to be tackled and Niles's conviction that his life is falling apart. Niles's despair that the academic world is no longer an ivory tower protected from reality is reflected in Doherty's accusation that Don is drawn to laboratory work as an escape.

In trying to convince Don that he has the equivalent of a priestly calling to serve his people through medicine, Doherty evokes an image with resonance for all of them. Niles's commitment to teaching is a calling, and Doherty points out that he never actually quit his job and will almost certainly return to it. Even Zappy can respond to the word, in an eloquent account of how the discovery of his athletic talent changed and defined his life. The final realization is Doherty's as he admits that the calling he is trying to force on Don is his own, and that the doctor must be free to define himself. These rediscoveries of the meaning in their lives do not radically change any of the characters; nobody leaves the play cured or significantly stronger for the experience. All they can really hope for is the ability to carry on, and late in the play Niles and his wife discover in the middle of a witticism that they have it:

> NILES   I seem to be coming apart at the seams on you, don't I?
>   Everything is coming unglued all at once.
> VITA   Not quite.
> NILES   Not quite all at once, or not quite everything?
> VITA   Not quite unglued.

'The only good thing that comes from these silly emergencies, these rehearsals for the end of the world,' concludes Doherty, 'is that it makes us get our act together.' Like many previous American plays, *Angels Fall* searches for reassurance that life can be endured, not triumphed over; and like some, it finds that capacity within the ability of the ordinary person.

Talley & Son (1985; an earlier version was staged in 1980 as *A Tale Told*) returns to Missouri on the same night as *Talley's Folly*, letting us see what is going on back at the house while Matt is courting Sally: essentially a lot of mutual backstabbing among the members of this power- and money-hungry family that resembles Lillian Hellman's Hubbards, though without their dramatic vitality or allegorical power. Wilson seems to have written this play for his own benefit, to give an off-stage reality to the other two Talley plays, without realizing that the story had little to say on its own. Most of the characters, particularly the women, are underwritten; and a comment that the soldiers who will soon be returning from the Second World War will not recognize America because it has changed so much does not really define the play, since the Talleys have not been identified with past or future. Sally's appearance at the beginning and end of the play helps make the rather weak point that she is wise to leave her family for Matt, but that confirms this play's status as little more than a footnote to *Talley's Folly*.

Burn This (Los Angeles, 1987) is an uncharacteristic departure for Wilson, a venture into the world of violent passions and bizarre behaviour more natural to Sam Shepard or David Mamet, and his success in this unfamiliar territory is only partial. The story of the uncontrollable sexual attraction between a somewhat repressed dancer and a near madman suffers from Wilson's inability to make them believably part of the same reality. Anna is a collection of attitudes and clichés (the sensitive but insecure artist, the brittle New Yorker, the sophisticate conquered by a man's tears, etc.) rather than a recognizable person. Pale is a more consistent and individual character, if only because he is defined by his violent self-contradictions: the passionate man driven mad by urban life. Even his most disconnected behaviour, such as interrupting a string of obscene curses at a half-dozen targets to take off his trousers because he is afraid of wrinkling them, is believable if you acknowledge the existence of such people; and certainly his uncontrollable careering about the stage has a theatrical excitement to it. But, for all their typical New York City neuroses, Anna and the secondary characters function on a moderate emotional plane, with no evidence of a capacity for intensity or obsession on Pale's level. Thus *Burn This* does not convince as the story of a mutual surrender to boundless passions, because no one in the play has boundless passions except Pale, and he is clearly an aberration. Instead, the audience is likely to experience it as the story of an emotionally vulnerable girl 'pillaged and raped' (her words) by the Byronic magnetism of an ultimately dangerous alien, and to believe her expressions of helpless foreboding at the end more than his.

It might be instructive to experience this play alongside Sam Shepard's *Fool for Love* which, despite flaws of its own, does succeed in depicting two people trapped by their obsessive emotions. Overpowering passion and aberrant behaviour are not really within Wilson's natural scope; his quietly poetic and Chekhovian style is better suited to capturing the chivalric yearning of Bill for The Girl in *The Hot l Baltimore*, the fairy tale romance of Matt and Sally in *Talley's Folly*, or the understated steadfastness of Jed's devotion to Ken in *5th of July*. Even more, the value of his most successful plays is in the way they gently remind us of truths and values we have lost sight of: the beauty of the past, the comfort of friendship, and the folly of rejecting any source of emotional support because it is imperfect.

Sam Shepard

During the 1970s Sam Shepard gradually abandoned the collage-like style of his early plays for a somewhat more consistent domestic realism, in which bizarre events might take place but the dramatic modes or reality levels would not change or overlap without warning. Among the remaining plays of the earlier style, *Angel City*, *Suicide in B^b* and *Seduced* are the most interesting. Each is at its core a criticism of some aspect of American culture, and each uses symbolism or violations of reality to dramatize its attack. In *Angel City* (San Francisco, 1976) Hollywood producers reaching for the ultimate special effect succeed only in turning themselves into monsters; it thus follows such earlier plays as *Red Cross*, *Icarus's Mother* and *Back Bog Beast Bait* in warning against the irresponsible use of the imagination. In *Suicide in B^b* (New Haven, 1976) a musician symbolically kills off the various false identities others have imposed on him, the play condemning the public's tendency to project its own needs, fears and fantasies on the artist. The central character of *Seduced* (Providence, 1978), based on the billionaire recluse Howard Hughes, is ancient, unkempt, half-mad, and living only in the fantasy-memories he pays others to supply for him. Like the other two plays, *Seduced* has no real plot or character development, but is an extended metaphor for the state of America ('I'm everywhere!. . . I'm all over the country . . . . A phantom they'll never get rid of . . . . Everything they ever aspired to. The nightmare of the nation!'), an image of the pioneering and entrepreneurial spirit turned into a lifeless but indestructible obscenity.

Curse of the Starving Class (London, 1977) is the first play in what would become Shepard's mature style; there are no magical phenomena, sudden character transformations or mixtures of reality and myth, just a family in their home, experiencing the events of a two-day period. Granted, family, home and events are all unusual, but they are not impossible; and when the play offers a metaphor for the human condition, it is through the representative power of realism, the same method used by Clifford Odets, Eugene O'Neill and the mainstream of American drama. Its subject, implied by the title, is a gnawing hunger, but not for food; Shepard repeatedly jokes with that image by bringing abundant quantities of food on stage. His characters are starved for some modest level of fulfilment, for just the chance at happiness, self-definition or self-esteem. Everyone in the family suffers from a sense of incompleteness, which Wesley blames on the faceless 'they' who run the world. Weston identifies them more explicitly with the institutions of American capitalism: 'I figured that's why everyone wants you to buy things. . . . They all want you to borrow anyhow. Banks, car lots, investors. . . .

So I figured if that's the case, why not take advantage of it? Why not go in debt . . . ?' So, on one level, *Curse of the Starving Class* is a variant on *Death of a Salesman*, an indictment of the American system for awakening a hunger it does not fill, and for then punishing the hungry.

The curse seems inescapable: Ella follows the empty promises of a trickster and is cheated; Weston dreams of a new start in Mexico, but the debt collectors are close behind; Emma's fantasized life of crime is just a further commitment to capitalism ('the perfect self-employment') and therefore doomed. Since this is a Sam Shepard play, it is not surprising that the one faint and ultimately chimerical hope lies in a reintegration with tradition and the land. Weston explains how a return to the farm gave him back his sense of self: 'Then it struck me that I actually was the owner. That somehow it was me and I was actually the one walking on my own piece of land. And that gave me a great feeling.' But Weston must run away again, to escape his creditors, and Wesley can only remain by putting on his father's clothes and identity; 'And every time I put one thing on it seemed like a part of him was growing on me. I could feel him taking over me.' Losing one's identity is not a solution to the problem of achieving one's identity; and Shepard can only end the play with the story of a fight between a cat and eagle, an unending and unwinnable struggle to the death.

Arguably Shepard's greatest play, *Buried Child* (San Francisco, 1978) offers a powerful dramatic metaphor for both the corruption of the American spirit and the hope for its salvation. In an assertively ordinary midwestern farmhouse, what would otherwise be an all-American family is marked by spiritual and physical decay. Grandfather Dodge is sick and virtually immobile; his wife Halie flirts drunkenly with the local priest; one son is crippled and the other brain-damaged. Grandson Vince is frightened by the family's bizarreness, but he is unable to deny his ties to them, and at Dodge's death Vince assumes his persona. Ominous hints are dropped through the play of a hidden scandal, eventually revealed as the incestuous child of Halie and her son Tilden, which the family killed and buried; in the final moments Tilden enters with the exhumed body as Halie describes a miraculous abundance of vegetables springing up from the hitherto dead farmland.

Except for those magical crops, the play is wholly realistic in style; these may be odd characters behaving oddly, but they could exist. But the play does not use domestic realism in the manner of Odets and Miller or of *Curse of the Starving Class*, addressing a larger subject through demonstrating its effects on a specific domestic situation. Rather, Shepard here adapts the method of *Operation Sidewinder*, *Seduced* and others of his non-realistic plays, making the specific stand directly for the general through the power of metaphor. This household is not America typified, but America personified: Tilden is identified as a former All-American athlete; the midwestern farm setting automatically suggests a universal;

and Shepard directly invokes the names of Norman Rockwell (the early twentieth-century illustrator who specialized in heartwarming Americana) and the 'Dick and Jane and Spot' of children's books.

If this family is what Norman Rockwell's America has become, it is as the direct result of a loss of connection to the past and a refusal to acknowledge its own past failings. The family exists on denial; Dodge will not admit he recognizes himself in old photos, Vince tries to run away from the family that does not live up to his fantasies, and Bradley insists, 'Nothing's wrong here! Nothin's ever been wrong! Everything's the way it's supposed to be! Nothing ever happened that's bad! Everything is all right here! We're all good people!' The central symbol of both dissociation and denial is the dead child: 'It wanted to grow up in this family. It wanted to be just like us. It wanted to be part of us. We couldn't allow that to grow up right in the middle of our lives. It made everything we'd accomplished look like it was nothin'. . . . I killed it.' One might hear echoes of David Rabe's *Sticks and Bones* in that speech, and Shepard does not have to press the metaphoric meaning any further. Dozens of examples will come to mind of the American cultural compulsion to bury our sins and to rewrite history so that we are always the good guys: slavery, the Indians, Vietnam. To preserve the family's sense of itself as pure, the family does the most un-family thing possible, killing a child, and thus destroys its capacity to be a family. By committing atrocities to deny its capacity to commit atrocities, America has decayed into an obscene parody of itself.

But the process is not irreversible. Vince runs away, but discovers that the past cannot be denied: 'I drove all night. . . . I could see myself in the windshield. . . . As though I was looking at another man. . . . And then his face changed. His face became his father's face. . . . And his father's face changed to his Grandfather's face. And it went on like that.' Through courage, honour or madness – and Shepard does not really seem to care which – Vince accepts his connection to the past and returns, declaring himself the new owner of the farm. At virtually the same moment Tilden enters with the exhumed child, and Halie's off-stage voice ends the play:

> I've never seen such corn. . . . Tall as a man already. This early in the year. Carrots, too. Potatoes. Peas. It's like a paradise out there. . . . It's a miracle, Dodge. I've never seen a crop like this in my whole life. Maybe it's the sun. Maybe that's it. Maybe it's the sun.

That last word is a pun, of course, referring to both Vince, who is going to save the family by drawing on his spiritual inheritance (earlier Halie called him 'an angel. A guardian angel. He'd watch over us. He'd watch over all of us.'), and to the baby, who will now finally be acknowledged and dealt with. Neither offers an easy or costless salvation; Vince appears to sacrifice his youth and even his sanity, sinking into his grandfather's immobility, while the baby will bring the shame and scandal it was killed to avoid. But this difficult, painful and uncertain path is the path to spiritual rebirth, as the sudden flowering of the farm makes clear. And on the metaphoric level Shepard repeats the assertion that is a *leitmotif* of his career: that the future of America lies in a reintegration with the best, and an acknowledgement of the worst, in its past.

In *True West* (San Francisco, 1980) Shepard invokes mythic imagery and power without once violating the bounds of domestic realism. Aspiring screenwriter Austin and his criminal, semi-literate brother Lee are trying to write a script based on an idea of Lee's. They ultimately fight, and Austin is trapped in the position of victor, unable to kill his brother but afraid to let him go. Much of the theatrical power comes from the simple display of animation; as in some other Shepard plays, notably *Fool for Love*, the characters spend a good part of the play careering violently about the stage, unable to control the raw energy within them. But beneath this surface the play is an inquiry into the subject of its title: is the uniquely American myth of the West valid and, if not, what is the reality that displaces it? (Clearly this question is of more than passing significance to Shepard, whose reverence for the mythic past drives so many of his plays.) Lee's script idea is a pure chase story, one man following another across country in a drive for vengeance with no clear beginning or end:

> So they take off after each other straight into an endless black prairie. . . . What they don't know is that each of 'em is afraid, see. Each one separately thinks that he's the only one that's afraid. . . . And the one who's chasin' doesn't know where the other is taking him. And the one who's being chased doesn't know where he's going.

That account, which ends the first act, is eerie and powerful, but the question remains whether it is 'true'. The answer comes in the final fight between the brothers, when Austin is temporarily the victor and then tries to find a way out of the impasse: 'I'll make ya' a deal. You let me outa' here. Just let me get to my car. All right, Lee? Gimme a little headstart and I'll turn you loose. Just gimme a little headstart. All right? . . . ' At that moment, without violating any of the rules of dramatic realism, *True West* leaps from domestic melodrama into myth and metaphor. What will follow this tableau, it is perfectly clear, is the real-life enactment of Lee's script. The fiction has come alive, and the living people have become characters in the fiction. Myth and reality combine, the True West encompassing both of them, as once more Shepard asserts his conviction that the dream of the American West is a truth that it is dangerous folly to deny.

Fool for Love (San Francisco, 1983) is a theatrical study in inescapable and uncontrollable human passions, as Eddie and May, long-time lovers and, we eventually learn, half-brother and sister, are trapped in a can't-stay-together-can't-stay-apart obsession. Even more than *True West*, the play is driven theatrically by the high energy Shepard demands in performance; his opening stage direction stresses that '*This play is to be performed relentlessly without a break*', and Eddie and May do nothing at half-steam. At various times she '*erupts furiously*', '*stares at him wild-eyed*', gives an '*agonized scream*', '*slams wall with her elbow*', '*pins him with her eyes*', is carried '*screaming and kicking*', and '*starts lashing out*'. He '*bangs his head into wall*', '*moves violently toward her*', '*crashes into stage-right wall*', '*drags chair violently*', and '*crashes to the floor*'. Both of them slam all doors repeatedly, and they take turns moving around the edges of the room, hugging the walls as if testing the power of the physical boundaries to hold them in. Quiet, controlled emotions are not within their repertoire; a '*Long, tender kiss*' is followed immediately by a vicious knee to the groin. *Fool for Love*, like many of Shepard's other plays, functions primarily as metaphor; it is not the narrated story of Eddie and May that the play is about, but their dramatized passion – and, by extension, any passion. The image of the motel at the edge of the desert, the pitifully small and fragile enclosure in the vastness with people bouncing off its inner walls, stands for the inevitably doomed attempt to keep infinite human emotion within the finite human frame. To be human, says the play, is to be made of forces so large they cannot be controlled, so essential they cannot be escaped, so extreme and contradictory that tenderness cannot be separated from violence or love from hate, so inherent in the fact of being human that their story can have no real beginning or end.

A Lie of the Mind (1985) has an almost O'Neill-like theme, the superiority of fantasy over realism as a means of coping with life. Insanely jealous Jake has viciously beaten his wife Beth, leaving her brain-damaged. He retreats to his family and to madness, while Beth slowly recovers in the bosom of her own dysfunctional family. When Jake's brother Frankie visits, Beth fantasizes him into a kinder, repentant Jake. Jake believes that Beth and Frankie are lovers, but in his madness he finds an escape from his jealousy, and he gives them his blessing. Once again Shepard builds his play on a metaphor, this time Beth's brain damage, which stands for the dissociation from self and distortion of relationships that is everyone's condition: Jake and Mike both see Beth only as extensions of themselves (Beth to Mike: 'You have a feeling I'm you.'); Lorraine, Sally and Meg all impose fictional identities on others and then relate to them (Beth to Meg: 'You don' know. Only love.'); Baylor withdraws ('This is my father. He's given up love.'). Thus, just as Beth must fight her way back to the use of language and coherent thought, everyone else in the play must find some means of defining self and surroundings; and for virtually all of them the process paradoxically involves a fantasy or escape from reality. By imagining Frankie to be a kind and loving Jake, Beth can find peace; by withdrawing into madness, Jake escapes his jealousy. Mike takes comfort in the role of protective and avenging brother; Sally and Lorraine run away to an imagined Utopia; and Meg and Baylor find serenity in the rituals and habits of a long marriage. Only Frankie, the one character trying to deal with the problems rationally and realistically, is left confused and alone, unable to take Beth's counsel: 'Pretend. Because it fills me. Pretending fills. Not empty. Other. Ordinary. Is no good. Empty. Ordinary is empty.'

It is striking that Shepard capped a long period of stylistic experiment with a return to domestic realism in his later plays. Of course his brand of realism is not the same as anyone else's, with unusual and even bizarre characters acting in ways that are not fully explained. But, with the occasional small exceptions, such as the magic vegetables in *Buried Child*, his best plays since *The Tooth of Crime* do not reach for new theatrical vocabularies, mix metaphors, offer isolated images in place of continuity, violate the laws of reality or change inexplicably from the tone and dramatic genre in which they begin. If the best of them – *Buried Child*, *True West*, perhaps *Fool for Love* – achieve mythic resonances, it is through exploiting the power of realism, not escaping from it. Like Elmer Rice, Maxwell Anderson, Eugene O'Neill and others before him, and like Lanford Wilson alongside him, Shepard found his way back to the American drama's natural mode.

David Mamet

David Mamet brings to the American theatre a particular sensitivity to the ways in which language is used, apart from its communicative function, to give shape and meaning to its users' lives. His characters tend to come from closed worlds with their own cultures, myths, codes and jargon – old men, swinging singles, minor criminals, high-pressure salesmen, Hollywood hustlers. Their lives are marked by frustrations and feelings of impotence that are likely to explode in bitter displays of rage unless they are controlled or diverted through something that gives the characters a reassuring sense of dignity: affectations of wisdom, of honour, or of moral superiority. In most cases, all it takes to achieve this comforting sense is language that *sounds* wise, honourable or moral; for Mamet's characters form is more convincing than content. Early in his career Mamet was celebrated for the accuracy of his ear and the perfection with which he captured the speaking styles of each subculture. Later it became apparent that Mamet-language is as artificial and stylized in its own way as, say, Tennessee Williams's lush prose poetry: a heightened style that captures the essence of its speakers through intensification rather than stenographic transcription.

The importance of self-definition and the use of language to achieve it are both apparent in Mamet's first successful play, the brief *The Duck Variations* (Plainfield, Vermont, 1972). In a series of short scenes two old men sitting in a park exchange inanities and misinformation on a variety of subjects, including ducks. Though virtually everything they say is empty or wrong, the ability to express themselves in the rhythms of epigrams or the vocabulary of profound thought is sufficient to give them a sense of value and dignity:

> The battle between the two is as old as time. The ducks propagating, the Herons eating them. . . . Each keeping the other in check, down through history, until a bond of unspoken friendship and respect unites them, even in the embrace of death. . . . Survival of the fittest. The never-ending struggle between heredity and environment. . . . Who can say to what purpose? . . . We do not know. But this much we *do* know. As long as the duck exists, he will battle day and night, sick and well with the Heron, for so is it writ.

Of course that does not mean anything, but it sounds as if it did, and that is enough to satisfy both speaker and listener.

In *Sexual Perversity in Chicago* (Chicago, 1974) this kind of meaning-in-empty-language is shown to have a dark side. The perversity of the title is a normal, healthy sexual romance which is broken up when the couple's friends invoke the codes of their respective societies. Bernie is a self-proclaimed swinger whose reduction of women to sex objects barely disguises a fear and hatred of their sexual power ('Coming out here on the beach. Lying all over the beach, flaunting their bodies.'). Joan is a feminist who is afraid of sex ('Look at the incidence of homosexuality . . . the number of violent, sex-connected crimes . . . all the anti-social behaviour that chooses sex as its form of expression.'). Separately they use their mastery of their jargons to lure Dan and Deborah away from their rather charming romance and back into their old habits of thinking:

> BERNIE   You getting serious? I mean she seemed like a hell of a girl, huh? The little I saw of her. . . . So what can you tell from seeing a broad one, two, ten times. You're seeing a lot of this broad. . . .
>
> JOAN   . . . the fact is if you take a grown man whose actions and whose outlook are those of a child, who wants nothing

more or better than to have someone who will lick his penis
and grin at his bizarre idea of wit. . . .

Eventually what *sounds* right becomes more real to the lovers than what
feels right, and the play ends with their separation, Deborah blaming
herself for falling, while Dan joins Bernie in ogling and cursing the girls
on the beach.

That language creates identity and also helps protect one from feelings of inadequacy and rage is central to *American Buffalo* (1977). Three
minor criminals planning a robbery are so insecure in their relationships
to each other, and so incompetent as criminals, that the jockeying for
power and the sheer logistics of the job overwhelm them. One finally
blows up in rage and frustration, but then finds his way back, with the
others, to the level of calm and friendship at which they began. The title
refers to a valuable coin that triggered the plan; it may suggest that these
characters, and their view of themselves as outlaws, are pitiful anachronisms. The men speak a *patois* that resembles the dialect invented by
Damon Runyon for his stories of the New York underworld in the
1920s: almost consciously artificial, combining extra-correct grammar
and courtesy with vulgarity, obscenity and a certain amount of verbiage
designed merely to fill the empty spaces. For those who really have
nothing, it is essential to *sound* as if they have values ('You're right, and
you do what you think is right, Don.'), dignity ('No, I am sorry, Don, I
cannot brush this off. They treat me like an asshole, they are an
asshole.'), and wisdom ('I want to tell you something. . . . Things are
not always what they seem to be.'). Language gives them the confidence
that they are capable of pulling off this job, even as their bumbling
proves that they are not – that is to say, language gives them the confidence that they are worth something, even if the facts of their lives
suggest otherwise. And, significantly, when things fall apart it is the language of forgiveness and reconciliation that leads them to the belief that
they have achieved reconciliation, and thus to peace: 'I fucked up.' –
'No. You did real good. . . . ' – 'Thank you.' – 'That's all right.'

As with some of Sam Shepard's plays, it is the danger of barely repressed violence that drives *American Buffalo* and several other Mamet
plays in the theatre, but what lingers in the audience's mind is likely to
be the hint of Tennessee Williams and Eugene O'Neill in the picture of
characters frightened by life and unsure of their ability to cope with its
ordinary demands. Several of Mamet's lesser plays have this same under-
lying observation: *A Life in the Theater* (Chicago, 1976) traces the small
rise of one actor and the small, sad decline of another through the subtle
power shifts in their backstage conversations; *The Woods* (Chicago, 1977)
shows a clearly incompatible couple driven by their fears to stay
together; *Edmond* (Chicago, 1982) shows a man conspiring in his own
degradation because the only shelter from the pain of existence is a

complete loss of ego. Other minor plays draw their energy from surprising and enlightening juxtapositions of language. In the radio play *The Water Engine* (1977) the exalted and optimistic language of a World's Fair guide and a riches-promising chain letter clashes ironically with the sordid tale (and classic American legend) of big business suppressing a lone inventor's discovery. *Prairie du Chien* (radio, 1979) juxtaposes a ghost story of high passions and violence with the more mundane emotions of reality; *Lakeboat* (Milwaukee, 1980) lets the inarticulate talk of a shipload of sailors create a sense of the milieu; and *The Shawl* (Chicago, 1985) enjoys the gap between a charlatan fortune-teller's professional patter and his plain-spoken explanations of the tricks of the trade.

The subculture of *Glengarry Glen Ross* (London, 1983) is that of high-pressure land salesmen. Two familiar Mamet themes are reiterated: the degree to which their language and thought processes limit and control them, and the importance to such marginal men of the fantasy that they have a calling and a code that set them apart from others. The play opens with brief scenes that constitute a virtual textbook lesson in selling modes: begging his boss for better 'leads', Levene ducks and weaves, trying to anticipate and counter every objection – ' . . . all I'm saying, put a *closer* on the job. There's more than one man for the . . . Put a . . . wait a second, put a *proven man out* . . . and you watch, now *wait* a second' [ellipses Mamet's] – while Moss, luring a colleague into a criminal plot, uses the trick of making him think he has already agreed; and Roma disguises his pitch so well that we think he is just rambling aimlessly to a stranger until 'You get befuddled by a middle-class morality' leads somehow to 'I do those things which seem correct to me *today*' and thence somehow to 'This is a piece of land. Listen to what I'm going to tell you now.'

But these skills are all that these men have, and they are forced to make them a basis of pride and self-definition, for want of any other material. When through the office manager's interference Roma loses a sale, the identification of salesmanship and manhood bursts out:

> ROMA   You stupid fucking cunt. . . . Whoever told you you
> could work with *men*? . . . What you're hired for is to *help* us
> . . . to help *men* who are going *out* there to try to earn a *living*. You *fairy*. . . .
> LEVENE   You have to learn it in the streets. You can't *buy* that.
> You have to *live* it. . . . 'Cause your partner *depends* on it
> . . . . you're *scum*.

And yet, despite this pride and sense of comradeship, these men cannot help cheating, lying and manipulating; it is what they do. The lead Williamson makes Levene demean himself for is a fake; Moss pushes his robbery plan until he finds someone he can con; Roma and Levene instantly invent a complex lie to befuddle a wavering customer; and

Roma, after declaring undying admiration for Levene, tries to cheat him out of commissions. The skills and instincts that give these characters their sense of identity and worth also cripple them, making them incapable of honesty, honour or even a simple, unpremeditated conversation.

Speed-the-Plow (1988) tells much the same story, this time in the somewhat less life-or-death context of Hollywood, as a producer and studio executive con each other with unctuous flattery and insincere intimacy. When a secretary tries to advance herself by joining the game, the producer whose project she threatens uses his superior skill to destroy her. Many of Mamet's familiar themes are here: the comradeship of fellow professionals and contempt for the outsider; the use of language that has the sound and rhythm of meaningful statement as a substitute for meaningful statement; the inability of the born conman to stop conning, with the paradox that the most skilled conmen may be the most easily cheated; and the need of these shallow characters to believe they are deeper and more sensitive than they really are. What is new, or has not been so apparent since *The Duck Variations,* is the humour; it is not only psychologically insightful that the men can convince themselves that they are deep thinkers and sensitive human beings –

> GOULD   Charl, I just hope.
> FOX   What?
> GOULD   The shoe was on the other foot, I'd act in such a . . .
> FOX   . . . hey . . .
> GOULD   Really, princely way towards *you.*
> FOX: I *know* you would, Bob, because lemme tell you: experiences like this, *films* like this . . . these are the films . . .
> GOULD   . . . Yes . . .
> FOX   *These* are the films, that whaddayacallit . . . [*long pause*] that make it all worthwhile.   [Ellipses Mamet's]

– it is also devastating satire. And still there is a point being made: if even these characters must play psychological and linguistic tricks on themselves to give themselves a sense of worth, then that need and that method must indeed be universal. Mamet may have a tendency to tell the same story over and over, but it is a good story, and he tells it with style, insight and theatrical vitality.

August Wilson

The most important new American dramatist of the 1980s is August Wilson, a black writer who has taken upon himself the task of dramatizing the experience of black Americans in the twentieth century through a series of plays, one for each decade (though not offered in historical order). It is part of Wilson's conceit that each play is written from the point of view of that decade, without the comforts or ironies hindsight might provide. So successful has Wilson been in this project that each of the four plays produced in the 1980s is both a powerful drama and a startling illumination of the black experience.

From a later perspective, the 1920s might be seen as a significant turning point in black American life, as the last remnants of the slavery world slowly gave way to the promises of the new century. But Wilson's historical insight is that only one of those movements was apparent at the time: clearly something was ending for black Americans, but there was no sense of anything replacing it. *Ma Rainey's Black Bottom* (1984) is set in 1927, as the blues singer Ma Rainey (a historical figure, fictionalized in the play) records some songs, and her musicians rehearse and kill time. One of them, Toledo, expresses the era's sense of black history:

> Everybody come from different places in Africa, right? Come from different tribes and things. Soonawhile they began to make one big stew. . . . Now it's over. . . . The colored man is the leftovers . . . . Done went and filled the white man's belly and now he's full and tired and wants you to get out the way.

The music that fills the play (which is not the familiar my-baby-left-me slow blues but the earlier, very earthy and life-affirming style of the 1920s) is a powerful identity-defining force, and the source of Ma Rainey's power:

> I always got to have some music going on in my head somewhere. It keeps things balanced. . . . White folks don't understand about the blues . . . You don't sing to feel better. You sing 'cause that's a way of understanding life. . . . The blues help you get out of bed in the morning. You get up knowing you ain't alone.

But it is also a commodity being bought and abused by the white world. Ma is aware of this, and has the intelligence to make sure she is paid well for selling her birthright: 'As soon as they get my voice down on them recording machines, then it's just like if I'd be some whore and they roll over and put their pants on.' The younger musician Levee is too blinded by ambition to realize that his music will be taken from him; and when the white man steals his songs and denies him the chance to record, he has no philosophy or historical perspective to fall back on. He experiences in an overpowering instant what Ma and Toledo had seen and accepted: the apparent end of a culture and a race.

Lashing out in frustration, he kills Toledo, ironically and tragically destroying his last connection with his racial heritage. If history has shown that things actually (if slowly) improved for black Americans after the 1920s, Wilson makes us understand that an unforeseeable future offered no comfort to a people whose only experience was the loss of a rich and life-defining past.

In *Fences* (1987), set in 1957, Wilson again chooses a historical moment which hindsight recognizes as coming just before a period of positive change for black Americans, and again he makes us see that the future was not apparent at the time. Troy Maxton represents the first generation of black Americans to progress into the middle class through pride and determination, but his instinct is to consolidate and protect what he has rather than risk it with further ambition; he sabotages his son Cory's hopes of college because they seem dangerously over-reaching. Troy *has* accomplished a great deal, and one of the play's purposes is to remove our memory of the even greater advances to come in the next decade so we can appreciate the plateau black Americans reached in the 1950s. But those who could only see how far they had come would have difficulty imagining an even grander future; and the inevitable clash between father and son becomes especially painful when both have reason to believe themselves in the right. One of the sad ironies of the 1950s that Wilson dramatizes is the fact that those who should have been heroes of black history, the first generation to achieve security and dignity, became villains in the eyes of the next generation because their fear of losing what they had gained made them conservative. That is the purpose of the coda-like final scene, in which Cory is made to understand that his generation's victories will be achieved because of those who came before, not in spite of them.

The second irony in the play is that Troy himself is unable to appreciate and enjoy his own accomplishments. Because he can only see it as something to lose, Troy's success weighs him down with responsibility, and this responsible family man is driven to violate the family in search of some respite from the burden: 'She gives me . . . a different understanding about myself. . . . I ain't got to wonder how I'm gonna pay the bills or get the roof fixed. I can just be a part of myself that I ain't never been.' Since at least as far back as *Death of a Salesman* dramatists have found a particularly American tragedy in the morality or social condition that forces a man to deny himself in order to do right. Troy Maxton fails the test – he violates his own principles in the name of self-fulfilment – and he pays the price. But like Arthur Miller, though somewhat less angrily, August Wilson recognizes that the fault lies in the times rather than the man; and, like most other plays on this theme, *Fences* will not condemn its hero-victim.

With *Joe Turner's Come and Gone* (1988), Wilson returns to the theme of lost identity, this time in personal terms. In 1911 any black American under the age of 45 was born into freedom, and even those older had spent most of their lives free. Wilson makes us see that this extraordinary advance had its price; as he explains in an introductory note, 'Isolated, cut off from memory, having forgotten the names of the gods, . . . they carry as part and parcel of their baggage a long line of separation and dispersement . . . as they search for ways to reconnect.' While the younger characters in the play function in an empty and hedonistic present, those with experience and memory look for some continuation or replacement of their lost cultural identity. The metaphor that Bynum, the conjure-man, offers for this missing element is the private song each person must create for himself out of himself and sing as a declaration of himself. Loomis, recently freed from the private chain gang of Joe Turner, has lost his: 'What he wanted was your song. . . . Now he's got you bound up to where you can't sing your own song. Couldn't sing it them seven years 'cause you was afraid he would snatch it from under you. But you still got it. You just forgot how to sing it.' Loomis rediscovers his selfhood almost by accident, in a moment of frustration at his wife's attempts to win him to her religion:

> MARTHA   Jesus bled for you . . . .
> LOOMIS   I don't need nobody to bleed for me! I can bleed for
> myself . . . .
> *(Loomis slashes himself across the chest. He rubs the blood over his face and comes to a realization.)*
> I'm standing! I'm standing! My legs stood up!

It is a significant dramatic weakness of this scene that Wilson must explain the meaning of the moment in a stage direction ('*Having found his song, the song of self-sufficiency, . . . he is free to soar. . . .* ') rather than making it fully clear on stage. That, along with the heavy reliance on mysticism, makes *Joe Turner's Come and Gone* the least effective of his plays so far. Nevertheless, the central image of the personal song is powerful; and the experience being described, of the first black generation faced with the task of self-definition, is a valuable chapter in the enriched history of America Wilson is writing.

The *Piano Lesson* (1990) also combines a resonant and evocative central imagery with an obscuring mysticism. In 1937 a black family owns an old piano filled with reverent associations: their slave ancestors were sold for it, family portraits are carved in it, and their father died stealing it from the white family that had owned it and them. But now that man's son has the opportunity to buy the farm his family had been slaves on, and, despite his sister's opposition, wants to sell the piano to raise the needed money. The audience must respond to the piano as an almost holy relic, and share Berniece's conviction that 'Money can't buy what that piano cost', but Boy Willie's dream is equally compelling; his quietly understated comment that 'This time I get to keep all the cotton' makes it clear that his triumph will be achieved in the name of those who preceded him.

The conflict between sister and brother presents one part of Wilson's definition of the black American experience of the 1930s: an opportunity, for the particularly fortunate, to have either a past or a future, but not both. To achieve his ambition, Boy Willie must, it seems, turn his back on the sacrifices of his ancestors ('You can always get you another piano'); in order to honour those ancestors, Berniece must not only block her brother but deny the validity of his ambition ('You right at the bottom with the rest of us'). Boy Willie hints at a way out of this impasse when he shows that he does recognize the piano's symbolic value, insisting only that the way to show respect to such an inheritance is to make use of it:

> The only thing my daddy had to give me was that piano. And he died over giving me that. I ain't gonna let it sit up there and rot without trying to do something with it. . . . Alright now, if you say to me, Boy Willie, I'm using that piano. I give out lessons on it and that help me make my rent or whatever. Then that be something else. I'd have to go on and say, well, Berniece using that piano. She building on it.

At the end, when Boy Willie must fight a vengeful ghost from the white family (a theatrically weak climax, since the mystical element seems imposed on the essentially realistic play, and the fight is off-stage), Berniece saves him by playing a song calling on the spirits of their ancestors to intervene. Now that Berniece has made use of the piano, Boy Willie acknowledges her right to keep it, and leaves to look elsewhere for his money; and Wilson ends this play with the most hopeful and reassuring note of his four plays so far: if the past is not just honoured but invoked, not just respected but used to serve the present, then it need not stand in opposition to the future.

Women dramatists: Wasserstein, Henley, Norman

Almost certainly more plays by women were produced in the 1970s and 1980s than during any other period, possibly more than in all other periods combined. Those of Wendy Wasserstein, Beth Henley and Marsha Norman stand out and complement each other. Wendy Wasserstein's plays focus on the stressful and confusing experience of the generation of American women who came of age in the 1970s, the first to experience the opportunities and frustrations of the feminist era. *Uncommon Women and Others* (1977) follows a group of over-achieving young women through their years in an exclusive college as they try to sort out the conflicting signals their culture, their families and their own emotions are sending them. The college repeatedly reminds them of their opportunities and of their obligation as an intellectual élite to be in the forefront of social revolution – 'Am I saying that anatomy is destiny? No . . . . Today all fields are open to women' – but at the same time offers courses in Gracious Living and suggests that worldly success 'can happen without loss of gaiety, charm or femininity'. The highest achiever in the graduating class is applauded for choosing law school, while the weakest is advised to take a typing course. Buffeted by these contradictions, given models ranging from wife-and-mother to bluestocking to professional to 'girl friday for an eastern senator', the young women flounder helplessly. One retreats into the brainless cheerleader mode of an earlier generation; one cuddles her dolls while dreaming of the handsome doctor who will save her from having to make choices; one retreats into near-catatonia; one moves forward, without enthusiasm or real direction, along the professional path: 'Just once it would be nice to wake up with nothing to prove. . . . But if I didn't fulfill obligations or weren't exemplary, then I really don't know what I'd do.' In a frame set six years later, some of the women meet to discover that nothing has become clearer; they still think of themselves as in transit, and the rallying cry of their college days – 'When we're thirty we're going to be pretty fucking amazing' – has merely been adjusted to' . . . forty-five . . . '.

Though it has an entirely new set of characters, *Isn't It Romantic?* (1983) essentially picks up the story where *Uncommon Women* left it. Struggling to begin her career, Janie Blumberg must juggle the distractions of equally struggling and frantic friends, the intrusive and smothering love of her parents, and the allure of what once might have been every woman's dream, a rich and loving doctor who wants nothing more than to marry her and absorb her into his life. Wasserstein's point is that choices have become harder, not easier; even in the post-feminist world the prospect of surrender to a protective man is very enticing, and all the things modern women have been taught to demand as their right are draining. Janie's friend Harriet asks her apparently successful mother whether the whole feminist agenda is just a fantasy: 'Mother, do you think it's possible to be married or live with a man, have a good relationship and children that you share equal responsibility for, build a career, and still read novels, play the piano, have women friends, and swim twice a week?' Her mother's answer is that it is impossible, but that a woman who chooses one or two items from that list and is willing to forgo the others without regret can find satisfaction. Janie and Harriet make their choices, career for one and marriage for the other, and begin the move forward with very unsteady optimism.

Wasserstein's *The Heidi Chronicles* (1988) continues the saga with a new group of characters. The life of evidently successful art historian Heidi Holland is told in flashbacks starting in the 1960s: self-consciously 'sensitive' adolescence, college idealism, seduction by an attractive sexist, feminism, watching activist friends burn out or sell out, and so on. Wasserstein shows that the problems that confused women in 1970 and 1980 are still unresolved; making what is supposed to be an inspirational speech at her school reunion, Heidi confesses, 'I'm afraid I haven't been happy for some time. . . . It's just that I feel stranded. And I thought the whole point was that we wouldn't feel stranded.' Particularly depressing is the discovery that her generation of women, those who began the struggle in the early 1970s, not only accomplished little for themselves, but merely made it easier for their younger sisters to conform, accepting the material benefits of their career opportunities with no sense of debt or of responsibility to continue the effort. And yet Heidi's story, like the others, ends with a quiet optimism. Heidi has adopted a baby girl, and she closes the play with the most traditional of comforts – that she has helped make the future a little better for her daughter: 'And [a man]'ll never tell her it's either/or, baby. And she'll never think she's worthless unless he lets her have it all. And maybe, just maybe, things will be a little better. And yes, that does make me happy.'

Beth Henley's plays are generally about ordinary southerners who turn out to have unexpected quirks or askew values, so that mundane events turn into bizarre adventures and bizarre adventures into unnoticed trivia. *Crimes of the Heart* (Louisville, 1979) is the story of the MaGrath sisters of Mississippi: Babe has just shot her husband, after he found her with a fifteen-year-old black boy; Lenny has decided on the life of an old maid; and Meg has come home from her failed attempt at a singing career for an affair with her old boyfriend. Filling any gaps in this already complicated situation are their antagonistic cousin, their dying grandfather, Babe's amorous lawyer, some compromising photos, a horse struck by lightning, and the memory of their mother, who committed suicide by hanging herself and the family cat. Clearly, Henley is drawing on the same tradition of gothic and grotesque that has inspired southern writers from Faulkner to Williams, though with a particularly benign and loving humour that assures all will be well.

The basic joke of *Crimes of the Heart* is a moral and emotional displacement that makes the sisters' response to events always somehow just off-centre:

> MEG   So, Babe shot Zackery Botrelle, the richest and most powerful man in all of Hazlehurst, slap in the gut. It's hard to believe.
> LENNY   It certainly is. Little Babe – shooting off a gun.

Repeatedly a fact or plot twist that should distress them is met with utter calm or hardly absorbed, while smaller things distract their attention or engage their emotions. Childhood grudges are more real than present dangers; and grief over their mother's death is overshadowed by curiosity about why she killed the cat. The waxing and waning tensions of the moment lead them to respond with hysterical laughter to the news that their grandfather is in a coma, while the thought of the lightning-struck horse moves them to tears. But beneath these jokes is a serious vision. Meg faces her failure as a singer and her inability to win her old swain back; Lenny overcomes the embarrassment that has stifled her romantic life; and Babe, driven to a failed suicide attempt, realizes why her mother killed the cat: because death might be lonely, and she needed the company. When Meg sums up the situation by saying, 'But, Babe, we've just got to learn how to get through these real bad days here, I mean, it's getting to be a thing in our family', Henley shows that the MaGrath sisters' curiously displaced reactions to reality actually protect them from the pains of reality. Unlike their mother, they will never find life too painful, and unlike her they will never be lonely. The play ends with the sisters laughing over the pleasure of eating birthday cake for breakfast, their inherent innocence guaranteeing them happiness.

Henley's next play has much the same quality, with slightly skewed characters having bizarre experiences but ultimately protected by their inability to distinguish between the trivial and the serious and by their inherent good natures. In *The Miss Firecracker Contest* (Buffalo, 1981) a poor girl looks for some vindication for her indignities in the local beauty contest while her rich cousins cope with their separately tangled love lives. She loses the contest, the love lives are not sorted out, and a few broken hearts seem possible in the future. But all is purified by the complete absence of malice, and the characters end the play innocently enjoying a fireworks display. *The Debutante Ball* (Costa Mesa, 1987) lays the gothic element on somewhat more thickly: a mother who has lived in scandal since killing her husband plans to use her daughter's formal presentation to society as the occasion of her own social rehabilitation. But baby is panicked by the approaching ball, and it is eventually revealed that she was the murderer. Secondary characters more than fill the play with additional bizarre touches and plot twists, but the saving innocence of the earlier plays is absent here, and the play is more grotesque than comic.

Indeed, it is true of both these plays that, at their weakest, they seem made up of leftover pieces of *Crimes of the Heart*, revisiting the same world and recycling the same jokes with decreasing effectiveness. Perhaps sensing this, Henley turned in *Abundance* (Costa Mesa, 1989) to a new setting and subject, tracing the lives of two mail-order brides in the nineteenth-century West. One meets nothing but hardship and disappointment, but attains a certain moral stature by resolutely honouring her commitment to her brutal and unproviding husband, while the other rises above her difficulties to achieve security and social success, but at a price to her soul. The play's title takes on multiple and sometimes ironic resonances as the promise implied in the myth of the American West is examined through the experience of women.

[The regional local-colour quality of Henley's earlier plays is present in several other successful dramas and comedies of the period. Both Alfred Uhry's *Driving Miss Daisy* (1987), about the friendship that develops between a southern gentlewoman and her black chauffeur over twenty-five years, and Robert Harling's *Steel Magnolias* (1987), about the mutual support provided by the women in a Louisiana beauty parlour, have some of the flavor of *Crimes of the Heart*. Earlier, Preston Jones's 'Texas Trilogy' of *The Last Meeting of the Knights of the White Magnolia* (Dallas, 1973), *The Oldest Living Graduate* (Dallas, 1974) and *Lu Ann Hampton Laverty Oberlander* (Dallas, 1974) offered a similar sentimentally comic picture of small-town Texas life.]

The third notable woman dramatist of the period is Marsha Norman, whose early plays show little people taking little steps in their search for happiness, steps that the plays cannot see as offering a great deal of promise or hope. *Getting Out* (Louisville, 1977) finds Arlene, released from prison after eight years, attempting to adjust to spiritual as well as physical freedom. The guarded, self-protective persona she had adopted in order to survive the brutality of prison is difficult to give up, especially since there are those, like her former pimp, ready to exploit any sign of softness in her. Overlapping and sometimes simultaneous scenes show her younger self, Arlie, entering prison as a dynamic and self-reliant, if undisciplined, girl and slowly learning to repress her personality. Norman thus shows Arlie turning to Arlene at the same time that she shows Arlene trying to find the remnants of Arlie in her; by the end Arlene has begun the reintegration of the two personalities, but there is clearly a long and uncertain way to go.

Third and Oak (Louisville, 1978) is made up of two slightly connected plays, 'The Laundromat' and 'The Pool Hall'. In the first an embittered middle-class widow and an unhappy working-class girl break through their reticence and the distance between them just enough to recognize some shared pain, but with no real hope that the discovery will change their lives. In 'The Pool Hall' a rebellious young black man and the older man who has been his responsible but intrusive father figure reach some respect for each other's values and boundaries, but again one senses a temporary truce rather than a resolution of their ongoing difficulties. *The Holdup* (San Francisco, 1983) uses an encounter between two young men and an older outlaw in 1914 to depict the passing of the Old West and the need to accept new realities; and *Traveler in the Dark* (Cambridge, 1984) shows a man who has tried to reduce life to a matter of fact and rationality tentatively rediscovering his capacity for faith.

Norman's most powerful play, *'night, Mother* (Cambridge, 1982) is about fortyish Jessie Cates, who announces to her mother Thelma that she intends to commit suicide later that evening, and then methodically goes through her chores, putting the house and her affairs in order while her mother moves from incredulity through attempts at reasoning, comforting, bargaining and begging. Jessie's reasons for ending her life are clearly elucidated, all the more forcefully for obviously being the result of cool and rational consideration. Life simply has nothing to offer her, and it makes more sense to end it than to endure: 'I'm just not having a very good time and I don't have any reason to think it'll get anything but worse.' It is not, as her mother guesses, that some specific disappointment or pattern of disappointments has depressed her; it is that there is no convincing argument in favour of life. What she is, what her life is, and what is likely to come are all just not enough: 'So, see, it doesn't much matter what else happens in the world or in this house, even. I'm what was worth waiting for and I didn't make it. Me . . . who might have made a difference to me . . . I'm not going to show up, so there's no reason to stay.' [Ellipses Norman's] She has no fantasy that things will be better after death; they will just be over: 'Dead is everybody and everything I ever knew, gone.'

'night, Mother is, however, less an argument for the legitimacy of suicide than it is an assertion of the individual's right to choose and control her own destiny. Even more satisfying to Jessie than the release death offers is the experience of taking possession of herself. When her mother cries that Jessie does not have to kill herself, she replies that having the choice is the whole point: 'No, I don't. That's what I like about it.' For the first time in an essentially passive life, Jessie is taking control – 'It's all I really have that belongs to me and I'm going to say what happens to it' – and that argument proves to be the unanswerable one. After the off-stage suicide Thelma can only acknowledge her daughter's right to make the decision: 'Forgive me. (*Pause*) I thought you were mine.'

Minority voices

The mainstream American theatre seems unable to accept more than one major black dramatist at a time so, with Ed Bullins dominating the 1970s and August Wilson the 1980s, only a few isolated plays by black authors reached the larger audience. Ntozake Shange's *for colored girls who have considered suicide/when the rainbow is enuf* (1975) is less a play than a staged reading of poems and set pieces, spoken by black women discovering their feminism and sisterhood through their relationships with men. Samm-Art Williams's *Home* (1979) tells of a black North Carolina farmer who leaves the land and loses his moral bearings until he returns home; an evocative mix of realism and folk styles expands the play into an allegory of the race's disconnection from its roots. Charles Fuller's *Zooman and the Sign* (1980) depicts the decay of middle-class black neighbourhoods as the residents lose the will to fight or save a lost generation of frighteningly amoral black youths. In Fuller's *A Soldier's Play* (1981), the murder of a black soldier in a southern army camp in 1944 leads to the discovery that racial pride can sometimes be an inadequate mask for racial self-hatred.

Of course many black writers, along with those of other ethnic or special interest groups, chose to write to and for their own limited audiences. Theatres such as the Negro Ensemble Company in New York and the East West Players in Los Angeles specialized in ethnic drama (and, not incidentally, gave employment to ethnic actors), only occasionally attracting the attention of the general public. Still some non-profit theatres, and the occasional commercial producer, attempted to bring these voices into the mainstream. Luis Valdez's *Zoot Suit* (Los Angeles, 1978) depicts a 1942 murder case tinged by racism and its effects on the Mexican–American community in a style that is a salute to the rhythms and vitality of that community. In David Henry Hwang's *FOB* (1980) the contempt of the Americanized second-generation Chinese for those Fresh Off the Boat is shown to cover an insecurity about the success of their own assimilation and an envy of the newcomers' living connection with Chinese tradition and culture. Hwang's *The Dance and the Railroad* (1981) corrects the popular image of the passive, exploited coolie workers in nineteenth-century America by showing how a continuing bond with their roots gave them the strength to survive and fight for better conditions.

That a minority writer can bring a special perspective to bear on the majority culture is demonstrated by Hwang's *M. Butterfly* (1988), based on the unlikely but true story of a French diplomat who carried on a twenty-year affair with a Chinese actress without knowing that she was both a spy and a man. Hwang's insight is that the story is one of cultural stereotyping more than of political or sexual confusion. In his version Rene Gallimard is so enraptured with the fantasy that he is acting out the archetypal story of *Madame Butterfly*, as the sexually irresistible Pinkerton worshipped by the submissive and self-effacing Butterfly, that he wilfully blinds himself to any evidence of the contrary in his affair with Song Liling. The westerner, insecure in his manhood and his culture, needs to believe in a woman from an exotic culture who is weaker than he and who will find her fulfilment in being dominated and exploited; and when he thinks he has found such an ideal, he will give her anything she asks just to keep up the illusion. Thus, Hwang sees, it is ultimately he who willingly submits to her domination; and the play ends with Gallimard's discovery that all along he was the Butterfly and Song the Pinkerton. In his courtroom testimony when the two are finally caught, Song makes the play's larger implications explicit:

> As soon as a Western man comes in contact with the East – he's already confused. . . . The West thinks of itself as masculine – big guns, big industry, big money – so the East is feminine – weak, delicate, poor. . . . Her mouth says no but her eyes say yes. The West believes the East, deep down, *wants* to be dominated.

The events of the play coincide with the period of the Vietnam War, and Hwang offers a metaphor for how completely America misjudged its role and power in Asia.

Minority drama is not merely a matter of race. As the subject of homosexuality came to be more openly discussed in the 1970s and 1980s, and as the homosexual community became more demanding of attention, several plays with homosexual characters or themes found their way into the mainstream theatre. The breadth of homosexual drama in the 1980s ranges from the casual inclusion of homosexuals among straight characters, in such plays as Lanford Wilson's *5th of July*; through plays in which the characters' sexuality is incidental to other issues, such as Terrence McNally's *Lisbon Traviata*; to plays specifically addressing gay issues like AIDS, such as William M. Hoffman's *As Is* (1985) and Larry Kramer's *The Normal Heart* (1985); to the flamboyantly campy drag extravaganzas and pastiches of Charles Ludlam (*Bluebeard*, *The Mystery of Irma Vep*) and Charles Busch (*Psycho Beach Party*, *Vampire Lesbians of Sodom*). Harvey Fierstein's *The Torch Song Trilogy* (1981), a long evening of three plays originally written and produced separately, operates fully within the mainstream tradition of domestic realism, using the life of the author's alter ego, Arnold Beckoff, to chart American homosexuals' evolution in the 1970s from impersonal promiscuity and self-depreciating humour to mature self-acceptance. The trilogy deals openly, if frequently comically, with the emotional difficulties of the homosexual life, showing how an unbearable loneliness drives Arnold to convince himself he enjoys the demeaning anonymous sexual encounters of the first play, while social prejudice makes him accept the patronization of heterosexuals who are shallower than he in the second; in the third play he mourns a lover killed by gay-bashing hoodlums and hears his mother deny the validity of his emotions. As he learns to honour himself and demand respect from others, he discovers that he is really a very ordinary and conventional person, whose dream is to have exactly what his mother had – a marriage, a family, and the right to mourn his lover openly. The trilogy reaches its resolution when that desire is honoured, as his mother accepts Arnold's widowhood as the equivalent of her own.

Mark Medoff's earlier plays had some theatrical vitality but little weight; *When You Comin' Back, Red Ryder?* (1973) is a thin reworking of *The Petrified Forest*, with a criminal holding several people hostage in a roadhouse, giving them the opportunity to display their true characters. But *Children of a Lesser God* (Los Angeles, 1979) is strong drama as well as good theatre. James Leeds, teacher of the deaf, falls in love with the proud and intelligent student Sarah Norman, and prods her to learn to speak rather than using sign language. But Sarah refuses, choosing to use a language in which she is eloquent rather than one in which she will always be inferior, and the conflict destroys their relationship. Some of the play's theatrical strength comes from the clear necessity to cast an actual deaf actress as Sarah, thus giving the events on stage a special reality. Medoff creates a multi-levelled stage vocabulary as James must sign all his dialogue to the deaf characters while speaking it aloud for the audience's benefit, and then speak the other characters' lines as they sign them. In a powerful emotional climax Sarah cries out in the barely intelligible sounds of the untrained deaf speaker, to demonstrate the violation of her dignity that James is demanding. Dignity is what the play is ultimately about; beneath the debate over speaking or signing is the hearing world's assumption that its ways are best. James's teaching is essentially paternalistic and patronizing, much the equivalent of racism; and Sarah's refusal to trade her proud and satisfying identity as a deaf person for the indignity of attempting to pass as hearing makes this play by a white male writer as powerful a repudiation of prejudice as any by minority dramatists.

An ethnic minority of a special sort is the subject of A.R. Gurney's plays. Gurney wrote some promising short plays in the 1960s, notably *The Golden Fleece* (Los Angeles, 1968), a retelling of the Medea myth in modern dress, with the off-stage tragedy reported and misinterpreted by Medea's very ordinary American neighbours. In the 1980s Gurney focused on the lives of American WASPS, well-to-do White Anglo–Saxon Protestants from old families, the Brahmin class that once ruled the country but now found itself reduced to a powerless and anachronistic minority. *The Dining Room* (1981) is a series of short sketches set in a variety of Brahmin dining rooms, each offering an insight into the culture: an adulterous couple are moved to discretion by the room's sense of history; a marriage breaks apart; an adult daughter tries to retreat into the past but is not welcomed; a father gives funeral instructions to his adult son. In *The Perfect Party* (1986) a man's attempt to give his life meaning by engineering a perfect social event is made, a little too explicitly, into an allegory of the fading American culture's attempt to retain its greatness through sheer will power. In *The Cocktail Hour* (San Diego, 1988) a playwright asks his Brahmin family's permission to produce a play about them, and the resulting debate exposes the culture's decay while still lovingly saluting its faded greatness. *Love Letters* (New Haven,

1988) is a reading for actor and actress of a lifetime's correspondence between a boy and girl from this community who are held together by a bond that can only be recognized afterwards as love. In one scene of *The Dining Room* a teenager treats his aunt's elegant dinner service and customs as quaint and primitive tribal artifacts, and that is essentially the point of view of Gurney's plays, more respectful than the boy but anthropological in nature, capturing and saluting a dying culture.

During the 1970s and 1980s Arthur Miller wrote a play indicting the totalitarian regimes of eastern Europe for invading the innermost core of their citizens' privacy; Sam Shepard offered a bizarre farm family as a microcosm of America's moral decay; Lanford Wilson showed a legless homosexual Vietnam veteran rediscovering the ability to love and hope; Marsha Norman presented suicide as the ultimate symbol of self-control; August Wilson showed a black family able to move forward with pride in their past; Neil Simon looked back on the Depression with warm and respectful humour – and every one of those plays was set in a living room.

The twentieth-century American drama was born in realism, as a few playwrights tentatively and almost accidentally brought a little extra substance to what had been a lightweight entertainment form by attempting to reflect the world as they saw it: with human behaviour that was sometimes unpredictable, and problems that could not all be resolved by the final curtain. That the drama's future would lie in realism was not at all clear from the start. In two particular periods – the years before 1930, when the American drama was young enough that no one could be sure what style fitted it best, and the 1960s, when cultural and artistic revolution was in the air – some of the century's most able and serious dramatists, from Percy MacKaye through Eugene O'Neill to Sam Shepard, tried to push the drama away from realism into other forms that would be more able to fulfil their artistic ambitions. Virtually all of them succeeded, at least in individual plays of merit and power, as did Maxwell Anderson, Thornton Wilder and other non-realistic playwrights.

And yet, in spite of all the experiments and all the individual successes, the backbone of American drama remains in realism. The continual discovery and rediscovery and re-rediscovery of this fact *is* the history of the twentieth-century American drama. It is in fact two parallel discoveries, of realism and of domestic drama. Realism – the use of art and artifice to create the effect of a direct reflection of the world outside – has proved remarkably adaptable. It is able to carry a thesis, as in the problem plays of Herne and Crothers; to depict life without comment, as in the earliest O'Neill plays; to introduce audiences to unfamiliar characters and perspectives on life, as Albee and various minority writers can; to let us see past the unfamiliar surface to a recognizable core, as Williams does; to capture, explain and even judge the largest social and political forces, as Odets and Miller do in their best plays. It is equally flexible, able to stretch its definition and rules to fit the styles and sensibilities of writers as individual and as different as O'Neill, Miller, Williams and Shepard. Above all, it works in the theatre: American audiences respond to it, it is understandable, and it meets an audience hunger to have their experience of life reflected and clarified through art.

Even more striking is the continuing power and adaptability of the domestic setting. Twentieth-century American playwrights did not invent domestic drama, but they – and their audiences – took to it from the start, recognizing not only that a variety of subjects could be addressed through the domestic focus, but that in fact it was the way these subjects affected the daily lives of ordinary Americans that was most worth addressing. Odets discovered in the 1930s that the true story of the Depression was not to be found in statistics and mass movements, but in how it permeated every aspect of everyday life. Miller in the 1940s and 1950s, Albee in the 1960s, and Shepard in the 1970s identified and condemned the failures of the American Dream by dramatizing the damaged lives of its victims. But American domestic drama is not limited to political and social comment. The special insight shared by Williams and O'Neill, in his last plays – that many Americans found the challenges of ordinary life almost beyond their capabilities – gave domestic realism a new focus that was to dominate the American drama in the second half of the century. O'Neill, Williams, Inge, Albee, Wilson, Wasserstein, Mamet, even Miller offer their audience spiritual comfort and counsel by depicting characters facing their own insecurities and self-condemnations. Realistic plays with a domestic setting can illuminate the inner world as well as the outer.

And so, while the twentieth-century American drama has had its talented mavericks and profitable diversions, the overall arc of its history is clear: a literature born in the impulse to describe the real world has always returned to that impulse – as, indeed, have its individual practitioners, as O'Neill, Rice, Anderson, Albee, Williams, Shepard and almost every other writer who challenged the hegemony of domestic realism eventually found it the most amenable vehicle for their individual styles and concerns. As the drama approaches the end of the century, in a theatrical context far more open and varied than it had at mid-century, it is inevitable that new writers, voicing new concerns in new styles, will appear; and there is every reason to believe that they will be able to say what they want to in plays with a realistic, contemporary, middle-class domestic setting.

Chronology

DATE	AMERICAN DRAMA	WORLD DRAMA	OTHER LITERATURE AND ART	HISTORICAL/CULTURAL EVENTS
1890	Herne *Margaret Fleming*	Ibsen *Hedda Gabler*	Howells *A Hazard of New Fortunes*	Ellis Island opens DAR founded Frazer *The Golden Bough*
		Strindberg: *The Stronger*	Wilde *The Picture of Dorian Gray*	
1891		Wedekind *Spring's Awakening*	Garland *Main-Travelled Roads*	First international copyright law Zipper invented
			Hardy *Tess of the D'Urbervilles*	
			Kipling *The Light that Failed*	
			Shaw *The Quintessence of Ibsenism*	
			Mahler: Symphony #1	
1892		Ibsen *The Master Builder*	Doyle *The Adventures of Sherlock Holmes*	Grover Cleveland elected US President Lizzie Borden case
		Shaw *Widowers' Houses*	Kipling *Barrack-Room Ballads*	

Year	Drama	Prose / Verse	Music	Events
1893	Wilde, *Lady Windermere's Fan* Thomas, *In Mizzoura* Pinero, *The Second Mrs Tanqueray* Wilde, *A Woman of No Importance*	Crane, *Maggie*	Dvorak: 'New World' Symphony Tchaikovsky: 'The Nutcracker'	World Exposition in Chicago Dreyfus trial in France Henry Ford builds first car
1894	Ibsen, *Little Eyolf* Shaw, *Arms and the Man*	Kipling, *The Jungle Book* Twain, *Pudd'nhead Wilson*	Debussy: 'Afternoon of a Faun'	Sears-Roebuck begins mail-order business
1895	Wilde, *The Importance of Being Earnest* Wilde, *An Ideal Husband* Gillette, *Secret Service*	Conrad, *Almayer's Folly* Crane, *The Red Badge of Courage* Wells, *The Time Machine* Yeats, *Poems*	Tchaikovsky: 'Swan Lake'	Roentgen discovers X-rays Gillette invents safety razor Freud *Studies in Hysteria*

DATE	AMERICAN DRAMA	WORLD DRAMA	OTHER LITERATURE AND ART	HISTORICAL/CULTURAL EVENTS
1896		Chekhov *The Seagull*	Hardy *Jude the Obscure*	McKinley elected president
				Nobel Prizes established
		Ibsen *John Gabriel Borkman*	Puccini: 'La Bohème'	First modern olympics, Athens
		Jarry *King Ubu*		
		Wilde *Salome*		
1897		Rostand *Cyrano de Bergerac*	Conrad *The Nigger of the Narcissus*	Queen Victoria's Diamond Jubilee
		Schnitzler *La Ronde*	James *The Spoils of Poynton*	Gold Rush in Alaska
		Shaw *The Devil's Disciple*	Kipling *Captains Courageous*	
			Sousa: 'The Stars and Stripes Forever'	
1898		Pinero *Trelawney of the 'Wells'*	Crane *The Open Boat*	Curies discover radium
		Strindberg *The Road to Damascus*	James *The Turn of the Screw*	Spanish–American War
				Hawaii annexed

			Wells *The War of the Worlds*	
1899	Gillette *Sherlock Holmes* Thomas *Arizona*	Chekhov *Uncle Vanya* Ibsen *When We Dead Awaken* Shaw *You Never Can Tell*	Norris *McTeague*	Boer War begins Veblen *Theory of the Leisure Class*
1900	Fitch *The Climbers*	Wedekind *The Marquis of Keith*	Baum *The Wizard of Oz* Conrad *Lord Jim* Dreiser *Sister Carrie* Puccini: 'Tosca'	Planck formulates quantum theory Freud *The Interpretation of Dreams*
1901	Barrie *Quality Street* Chekhov *The Three Sisters* Strindberg *The Dance of Death*	Kipling *Kim* Norris *The Octopus* Washington *Up from Slavery*		Queen Victoria dies; Edward VII king McKinley assassinated; Theodore Roosevelt elected president

DATE	AMERICAN DRAMA	WORLD DRAMA	OTHER LITERATURE AND ART	HISTORICAL/CULTURAL EVENTS
			Rachmaninoff: Piano Concerto #2	
1902	Fitch *The Girl With Green Eyes*	Barrie *The Admirable Crichton*	Doyle *The Hound of the Baskervilles*	Boer War ends W. James *The Varieties of Religious Experience*
		Gorki *The Lower Depths*	James *The Wings of the Dove*	
		Shaw *Mrs Warren's Profession*	Kipling *Just So Stories*	
		Strindberg *The Dream Play*	Potter *Peter Rabbit*	
			Wister *The Virginian*	
1903		Gorki *Summer Folk*	James *The Ambassadors*	Wright brothers fly Ford Motor Company founded First baseball World Series
		Synge *In the Shadow of the Glen*	London *The Call of the Wild*	
			Norris *The Pit*	
			film: 'The Great Train Robbery'	

Year				
1904	Cohan *Little Johnny Jones*	Barrie *Peter Pan* Chekhov *The Cherry Orchard* Molnar *Liliom* Shaw *John Bull's Other Island* Synge *Riders to the Sea*	Conrad *Nostromo* James *The Golden Bowl* London *The Sea Wolf* Puccini: 'Madame Butterfly'	Panama Canal begun Abbey Theatre founded, Dublin
1905	Belasco *The Girl of the Golden West* Fitch *The Woman in the Case* Walter *The Easiest Way*	Shaw *Man and Superman* Shaw *Major Barbara*	Wharton *The House of Mirth* Lehar: 'The Merry Widow'	Einstein formulates Special Theory of Relativity
1906	Cohan *Forty-five Minutes from Broadway* Crothers *The Three of Us*	Shaw *Caesar and Cleopatra* Shaw *The Doctor's Dilemma*	Galsworthy *The Man of Property* Sinclair *The Jungle*	San Francisco earthquake

DATE	AMERICAN DRAMA	WORLD DRAMA	OTHER LITERATURE AND ART	HISTORICAL/CULTURAL EVENTS
	MacKaye *Jeanne d'Arc*			
	Mitchell *The New York Idea*			
1907	MacKaye *Sappho and Phaon*	Strindberg *The Ghost Sonata*	Conrad *The Secret Agent*	Boy Scouts founded First Ziegfeld Follies Adams *The Education of Henry Adams* W. James *Pragmatism*
		Synge *The Playboy of the Western World*	Picasso: 'Demoiselles d'Avignon'	
1908		Barrie *What Every Woman Knows*	Bennett *The Old Wives' Tale*	Taft elected President First Model T Ford General Motors Corporation founded
			Grahame *The Wind in the Willows*	
1909	MacKaye *The Canterbury Pilgrims*		Stein *Three Lives*	Peary reaches North Pole
	MacKaye *The Scarecrow*			
	Sheldon *Nigger*			

1910	Crothers *A Man's World*	Molnar *The Guardsman* Shaw *Misalliance* Synge *Deirdre of the Sorrows*	Forster *Howard's End* Stravinsky: 'The Firebird'	Edward VII dies; George V king
1911	Crothers *He and She* Knoblock *Kismet* Sheldon *The Boss*		Wharton *Ethan Frome*	Amundsen reaches South Pole Chinese revolution ends Manchu dynasty
1912			Grey *Riders of the Purple Sage*	Wilson elected President Titanic sinks F. W. Woolworth Company founded
1913	MacKaye *A Thousand Years Ago*	Shaw *Androcles and the Lion* Shaw *Pygmalion*	Cather *O, Pioneers!* Lawrence *Sons and Lovers* Mann *Death in Venice*	US institutes income tax

DATE	AMERICAN DRAMA	WORLD DRAMA	OTHER LITERATURE AND ART	HISTORICAL/CULTURAL EVENTS
			Proust *Swann's Way* Stravinsky: 'The Rite of Spring'	
1914	Mackaye *St. Louis* Rice *On Trial*	Molnar *The Swan*	Burroughs *Tarzan of the Apes* Joyce *Dubliners*	First World War begins Panama Canal opens First Charlie Chaplin films
1915			Conrad *Victory* Lawrence *The Rainbow* Masters *Spoon River Anthology* Maugham *Of Human Bondage* film: 'Birth of a Nation'	Einstein formulates General Theory of Relativity

1916	Glaspell *Trifles*	Gorki *Enemies*	Joyce *Portrait of the Artist as a Young Man*	
	MacKaye *Washington*	Pirandello *Liola*	Sandburg *Chicago Poems*	
	O'Neill *Before Breakfast*		Tarkington *Seventeen*	
	O'Neill *Bound East for Cardiff*		film: 'Intolerance'	
1917	Glaspell *The Outside*	Barrie *Dear Brutus*	Eliot *Prufrock and Other Observations*	US enters First World War Russian revolution Jung *Psychology of the Unconscious*
	O'Neill *Ile*	Pirandello *Right You Are!*		
	O'Neill *In the Zone*	Yeats *At the Hawk's Well*		
	O'Neill *The Long Voyage Home*			
1918	MacKaye *The Roll Call*	Joyce *Exiles*	Cather *My Antonia*	First World War ends Wordwide influenza epidemic kills 22 million Theatre Guild founded
	O'Neill *Moon of the Caribbees*		Hopkins *Poems*	

DATE	AMERICAN DRAMA	WORLD DRAMA	OTHER LITERATURE AND ART	HISTORICAL/CULTURAL EVENTS
	O'Neill *The Rope*		Tarkington *The Magnificent Ambersons*	
	O'Neill *Where the Cross is Made*			
1919	Field *Wedding Bells*		Anderson *Winesburg, Ohio*	League of Nations founded 'Black Sox' scandal in baseball
	Glaspell *Bernice*		Maugham *The Moon and Sixpence*	
	Tarkington *Clarence*			
1820	O'Neill *Beyond the Horizon*	Capek *R.U.R.*	Eliot *Poems*	Harding elected President Prohibition begins Women get the vote Joan of Arc canonized
	O'Neill *The Emperor Jones*	Shaw *Heartbreak House*	Fitzgerald *This Side of Paradise*	
			Lawrence *Women in Love*	
			Lewis *Main Street*	

			Wharton	
			The Age of Innocence	
			Holst: 'The Planets'	
			film: 'The Cabinet of Dr Caligari'	
1921	Glaspell *Inheritors*	Capek *The Insect Play*	Dos Passos *Three Soldiers*	First scheduled radio broadcasts, KDKA, Pittsburgh
	Glaspell *The Verge*	Maugham *The Circle*	Moore *Poems*	BBC founded
	Kaufman & Connelly *Dulcy*	Pirandello *Six Characters in Search of an Author*	Robinson *Collected Poems*	Sacco and Vanzetti case
	O'Neill *Anna Christie*	Shaw *Back to Methuselah*	Picasso: 'Three Musicians'	
1922	Kaufman & Connelly *Merton of the Movies*	Brecht *Baal*	Cather *One of Ours*	Irish Free State proclaimed
	Kaufman & Connelly *To the Ladies!*	Brecht *Drums in the Night*	Eliot *The Waste Land*	Mussolini forms Fascist goverment in Italy
	Marquis *The Old Soak*	Pirandello *Henry IV*	Joyce *Ulysses*	Emily Post *Etiquette*
	Nichols *Abie's Irish Rose*	Witkiewicz *The Water Hen*	Lewis *Babbitt*	

DATE	AMERICAN DRAMA	WORLD DRAMA	OTHER LITERATURE AND ART	HISTORICAL/CULTURAL EVENTS
	O'Neill *The Hairy Ape*		Sitwell *Facade*	
1923	Barry *You and I* Rice *The Adding Machine*	O'Casey *The Shadow of a Gunman* Shaw *St Joan*	Gershwin: 'Rhapsody in Blue'	Teapot Dome scandal *Time* magazine founded *Reader's Digest* founded Keynes *A Tract on Monetary Reform*
1924	Anderson & Stallings *What Price Glory?* Barry *The Youngest* Howard *They Knew What They Wanted* Kaufman & Connelly *Beggar on Horseback* Kaufman & Ferber *Minick* O'Neill *All God's Chillun Got Wings*	Coward *The Vortex* O'Casey *Juno and the Paycock*	Dickinson *Complete Poems* Forster *A Passage to India* Hemingway *In Our Time* Melville *Billy Budd*	Coolidge elected President First winter olympics J. Edgar Hoover named head of FBI

	O'Neill *Desire Under the Elms*			
	O'Neill *Welded*			
	Selwyn & Goulding *Dancing Mothers*			
1925	Kaufman *The Butter and Egg Man*	Coward *Hay Fever*	Dos Passos *Manhattan Transfer*	Scopes Trial (on teaching of evolution) Hitler *Mein Kampf*
	Kelly *Craig's Wife*		Dreiser *An American Tragedy*	
	Kennedy & Hawthorne *Mrs. Partridge Presents*		Fitzgerald *The Great Gatsby*	
	O'Neill *The Fountain*		Lewis *Arrowsmith*	
			Pound *Cantos*	
			Woolf *Mrs. Dalloway*	
			film: 'Battleship Potemkin'	

DATE	AMERICAN DRAMA	WORLD DRAMA	OTHER LITERATURE AND ART	HISTORICAL/CULTURAL EVENTS
1926	Howard *The Silver Cord* O'Neill *The Great God Brown*	O'Casey *The Plough and the Stars*	Faulkner *Soldiers' Pay* Hemingway *The Sun Also Rises* Lawrence *The Plumed Serpent* Milne *Winnie the Pooh* film: 'Metropolis'	Hirohito becomes emperor of Japan General Strike in England Goddard launches first rocket T.E. Lawrence *Seven Pillars of Wisdom*
1927	Barry *Paris Bound* Heyward *Porgy* Kaufman & Ferber *The Royal Family* Kern & Hammerstein *Show Boat*	Brecht *Man is Man*	Lewis *Elmer Gantry* Marquis *archy and mehitabel* Wilder *The Bridge of San Luis Rey* Woolf *To the Lighthouse* film: 'The Jazz Singer' (first talkie) Stravinsky: 'Oedipus Rex'	Lindbergh makes first solo transatlantic flight Sacco and Vanzetti executed Babe Ruth hits 60 home runs

1928	Barry *Holiday*	Brecht *The Threepenny Opera*	Benet *John Brown's Body*	Hoover elected President
	Hecht & MacArthur *The Front Page*		Huxley *Point Counterpoint*	Fleming discovers penicillin
	O'Neill *Lazarus Laughed*		Lawrence *Lady Chatterley's Lover*	First Mickey Mouse cartoon
	O'Neill *Marco Millions*		Woolf *Orlando*	Mead *Coming of Age in Samoa*
	O'Neill *Strange Interlude*		Gershwin: 'An American in Paris'	
1929	Kaufman & Lardner *June Moon*	Giraudoux *Amphitryon 38*	Aiken *Selected Poems*	Stock market crash triggers decade-long Depression
	O'Neill *Dynamo*	Mayakovsky *The Bedbug*	Faulkner *The Sound and the Fury*	
	Rice *Street Scene*		Hemingway *A Farewell to Arms*	
			Lewis *Dodsworth*	
			Remarque *All Quiet on the Western Front*	
			Wolfe *Look Homeward, Angel*	

DATE	AMERICAN DRAMA	WORLD DRAMA	OTHER LITERATURE AND ART	HISTORICAL/CULTURAL EVENTS
			Woolf *A Room of One's Own*	
1930	Anderson *Elizabeth the Queen*	Brecht *The Measures Taken*	Crane *The Bridge*	Haile Selassie becomes Emperor of Ethiopia
	Connelly *The Green Pastures*	Coward *Private Lives*	Dos Passos *42nd Parallel*	Constantinople renamed Istanbul
	Glaspell *Alison's House*		Faulkner *As I Lay Dying*	Planet Pluto discovered
	Kaufman & Hart *Once in a Lifetime*		Frost *Collected Poems*	Freud *Civilization and its Discontents*
	Weitzenkorn *Five Star Final*		Hammett *The Maltese Falcon*	
			Wood: 'American Gothic'	
1931	Behrman *Brief Moment*	Giraudoux *Judith*	Buck *The Good Earth*	Empire State Building completed
	O'Neill *Mourning Becomes Electra*	Lorca *The Love of Don Perlimplin and Belisa in the Garden*	Faulkner *Sanctuary*	'Star Spangled Banner' made national anthem
			Dali: 'Persistence of Memory'	
			film: 'Frankenstein'	

1932	Barry *The Animal Kingdom* Behrman *Biography* Hecht & MacArthur *Twentieth Century*	Anouilh *Thieves' Carnival* Priestley *Dangerous Corner* Shaw *Too True to be Good*	Dos Passos *1919* Eliot *Selected Essays* Faulkner *Light in August* Huxley *Brave New World*	Roosevelt elected President
1933	M. Anderson *Mary of Scotland* Hagan *One Sunday Afternoon* Kingsley *Men in White* O'Neill *Ah, Wilderness!* O'Neill *Days Without End* Rice *We the People*	Coward *Design for Living* Lorca *Blood Wedding*	Crane *Collected Poems* Orwell *Down and Out in Paris and London* Stein *Autobiography of Alice B. Toklas* West *Miss Lonelyhearts* Yeats *Collected Poems*	Hitler appointed Chancellor of Germany Prohibition repealed

DATE	AMERICAN DRAMA	WORLD DRAMA	OTHER LITERATURE AND ART	HISTORICAL/CULTURAL EVENTS
1934	M. Anderson *Valley Forge*	Lorca *Yerma*	Auden *Poems*	Dionne quintuplets born
	Behrman *Rain From Heaven*		Fitzgerald *Tender is the Night*	
	Hellman *The Children's Hour*		Graves *I, Claudius*	
	Kaufman & Hart *Merrily We Roll Along*		Miller *Tropic of Cancer*	
	Raphaelson *Accent on Youth*		W.C.Williams *Collected Poems*	
	Thomas *No More Ladies*			
1935	M. Anderson *Winterset*	Coward *Tonight at 8:30*	Farrell *Studs Lonigan*	Social Security Act
	Kingsley *Dead End*	Eliot *Murder in the Cathedral*	Moore *Selected Poems*	
	Odets *Waiting for Lefty*	Giraudoux *The Trojan War Will Not Take Place*	Steinbeck *Tortilla Flat*	
	Odets *Awake and Sing!*		Gershwin: *'Porgy and Bess'*	

	Odets *Till the Day I Die*		
	Odets *Paradise Lost*		
	Sherwood *The Petrified Forest*		
	Spewack *Boy Meets Girl*		
1936	M. Anderson *The Wingless Victory*	Lorca *The House of Bernarda Alba*	Dos Passos *The Big Money*	Spanish Civil War begins
	Behrman *End of Summer*	Rattigan *French Without Tears*	Eliot *Collected Poems*	George V dies; Edward VIII abdicates; George VI king
	Boothe *The Women*		Faulkner *Absalom, Absalom!*	O'Neill wins Nobel Prize
	Ferber & Kaufman *Stage Door*		Mitchell *Gone With the Wind*	Ford Foundation established
	Kaufman & Hart *You Can't Take It With You*			Life magazine founded
	Sherwood *Idiot's Delight*			Carnegie *How To Win Friends and Influence People*

DATE	AMERICAN DRAMA	WORLD DRAMA	OTHER LITERATURE AND ART	HISTORICAL/CULTURAL EVENTS
1937	M. Anderson *The Masque of Kings* M. Anderson *High Tor* M. Anderson *The Star-Wagon* Odets *Golden Boy*	Giraudoux *Electra* Priestley *Time and the Conways*	Hemingway *To Have and Have Not* Steinbeck *Of Mice and Men* Picasso: 'Guernica' film: 'Snow White'	Japan invades China Dirigible 'Hindenburg' burns Golden Gate Bridge opens
1938	Conkle *Prologue to Glory* Goldsmith *What a Life* Odets *Rocket to the Moon* Osborn *On Borrowed Time* Sherwood *Abe Lincoln in Illinois*		cummings *Collected Poems* Hemingway *The Fifth Column* Isherwood *Goodbye to Berlin*	Germany annexes Austria, occupies Sudetenland House Unamerican Activities Committee formed

	Wilder *Our Town*			
	Wilder *The Merchant of Yonkers*			
1939	M. Anderson *Key Largo*	Brecht *Galileo*	Frost *Collected Poems*	Second World War begins as Germany invades Poland New York World's Fair
	Barry *Philadelphia Story*	Eliot *The Family Reunion*	Joyce *Finnegans Wake*	
	Behrman *No Time for Comedy*	Giraudoux *Ondine*	Steinbeck *The Grapes of Wrath*	
	Hellman *The Little Foxes*		West *The Day of the Locust*	
	Kaufman & Hart *The Man Who Came to Dinner*		films: 'Gone With the Wind', 'The Wizard of Oz'	
	Lindsay & Crouse *Life With Father*			
	Osborn *Morning's at Seven*			
	Saroyan *The Time of Your Life*			

DATE	AMERICAN DRAMA	WORLD DRAMA	OTHER LITERATURE AND ART	HISTORICAL/CULTURAL EVENTS
1940	Fields & Chodorov *My Sister Eileen*	E. Williams *The Corn is Green*	cummings *Fifty Poems*	Germany conquers most of western Europe
	Kaufman & Hart *George Washington Slept Here*		Faulkner *The Hamlet*	
	Sherwood *There Shall Be No Night*		Hemingway *For Whom the Bell Tolls*	
	Williams *Battle of Angels*		Koestler *Darkness at Noon*	
			Van Doren *Collected Poems*	
			Wright *Native Son*	
1941	M. Anderson *Candle in the Wind*	Brecht *Arturo Ui*	Fitzgerald *The Last Tycoon*	Japanese attack Pearl Harbour; US enters war
	Chodorov & Fields *Junior Miss*	Brecht *The Good Woman of Sezuan*	Millay *Collected Sonnets*	
	Hellman *Watch on the Rhine*	Brecht *Mother Courage*	film: 'Citizen Kane'	
	Kesselring *Arsenic and Old Lace*	Coward *Blithe Spirit*		

1942	M. Anderson *The Eve of St. Mark*	Coward *Present Laughter*	Camus *The Stranger*	Fermi splits the atom Internment of Japanese–Americans
	Fields *The Doughgirls*	O'Casey *Red Roses for Me*	Eliot *Four Quartets*	
	James *Winter Soldiers*		Faulkner *Go Down, Moses*	
	Steinbeck *The Moon is Down*		Copland: 'Rodeo'	
	Wilder *The Skin of Our Teeth*			
1943	Gow & d'Usseau *Tomorrow the World*	Sartre *The Flies*	Saroyan *The Human Comedy*	Allied invasion of Italy
	Herbert *Kiss and Tell*			
	Kingsley *The Patriots*			
	Van Druten *The Voice of the Turtle*			
	Rodgers & Hammerstein *Oklahoma!*			

DATE	AMERICAN DRAMA	WORLD DRAMA	OTHER LITERATURE AND ART	HISTORICAL/CULTURAL EVENTS
1944	Behrman *Jacobowsky and the Colonel*	Anouilh *Antigone*	Bellow *The Dangling Man*	D-Day, allied invasion of Europe
	Chase *Harvey*	Camus *Caligula*	Borges *Ficiones*	
	Hellman *The Searching Wind*		Copland: 'Appalachian Spring'	
	Krasna *Dear Ruth*			
	Marquand & Kaufman *The Late George Apley*			
	Miller *The Man Who Had All the Luck*			
	Osborn *A Bell for Adano*			
	Van Druten *I Remember Mama*			
1945	Laurents *Home of the Brave*	Anouilh *Romeo and Jeanette*	Orwell *Animal Farm*	Roosevelt dies; Truman becomes President

	Patrick *The Hasty Heart*	Giraudoux *The Madwoman of Chaillot*	Steinbeck *Cannery Row*	US drops atom bombs on Japan Second World War ends
	Rice *Dream Girl*	Sartre *No Exit*	Waugh *Brideshead Revisited*	
	Williams *The Glass Menagerie*		Wright *Black Boy*	
			Britten: 'Peter Grimes'	
1946	M. Anderson *Joan of Lorraine*	Anouilh *Medea*	Warren *All the King's Men*	United Nations founded Spock *Baby and Child Care*
	Hellman *Another Part of the Forest*	De Filippo *Filumena Marturano*		
	Kanin *Born Yesterday*	Fry *A Phoenix Too Frequent*		
	O'Neill *The Iceman Cometh*	Rattigan *The Winslow Boy*		
1947	Goetz *The Heiress*	Genet *The Maids*	Camus *The Plague*	India granted independence Dead Sea Scrolls discovered Transistor invented CIA formed
	Haines *Command Decision*		Capote *Other Voices, Other Rooms*	

DATE	AMERICAN DRAMA	WORLD DRAMA	OTHER LITERATURE AND ART	HISTORICAL/CULTURAL EVENTS
	Krasna *John Loves Mary*		Frank *The Diary of Anne Frank*	
	Miller *All My Sons*		Michener *Tales of the South Pacific*	
	O'Neill *A Moon for the Misbegotten*			
	Williams *A Streetcar Named Desire*			
1948	M. Anderson *Anne of the Thousand Days*	Brecht *The Caucasian Chalk Circle*	Faulkner *Intruder in the Dust*	Ghandi assassinated Truman elected President Israel founded
	Heggen & Logan *Mr. Roberts*	Fry *The Lady's Not For Burning*	Mailer *The Naked and the Dead*	Berlin airlift Kinsey *Sexual Behavior in the Human Male*
	Lindsay & Crouse *Life With Mother*	Rattigan *The Browning Version*	Paton *Cry, the Beloved Country*	
	McEnroe *The Silver Whistle*			
	Williams *Summer and Smoke*			

1949	Kingsley *Detective Story* Miller *Death of a Salesman* Odets *The Big Knife* Spewack *Two Blind Mice* Rodgers & Hammerstein *South Pacific*	Genet *Deathwatch* O'Casey *Cock-a-Doodle Dandy*	Orwell *1984* film: 'The Third Man'	Republic of Ireland founded Communist revolution in China NATO Treaty signed
1950	Archibald *The Innocents* Inge *Come Back, Little Sheba* McCullers *The Member of the Wedding* Miller *An Enemy of the People* Odets *The Country Girl*	Eliot *The Cocktail Party* Fry *Venus Observed* Ionesco *The Bald Soprano*	Hemingway *Across the River and Into the Trees* Williams *The Roman Spring of Mrs Stone* Pollock 'Lavender Mist'	Korean War begins
1951	M. Anderson *Barefoot in Athens*	Ionesco *The Lesson*	Faulkner *Requiem for a Nun*	2nd Amendment limits President to two terms

DATE	AMERICAN DRAMA	WORLD DRAMA	OTHER LITERATURE AND ART	HISTORICAL/CULTURAL EVENTS
	Bevin & Trzcinski *Stalag 17*		Frost *Complete Poems*	
	Hellman *The Autumn Garden*		Jones *From Here to Eternity*	
	Williams *The Rose Tattoo*		Moore *Collected Poems*	
			Salinger *The Catcher in the Rye*	
			Sandburg *Complete Poems*	
1952	Axelrod *The Seven Year Itch*	Anouilh *Waltz of the Toreadors*	Capote *The Grass Harp*	George VI dies; Elizabeth II queen
	Behrman *Jane*	Christie *The Mousetrap*	Ellison *Invisible Man*	Eisenhower elected President Revised Standard Version of Bible published
	Laurents *The Time of the Cuckoo*	Ionesco *The Chairs*	Hemingway *The Old Man and the Sea*	First H-bomb test Peale *The Power of Positive Thinking*
		Rattigan *The Deep Blue Sea*	Malamud *The Natural*	
			Steinbeck *East of Eden*	

film: 'High Noon'

1953	R. Anderson *Tea and Sympathy*	Anouilh *The Lark*	Bellow *The Adventures of Augie March*	Korean War ends Hillary and Tenzing climb Mt. Everest
	Inge *Picnic*	Beckett *Waiting for Godot*	Fleming *Casino Royale*	Playboy magazine founded Kinsey *Sexual Behavior in the* *Human Female*
	Miller *The Crucible*	Rattigan *The Sleeping Prince*	Salinger *Nine Stories*	
	Patrick *The Teahouse of the August Moon*			
	Teichmann & Kaufman *The Solid Gold Cadillac*			
	Williams *Camino Real*			
1954	M. Anderson *Bad Seed*	Behan *The Quare Fellow*	Amis *Lucky Jim*	Supreme Court, in Brown v Board of Education, bars school segregation
	Hayes *The Girl on the Via Flaminia*	Eliot *The Confidential Clerk*	Faulkner *A Fable*	Salk introduces anti-polio vaccine
	Odets *The Flowering Peach*	Ionesco *Amédée*	Golding *Lord of the Flies*	
	Wilder *The Matchmaker*	Rattigan *Separate Tables*	Stevens *Collected Poems*	

DATE	AMERICAN DRAMA	WORLD DRAMA	OTHER LITERATURE AND ART	HISTORICAL/CULTURAL EVENTS
			Thomas *Under Milk Wood*	
			Britten: 'The Turn of the Screw'	
			film: 'On The Waterfront'	
1955	Axelrod *Will Success Spoil Rock Hunter?*		Donleavy *The Ginger Man*	Montgomery, Alabama bus boycott energizes Civil Rights movement, produces Martin Luther King as leader
	Goodrich & Hackett *The Diary of Anne Frank*		Mailer *Deer Park*	Rock and roll music appears McDonald's founded
	Inge *Bus Stop*		Nabokov *Lolita*	
	Levin *No Time for Sergeants*		O'Hara *Ten North Frederick*	
	Marchant *The Desk Set*			
	Miller *A View From the Bridge*			
	Miller *A Memory of Two Mondays*			

	Williams *Cat on a Hot Tin Roof*			
1956	Chayefsky *Middle of the Night*	Anouilh *Poor Bitos*	Bellow *Sieze the Day*	Suez Canal crisis Soviet invasion of Hungary Churchill *History of the English-Speaking Peoples*
	Lawrence & Lee *Auntie Mame*	Durrenmatt *The Visit*	Ginsberg *Howl*	Kennedy *Profiles in Courage* Mills *The Power Elite* Whyte *The Organization Man*
	O'Neill *Long Day's Journey into Night*	Genet *The Balcony*	Moore: 'The Ballad of Baby Doe'	
	Lerner & Loewe *My Fair Lady*	Osborne *Look Back in Anger*	films: 'Around the World in Eighty Days', 'The Seventh Seal'	
1957	Frings *Look Homeward, Angel*	Beckett *Endgame*	Cheever *The Wapshot Chronicle*	USSR launches first space satellite
	Inge *The Dark at the Top of the Stairs*	Osborne *The Entertainer*	Kerouac *On the Road*	
	Laurents *A Clearing in the Woods*	Pinter *The Room*	Rand *Atlas Shrugged*	
	Vidal *Visit to a Small Planet*		Seuss *The Cat in the Hat*	
	Williams *Orpheus Descending*			
	Bernstein & Sondheim *West Side Story*			

DATE	AMERICAN DRAMA	WORLD DRAMA	OTHER LITERATURE AND ART	HISTORICAL/CULTURAL EVENTS
1958	MacLeish *J.B.*	Arden *Live Like Pigs*	Capote *Breakfast at Tiffany's*	Alaska becomes 49th state
	O'Neill *A Touch of the Poet*	Beckett *Krapp's Last Tape*	Ferlinghetti *A Coney Island of the Mind*	US launches first satellite European Common Market formed
	Schary *Sunrise at Campobello*	Behan *The Hostage*	O'Hara *From the Terrace*	Galbraith *The Affluent Society*
	Stevens *The Marriage-Go-Round*	Delaney *A Taste of Honey*	Pasternak *Dr. Zhivago*	
	Taylor & Skinner *The Pleasure of His Company*	Frisch *The Firebugs*		
	Williams *Suddenly Last Summer*	Genet *The Blacks*		
		Pinter *The Birthday Party*		
		P. Shaffer *Five Finger Exercise*		
		Wesker *Chicken Soup With Barley*		

Year				
1959	Albee *The Zoo Story* R. Anderson *Silent Night, Lonely Night* Chayefsky *The Tenth Man* Gelber *The Connection* Gibson *The Miracle Worker* Hansberry *A Raisin in the Sun* Williams *Sweet Bird of Youth*	Anouilh *Becket* Arden *Serjeant Musgrave's Dance* Ionesco *Rhinoceros* Wesker *Roots*	Bellow *Henderson the Rain King* Burroughs *Naked Lunch* Grass *The Tin Drum* Mailer *Advertisements for Myself* Roth *Goodbye, Columbus* films: 'La Dolce Vita', 'Ben Hur'	Hawaii becomes fiftieth state Fidel Castro becomes Premier of Cuba
1960	Albee *Fam and Yam* Albee *The Sandbox* Hellman *Toys in the Attic* Williams *Period of Adjustment*	Bolt *A Man for All Seasons* Pinter *The Caretaker* Pinter *The Dumb Waiter* Rattigan *Ross*	Barth *The Sot-Weed Factor* Lee *To Kill a Mockingbird* Sillitoe *The Loneliness of the Long Distance Runner* Updike *Rabbit, Run*	Kennedy elected President Laser invented Goodman *Growing Up Absurd*

DATE	AMERICAN DRAMA	WORLD DRAMA	OTHER LITERATURE AND ART	HISTORICAL/CULTURAL EVENTS
		Sartre *The Condemned of Altona*	film: 'Psycho'	
		Wesker *I'm Talking About Jerusalem*		
1961	Albee *The American Dream*	Beckett *Happy Days*	Ginsberg *Kaddish*	Peace Corps founded Berlin Wall erected Bay of Pigs, failed invasion of Cuba
	Albee *Bartleby*	Fugard *The Blood Knot*	Heller *Catch-22*	
	Albee *The Death of Bessie Smith*	Jellicoe *The Knack*	Salinger *Franny and Zooey*	
	Kerr *Mary Mary*	Osborne *Luther*	Steinbeck *The Winter of Our Discontent*	
	Simon *Come Blow Your Horn*	Pinter *The Collection*		
	Williams *The Night of the Iguana*	Pinter *A Slight Ache*		
		Wesker *The Kitchen*		
		Whiting *The Devils*		

1962	Albee *Who's Afraid of Virginia Woolf?* Kingsley *Night Life* Kopit *Oh Dad, Poor Dad, . . .*	P. Shaffer *The Private Ear and The Public Eye* Wesker *Chips With Everything*	Faulkner *The Reivers* Kesey *One Flew Over the Cuckoo's Nest* Nabokov *Pale Fire* Porter *Ship of Fools* Steinbeck *Travels With Charlie* Britten: 'War Requiem'	Cuban missile crisis Thalidomide produces deformed children Pop Art appears Carson *Silent Spring*
1963	Albee *The Ballad of the Sad Cafe* Brown *The Brig* Hellman *My Mother, My Father and Me* Simon *Barefoot in the Park* Williams *The Milk Train Doesn't Stop Here Anymore*	Beckett *Play* Hochhuth *The Deputy* Ionesco *Exit the King* Pinter *The Dwarfs* Pinter *The Lover*	Baldwin *The Fire Next Time* LeCarre *The Spy Who Came In From the Cold* Plath *The Bell Jar* Pynchon *V*	Kennedy assassinated; Johnson becomes President Civil Rights March on Washington; King's 'I have a dream' speech

DATE	AMERICAN DRAMA	WORLD DRAMA	OTHER LITERATURE AND ART	HISTORICAL/CULTURAL EVENTS
	L. Wilson *So Long at the Fair*		Vonnegut *Cat's Cradle*	
	L. Wilson *The Bottle Harp*		film: 'Dr. Strangelove'	
1964	Albee *Tiny Alice*	Arden *Armstrong's Last Goodnight*	Bellow *Herzog*	Johnson elected President Beginnings of US involvement in Vietnam War
	Behrman *But For Whom Charlie*	Orton *Entertaining Mr. Sloane*	Golding *The Spire*	Beginnings of several summers of race riots in various US cities
	Hansberry *The Sign in Sidney Brustein's Window*	Osborne *Inadmissable Evidence*	Hemingway *A Moveable Feast*	Major Civil Rights legislation passed Beatles popular
	Jones *Dutchman*	P. Shaffer *Royal Hunt of the Sun*		McLuhan *Understanding Media*
	Jones *The Slave*	Weiss 'Marat/Sade'		
	Jones *The Toilet*			
	Manhoff *The Owl and the Pussycat*			

	Miller *After the Fall*		
	Miller *Incident at Vichy*		
	O'Neill *Hughie*		
	Shepard *Cowboys*		
	Williams *Eccentricities of a Nightingale*		
	L. Wilson *Home Free!*		
	L. Wilson *The Madness of Lady Bright*		
1965	Bullins *Clara's Old Man*	Bond *Saved*	Capote *In Cold Blood*	Civil Rights march in Selma, Alabama
	Burrows *Cactus Flower*	Fugard *Hello and Goodbye*	Mailer *An American Dream*
	Shepard *Chicago*	Marcus *The Killing of Sister George*	Plath *Ariel*
	Shepard *Icarus's Mother*	Orton *Loot*	films: 'Dr. Zhivago.' 'The Sound of Music'

DATE	AMERICAN DRAMA	WORLD DRAMA	OTHER LITERATURE AND ART	HISTORICAL/CULTURAL EVENTS
	Simon *The Odd Couple*	Osborne *A Patriot for Me*		
	Terry *Calm Down Mother*	Pinter *The Homecoming*		
	Terry *Keep Tightly Closed in a Clean Dry Place*	P. Shaffer *Black Comedy*		
	Ward *Day of Absence*			
	Ward *Happy Ending*			
	L. Wilson *Balm in Gilead*			
	L. Wilson *Days Ahead*			
	L. Wilson *Ludlow Fair*			
	L. Wilson *This is the Rill Speaking*			
	Zindel *The Effects of Gamma Rays . . . .*			

1966

Albee
Breakfast at Tiffany's

Albee
A Delicate Balance

Albee
Malcolm

Shepard
Fourteen Hundred Thousand

Shepard
Red Cross

Simon
The Star-Spangled Girl

Terry
Viet Rock

van Itallie
America Hurrah

L. Wilson
The Rimers of Eldritch

Williams
The Gnadiges Fraulein

Williams
The Mutilated

Barth
Giles Goat-Boy

Greene
The Comedians

Malamud
The Fixer

Pynchon
The Crying of Lot 49

US and USSR land
unmanned spacecraft on
moon

DATE	AMERICAN DRAMA	WORLD DRAMA	OTHER LITERATURE AND ART	HISTORICAL/CULTURAL EVENTS
1967	Albee *Everything in the Garden*	Ayckbourn *Relatively Speaking*	Brautigan *Trout Fishing in America*	Six-day Arab-Israeli War First human heart transplant
	R. Anderson *You Know I Can't Hear You When the Water's Running*	Nichols *A Day in the Death of Joe Egg*	Mailer *Why Are We in Vietnam?*	
	Friedman *Scuba Duba*	Stoppard *Rosencrantz and Guildenstern Are Dead*	Styron *The Confessions of Nat Turner*	
	Garson *MacBird*		Wilder *The Eighth Day*	
	Horovitz *Line*		film: 'The Graduate'	
	O'Neill *More Stately Mansions*			
	Shepard *La Tourista*			
	Shepard *Melodrama Play*			
	Williams *The Two-Character Play*			

1968	Albee	Ayckbourn	Dickey	Soviet invasion of
	Box-Mao-Box	*How the Other Half Loves*	*Poems*	Czechoslovakia
				Assassinations of Robert
	Bullins	Barnes	Mailer	Kennedy and Martin Luther
	The Electronic Nigger	*The Ruling Class*	*The Armies of the Night*	King
				Demonstrations at
	Bullins	Bond	Portis	Democratic Convention in
	Goin' a Buffalo	*Narrow Road to the Deep North*	*True Grit*	Chicago bring anti-war
				movement to a head
	Bullins	Osborne	Spark	Student riots throughout
	In the Wine Time	*A Hotel in Amsterdam*	*The Prime of Miss Jean Brodie*	Europe
				Nixon elected President
	Crowley			
	The Boys in the Band			
	Gurney			
	The Golden Fleece			
	Horovitz			
	The Indian Wants the Bronx			
	Kopit			
	Indians			
	Miller			
	The Price			
	Simon			
	Plaza Suite			
	van Itallie			
	The Serpent			

DATE	AMERICAN DRAMA	WORLD DRAMA	OTHER LITERATURE AND ART	HISTORICAL/CULTURAL EVENTS
	Williams *Kingdom of Earth*			
1969	Elder *Ceremonies in Dark Old Men*	Fugard *Boesman and Lena*	Puzo *The Godfather*	First manned moon landing Woodstock rock festival
	Gordone *No Place to be Somebody*	Nichols *The National Health*	Roth *Portnoy's Complaint*	
	McNally *Next*	Orton *What the Butler Saw*	Vonnegut *Slaughterhouse Five*	
	May *Adaptation*	Pinter *Landscape*	film: 'Easy Rider'	
	Russell *Five on the Black Hand Side*	Pinter *Silence*		
	Shepard *The Holy Ghostly*	Storey *In Celebration*		
	Shepard *The Unseen Hand*			
	Simon *The Last of the Red-Hot Lovers*			

	Williams *In the Bar of a Tokyo Hotel* Williams *Out Cry* MacDermot, Ragni & Rado *Hair*			
1970	Friedman *Steambath* Shepard *Operation Sidewinder* Shepard *Shaved Splits* Simon *The Gingerbread Lady* L. Wilson *Lemon Sky*	Hampton *The Philanthropist* A. Shaffer *Sleuth* Storey *Home* Wesker *The Friends*	Angelou *I Know Why the Caged Bird Sings* Bellow *Mr Sammler's Planet* Dickey *Deliverance* Hemingway *Islands in the Stream* Olson *Collected Poems* Pound *Cantos*	Anti-war demonstrations on college campuses; students killed at Kent State University
1971	Albee *All Over* Bullins *In New England Winter*	Bond *Lear* Gray *Butley*	Segal *Love Story* Updike *Rabbit Redux*	Eighteen-year-olds given the vote

DATE	AMERICAN DRAMA	WORLD DRAMA	OTHER LITERATURE AND ART	HISTORICAL/CULTURAL EVENTS
	Guare *The House of Blue Leaves*	Osborne *West of Suez*		
	McNally *Where Has Tommy Flowers Gone?*	Pinter *Old Times*		
	Rabe *The Basic Training of Pavlo Hummel*	Storey *The Changing Room*		
	Rabe *Sticks and Bones*			
	Shepard *Cowboy Mouth*			
	Shepard *Back Bog Beast Bait*			
	Shepard *Mad Dog Blues*			
	Simon *The Prisoner of Second Avenue*			
	L. Wilson *The Great Nebula in Orion*			

1972	Mamet *The Duck Variations*	Ayckbourn *Absurd Person Singular*	film: 'The Godfather'	US ends draft, begins all-volunteer army Break-in at Democratic headquarters begins Watergate scandal
	Miller *The Creation of the World and Other Business*	Fugard *Sizwe Banzi is Dead*		
	J. Miller *That Championship Season*	Osborne *A Sense of Detachment*		
	Randall *6 Rms Riv Vu*	Stoppard *Jumpers*		
	Shepard *The Tooth of Crime*	Wesker *The Old Ones*		
	Simon *The Sunshine Boys*			
	Walker *The River Niger*			
	L. Wilson *Ikke, Ikke, Nye, Nye, Nye*			
	Williams *Small Craft Warnings*			
1973	Jones *The Last Meeting of the Knights of the White Magnolia*	Ayckbourn *The Norman Conquests*	Jong *Fear of Flying*	Vietnam War ends Arab oil embargo triggers worldwide energy crisis

DATE	AMERICAN DRAMA	WORLD DRAMA	OTHER LITERATURE AND ART	HISTORICAL/CULTURAL EVENTS
	Medoff *When You Comin' Back, Red Ryder?*	Beckett *Not I*	Pynchon *Gravity's Rainbow*	Supreme Court legalizes abortion Watergate scandal spreads
	Patrick *Kennedy's Children*	Hampton *Savages*	Vidal *Burr*	
	Simon *The Good Doctor*	P. Shaffer *Equus*	Vonnegut *Breakfast of Champions*	
	L. Wilson *The Hot l Baltimore*		Wilder *Theophilus North*	
1974	Jones *Lu Ann Hampton Laverty Oberlander*	Ayckbourn *Absent Friends*		Nixon resigns US Presidency in Watergate scandal; Ford becomes president
	Jones *The Oldest Living Graduate*	Barnes *The Bewitched*		
	Mamet *Sexual Perversity in Chicago*	Brenton *The Churchill Play*		
	Moore *The Sea Horse*	Stoppard *Travesties*		
	Rabe *In the Boom Boom Room*			

Shepard
Action

Shepard
*Geography of a Horse
    Dreamer*

Simon
God's Favorite

1975	Albee *Seascape*	Ayckbourn *Bedroom Farce*	Adams *Watership Down*	Vietnam War ends
	Bullins *The Taking of Miss Janie*	Berkoff *East*	Bellow *Humboldt's Gift*	
	Horovitz *The Primary English Class*	Gray *Otherwise Engaged*	Doctorow *Ragtime*	
	Shange *for colored girls . . . . .*	Griffith *Comedians*		
	Shepard *Killer's Head*	Pinter *No Man's Land*		
	Slade *Same Time, Next Year*			
	L. Wilson *The Mound Builders*			
	Williams *The Red Devil Battery Sign*			

DATE	AMERICAN DRAMA	WORLD DRAMA	OTHER LITERATURE AND ART	HISTORICAL/CULTURAL EVENTS
	Hamlisch, Kirkwood, Dante & Kleban *A Chorus Line*			
1976	Albee *Counting the Ways*	Beckett *That Time*	Haley *Roots*	Carter elected President US Bicentennial
	Albee *Listening*	Brenton *Weapons of Happiness*	Vidal *1876*	
	Mamet *A Life in the Theater*	Osborne *Watch It Come Down*	Warren *Selected Poems*	
	Rabe *Streamers*	Stoppard *Dirty Linen*	film: 'Rocky'	
	Shepard *Angel City*	Wesker *The Merchant*		
	Shepard *Suicide in B♭*			
	Simon *California Suite*			
	L. Wilson *Seranading Louie*			

1977

Kopit
Wings

Mamet
American Buffalo

Mamet
The Water Engine

Mamet
The Woods

Miller
The Archbishop's Ceiling

Norman
Getting Out

Shepard
Curse of the Starving Class

Simon
Chapter Two

Wasserstein
*Uncommon Women and
Others*

Williams
Vieux Carré

Nichols
Privates on Parade

Rattigan
Cause Célèbre

Stoppard
*Every Good Boy Deserves
Favour*

McCullough
The Thorn Birds

Morrison
Song of Solomon

films: 'Annie Hall,'
'Star Wars'

DATE	AMERICAN DRAMA	WORLD DRAMA	OTHER LITERATURE AND ART	HISTORICAL/CULTURAL EVENTS
1978	Durang *A History of the American Film* Norman *Third and Oak* Shepard *Buried Child* Shepard *Seduced* Valdez *Zoot Suit* L. Wilson *5th of July*	Ayckbourn *Joking Apart* Bond *The Woman* Hare *Plenty* Pinter *Betrayal* Stoppard *Night and Day*	Irving *The World According to Garp*	First 'test-tube baby' born in England
1979	Durang *Sister Mary Ignatius Explains It All For You* Henley *Crimes of the Heart* Mamet *Prairie du Chien*	Ayckbourn *Sisterly Feelings* Churchill *Cloud Nine* P. Shaffer *Amadeus*	Heller *Good as Gold* Mailer *The Executioner's Song* Roth *The Ghost Writer*	US establishes diplomatic relations with China Soviet invasion of Afghanistan Fundamentalist revolution in Iran

1979	Medoff *Children of a Lesser God*	Stoppard *Dogg's Hamlet, Cahoot's Macbeth*	Styron *Sophie's Choice*	
	Williams *A Lovely Sunday for Creve Coeur*			
	S. Williams *Home*			
	L. Wilson *Talley's Folly*			
1980	Albee *The Lady from Dubuque*	Ayckbourn *Season's Greetings*	Toole *A Confederacy of Dunces*	Reagan elected President
	Fuller *Zooman and the Sign*	Brenton *The Romans in Britain*	Welty *Collected Stories*	
	Hwang *FOB*	Pinter *The Hothouse*		
	Mamet *Lakeboat*	Russell *Educating Rita*		
	Mastrosimone *The Woolgatherer*			
	Miller *The American Clock*			
	Shepard *True West*			

DATE	AMERICAN DRAMA	WORLD DRAMA	OTHER LITERATURE AND ART	HISTORICAL/CULTURAL EVENTS
	Simon *I Ought To Be In Pictures*			
	Williams *Clothes for a Summer Hotel*			
1981	Albee *Lolita*	Beckett *Catastrophe*	Helprin *Ellis Island*	AIDS identified as world health threat
	Durang *Beyond Therapy*	Beckett *Ohio Impromptu*	Irving *The Hotel New Hampshire*	
	Fierstein *The Torch Song Trilogy*	Beckett *Rockaby*	Morrison *Tar Baby*	
	Fuller *A Soldier's Play*	Bond *Restoration*	Plath *Collected Poems*	
	Gurney *The Dining Room*	Gray *Quartermaine's Terms*	Updike *Rabbit is Rich*	
	Henley *The Miss Firecracker Contest*			
	Hwang *The Dance and the Railroad*			

McKay
Sea Marks

Shue
The Nerd

Simon
Fools

Walker
The Color Purple

Falklands War between
Britain and Argentina

Churchill
Top Girls

Hare
A Map of the World

Pinter
Other Places

1982   Albee
*The Man Who Had Three
Arms*

Mamet
Edmond

Miller
Elegy for a Lady

Miller
Some Kind of Love Story

Norman
'night, Mother

L. Wilson
Angels Fall

DATE	AMERICAN DRAMA	WORLD DRAMA	OTHER LITERATURE AND ART	HISTORICAL/CULTURAL EVENTS
1983	Mamet *Glengarry Glen Ross* Norman *The Holdup* Shepard *Fool for Love* Shue *The Foreigner* Simon *Brighton Beach Memoirs* Wasserstein *Isn't It Romantic?*	Stoppard *The Real Thing*		
1984	Norman *Traveler in the Dark* Rabe *Hurlyburly* Shanley *Danny and the Deep Blue Sea* A. Wilson *Ma Rainey's Black Bottom*	Ayckbourn *A Chorus of Disapproval* Frayn *Benefactors* Gray *The Common Pursuit* Pinter *One for the Road*	Ginsberg *Collected Poems*	

1985	Durang *The Marriage of Bette and Boo*	Barnes *Red Noses*	Spender *Collected Poems*	
		Bond *The War Plays*		
	Hoffman *As Is*			
	Kramer *The Normal Heart*	Brenton & Hare *Pravda*		
	McNally *It's Only a Play*	Carrière *Mahabharata*		
	Mamet *The Shawl*			
	Shepard *A Lie of the Mind*			
	Simon *Biloxi Blues*			
	L. Wilson *Talley & Son*			
1986	Gurney *The Perfect Party*	Ayckbourn *Woman in Mind*	Capote *Answered Prayers*	Accident at Soviet nuclear plant, Chernobyl US air attack on Libya in response to terrorism
	Simon *Broadway Bound*			

DATE	AMERICAN DRAMA	WORLD DRAMA	OTHER LITERATURE AND ART	HISTORICAL/CULTURAL EVENTS
1987	Harling *Steel Magnolias*	Ayckbourn *A Small Family Business*	Morrison *Beloved*	Stock Market drops 23% in one day
	Henley *The Debutante Ball*	P. Shaffer *Lettice and Lovage*		
	McNally *Frankie and Johnny in the Clair de Lune*			
	Miller *Clara*			
	Miller *I Can't Remember Anything*			
	Uhry *Driving Miss Daisy*			
	A. Wilson *Fences*			
	L. Wilson *Burn This*			

1988	Gurney *The Cocktail Hour* Gurney *Love Letters* Hwang *M. Butterfly* Mamet *Speed-the-Plow* Wasserstein *The Heidi Chronicles* A. Wilson *Joe Turner's Come and Gone*	Wertenbaker *Our Country's Good*	Larkin *Collected Poems* Rushdie *The Satanic Verses* Wolfe *The Bonfire of the Vanities*	Bush elected President USSR begins major restructuring of government and economy
1989	Henley *Abundance* McNally *The Lisbon Traviata* Simon *Rumors*			Soviet domination of Eastern Europe ends Berlin Wall down US invades Panama
1990	Guare *Six Degrees of Separation* A. Wilson *The Piano Lesson*			East and West Germany united

DATE	AMERICAN DRAMA	WORLD DRAMA	OTHER LITERATURE AND ART	HISTORICAL/CULTURAL EVENTS
1991	McNally *Lips Together, Teeth Apart* Miller *The Ride Down Mt. Morgan* Shepard *The War in Heaven* Simon *Lost in Yonkers*			Soviet Union dissolved 'Desert Storm' war in Iraq

General Bibliographies

Note: Each section is arranged alphabetically. Place of publication is New York City unless otherwise noted.

(i) Bibliographies and reference works

(Note: Many major dramatists are the subjects of individual bibliographies or reference guides; see the biographical section.)

Adelman, Irving and Dworkin, Rita
Modern Drama: A Checklist of Critical Literature on Twentieth Century Plays (Metuchen, NJ, 1967). (Covers world drama, focusing on books and popular periodicals.)

Arata, Esther Spring and Rotoli, Nicholas John
Black American Playwrights 1800 to the Present: A Bibliography (Metuchen, NJ, 1976). (Primary and secondary listings; see supplementary volume below.)

Arata, Esther Spring
More Black American Playwrights: A Bibliography (Metuchen, NJ, 1978). (Supplement to the previous volume.)

Bonin, Jane F.
Prize-Winning American Drama: A Bibliography and Descriptive Guide (Metuchen, NJ, 1973). (Plot summaries and brief lists of reviews of winners of Pulitzer, Tony, Obie and other awards 1917–70.)

Bordman, Gerald
The Oxford Companion to the American Theatre (1984). (Encyclopedia-style entries for authors, plays, etc.)

Bronner, Edwin   *The Encyclopedia of the American Theatre 1900–1975* (1980). (Entries for all Broadway and many other plays, with brief plot, cast list and other data.)

Carpenter, Charles A. (ed).   *Modern Drama: Scholarship and Criticism 1966–1980* (Toronto, 1986). (Extensive bibliographies arranged by dramatist.)

Coleman, Arthur and Tyler, Gary R.   *Drama Criticism: A Checklist of Interpretations Since 1940 of English and American Plays* (Denver, 1966). (Includes journal articles and book sections.)

Coven, Brenda   *American Women Dramatists of the Twentieth Century: A Bibliography* (Metuchen, NJ, 1982). (Primary and secondary listings.)

Eddleman, Floyd Eugene (ed.)   *American Drama Criticism: Interpretations 1890–1977* (Hamden, CT, 1979). (Primarily theatre reviews; this volume supplants an earlier edition edited by Helen H. Palmer. See supplement below.)

Eddleman, Floyd Eugene (ed.)   *American Drama Criticism: Supplement I* (Hamden, CT, 1984).

French, William P. (ed.)   *Afro-American Poetry and Drama 1760–1975: A Guide to Information Sources* (Detroit, 1979). (Primary bibliographies.)

Harris, Richard H.   *Modern Drama in America and England, 1950–1970: A Guide to Information Sources* (Detroit, 1982). (Primary and secondary bibliographies.)

Hatch, James V. and Abdullah, OMANii   *Black Playwrights 1823–1977: An Annotated Bibliography of Plays* (1977). (Primary only.)

Helbing, Terry (ed.)   *Gay Theatre Alliance Directory of Gay Plays* (1980). (Brief descriptions and plot summaries.)

King, Kimball   *Ten Modern American Playwrights: An Annotated Bibliography* (1982). (Covers Albee, Baraka, Bullins, Gelber, Kopit, Mamet, Rabe, Shepard, Simon, L. Wilson with detailed and annotated primary and secondary listings.)

Kirkpatrick, D. L. (ed.)   *Contemporary Dramatists*, 4th edition (London, 1988). (Covers world drama with primary bibliographies and brief critical essays.)

Kolin, Philip C. (ed.)   *American Playwrights Since 1945: A Guide to Scholarship, Criticism and Performance* (1989). (Primary and secondary bibliographies and summary essays on plays and criticism, for 40 dramatists from Williams and Miller through August Wilson.)

Leiter, Samuel L. (ed.)   *The Encyclopedia of the New York Stage: 1920–1930*, 2 vols (Westport, CT, 1985); *1930–1940* (Westport, 1989). (Alphabetic listing of plays with plot outlines, excerpts from reviews, etc.)

Long, E. Hudson	*American Drama From Its Beginnings to the Present* (1970). (Brief bibliographies arranged by subject and by dramatist.)
Lovell, John Jr	*Digests of Great American Plays* (1961). (Detailed plot summaries of plays from 1766 to 1959.)
Mantle, Burns and subsequent editors	*The Best Plays of 1919–1920* [and subsequent years]. (Annual volume with abridged texts of ten plays, essays summarizing the New York season, and complete production details – casts, etc. – for Broadway and, in later volumes, Off-Broadway and regional theatres. Edited in turn by Mantle, 1919–46; John Chapman, 1947–51; Louis Kronenberger, 1952–60; Henry Hewes, 1961–3; Otis L. Guernsey Jr, 1964–84; Guernsey and Jeffrey Sweet, 1985–.)
Millett, Fred B.	*Contemporary American Authors* (1940). (Biographies, primary and secondary bibliographies; good coverage of minor writers.)
Petersen, Bernard L. Jr	*Contemporary Black American Playwrights and Their Plays: A Biographical Directory and Dramatic Index* (1988). (Biographies and primary bibliographies.)
Rigdon, Walter	*The Biographical Encyclopedia and Who's Who of the American Theatre* (1966). (Who's-Who-style entries for dramatists, actors, producers, etc.)
Salem, James M.	*A Guide to Critical Reviews, Volume I: American Drama 1909–1982* (London, 1984). (Listings of theatre reviews.)
Seller, Maxine Schwartz (ed.)	*Ethnic Theatre in the United States* (Westport, CT, 1981). (Essays and extensive bibliographies on Armenian–American, Black, Yiddish, etc., theatre.)
Stein, Rita and Rickert, Friedhelm (eds)	*Major Modern Dramatists*, 2 vols (1984). (Brief excerpts from reviews, books, etc., for each author.)
Woll, Allen	*Dictionary of the Black Theatre* (Westport, CT. 1983) (Casts, plots, reviews of plays 1898–1981).

(ii) General drama histories

Bigsby, C.W.E.	*A Critical Introduction to Twentieth-Century American Drama*. Vol. One: *1900–1940* (1982); Vol. Two: *Williams/Miller/Albee* (1984); Vol. Three: *Beyond Broadway* (1986). (Extensive critical analysis of major plays and playwrights.)

Dickinson, Thomas H. | *Playwrights of the New American Theater* (1925). (Covers MacKaye through O'Neill; though obviously dated, offers a valuable contemporary view, particularly of minor writers.)

Downer, Alan S. (ed.) | *American Drama and Its Critics: A Collection of Critical Essays* (Chicago, 1965). (Seventeen essays on writers from Herne to Albee.)

Downer, Alan S. | *Fifty Years of American Drama 1900–1950* (Chicago, 1951). (A short but useful overview and summary.)

Dukore, Bernard F. | *American Dramatists 1918–1945* (1984). (A short history with some analyses.)

Gould, Jean | *Modern American Playwrights* (1966) (Biographical sketches of writers from Rice to Albee.)

Krutch, Joseph Wood | *The American Drama Since 1918*, revised edition (1957). (First published in 1939, valuable for its contemporary viewpoint.)

Lewis, Allan | *American Plays and Playwrights of the Contemporary Theatre*, revised edition (1970). (Chapters on major writers from O'Neill to Albee.)

Mantle, Burns | *American Playwrights of Today* (1929). (Brief biographical sketches and analyses of plays, particularly valuable for minor figures. See next item.)

Mantle, Burns | *Contemporary American Playwrights* (1938) (Follow-up to the previous volume, covering major and minor writers of the 1930s.)

Meserve, Walter J. | *An Outline History of American Drama* (Totowa, NJ, 1965). (Useful brief review, covering from pre-revolutionary writers to early Albee.)

Moses, Montrose J. | *The American Dramatist* (Boston 1925) (From the beginnings to early O'Neill; though obviously dated, valuable for its contemporary view of early twentieth-century writers.)

Moses, Montrose J. and Brown, John Mason (eds) | *The American Theatre As Seen By Its Critics, 1752–1934* (1934). (Reprints contemporary reviews of major plays.)

Quinn, Arthur Hobson | *A History of the American Drama from the Civil War to the Present Day*, revised edition (1936). (First published 1923; like the Dickinson and Moses books it remains valuable for its contemporary view and its coverage of minor writers.)

Slide, Anthony (ed.) | *Selected Theatre Criticism*, three volumes: 1900–1919; 1920–1930; 1931–1950 (Metuchen, NJ, 1985–6). (Reprints contemporary reviews of major and minor plays.)

Wilson, Garff B.	*Three Hundred Years of American Drama and Theatre* (Englewood Cliffs, NJ, 1973). (A readable general history textbook.)

(iii) Special period studies

(Note: For books focusing on the early years of the century, see the older volumes in the preceding section.)

Bigsby, C.W.E.	*Confrontation and Commitment: A Study of Contemporary American Drama 1959–1966* (Missouri, 1968). (Focus on political and social critics: Miller, Albee, Jones, Hansberry, etc.)
Cohn, Ruby	*New American Dramatists 1960–1980* (1982) (Primarily Off- and Off Off-Broadway writers, but also Neil Simon.)
Goldstein, Malcolm	*The Political Stage: American Drama and Theater of the Great Depression* (1974). (A history of the left-wing theatre with analysis of major and minor political plays.)
Hughes, Catharine	*American Playwrights 1945–75* (London, 1976). (A brief introduction to Williams, Miller, Inge, Albee, Simon, Shepard and Rabe.)
Kirby, Michael (ed.)	*The New Theatre* (1974). (Descriptions and texts of some experimental productions of the 1960s and 1970s.)
Marranca, Bonnie and Dasgupta, Gautam, (eds)	*American Playwrights: A Critical Survey* (1981). (Critical essays on 18 Off- and Off Off-Broadway writers from Gelber to Shepard.)
Rabkin, Gerald	*Drama and Commitment: Politics in the American Theatre of the Thirties* (Bloomington, IN, 1964). (On politically committed theatres and writers: Odets, Rice, Anderson, etc.)
Weales, Gerald	*American Drama Since World War II* (1962) (Covers the 1945–60 period.)
Weales, Gerald	*The Jumping Off Place: American Drama in the 1960s* (1969). (Williams, Miller, Albee and many secondary Off-Broadway writers.)

(iv) Books focusing on special topics

Abramson, Doris E.	*Negro Playwrights in the American Theatre, 1925–1959* (1969). (Particularly valuable on secondary writers.)
Adler, Thomas	*Mirror on the Stage: The Pulitzer Play as an Approach to American Drama* (West Lafayette, IN, 1987). (Analysis of recurring themes in Pulitzer Prize plays.)
Broussard, Louis	*American Drama: Contemporary Allegory from Eugene O'Neill to Tennessee Williams* (Norman, OK, 1962). (On expressionism and other non-realistic styles.)
Laufe, Abe	*Anatomy of a Hit: Long-run Plays on Broadway from 1900 to the Present Day* (1966). (Descriptions and analyses of popular successes.)
Murphy, Brenda	*American Realism and American Drama, 1880–1940* (Cambridge, 1987). (Traces the rise of domestic realism as the dominant dramatic mode.)
Sanders, Leslie Catherine	*The Development of Black Theater in America* (Baton Rouge, LA, 1988). (Analysis of black drama with focus on Langston Hughes, LeRoi Jones and Ed Bullins.)
Schlueter, June (ed.)	*Modern American Drama: The Female Canon* (Rutherford, NJ, 1990). (Essays on women dramatists from Glaspell to Norman.)
Sievers, W. David	*Freud on Broadway: A History of Psychoanalysis and the American Drama* (1955). (Plays about psychology or built on Freudian characterizations.)

(v) Theatre histories

Atkinson, Brooks	*Broadway*, revised edition (1974). (A readable and authoritative history 1900–74.)
Berkowitz, Gerald M.	*New Broadways: Theatre Across America 1950–1980* (Totowa, NJ, 1982). (On the rise of Off- and Off Off-Broadway, and of regional and non-commercial theatre.)
Brown, John Mason	*Upstage: The American Theatre in Performance* (1930). (Essays on key actors, critics, directors, playwrights, etc.)

Chinoy, Helen Krich and Jenkins, Linda Walsh (eds)	*Woman in American Theatre* (1981). (Articles on actresses, playwrights, directors, theatre companies, etc.)
Clurman, Harold	*The Fervent Years* (1945). (A memoir of the Group Theatre in the 1930s.)
Durham, Weldon B. (ed.)	*American Theatre Companies, 1888–1930* (Westport, CT, 1987) and *American Theatre Companies, 1931–1986* (Westport, CT, 1989). (Descriptions, histories and performance records.)
Flanagan, Hallie	*The History of the Federal Theatre* (1940). (Memoir of the government-sponsored company of the 1930s, by its director.)
Goldman, William	*The Season* (1969). (Close study of a single Broadway season, 1967–68, by an insightful critic.)
Gottfried, Martin	*A Theatre Divided: The Postwar American Stage* (Boston, 1967). (Premise: Broadway retreated into shallow popular fare, leaving serious drama to other venues.)
Guernsey, Otis L. Jr	*Curtain Times: The New York Theater 1965–1987* (1987). (Reprints his Introductions to the annual *Best Plays* volumes, excellent contemporary accounts of the New York theatre.)
Himelstein, Morgan Y.	*Drama Was a Weapon: The Left-Wing Theatre in New York 1929–1941* (New Brunswick, NJ, 1963). (Focus more on personalities and theatre companies than plays.)
Hughes, Glenn	*A History of the American Theatre 1700–1950* (1951). (Focus on managers, actors, etc., more than plays.)
Little, Stuart W.	*Off-Broadway: The Prophetic Theater* (1972). (History 1950–70.)
Little, Stuart W. and Cantor, Arthur	*The Playmakers* (1970). (A primer on how Broadway works, with chapters on producers, critics, theatre owners, etc.)
Mordden, Ethan	*The American Theatre* (1981) (Anecdotal history placing Broadway in cultural and historical perspective.)
Novick, Julius	*Beyond Broadway* (1968). (On the beginnings of regional theatre.)
Poggi, Jack	*Theater in America: The Impact of Economic Forces 1870–1967* (Ithaca, NY, 1968). (On the fall of regional theatre, the dominance of Broadway, the rise of Off-Broadway and the reappearance of regional theatre, explained in economic terms.)

Sainer, Arthur — *The Radical Theatre Notebook* (1975). (Histories and descriptions of experimental theatres of the 1960s and 1970s.)

Sarlós, Robert Károly — *Jig Cook and the Provincetown Players* (Amherst, MA, 1982). (History of the company that produced O'Neill's first plays.)

Shank, Theodore — *American Alternative Theatre* (London, 1982). (Experimental companies of the 1960s and 1970s.)

Taubman, Howard — *The Making of the American Theatre* (1965). (A readable general history.)

Waldau, Roy S. — *Vintage Years of the Theatre Guild* (Cleveland, OH, 1972). (Early history of the important Broadway producers.)

Williams, Jay — *Stage Left* (1974). (Memoir of left-wing companies of the 1930s.)

Williams, Mance — *Black Theater in the 1960s and 1970s* (Westport, CT, 1985). (Accounts of companies, theatres, playwrights, etc.)

Zeigler, Joseph Wesley — *Regional Theatre* (Minneapolis, 1973). (On the growth of resident companies around the country from 1947 onwards.)

Individual Authors

ALBEE, Edward (1928–), born in Virginia and adopted as an infant by Reed and Frances Albee, members of the vaudeville theatre-owning family. Albee was raised in luxury, attending a series of boarding schools and spending three semesters at Trinity College in Connecticut (1946–47). He moved to New York City in 1950, living in relative poverty while working in a variety of jobs including Western Union messenger (1955–58). His first play, *The Zoo Story*, was produced in Berlin in 1959 and Off-Broadway in 1960. It was followed by *The Death of Bessie Smith* (Berlin 1960, New York 1961), *The Sandbox* (1960), *Fam and Yam* (1960) and *The American Dream* (1961). With *Who's Afraid of Virginia Woolf?* (1962) Albee became the first Off-Broadway dramatist to move to Broadway, where most of his subsequent plays were produced: *Tiny Alice* (1964), *A Delicate Balance* (Pulitzer Prize 1966), *Box and Quotations from Mao Tse-Tung* (1968), *All Over* (1971), *Seascape* (Pulitzer 1975), *Listening* and *Counting the Ways* (1977), *The Lady from Dubuque* (1980), *The Man Who Had Three Arms* (1982), *Finding the Sun* (1982), *Walking* (1984), *Marriage Play* (1986). Albee also wrote several adaptations: of Melville's *Bartelby* (1961), McCullers's *The Ballad of the Sad Cafe* (1963), Purdy's *Malcolm* (1966), Capote's *Breakfast at Tiffany's* (1966), Cooper's *Everything in the Garden* (1967), Nabokov's *Lolita* (1984); with the partial exception of the McCullers, all were critical and commercial failures. During the 1960s Albee and his producers used profits from *. . . Virginia Woolf?* to subsidize a playwrights' workshop that developed and produced the plays of many younger Off-Broadway writers.

See: Amacher, Richard E. and Margaret Rule, *Edward Albee at Home and Abroad* (1973) (Bibliography of criticism).

Amacher, Richard E., *Edward Albee*, revised edition (Boston, 1982).

Bigsby, C.W.E., *Edward Albee: Bibliography, Biography, Playography* (London, 1980).

Bigsby, C.W.E., *Albee* (Edinburgh, 1969).

Bloom, Harold, (ed.), *Edward Albee: Modern Critical Views* (1987).

De La Fuente, Patricia, (ed.), *Edward Albee: Planned Wilderness; Interviews, Essays and Bibliography* (Edinburg, TX, 1980).

Giantvalley, Scott, *Edward Albee: A Reference Guide* (Boston, 1987).

Green, Charles Lee, *Edward Albee: An Annotated Bibliography, 1968–77* (1980).

Kolin, Philip C. and J. Madison Davis (eds), *Critical Essays on Edward Albee* (Boston, 1986).

Tyce, Richard, *Edward Albee: A Bibliography* (Metuchen, NJ, 1986).

ANDERSON, Maxwell (1888–1959), born in Atlantic, Pennsylvania, son of a
Baptist minister, and raised in Iowa and North Dakota. With degrees from
the University of North Dakota (BA 1911) and Stanford (MA 1914), he
taught at Whittier College before becoming a newspaper writer in San
Francisco and New York. His first produced play, *White Desert* (1923) is a
verse tragedy about North Dakota farmers; his first success, *What Price Glory?*
(1924, with Laurence Stallings) a realistic comedy-drama about men at war. A
series of unsuccessful plays followed in the 1920s until he returned to verse
with *Elizabeth the Queen* (1930), *Night over Taos* (1932), *Mary of Scotland*
(1933), *Valley Forge* (1934), *Winterset* (1935), *The Masque of Kings* (1936), *The
Wingless Victory* (1936), *High Tor* (1937), and *Key Largo* (1939). Interspersed
with these were the prose plays *Both Your Houses* (Pulitzer Prize, 1933), *The
Star-Wagon* (1937), *Candle in the Wind* (1941), *The Eve of St Mark* (1942) and
Storm Operation (1944); and the musical *Knickerbocker Holiday* (1938). Of
Anderson's post-war plays, only *Joan of Lorraine* (1946), *Anne of the Thousand
Days* (1948), the musical *Lost in the Stars* (1949) and *Bad Seed* (1954) were
successful. Anderson also wrote eight films, including *All Quiet on the Western
Front* (1930), *Rain* (1932), *Death Takes a Holiday* (1934) and *The Wrong Man*
(1957); and a volume of poetry, *You Who Have Dreams* (1925).

> *Dramatist in America: Letters of Maxwell Anderson 1912–56* (Chapel Hill, NC,
> 1958).
> *The Essence of Tragedy* (1939).
> *Off Broadway: Essays about the Theatre* (1947).
> Shivers, Alfred S., *The Life of Maxwell Anderson* (Briarcliff Manor, NY, 1983).

> See: Bailey, Mabel Driscoll, *Maxwell Anderson: The Playwright as Prophet*
>   (1957).
>   Clark, Barrett H., *Maxwell Anderson: The Man and His Plays* (1933).
>   Klink, William, *Maxwell Anderson and S. N. Behrman: A Reference Guide*
>   (Boston, 1977).
>   Shivers, Alfred S., *Maxwell Anderson* (Boston, 1976).
>   Shivers, Alfred S., *Maxwell Anderson: An Annotated Bibliography*
>   (Metuchen, NJ, 1985).

ANDERSON, Robert Woodruff (1917–   ), born in New York City, attended
Philips Exeter Academy and Harvard (BA 1939, MA 1940). Served as Navy
intelligence officer 1942–46; *Come Marching Home*, written while in the Navy,
was his first produced play. From 1945 to 1953 Anderson adapted such plays
as *The Petrified Forest* and *The Glass Menagerie* for radio and television, while
several of his own plays were produced outside New York. His first critical
success, *All Summer Long* (Washington, 1953) led to his Broadway debut and
best-known play, *Tea and Sympathy* (1953). Others are *Silent Night, Lonely
Night* (1959), *The Days Between* (Dallas, 1965), *You Know I Can't Hear You
When the Water's Running* (1967), *I Never Sang for my Father* (1968),
Solitaire/Double Solitaire (1971) and *Free and Clear* (1983). Anderson also wrote
several films, including *Tea and Sympathy* (1956), *The Nun's Story* (1959), *The
Sand Pebbles* (1966) and *I Never Sang . . .* (1970); as well as two novels,
After (1973) and *Getting Up and Going Home* (1978). He is co-editor of a
series of textbooks, *Elements of Literature* (1988).

> See: Adler, Thomas P., *Robert Anderson* (Boston, 1978).

BARAKA, Amiri. *See* Jones, LeRoi.

BARRY, Philip (1896–1949), born in Rochester, NY, educated in Catholic schools, Yale (BA 1919) and Harvard (1919–21). His first play, written at Harvard, is *A Punch for Judy* (1921); his first professional production *You and I* (1923). Barry's strength was in sophisticated social comedy, as in *The Youngest* (1924), *Paris Bound* (1927), and particularly *Holiday* (1928) and *The Philadelphia Story* (1939). He was more interested, however, in writing symbolic and expressionistic plays on religious and spiritual subjects, such as *John* (1927), *Hotel Universe* (1930) and *Here Come the Clowns* (1938); most of these were commercial and critical failures. His novel *War in Heaven* appeared in 1938; his last play, *Second Threshold*, was revised by Robert E. Sherwood and produced posthumously in 1951.

See: Hamm, Gerald, *The Drama of Philip Barry* (Philadelphia, 1948).
Roppolo, Joseph P., *Philip Barry* (1965).

BEHRMAN, S[amuel] N[athan] (1893–1973), born in Worcester, MA, educated at Clark College, Harvard (BA 1916) and Columbia (MA 1918). Work as a freelance writer and as press agent for Broadway shows led to a couple of unsuccessful plays in the early 1920s. With his first success, *The Second Man* (1927), he found his niche in urbane, sophisticated social comedy frequently involving the Shavian discussion of political and social issues. Notable plays are *Meteor* (1929), *Biography* (1932), *End of Summer* (1936), *Amphitryon 38* (1937), *No Time for Comedy* (1939), *The Pirate* (1942), *Jacobowsky and the Colonel* (1944), and his last play *But For Whom Charlie* (1964). Behrman wrote about thirty films including *Queen Christina* (1933), *A Tale of Two Cities* (1935), *Waterloo Bridge* (1940) and *Quo Vadis* (1951); two novels, *The Suspended Drawing Room* (1965) and *The Burning Glass* (1969); and a biography, *Portrait of Max* (1960).

The Worcester Account (1954) (memoir).
People in a Diary: A Memoir (1972).

See: Klink, William, *Maxwell Anderson and S.N. Behrman: A Reference Guide* (Boston, 1977).
Klink, William, *S. N. Behrman: The Major Plays* (Amsterdam, 1978).
Reed, K. T., *S. N. Behrman* (Boston, 1975).

BULLINS, Ed (1935–   ), born in Philadelphia, dropped out of high school to join the Navy 1952–55. In the 1960s Bullins was active in the Black Power movement, serving as Culture Minister of the Black Panther Party until 1967, when he moved to New York as playwright-in-residence at the New Lafayette Theatre and other Off-Broadway companies. His plays fall into two general groups: revolutionary and consciousness-raising pieces such as *How Do You Do?* (1965), *The Theme is Blackness* (1966), *The Gentleman Caller* (1969) and *Death List* (1970); and less overtly political depictions of black life, such as *The Electronic Nigger* (1968), *Goin' a Buffalo* (1968), *In the Wine Time* (1968) *In New England Winter* (1971) and *The Taking of Miss Janie* (1975). He has taught drama, playwriting or black studies at such universities as Fordham, Columbia and Berkeley; edited the magazine *Black Theatre*; and published a novel, a book of short stories, a volume of poetry, and two anthologies of plays by black writers.

See: King, Kimball, *Ten Modern American Playwrights: An Annotated Bibliography* (1982).

CHAYEFSKY, Paddy (1923–81), born Sidney Chayefsky in New York City to a Russian immigrant family; BA City College 1943. Served in the Army, where he wrote the musical *No T.O. for Love* (1945). Of Chayefsky's six stage plays only *Middle of the Night* (1956) and *The Tenth Man* (1959), both effective comedy-dramas of small people finding small hope, are noteworthy; his major works were written for television – *Marty* (1953), *The Bachelor Party* (1953), *The Catered Affair* (1955) – and film – *Marty* (1955), *The Americanization of Emily* (1964), *Network* (1976), *Altered States* (1979).

    See: Clum, John M., *Paddy Chayefsky* (Boston, 1976).

CONNELLY, Marc (1890–80), born in McKeesport, PA, to a theatrical family, and wrote for newspapers in Pittsburgh and New York, and later for *The New Yorker*. His plays fall into two groups, a series of successful farces written with George S. Kaufman in the 1920s, and later works written alone or in collaboration with others. The Kaufman comedies include *Dulcy* (1921), *To the Ladies!* (1922), *Merton of the Movies* (1922) and *Beggar on Horseback* (1924); the only success among the post-Kaufman plays is *The Green Pastures* (Pulitzer Prize, 1930). Connelly wrote a number of films, including *Captains Courageous* (1937) and *I Married a Witch* (1942); a radio play, *The Mole on Lincoln's Cheek* (1941); and a novel, *A Souvenir from Qam* (1965).

    Voices Off-Stage: A Book of Memoirs (1968).

    See: Nolan, Paul T., *Marc Connelly* (Boston, 1969).

CROTHERS, Rachel (1878–1958), born in Bloomington, Illinois, daughter of two physicians. After attending Illinois Normal School, she became an actress, eventually training and teaching at the Stanhope-Wheatcroft School of Acting in New York. After some plays written for her students, her first professional production was the one-act comedy *The Rector* (1902). More than twenty-five full-length plays followed, most of them built on conventional plot situations, but with an unusual awareness of psychology or moral issues, particularly relating to women. Such plays as *The Three of Us* (1906), *A Man's World* (1909), *He and She* (1911) and *Mary the Third* (1923) dramatize the constraints on women in a male-dominated world; while *Let Us Be Gay* (1929), *As Husbands Go* (1931), *When Ladies Meet* (1932) and *Susan and God* (1938) explore the mutual obligations of married couples, in the context of social comedy. A series of lectures was published as *The Art of Playwriting* (1928).

    See: Gottlieb, Lois C., *Rachel Crothers* (1979).

GELBER, Jack (1932–   ), born in Chicago, (BA University of Illinois 1953). *The Connection* (1959), one of the first original plays produced Off-Broadway, is his most significant work; of his ten subsequent plays only *The Apple* (1961), *The Cuban Thing*, (1968) and *Jack Gelber's New Play: Rehearsal* (1976) have attracted much attention. Gelber has been a successful director of his plays and others, and has taught at City College, Columbia and Brooklyn College, where he is Professor of Drama. He has two novels, *On Ice* (1964) and *Rehearsal* (1976).

    See: Gale, Steven, 'Jack Gelber: An Annotated Bibliography', *Bulletin of Bibliography* 44 (1987), 102–10.

GLASPELL, Susan (1882–1948), born in Davenport, IA, attended Drake and Chicago Universities, and worked as political reporter for an Iowa newspaper.

Married George Cram Cook 1913 and joined the circle of leftist intellectuals that formed the Provincetown Players. Plays include *Suppressed Desires* (1915), a parody of Freud written with Cook; and *Trifles* (1916), *The Outside* (1917), *Inheritors* (1921), *The Verge* (1921) and *Alison's House* (Pulitzer Prize 1930), most of which deal with women alienated from society and self. Glaspell also wrote ten novels, two volumes of short stories, and a biography of her husband.

See: Waterman, Arthur E., *Susan Glaspell* (1966).

GUARE, John (1938–   ), born in New York City, educated at Georgetown (BA 1961) and Yale Drama School (MFA 1963). After some early plays produced at Yale and Off Off-Broadway, Guare made his mark with *Muzeeka* (1967), the musical *Two Gentlemen of Verona* (1971) and particularly *The House of Blue Leaves* (1971). Subsequent plays were generally poorly received, though *Landscape of the Body* (1977), *Marco Polo Sings a Solo* (1977) and *Bosoms and Neglect* (1979) are worth attention, and *Six Degrees of Separation* (1990) is an effective social satire. Guare wrote the films *Taking Off* (1971) and *Atlantic City* (1981).

HANSBERRY, Lorraine (1930–65), born in Chicago, daughter of a prosperous black businessman who challenged convention by moving into a white neighbourhood in 1938. Educated at the University of Wisconsin, the Art Institute of Chicago and Roosevelt College, and worked as journalist and editor. *A Raisin in the Sun* (1959), about a black family moving to a white neighbourhood, is her best play; the unsuccessful *The Sign in Sidney Brustein's Window* (1964), about a white liberal, was produced as she was dying of cancer. Her husband Howard Nemiroff adapted and edited her uncompleted works as *To Be Young, Gifted, and Black* (1969), *Les Blancs* (1970), *The Drinking Gourd* (1972) and *What Use are Flowers?* (1972).

See: Cheney, Anne, *Lorraine Hansberry* (Boston, 1984).
Kaiser, Ernest and Robert Nemiroff, 'A Lorraine Hansberry Bibliography', *Freedomways* 19 (1979), 285–304.

HART, Moss (1904–1961), born in New York City and educated in city schools. Early work in amateur theatre and as social director at a summer resort led to playwriting; a producer teamed him with George S. Kaufman, and the pair wrote some of the most successful comedies of the 1930s, Hart generally providing the story and Kaufman the structure and jokes: *Once in a Lifetime* (1929), *Merrily We Roll Along* (1934), *You Can't Take It With You* (Pulitzer Prize 1936), *The Man Who Came to Dinner* (1939) and *George Washington Slept Here* (1940); they also wrote the books for several musicals, including *As Thousands Cheer* (1933), *I'd Rather Be Right* (1937) and *Lady in the Dark* (1941). On his own Hart wrote some serious plays – *Winged Victory* (1943), *Christopher Blake* (1946) and *The Climate of Eden* (1948) – and the comedy *Light Up the Sky* (1948); he also wrote several films, including *Gentlemen's Agreement* (1947) and *A Star is Born* (1954), and directed the musical *My Fair Lady* (1956).

Act One: An Autobiography (1959).

HECHT, Ben (1894–1964) and MACARTHUR, Charles (1895–1956), former newspapermen who collaborated on two classic comedies. Hecht was born in New York and raised in Wisconsin; MacArthur was born and raised in

Scranton, PA. Both worked on Chicago newspapers from about 1910 through the early 1920s before moving to New York. Each had written a couple of plays with others before teaming for the high-energy, wisecracking *The Front Page* (1928) and *The Twentieth Century* (1932). They also wrote the musical *Jumbo* (1935) and, together or separately, such films as *Scarface* (1932), *Design for Living* (1933), *Rasputin and the Empress* (1933), *Wuthering Heights* (1939) and *Gunga Din* (1939). Each wrote several lesser plays alone or with other collaborators, and each published several volumes of reportage – Hecht, *1001 Afternoons in Chicago* (1922); MacArthur, *A Bug's-Eye View of the War* (1919). Hecht also wrote several novels.

Hecht, *A Child of the Century* (1954) (autobiography).
Hecht, *Charlie* (1957) (biography of MacArthur).
Hecht, *Gaily, Gaily* (1963) (autobiography).
Fetherling, D., *The Five Lives of Ben Hecht* (Toronto, 1977).

HELLMAN, Lillian (1905–84), born in New Orleans and raised there and in New York City; studied at NYU and Columbia. Worked as book editor and reviewer, play reader for Broadway producers and script reader in Hollywood. After a failed marriage to Arthur Kober she began a lifelong relationship with mystery writer Dashiell Hammett, who encouraged her writing. Major plays include *The Children's Hour* (1934), *The Little Foxes* (1939), *Watch on the Rhine* (1941), *Another Part of the Forest* (1946), *The Lark* (1955), the musical *Candide* (1956) and *Toys in the Attic*, 1960). Films include *Dead End* (1937) and *The Chase* (1966); she also edited *The Selected Letters of Anton Chekhov* (1955) and *The Big Knockover* (1966) a collection of Hammett's stories. The historical accuracy of her three volumes of memoirs (see below) has been questioned.

An Unfinished Woman (1969).
Pentimento (1973).
Scoundrel Time (1976).
Rollyson, Carl, *Lillian Hellman: Her Legend and Her Legacy* (1988).
Wright, William, *Lillian Hellman: The Image, The Woman* (1986).

See: Bills, Steven H., *Lillian Hellman: An Annotated Bibliography* (1979).
Estrin, M. W., *Lillian Hellman: A Reference Guide* (Boston, 1980).
Falk, Doris V., *Lillian Hellman* (1978).
Holmin, Lorena R., *The Dramatic Works of Lillian Hellman* (Austin, 1973).
Lederer, Katherine, *Lillian Hellman* (Boston, 1979).
Moody, Richard, *Lillian Hellman, Playwright* (1972).
Riordan, Mary M., *Lillian Hellman, A Bibliography* (1980).

HENLEY, Beth (1952–   ), born in Jackson, MS, daughter of a state politician; set out to be an actress, studying at Southern Methodist University (BFA 1974) and the University of Illinois, and acting in Dallas and Los Angeles. *Crimes of the Heart* was entered by a friend in the annual competition of the Actors Theatre of Louisville; it won and, after a Louisville production in 1979 and several other regional productions, went to Broadway and a Pulitzer Prize in 1981. Other plays are *The Wake of Jamey Foster* (1982), *The Miss Firecracker Contest* (1984), *The Debutante Ball* (1985), *The Lucky Spot* (1987) and *Abundance* (1989); she also wrote the film *Nobody's Fool* (1986) and the film versions of *Crimes* (1986) and *Miss Firecracker* (1989).

HERNE, James A. (1839–1901), born in West Troy, New York, and educated in local schools. He became an actor, with seasons in Troy, Baltimore, Washington (where he delivered the opening address at the inauguration of Ford's Theatre), Philadelphia and on tour of Canada, eventually establishing himself in San Francisco and later New York. Like most other actor-dramatists he began writing to provide good roles for himself and for his second wife, actress Katherine Corcoran, adapting such works as *Oliver Twist* and *Rip Van Winkle*, sometimes in collaboration with producer-dramatist David Belasco. His plays – *Hearts of Oak* (1879), *The Minute Men* (1886), *Drifting Apart* (1888), *Margaret Fleming* (1890), *Shore Acres* (1892), *Griffith Davenport* (1899) and *Sag Harbor* (1899) – are generally realistic, though not without the melodramatic flourishes of nineteenth-century drama. *Margaret Fleming* is usually cited as the first modern American play, for its serious treatment of complex moral issues.

See: Perry, J., *James A. Herne – The American Ibsen* (Chicago, 1978).

HOWARD, Sidney (1891–1939), born in Oakland, CA, studied at Berkeley (AB 1915) and Harvard (MA 1916). After service as ambulance driver and pilot in the First World War, he joined *Life* magazine, becoming its literary editor in 1922. Half of his twenty-eight produced plays are journeyman translations or adaptations – e.g. *The Last Night of Don Juan* (1925), *Dodsworth* (1934). Among his original plays are *They Knew What They Wanted* (Pulitzer Prize 1924), *Lucky Sam McCarver* (1925), *Ned McCobb's Daughter* (1926), *The Silver Cord* (1926) and *Alien Corn* (1933). He also wrote eleven films, including *Gone With the Wind* (1939); a book of short stories; and two volumes of non-fiction.

See: White, Sidney H., *Sidney Howard* (Boston, 1977).

INGE, William (1913–73), born in Independence, Kansas to a family much like that in his *The Dark at the Top of the Stairs* – distant father, over-protective mother. Degrees from the University of Kansas (BA 1935) and George Peabody College (MA 1938) led to positions teaching English at Stephens College and Washington University, and reviewing theatre for a St Louis newspaper. A meeting in that capacity with Tennessee Williams encouraged his play writing; his first production was *Further Off From Heaven* (an early version of *Dark . . .*) in Dallas, 1947. Inge's next four plays, all about little people making little compromises to achieve little happinesses, were Broadway successes: *Come Back, Little Sheba* (1950), *Picnic* (Pulitzer Prize, 1953), *Bus Stop* (1955), *The Dark at the Top of the Stairs* (1957); he also wrote the films *Splendor in the Grass* (1961) and *All Fall Down* (1962). Unfortunately none of his subsequent plays was a success, nor were his novels *Good Luck, Miss Wyckoff* (1970) and *My Son Is a Splendid Driver* (1971); and depression and alcoholism led to his suicide.

Voss, Ralph F., *A Life of William Inge* (Lawrence, KS, 1989).
See: McClure, Arthur F., *William Inge: A Bibliography* (1982).
Shuman, Robert B., *William Inge* (Boston, 1989).

JONES, LeRoi (BARAKA, Amiri) (1934–) born in Newark, NJ, educated at Howard University (BA 1954), served in the Air Force 1954–57. Edited the literary magazine *Yugen* (1958–63) while writing music criticism and teaching creative writing at the New School, Columbia and SUNY Buffalo; he would later teach at San Francisco State, Yale, George Washington, Rutgers and SUNY Stony Brook, where he is Professor of African Studies. Early plays *A Good Girl is Hard to Find* (1958) and *Dante* (1961) preceded his first successes *Dutchman, The Baptism, The Slave* and *The Toilet* (all 1964). Soon afterwards Jones left the literary world to devote himself to social and political activism in the black community of Newark; in 1968 he took the name Amiri Baraka. Subsequent plays, such as *A Black Mass* (1966), *Slave Ship* (1967) and *Arm Yourself, or Harm Yourself!* (1967) are consciousness-raising or agitprop pieces designed for inner city black audiences. Most of his publications since 1968 have been political – e.g. *Raise Race Rays Raze* (1971), a collection of essays – though he has edited collections of black literature and published volumes of fiction and poetry. The convention of retaining the name Jones for the works written before 1968 is one Baraka himself follows.

Autobiography of LeRoi Jones/Amiri Baraka (1984).

See: Benston, Kimberly W., *Baraka* (New Haven, 1976).
      Brown, Lloyd W., *Amiri Baraka* (Boston, 1980).
      Dace, Letitia, *LeRoi Jones (Imamu Amiri Baraka): A Checklist of Works By and About Him* (London, 1971).
      Hudson, Theodore R., *From LeRoi Jones to Amiri Baraka* (Durham, NC, 1973).
      King, Kimball, *Ten Modern American Playwrights: An Annotated Bibliography* (1982).
      Lacey, Henry C., *To Raise, Destroy, and Create: The Poetry, Drama and Fiction of Amamu Amiri Baraka* (Troy, NY, 1981).
      Sollors, Werner, *Amiri Baraka/LeRoi Jones* (1978).

KAUFMAN, George S[imon] (1889–1961), born in Pittsburgh, briefly studied law and held a variety of jobs until his freelance contributions to newspaper columnists led to his own columns in Washington and New York papers and to the position of drama critic for the *New York Times* 1917–30. From *Someone in the House* (1918) he wrote more than fifty plays, virtually all comedies, and most in collaboration with others; generally the partner supplied the plot and Kaufman the jokes and comic structure. His major collaborations were with Marc Connelly – *Dulcy* (1921), *To the Ladies!* (1922), *Merton of the Movies* (1922), *Helen of Troy, New York* (1923) and *Beggar on Horseback* (1924) – Edna Ferber – *Minick* (1924), *The Royal Family* (1927), *Dinner at Eight* (1932), *Stage Door* (1936) and others – and Moss Hart – *Once in a Lifetime* (1929), *You Can't Take It With You* (Pulitzer Prize 1936), *The Man Who Came to Dinner* (1939), *George Washington Slept Here* (1940) and others. Other successes include *The Butter and Egg Man* (1924), *The Solid Gold Cadillac* (1953, with Howard Teichmann), and the musicals (with various collaborators) *The Cocoanuts* (1925), *Animal Crackers* (1928), *The Band Wagon* (1931), *Of Thee I Sing* (Pulitzer 1931), *I'd Rather Be Right,* (1937) and *Silk Stockings* (1955). Kaufman also wrote several films, notably *A Night at the Opera* (1935), and directed many of his own plays and others.

Hart, Moss, *Act One* (1959) (Hart's autobiography, with much about Kaufman).
Meredith, Scott, *George S. Kaufman and his Friends* (1974).
Teichmann, Howard, *George S. Kaufman: An Intimate Portrait* (1977).

See: Goldstein, Malcolm, *George S. Kaufman: His Life, His Theatre* (1979).
      Pollack, Rhoda-Gale, *George S. Kaufman* (Boston, 1988).

KINGSLEY, Sidney (1906–   ), born Sidney Kirshner in New York City; he began
writing after college (Cornell, 1928) and brief careers as actor and script
reader. His strongest plays are fairly conventional melodramas in intensely
realistic slice-of-life settings: *Men in White* (Pulitzer Prize 1933), *Dead End*
(1935), *The World We Make* (1939), *Detective Story* (1949). *The Patriots* (1943)
about the rivalry of Hamilton and Jefferson, and *Darkness at Noon* (1951),
from Koestler's novel, were also successful.

KOPIT, Arthur (1937–   ), born in New York City, raised on Long Island, began
writing plays at Harvard (BA 1959). *Oh Dad, Poor Dad, Mamma's Hung You in
the Closet and I'm Feeling So Sad* (1962) was one of the first original plays to
be an Off-Broadway hit, but none of his subsequent plays succeeded until
Indians (1968) and then again until *Wings* (1978). Among the others *The Day
the Whores Came Out to Play Tennis* (1965) and *End of the World* (1984) are
worth attention, as is his version of Ibsen's *Ghosts* (1982). He also wrote the
book for the musical *Nine* (1982) and a television (1990) and stage (1991)
version of *The Phantom of the Opera*.

> See: Auerbach, Doris, *Sam Shepard, Arthur Kopit and the Off-Broadway
> Theatre* (Boston, 1982).
> King, Kimball, *Ten Modern American Playwrights: An Annotated
> Bibliography* (1982).

MACARTHUR, Charles. *See* HECHT, Ben.

MACKAYE, Percy Wallace (1875–1956), born in New York City, son of
playwright-director Steele MacKaye; attended Harvard (BA 1897), toured
Europe, and taught at a private school in New York until devoting himself
full time to writing in 1904. Early plays were verse comedies – *The Canterbury
Pilgrims* (1903) – and tragedies – *Fenris the Wolf* (1905), *Jeanne d'Arc* (1906),
Sappho and Phaon (1907), but he also wrote romantic prose comedy – *The
Scarecrow* (1908) – political and social satire – *Mater* (1908), *Anti-Matrimony*
(1910) – and problem plays – *Tomorrow* (1913). Much of his work,
particularly in the second decade of the century, was in large-scale pageant
plays, with casts numbering in the thousands: *St Louis* (1914), *Sanctuary, a Bird
Masque* (1913), *Washington, the Man Who Made Us* (1916), *The Evergreen Tree*
(1917), *The Roll Call* (1918), among others. MacKaye subsequently taught at
Miami University, Ohio, and published several volumes of essays and lectures
on theatre, along with a biography of his father and two collections of poetry,
generally celebratory odes. His last major work, *The Mystery of Hamlet* (1949)
was a tetralogy of verse plays set in the years before the opening of
Shakespeare's version.

MCNALLY, Terrence (1939–   ), born in St Petersburg, FL, and raised in Corpus
Christi, TX. After college (Columbia, 1960) worked as stage manager at the
Actors Studio (1960-61), travelling tutor for John Steinbeck's family
(1961-62), film critic for *Seventh Art* magazine (1963-65) and assistant editor
of the Columbia alumni magazine (1965-66). His early plays, among them
And Things That Go Bump in the Night (1964), *Next* (1968), *Botticelli* (1968),
Sweet Eros (1968) and *Where Has Tommy Flowers Gone?* (1971), are generally
anti-war or social criticism pieces in the spirit of the times, though a strong
farcical sense is apparent in *Next* and *Noon* (1968) that prepared for the
apolitical farce *The Ritz* (1975). Few of his plays of the next decade are
noteworthy until the comic *It's Only a Play* (1986), the romantic *Frankie and*

Johnny in the Clair de Lune (1988); and the character studies *The Lisbon Traviata* (1989) and *Lips Together, Teeth Apart* (1991). McNally wrote the musical *The Rink* (1984), the film *Frankie and Johnny* (1991), and several short plays for television.

MAMET, David (1947-), born in Chicago, attended private schools and Goddard College (BA 1969), studied acting in New York and taught at Marlboro College (1969–70) and Goddard (1971–73). A theatre company he directed at Goddard regrouped as the St Nicholas Players in Chicago in 1974, and thereafter most of Mamet's plays were first staged by various Chicago theatres. Plays include *Lakeboat* (1970), *The Duck Variations* (1972), *Sexual Perversity in Chicago* (1974), *American Buffalo* (1975), *The Water Engine* (1977), *A Life in the Theatre* (1977), *Edmond* (1982), *Glengarry Glen Ross* (Pulitzer Prize 1984), *Speed-the-Plow* (1987), and translations of *The Cherry Orchard* (1987) and *Uncle Vanya* (1989). Mamet wrote the films *The Postman Always Rings Twice* (1979), *The Verdict* (1980), *The Untouchables* (1986), *House of Games* (1986), *Things Change* (1987), *We're No Angels* (1987) and *Homicide* (1991); two collections of essays – *Writing in Restaurants* (1986) and *Some Freaks* (1989) – and two children's books – *Warm and Cold* (1985) and *The Owl* (with Lindsay Crouse, 1987).

> See: Bigsby, C.W.E., *David Mamet* (1985).
> Carroll, Dennis, *David Mamet* (London, 1987).
> Davis, J. Madison and John Coleman, 'David Mamet: A Classified Bibliography', *Studies in American Drama 1945- Present* 1 (1986), 83–101.

MILLER, Arthur (1915–), born in New York City, son of a prosperous clothing manufacturer who lost his money just before the onset of the Depression, an event alluded to in *A Memory of Two Mondays* (1955), *After the Fall* (1964), *The Price* (1968) and *The American Clock* (1980). Miller worked at various menial jobs before attending the University of Michigan (BA 1938), where his first plays won several prizes. During the 1940s he wrote for radio and films; his first professional stage play, *The Man Who Had All the Luck*, failed in 1944. It was followed by the successful *All My Sons* (1947) and his best play *Death of a Salesman* (Pulitzer Prize 1949). Miller was of the generation whose youthful politics endangered them in the anti-communist hysteria of the 1950s; he dealt with this subject in his version of Ibsen's *An Enemy of the People* (1950) and in *The Crucible* (1953). Blacklisted in 1955 and convicted of contempt of Congress for not naming names in 1957 (the conviction was reversed on appeal), Miller wrote only one other play during the decade, *A View from the Bridge* (1956). His first marriage (to Mary Grace Slattery, 1940-55) ending in divorce, Miller married actress Marilyn Monroe in 1956, and spent the next six years aiding her career; he wrote the film *The Misfits* (1961) for her. After their divorce in 1961 he married photo-journalist Inge Morath; they have collaborated on several books of photography and reportage. Plays of the next decade include *After the Fall, Incident at Vichy* (1964), *The Price* and *The Creation of the World and Other Business* (1972). Another gap, during which Miller was active in international writers' organizations, ended with *The Archbishop's Ceiling* (1977), followed by *The American Clock* (1980), the double bill *Elegy for a Lady* and *Some Kind of Love Story* (1982), the double bill *I Can't Remember Anything* and *Clara* (1987), and *The Ride Down Mt Morgan* (1991). Other works include a novel, *Focus* (1945); a children's book, *Jane's Blanket* (1963); a volume of short stories, *I Don't*

Need You Anymore (1967), the television film *Playing for Time* (1980), and a film adaptation of *Some Kind of Love Story*, *Everybody Wins* (1990).

The Theatre Essays of Arthur Miller (1978).
Salesman in Beijing (1984). (An account of directing the play in China.)
Timebends (1987). (A memoir.)
Roudane, Matthew, (ed.), *Conversations with Arthur Miller* (Jackson, MS, 1988). (Collects 37 interviews from five decades.)

See: Carson, Neil, *Arthur Miller* (London, 1982).
Ferres, John H., *Arthur Miller: A Reference Guide* (Boston, 1979).
Hayashi, Tetsumaro, *An Index to Arthur Miller Criticism* (Metuchen, NJ, 1976).
Hayman, Ronald, *Arthur Miller* (1970).
Jensen, George, *Arthur Miller: A Bibliographical Checklist* (Columbia, SC, 1976).
Moss, Leonard, *Arthur Miller* (Boston, 1980).
Nelson, Benjamin, *Arthur Miller: Portrait of a Playwright* (1970).
Schleuter, June and James K. Flanagan, *Arthur Miller* (1987).
Welland, Dennis, *Arthur Miller: The Playwright* (London, 1983).

NORMAN, Marsha (1947–   ), born Marsha Williams in Louisville, KY, studied at Agnes Scott College (BA 1969) and University of Louisville (MAT 1971). Married Michael Norman 1969 (divorced 1974; married Dann C. Byck Jr 1978) and kept his name. Taught disturbed adolescents at Kentucky Central State Hospital and gifted children at the Brown School; created the children's page of the Louisville *Times* 1976. Her first play, *Getting Out* (1977), was a winner in the Actors Theatre of Louisville competition, leading to productions there and elsewhere. Subsequent plays include *Third and Oak* (1978), *Circus Valentine* (1979), *The Hold-up* (1980), the Pulitzer Prize winning *'night, Mother* (1983), *Traveler in the Dark* (1984) and the book and lyrics for the musical *The Secret Garden* (1991). She has also written two television plays and a novel, *The Fortune Teller* (1987).

See: Wolfe, Irmgard H., 'Marsha Norman: A Bibliography', *Studies in American Drama 1945–Present* 3 (1988).

ODETS, Clifford (1906–63), born in Philadelphia, son of a printer who later prospered, though Odets always considered himself a worker's son. Raised in New York City, he quit high school to become a radio and stage actor, joining the newly formed Group Theatre in 1930. His first play, *Waiting for Lefty* (1935), was first done by the New Theatre League, another leftist company, then staged by the Group Theatre, as were his next several plays, almost all reflections of the Depression through domestic melodrama: *Awake and Sing* (1935), *Till the Day I Die* (1935), *Paradise Lost* (1935), *Golden Boy* (1937), *Rocket to the Moon* (1938). Subsequent plays – *Night Music* (1940), *Clash by Night* (1941), *The Russian People* (1942), *The Big Knife* (1949), *The Flowering Peach* (1954) – were generally unsuccessful, though *The Country Girl* (1950) proved an effective dissection of marital politics. Odets worked briefly in Hollywood in the 1930s (*The General Died at Dawn*, 1936) and more extensively in the next two decades – his films include *None But the Lonely Heart* (1944), *The Sweet Smell of Success* (1957) and *The Story on Page One* (1960) – and remained ambivalent about easy money's effect on his work.

The Time is Ripe: The 1940 Journal of Clifford Odets (1989).

See: Brenman-Gibson, M., *Clifford Odets, American Playwright* (1981).
   Cantor, Harold, *Clifford Odets, Playwright-Poet* (Metuchen, NJ, 1978).
   Clurman, Harold, *The Fervent Years* (1945). (Memoir of the Group
      Theatre, with discussion of Odets.)
   Mendelsohn, Michael J., *Clifford Odets, Humane Dramatist* (Deland, FL,
      1969).
   Murray, Edward, *Clifford Odets: The Thirties and After* (1968).
   Shuman, R. Baird, *Clifford Odets* (1962).
   Weales, Gerald, *Odets the Playwright* (1985).

O'NEILL, Eugene (1888–1953), born in New York City, youngest son of popular
actor James O'Neill, educated in Catholic schools, with a year at Princeton
(1906–07) and later at Harvard (1914–15). A period of rootlessness and
dissipation, briefly interrupted by marriage, menial jobs in New York and
Latin America, and two seasons touring with his father, ended with a
sanatarium stay for tuberculosis in 1912–13, when he read heavily and
decided to be a writer. Several short plays written 1913–16 remain
unproduced or unpublished; his first production, *Bound East for Cardiff* (1916)
was the result of his association with the young radicals and artists who made
up the Provincetown Players. Other short plays followed, in Provincetown
and New York, leading to his Broadway debut with *Beyond the Horizon*
(1920). His plays of the 1920s are marked by experiments in form, virtually
no two written in the same style: *The Emperor Jones* (1920), *Anna Christie*
(1921), *The Hairy Ape* (1922), *All God's Chillun Got Wings* (1924), *Desire
Under the Elms* (1924), *The Fountain* (1925), *The Great God Brown* (1926),
Marco Millions (1928), *Strange Interlude* (1928), *Lazarus Laughed* (1928), *Dynamo*
(1929). Only three plays appeared in the 1930s – *Mourning Becomes Electra*
(1931), *Ah, Wilderness!* (1933) and *Days Without End* (1933) – and only two
more during his lifetime – *The Iceman Cometh* (1946) and *A Moon for the
Misbegotten* (1947) – as O'Neill withdrew into depression and a degenerative
nerve disease. At his death it was revealed that he had continued writing, and
Long Day's Journey into Night (1956) is now considered his masterpiece; other
posthumous plays are *A Touch of the Poet* (1957), *Hughie* (1958) and the
incomplete *More Stately Mansions* (1967). O'Neill was married three times, to
Kathleen Jenkins 1909–12, Agnes Boulton 1918–29 and Carlotta Monterey
1929–53. *Beyond the Horizon*, *Anna Christie*, *Strange Interlude* and *Long Day's
Journey* won Pulitzer Prizes; and O'Neill was awarded the Nobel Prize for
Literature in 1936.

Work Diary 1924–43 (New Haven, 1981).
'*As Ever, Gene': The Letters of Eugene O'Neill to George Jean Nathan* (Ruther-
   ford, NJ, 1987).
'*Love and Admiration and Respect': The O'Neill–Commins Correspondence* (Dur-
   ham, NC, 1986).
Selected Letters of Eugene O'Neill (New Haven, 1988).
'*The Theatre We Worked For': The Letters of Eugene O'Neill to Kenneth Macgo-
   wan* (New Haven, 1982).
Gelb, Arthur and Barbara, *O'Neill* (1973).
Sheaffer, Louis, *O'Neill: Son and Playwright* (Boston, 1968).
Sheaffer, Louis, *O'Neill: Son and Artist* (Boston, 1973).

See: Atkinson, Jennifer McCabe, *Eugene O'Neill: A Descriptive Bibliography*
   (Pittsburgh, 1974).

Berlin, Normand, *Eugene O'Neill* (1988).

Bogard, Travis, *Contour in Time: The Plays of Eugene O'Neill* (1972).

Cargill, Oscar *et al.* (eds), *O'Neill and His Plays: Four Decades of Criticism* (1961). (Collection of reviews and analyses.)

Carpenter, Frederick, *Eugene O'Neill* (Boston, 1979)

Floyd, Virginia (ed.), *Eugene O'Neill: A World View* (1979). (Collection of foreign criticism.)

Griffin, Ernest (ed.), *Eugene O'Neill: A Collection of Criticism* (1976).

Miller, Jordan Y., *Eugene O'Neill and the American Critic: A Bibliographical Checklist* (Hamden, CT, 1973).

Ranald, Margaret Loftus, *The Eugene O'Neill Companion* (Westport, CT, 1984). (Encyclopedia-style entries for plays, characters, family, etc.)

Reaver, J. Russell, *An O'Neill Concordance*, 3 vols (Detroit, 1969).

RABE, David (1940–   ), born in Dubuque, Iowa, educated in Catholic schools, Loras College (BA 1962) and Villanova. Drafted in 1965, he spent one of his two army years in Vietnam, returning to Villanova for an MA in theatre 1968. He worked as a journalist 1969–70 and taught at Villanova 1970–72. His reputation rests on three powerful plays about the Vietnam War, *The Basic Training of Pavlo Hummel* (1971), *Sticks and Bones* (1971) and *Streamers* (1976). Other plays – *The Orphan* (1973), *In the Boom Boom Room* (1974), *Goose and Tomtom* (1982) and *Hurlyburly* (1984) – are less effective. He wrote the films *I'm Dancing as Fast as I Can* (1982), *Streamers* (1983) and *Casualties of War* (1989).

See: Kolin, Philip C., *David Rabe: A Stage History and Primary and Secondary Bibliography* (1988).

RICE, Elmer (1892–1967), born Elmer Reizenstein in New York City, he dropped out of high school but studied law while working in a law office, and was admitted to the bar 1913. He turned immediately to writing, taking the name Rice; his first play, *On Trial* (1914) contains the first use of flashbacks in American drama. The rest of his more than forty produced plays fall into three groups: conventional and generally minor melodramas and comedies such as *Cock Robin* (with Philip Barry 1928), *Counsellor-at-Law* (1931) and *Love Among the Ruins* (1963); plays with a strong social or political content, such as *Street Scene* (Pulitzer Prize 1929), *We, the People* (1933) and *Flight to the West* (1940); and a few experiments in style and form, notably the expressionistic *The Adding Machine* (1923) and *Dream Girl* (1945). Rice directed the New York branch of the Federal Theatre Project 1935–36, helping to create the 'Living Newspaper' style. He directed all his own plays after 1929, and wrote several films and two novels.

The Living Theatre (1959).
Minority Report: An Autobiography (1963).

See: Durham, Frank, *Elmer Rice* (Boston, 1970).

Hogan, Robert, *The Independence of Elmer Rice* (Carbondale, IL, 1965).

SHEPARD, Sam (1943–   ), born Samuel Shepard Rogers in Fort Sheridan, Illinois, and raised in Duarte, California. After one year of junior college he moved to New York City in 1963, supporting himself with menial jobs and as a rock musician. Shepard was one of the first Off Off-Broadway writers to attract attention, first with Theatre Genesis, then with the Open Theatre; he later became playwright-in-residence for San Francisco's Magic Theatre. He wrote more than 25 short plays in his first decade, many of them unpublished. Among the most significant are *Cowboys* (1964), *Chicago* (1965), *Icarus's Mother* (1965), *Red Cross* (1966), *Forensic and the Navigators* (1967), *The Unseen Hand* (1969) and *Cowboy Mouth* (1971). Longer plays from this period include *Operation Sidewinder* (1970), *The Tooth of Crime* (1972) and *Geography of a Horse Dreamer* (1974). Shepard's plays after 1975 are generally more realistic in style, and generally more powerful than his early work: *Curse of the Starving Class* (1977), *Buried Child* (Pulitzer Prize 1978), *True West* (1980), *Fool for Love* (1983), *A Lie of the Mind* (1985) and *The War in Heaven* (1991). Shepard has written for films, and has a second career as film actor (*Days of Heaven*, *The Right Stuff*, *Country*, *Fool for Love*, *Crimes of the Heart*, etc.). His non-dramatic writing includes two volumes of stories and verse, *Hawk Moon* (1972) and *Motel Chronicles* (1982), and an impressionistic report on a rock concert tour, *Rolling Thunder Logbook* (1978).

Oumano, Ellen, *Sam Shepard: The Life and Work of an American Dreamer* (1986).

Shewey, Don, *Sam Shepard* (1985).

See: Auerbach, Doris, *Sam Shepard, Arthur Kopit, and the Off-Broadway Theatre* (Boston, 1982).
   Hart, Lynda, *Sam Shepard's Metaphorical Stages* (Westport, 1987).
   King, Kimball, *Ten Modern American Playwrights: An Annotated Bibliography*, (1982).
   Marranca, Bonnie (ed.), *American Dreams: The Imagination of Sam Shepard* (1981).
   Mottram, Ron, *Inner Landscapes: The Theatre of Sam Shepard* (Columbia, MO, 1984).

SHERWOOD, Robert E. (1896–1955), born in New Rochelle, NY, his education at Harvard (BA 1918) interrupted for service in the Canadian army. Wrote for *Vanity Fair* (1919) and *Life* (1920–28). Sherwood could write romance – *Waterloo Bridge* (1930) – and light comedy – *Reunion in Vienna* (1931) – but his best plays have a liberal social or political edge: *The Petrified Forest* (1934), *Idiot's Delight* (Pulitzer Prize 1936), *Abe Lincoln in Illinois* (Pulitzer 1938), *There Shall Be No Night* (Pulitzer 1940). Sherwood was active in theatrical and political circles, serving as President of the Dramatists Guild and later of ANTA; during the Second World War he held several government posts. He wrote twelve films, including *The Scarlet Pimpernel* (1935), *Rebecca* (1940) and *The Best Years of Our Lives* (1946); and a Pulitzer Prize biography, *Roosevelt and Hopkins* (1948).

Brown, John Mason, *The Worlds of Robert E. Sherwood* (1965).
Brown, John Mason, *The Ordeal of a Playwright* (1970).

See: Meserve, Walter J., *Robert E. Sherwood, Reluctant Moralist* (1970).
   Shuman, R. Baird, *Robert E. Sherwood* (1964).

SIMON, Neil (1927–   ), born in New York as Marvin Neil Simon, attended New York schools and NYU, and served in the Air Force in Colorado during the Second World War. With his older brother Danny, he wrote comic sketches and scripts for radio and television 1948–52, notably the Sid Caesar *Your Show of Shows* and the Phil Silvers *Sgt Bilko* series. The brothers contributed sketches to two Broadway revues, *Catch a Star!* (1955) and *New Faces of 1956* (1956). Neil Simon's first stage comedy, *Come Blow Your Horn* (1960) began an unprecedented string of successes; for the next three decades there was hardly a season without one or as many as four Simon comedies on Broadway: *Barefoot in the Park* (1963), *The Odd Couple* (1965), *The Star-Spangled Girl* (1966), *Plaza Suite* (1968), *Last of the Red Hot Lovers* (1969), *The Prisoner of Second Avenue* (1971), *The Sunshine Boys* (1972), *The Good Doctor* (1973), *God's Favorite* (1974), *California Suite* (1976), *Chapter Two* (1977), *I Ought To Be in Pictures* (1980), *Fools* (1981), *Rumors* (1988). Simon's first attempt at a serious play, *The Gingerbread Lady* (1970), was unsuccessful, but his later trilogy of autobiographical comedies *Brighton Beach Memoirs* (1983), *Biloxi Blues* (1985) and *Broadway Bound* (1986) had a realism and emotional depth hitherto missing from his work, as did *Lost in Yonkers* (Pulitzer Prize 1991). Simon wrote the books for the musicals *Little Me* (1962), *Sweet Charity* (1966), *Promises, Promises* (1968) and *They're Playing Our Song* (1979). He has written more than twenty films, including adaptations of many of his own plays and *After the Fox* (1966), *The Out-of-Towners* (1970), *The Heartbreak Kid* (1972), *The Goodbye Girl* (1977), *The Cheap Detective* (1978) and *The Lonely Guy* (1984). He is known as a play doctor, and is reported to have edited or rewritten many scripts by others without credit.

See: Johnson, Robert K., *Neil Simon* (Boston, 1983).
   King, Kimball, *Ten Modern American Playwrights: An Annotated Bibliography* (1982).
   McGovern, Edythe M., *Neil Simon: A Critical Study* (Van Nuys, CA, 1978).

VAN ITALLIE, Jean-Claude (1936–   ), born in Brussels, came to America 1940, educated at Harvard (BA 1958). He studied acting in New York, and edited the *Transatlantic Review* 1963–68. During the same period he was playwright-in-residence at the Open Theatre, an experimental company specializing in improvisations and group creations; many of his plays were actually developed in collaboration with the actors. Among his early plays the three eventually combined as *America Hurrah* (1966) are the most notable; later *The Serpent* (1969) proved a particularly impressive group creation. While continuing to write original plays, among them *Bag Lady* (1979) and *The Tibetan Book of the Dead* (1983), van Itallie produced a series of well-regarded translation-adaptations: *The Sea Gull* (1973), *The Cherry Orchard* (1977), *The Three Sisters* (1979), *Uncle Vanya* (1983) and *The Balcony* (1986). He wrote several television documentaries in the 1960s, and has taught theatre or playwriting at Yale, the New School, the Naropa Institute, Amhurst, Princeton, NYU, Colorado and Columbia.

See: Brittain, Michael J., 'A Checklist of Jean-Claude van Itallie 1961–72', *Serif* 9 (1972), 75-77.
   Pasolli, Robert, *A Book on the Open Theatre* (1970).

WASSERSTEIN, Wendy (1950–   ), born in Brooklyn, raised there and in Manhattan, attending private schools and Mount Holyoke (BA 1971), City University of New York (MA in creative writing 1973) and Yale Drama School (MFA 1976). Her first plays were written at Yale and produced there or Off Off-Broadway: *Any Woman Can't* (1973), *Montpelier Pazazz* (a musical, with David Hollister, 1976), *When Dinah Shore Ruled the Earth* (revue, with Christopher Durang, 1977). Wasserstein found her subject, the experience of her own generation of women, in *Uncommon Women and Others* (1977), continuing the exploration in *Isn't It Romantic* (1981) and *The Heidi Chronicles* (Pulitzer Prize 1987). Along with some minor plays, Wasserstein has also written for television, is contributing editor of *New York Woman* magazine, and published a book of essays, *Bachelor Girls* (1990).

WILDER, Thornton (1897–1975), born in Madison, Wisconsin, the survivor of a pair of twins. In 1906 his father became US Consul General in Hong Kong; the family lived there and in Shanghai between stays in California. Wilder studied at Oberlin and Yale (AB 1920), and taught at a New Jersey boys' school (1921-28) and the University of Chicago (1930-36). He made his name as a novelist with *The Cabala* (1926) and *The Bridge of San Luis Rey* (Pulitzer Prize 1928), and continued to write fiction throughout his life: *The Woman of Andros* (1930), *Heaven's My Destination* (1935), *The Ides of March* (1948), *The Eighth Day* (1967), *Theophilus North* (1973). A collection of early short plays was published in 1928 as *The Angel That Troubled the Waters*; it was followed by another collection, *The Long Christmas Dinner* (1931). After a few minor works came *Our Town* (Pulitzer Prize 1938), *The Merchant of Yonkers* (1939), *The Skin of Our Teeth* (Pulitzer 1943), *The Matchmaker* (1954), *The Alcestiad* (1955) and *Plays for Bleeker Street* (1962). He wrote the films *Our Town* (1940) and *Shadow of a Doubt* (1943), served as Lieutenant-Colonel in Army Air Intelligence in the Second World War, and was Norton Professor of Poetry at Harvard 1950-51.

Goldstone, Richard H., *Thornton Wilder* (1975).
Harrison, Gilbert A., *The Enthusiast: A Life of Thornton Wilder* (1983).

See: Burbank, Rex J., *Thornton Wilder* (Boston, 1978).
Castronovo, D., *Thornton Wilder* (1986).
Goldstein, Malcolm, *The Art of Thornton Wilder* (Lincoln, NB, 1965).
Goldstone, Richard H. and G. Anderson, *Thornton Wilder: An Annotated Bibliography* (1982).
Haberman, Donald, *The Plays of Thornton Wilder* (Middletown, CT, 1967).
Papajewski, Helmut, *Thornton Wilder* (1968).
Simon, Linda, *Thornton Wilder* (Garden City NY, 1979).

WILLIAMS, Tennessee (1911–83), born in Columbus, Mississippi, to a minister's daughter and a travelling salesman; his parents would appear both as characters and as conflicting moral energies in his work. The family moved to St Louis 1919, and Williams attended the University of Missouri 1929-32, but finances forced his withdrawal to work in various jobs, including a shoe warehouse. He briefly attended Washington University, writing his first plays there, and ultimately graduated from Iowa (1938). In 1937 his sister Rose was diagnosed as schizophrenic, probably falsely, and subjected to a lobotomy; Williams would support her for the rest of his life. In 1939 he went to New Orleans hoping to find work with the Federal Writers Project, but found bohemian poverty instead. It was at this time that he took the name Tennessee, submitting some early plays to a national contest, where they came to the attention of agent Audrey Wood, who would manage most of his career. His first professional production, *Battle of Angels* (1940), closed out of town; a contract writing films for MGM gave him time to write his first success, *The Glass Menagerie* (1945). This was followed by his best play, *A Streetcar Named Desire* (Pulitzer Prize 1947), and a string of plays that, along with those of

Arthur Miller, dominated the next decade: *Summer and Smoke* (1948), *The Rose Tattoo* (1951), *Camino Real* (1953), *Cat on a Hot Tin Roof* (Pulitzer 1955), *Orpheus Descending* (1957), *Suddenly Last Summer* (1958), *Sweet Bird of Youth* (1959), *Period of Adjustment* (1960), and *The Night of the Iguana* (1961). In 1963 the death of Frank Merlo, his long-time lover, triggered a depression which would be compounded by alcoholism and drug dependency, and Williams never again regained the artistic control of his early work, though he continued to write almost compulsively for two decades. Of the later plays *The Milk Train Doesn't Stop Here Anymore* (1963), *Small Craft Warnings* (1972), *Out Cry* (1973) and *Vieux Carré* (1977) show the clearest remnants of his lost talent. Williams also wrote two volumes of poetry, two novels (*The Roman Spring of Mrs Stone*, 1950; *Moise and the World of Reason*, 1976), five volumes of short stories (ultimately assembled in *Collected Stories* 1985), and the film versions of several of his plays.

Memoirs (1975).
Where I Live (1978) (theatrical and personal essays).
Tennessee Williams's Letters to Donald Windham (1976).
Leavitt, Richard Freeman, (ed.), *The World of Tennessee Williams* (1978., (A biography through montage of photos, documents and text.)
Spoto, Donald, *The Kindness of Strangers: The Life of Tennessee Williams* (Boston, 1985).

See: Boxill, Roger, *Tennessee Williams* (1987).
    Devlin, Albert J., (ed), *Conversations With Tennessee Williams* (Jackson, MS, 1986). (36 interviews from 1940 to 1981.)
    Falk, Signi, *Tennessee Williams* (Boston, 1978).
    Fayard, Jeanne, *Tennessee Williams* (Paris, 1972).
    Gunn, Drewey Wayne, *Tennessee Williams: A Bibliography* (Metuchen, NJ, 1980).
    Londré, Felicia Hardison, *Tennessee Williams* (1979).
    McCann, John S., *The Critical Reputation of Tennessee Williams: A Reference Guide* (Boston, 1983).
    Phillips, Gene D., *The Films of Tennessee Williams* (London, 1980).
    Stanton, Stephen S. (ed.), *Tennessee Williams: A Collection of Critical Essays* (Englewood Cliffs, NJ, 1977).
    Tharpe, Jac (ed.), *Tennessee Williams: A Tribute* (Jackson, MS, 1977). (Critical essays.)

WILSON, August (1945–), born in a black slum in Pittsburgh, son of a white father who had little to do with the family; Wilson was raised by his mother and stepfather. He quit school at 15 and held various odd jobs. In the 1960s Wilson became active in the Black Power movement, founding the Black Horizons Theatre Company in Pittsburgh in 1968. In 1978 he moved to St Paul, writing educational scripts for the Science Museum of Minnesota and working with the Minneapolis Playwrights Center. After some early plays he committed himself to the project of depicting the black American experience in the twentieth century, one play for each decade. Four plays have appeared so far: *Ma Rainey's Black Bottom* (1984), *Fences* (Pulitzer Prize 1987), *Joe Turner's Come and Gone* (1988) and *The Piano Lesson* (Pulitzer Prize 1990). Typically, Wilson's plays go through several years of development involving workshop stagings and preliminary productions before their final versions.

WILSON, Lanford (1937–), born in Lebanon, Missouri, and raised, after his parents' divorce in 1942, in Springfield and Ozark, Missouri. Briefly attended Southwest Missouri State College and San Diego State College. Worked in Chicago as a graphic artist for an advertising agency 1956–62; moved to New York 1962 and discovered the Caffe Cino, one of the first Off Off-Broadway theatres. His first plays, including *So Long at the Fair* (1963), *Home Free!* (1964) and *The Madness of Lady Bright* (1964), were staged at the Caffe Cino; others from this period include *Balm in Gilead* (1965), *The Rimers of Eldrich* (1966) and *The Gingham Dog* (1968). In 1969 he joined director Marshall W. Mason and others in forming the Circle Theatre, later the Circle Repertory Company; most of his subsequent plays would be written for specific actors and directed by Mason. Major plays include *The Hot l Baltimore* (1973), *The Mound Builders* (1975), *5th of July* (1978), *Talley's Folly* (Pulitzer Prize 1979), *Angels Fall* (1983) and *Burn This* (1987). Wilson also wrote the libretto for an operatic version of Williams's *Summer and Smoke* (1971), an adaptation of *The Three Sisters* (1984) and some television plays.

See: Barnett, Gene, *Lanford Wilson* (Boston, 1987).

King, Kimball, *Ten Modern American Playwrights: An Annotated Bibliography* (1982).

Ryzuk, Mary S., *The Circle Repertory Company* (Ames, IA, 1989).

Index